SUBALTERN STUDIES IX
Writings on South Asian History and Society

SUBALTERN STUDIES IX

Writings on South Asian History and Society

edited by

SHAHID AMIN

and

DIPESH CHAKRABARTY

DELHI

OXFORD UNIVERSITY PRESS

CALCUTTA   CHENNAI   MUMBAI

Oxford University Press, Great Clarendon Street, Oxford OX2 6DP

Oxford New York
Athens Auckland Bangkok Calcutta
Cape Town Chennai Dar es Salaam Delhi
Florence Hong Kong Istanbul Karachi
Kuala Lumpur Madrid Melbourne Mexico City
Mumbai Nairobi Paris Singapore
Taipei Tokyo Toronto

and associates in

Berlin Ibadan

ISBN 0 19 564334 8

Printed in India at Rekha Printers Pvt. Ltd., New Delhi 110 020
and published by Manzar Khan, Oxford University Press
YMCA Library Building, Jai Singh Road, New Delhi 110 001

Contents

Preface

This volume continues some of the past practices of Subaltern Studies. We carry articles embodying new and original research on aspects of subalternity in colonial and contemporary South Asia at the same time as we try to expand our intellectual horizons. Started with a specific agenda bearing on developments within modern South Asian history, Subaltern Studies have now expanded beyond the discipline of history. The essays here retain that original connection with history but also display our engagements with more contemporary problems and theoretical formations.

Some of the papers published here—those by Vivek Dhareshwar and R. Srivatsan, and Susie Tharu and Tejaswini Niranjana—were originally presented at the conference on Subalternity and Culture organized jointly at Hyderabad in January 1993 by the Subaltern Studies Collective and the Anveshi Research Centre for Women's Studies. We also include the text of a public lecture by Ranajit Guha also delivered in Hyderabad on 11 January 1993. The five remaining papers—by Ajay Skaria, Gyan Prakash, Kamala Visweswaran and Kancha Illaih—have been independently contributed for this volume. The essay by Kancha Illaih represents a first for Subaltern Studies: it is the first time Subaltern Studies have engaged with contemporary discussions of Dalitbahujan politics in India, and we look forward to more of this in our pages. The essay by David Lloyd in the 'Discussion' section explores parallels, similarities and divergences between subaltern historiography here and that developed in the context of Irish anti-imperialism.

This volume is the result of a collaborative effort on the part of an enlarged Subaltern Studies Collective. As usual two members have undertaken the task of editing the volume on behalf of the Editorial Collective which has been actively involved in determining the overall character and contents of the volume. All correspondence as well as contributions for inclusion in future volumes may be sent to one of the four Executive Editors.

Our thanks go to the Oxford University Press, Delhi for continuing to support this project.

Delhi and Chicago   SHAHID AMIN
June 1996   DIPESH CHAKRABARTY

Notes on Contributors

RANAJIt GUHA is the author of *A Rule of Property for Bengal* (1963) and *Elementary Aspects of Peasant Insurgency in Colonial India* (1983), and has edited the first six volumes of *Subaltern Studies*.

VIVEK DHARESHWAR is Fellow at the Centre for Studies in Social Sciences, Calcutta.

KANCHA ILAIH is Reader in Political Science, Osmania University, Hyderabad. His most recent publication is *Why I am not a Hindu* (1996).

DAVID LLOYD is Professor of English at the University of California, Berkeley. He is the author of *Anomalous States: Irish Writing and the Post-colonial Moment* (1993) and co-editor with Lisa Lowe of *World's Aligned* (forthcoming).

SHAIL MAYARAM is Fellow at the Institute of Development Studies, Jaipur. She is the author of *Resisting Require: Myth, Memory and the Shaping of a Muslim Identity* (forthcoming).

GYAN PRAKASH is Associate Professor of History at Princeton University. He is the author of *Bonded Histories: Genealogies of Labour Servitude* in Colonial India (1990) and editor of *After Colonialism* (1995).

TEJASWINI NIRANJANA is with the English Department at the University of Hyderabad and the author of *Siting Translation: History, Post-structuralism and the Colonial Context.*

AJAY SKARIA is Assistant Professor of History, University of Virginia, Charlottsville. He is the author of *Hybrid Histories: Forests, Frontiers and Wildness in Western India* (forthcoming).

R. SRIVATSAN is an Engineering Consultant and computer software designer. He is currently completing a book on Visual Politics in India.

SUSIE THARU is a Reader in the Department of English at the Central Institute of English and Foreign Languages, Hyderabad. She has edited with K. Lalita, *Women Writing in India*, vol. I & II (1991).

KAMALA VISWESWARAN teaches Anthropology at the University of Texas, Austin. She is the author of *Fictions of Feminist Ethnography* (1994).

1

The Small Voice of History*

RANAJIT GUHA

There are phrases in many languages, Indian as well as others, which speak of historic events and historic deeds. These phrases enjoy the status of common sense and an understanding of their meaning by members of the respective speech communities is presupposed without question. However, the crust of common sense begins to crumble as soon as one asks what precisely the adjective 'historic' is supposed to be doing in such expressions. Its function is of course to assign certain events and deeds to history. But who is it that nominates these for history in the first place? For some discrimination is quite clearly at work here—some unspecified values and unstated criteria—to decide why any particular event or deed should be regarded as historic and not others. Who decides, and according to what values and what criteria? If these questions are pressed far enough, it should be obvious that in most cases the nominating authority is none other than an ideology for which the life of the state is all there is to history. It is this ideology, henceforth to be called statism, which is what authorizes the dominant values of the state to determine the criteria of the historic.

That is why the common sense of history may be said generally to be guided by a sort of statism which thematizes and evaluates the past for it. This is a tradition which goes back to the beginnings of modern historical thinking in the Italian Renaissance. For the ruling elements of the fifteenth-century city–states the study of history served as a schooling in politics and government so indispensable to their role as citizens and

---

* Text of a public lecture originally delivered in Hyderabad on 11 January 1993.

monarchs. It is entirely appropriate therefore that to Machiavelli, the intellectual most representative of those elements, 'historical study and the study of statecraft should have been essentially the same'.[1]

The ascendancy of the bourgeoisie in Europe during the next three hundred years did little to weaken this bonding of statism and historiography. On the contrary, it was reinforced both by absolutism and republicanism, so that by the nineteenth century, as every schoolboy knows thanks to Lord Acton, politics had become the very staple of historical scholarship. What is no less important is that by then the study of history had become fully institutionalized in Western Europe, perhaps more so in England than elsewhere because of the relatively greater maturity of the English bourgeoisie.

Institutionalization under these conditions meant, first, that the study of history developed into a sort of 'normal science' in the Kuhnian sense. It was integrated into the academic system as a fully secularized body of knowledge with its own curricula and classrooms as well as a profession devoted entirely to its propagation by teaching and writing. Secondly, it now acquired a place of its own in the increasingly expanding public space where the hegemonic process often appealed to history in order to realize itself in the interaction between citizens and the state. It was here, again, that the study of history found its public—a reading public, progeny of the printing technology and avid consumers of such of its products as catered to a new bourgeois taste for historical literature of all kinds. Thirdly, it was this literature ranging from school manuals to historical novels which helped to institutionalize the writing of history by constituting it into imaginative and discursive genres equipped with their distinctive canons and narratologies. The institutionalization of the study of history had the effect, on the whole, of securing a stable base for statism within the academic disciplines and promoting hegemony.

So it was as a highly institutionalized and statist knowledge that the study of history was introduced by the British in nineteenth-century India. However, in a colonial condition neither institutionalization nor statism could be what it was in metropolitan Britain. The relationship of dominance and subordination made for some critical difference here in both respects. Education, the principal instrument used by the Raj to 'normalize' the study of history in India, was limited to a very small minority of the population, and correspondingly, the reading public too was small in size, as was the output of books and periodicals.

[1] Lauro Martines, *Power and Imagination: City–states in Renaissance Italy* (Penguin Books, Harmondsworth, 1983), pp. 268–9.

Institutionalization was therefore of little help to the rulers in their bid for hegemony. It was, on the contrary, simply a measure of the containment of this knowledge within the colonized élite who were the first to benefit from Western education in our subcontinent.

Statism in Indian historiography was a gift of this education. The intelligentsia, its purveyors within the academic field and beyond, had been schooled in their understanding of the history of the world and especially of modern Europe as a history of state systems. In their own work within the liberal professions therefore they found it easy to conform to the official interpretation of contemporary Indian history simply as a history of the colonial state. But there was a fallacy about this interpretation. The consent which empowered the bourgeoisie to speak for all citizens in the hegemonic states of Europe was also the licence used by the latter to assimilate the respective civil societies to themselves. But no such assimilation was feasible under colonial conditions where an alien power ruled over a state without citizens, where the right of conquest rather than the consent of its subjects constituted its charter, and where, therefore, dominance would never gain the hegemony it coveted so much. So it made no sense to equate the colonial state with India as constituted by its own civil society. The history of the latter would always exceed that of the Raj, and consequently an Indian historiography of India would have little use for statism.

The inadequacy of statism for a truly Indian historiography follows from its tendency to forbid any interlocution between us and our past. It speaks to us in the commanding voice of the state which by presuming to nominate the historic for us leaves us with no choice about our own relation to the past. Yet the narratives which constitute the discourse of history are dependent precisely on such choice. To choose means, in this context, to try and relate to the past by listening to and conversing with the myriad voices in civil society. These are small voices which are drowned in the noise of statist commands. That is why we don't hear them. That is also why it is upto us to make that extra effort, develop the special skills and above all cultivate the disposition to hear these voices and interact with them. For they have many stories to tell—stories which for their complexity are unequalled by statist discourse and indeed opposed to its abstract and oversimplifying modes.

Let us consider four such stories.[2] Our source for them is a series of

---

[2] Panchanan Mandal (ed.), *Chitthipatre Samajchitra, vol. 2* (Viswabharati, Calcutta & Santiniketan, 1953), no. 249 (pp. 181–2), no. 255 (p. 185), no. 257 (pp. 185–6), no. 258 (p. 186).

petitions addressed to the local communities of Brahman priests in some West Bengal villages asking for absolution from the sin of affliction. The sin, supposed to have been testified by the disease itself, called, in each case, for such purificatory rituals as only the Brahmans could prescribe and perform. The offence, no less spiritual than pathological, was identified either by name or symptom or a combination of both. There were two cases of leprosy and one each of asthma and tuberculosis—all diagnosed apparently without the help of specialist advice which, in those days during the first half of the nineteenth century, was perhaps not easily available for the rural poor.

The afflicted were all agriculturists by caste, so far as one can tell by the surnames. For at least one of them occupation was indexed by illness as he traced the ravages of leprosy on his hand to being bitten by a mouse while at work on his paddy field. Nothing could be more secular, indeed down-to-earth, if not quite convincing as an explanation of the disease, and yet the victim himself looked upon the latter as a suffering caused by some unspecified spiritual offence. What is it, one wonders, that made it necessary for a malady of the body to be understood as a malfunction of the soul? For an answer, it must be recognized in the first place that a question such as this could hardly be asked in rural Bengal at the time. With all that had happened geopolitically by then to consolidate British paramountcy, its organ the colonial state was still rather limited in its penetration of Indian society even in that region where the process of colonization had gone the farthest. Insofar as that penetration was a measure of the hegemonic claims of the Raj, the latter were, on this evidence, unrealized in some important respects.

The first of these claims relate to questions of health and medicine. The colonial rulers are said to have won the minds of the natives everywhere by helping them to improve their bodies. This is a commonplace of imperialist discourse meant to elevate European expansion to the level of a global altruism. The control of disease by medicine and the sustenance of health by hygiene were, according to it, the two great achievements of a moral campaign initiated by the colonizers entirely for the benefit of the colonized. But morality was also a measure of the benefactor's superiority, and these achievements were flaunted as the triumph of science and culture. It was a triumph of Western civilization symbolized for the simple-minded peoples of Asia, Africa and Australasia touchingly by soap.

The soap and the Bible were the twin engines of Europe's cultural conquest. For historical reasons specific to the Raj the soap prevailed over the Bible in our subcontinent, and medicine and public health figured more and more prominently on the record of England's Work in India during the last decades of the nineteenth century. That was a record in which the statement of good deeds served as an announcement of hegemonic intentions as well. Its aim, amongst other things, was to make foreign rule tolerable for the subject population, and science had a part to play in that strategy. Science—the science of war and the science of exploration—had won for Europe its first overseas empires in the mercantile era. Now in the nineteenth century it was for science again to establish a second-order empire by subjugating the bodies of the colonized to the disciplines of medicine and hygiene.

The small voices of the sick in rural India speak of a degree of resistance to that imperial design. They demonstrate how difficult it still was for medicine to rely on that objectification of the body so essential for its success in diagnosis and healing. Although it had already been institutionalized during this period by a medical college and a number of hospitals set up in Calcutta, the clinical gaze had not beamed on to the neighbouring districts yet. Symptomatology would continue to inform pathology there for some time to come and no secular understanding of disease, however necessary, would suffice unless backed by transcendental explanation.

The latter is where science met tradition in a cultural contest. Its outcome was to remain undecided so long as the afflicted turned for help to the law of faith rather than the law of reason in the conviction that the body was merely a register for the gods to inscribe their verdicts against sinners. What our petitioners sought therefore was moral prescriptions for absolution rather than medical ones for cure, and the authority they turned to was not doctors but priests. They were persuaded to do so no less by their individual judgment than by the counsel of their respective communities. The petitions were all witnessed by signatories from the same or neighbouring villages, and in three out of four by those from the same caste. In fact, the petitioners were not necessarily the diseased themselves, but a kinsman in one instance and a number of fellow villagers in another.[3] Absolution was for them as important as cure. Hence the sense of urgency about ritual expiation (*prayaschitta*). The latter was doubly efficacious. Its function was to absolve not only a particular offender from the polluting effect of his sin, but also others who had incurred

[3] The five petitioners in the case of tuberculosis are all from the sick man's own village Singarpur (op. cit., no. 255), while the petitioner in the other case describes the patient as his mother-in-law (ibid., no. 257).

impurity by association (*samsarga*). Since certain kinds of diseases, such as leprosy, were thought to be highly polluting, the need for ritual purification was always a communal concern.

That concern has much to tell us about the history of power. At one level, it is evidence of the limitations of colonialism—that is, of the resistance its science, its medicine, its civilizing institutions and administrative policies, in short, its reason encountered in rural India even as late as the 1850s. That is a level quite accessible to statist discourse: it is never happier than when its globalizing and unifying tendency is allowed to deal with the question of power in gross terms. It is a level of abstraction where all the many stories these petitions have to tell are assimilated to the story of the Raj. The effect of such lumping is to oversimplify the contradictions of power by reducing them to an arbitrary singularity—the so-called principal contradiction, that between the colonizer and the colonized.

But what about the contradiction between priest and peasant in rural society, the contradiction between those dispensers of *shastric* injunction for whom to touch a plough is *adharma* and their victims for whom the labour on the rice fields is dharma itself, the contradiction between a caste association (*samaj*) led more often than not by its élite and the sick amongst its members handed over to sacerdotal authority as a gesture of willing subordination to Brahmanism and landlordism? When Abhoy Mandal of Momrejpur, considered polluted by the asthmatic attacks suffered by his mother-in-law, submits himself for expiation to the local council of priests and says, 'I am utterly destitute; would the revered gentlemen be kind enough to issue a prescription that is commensurate to my misery?'[4] or when Panchanan Manna of Chhotobainan, his body racked by anal cancer, pleads before a similar authority in his own village, 'I am very poor; I shall submit myself to the purificatory rites of course; please prescribe something suitable for a pauper,'[5]—are we to allow these plaintive voices to be drowned in the din of a statist historiography? What kind of history of our people would that make, were it to turn a deaf ear to these histories which constitute, for that period, the density of power relations in a civil society where the colonizer's authority was still far from established?

Yet who amongst us as historians of India can claim not to have been compromised by élitism of this particular kind—namely, statism? It pervades so obviously the work of scholars who follow the colonialist model that I would rather not take your time over it: in any case, I have

---

[4] Ibid., no. 257.
[5] Ibid., no. 258.

already discussed that question elsewhere at some length.[6] All that need be said here is simply that the statist point of view which informs the colonialist model is identical with the colonizer's own standpoint: the state it refers to is none other than the Raj itself. However there is a statism which prevails in nationalist and Marxist discourses as well. The referent in both of these is a state that differs in a significant respect from that in colonialist writing. The difference is one between power realized in a well-formed and well-established regime of many years' standing and power that is yet to actualize; a dream of power. It is a dream that anticipates a nation–state with emphasis laid primarily on self-determination defined in liberal–nationalist writing by only the most general liberal–democratic terms, and in left-nationalist and Marxist writing by state–socialist terms. In either case historiography is dominated by the hypothesis of a principal contradiction which once resolved would convert the vision of power into its substance. Between the two it is the latter that is considerably more complex in its articulation of statism and I shall concentrate on it for the rest of my talk if only because its intellectual challenge for any critique is more sophisticated, hence more formidable, than that of nationalist discourse.

It is well known how for many academics and activists concerned with the problem of social change in the subcontinent the historical experience of peasant insurgency has been the paradigmatic instance of an anticipation of power. And that instance has nowhere been more fully documented than in P. Sundarayya's monumental history of the Telangana uprising.[7] This was an uprising of the mass of peasants and agricultural labourers in the south-eastern region of the Indian peninsula called Telangana, now a part of Andhra Pradesh. The uprising, led by the Communist Party, assumed the form of an armed struggle directed first against the princely state of the Nizam of Hyderabad and then against the Government of India when the latter annexed the kingdom to the newly founded republic. The rebellion ran its course from 1946 to 1951 and won some important victories for the rural poor before being put down by the Indian army. An authoritative account of the event was published twenty years later by P. Sundarayya, the principal leader of the insurrection, in his book *Telangana People's Struggle and Its Lessons*.

The unifying element in Sundarayya's account is power—a vision of

[6] In 'Dominance without Hegemony and its Historiography': *Subaltern Studies VI* (Oxford University Press, Delhi, 1989), pp. 210–309.
[7] P. Sundarayya, *Telangana People's Struggle and Its Lessons* (Communist Party of India–Marxist, Calcutta, 1972).

power in which the fight for land and fair wages was significantly over-determined by certain administrative, judicial and military functions. These, properly speaking, are state-like functions, but were reduced in this instance to the level of local authority because of the character and scope of the struggle. Yet the latter with all its limitations was oriented towards a contest for state power as acknowledged by its adversaries—the landlord state of the Nizam and the bourgeois state of Independent India. The organs of its authority and the nature of the programmes envisaged for the areas under its control also testified to such an orientation. Power, anticipated thus, was to be won in the form of an embryonic state by the resolution of that 'principal contradiction' which, apparently, was not quite the same under the Nizam's rule as under Nehru's. Whatever that was—and Party theoreticians were locked in an interminable wrangle over the issue—its resolution in a manner favourable to the people could be achieved, according to them, only by means of armed resistance. It followed, therefore, that the values most appreciated in this struggle—values such as heroism, sacrifice, martyrdom, etc.—were those that informed such resistance. In a history written to uphold the exemplary character of that struggle one would expect those values and the corresponding deeds and sentiments to dominate.

All these three aspects of the Telangana movement—that is, an anticipation of state power, strategies and programmes designed for its realization, and the corresponding values—are neatly integrated in Sundarayya's narrative. It is significant, however, that the condition for such coherence is a singularity of purpose which has been presupposed in his account of the struggle and which provides it with its discursive unity and focus. What would happen to coherence and focus if one were to question that singularity and ask whether that single struggle was all that gave the Telangana movement its content?

This disturbing question has indeed been asked. It has been asked by some of the women who had themselves been active in the uprising. Heard first in a series of interviews it has been recorded as material for a feminist reading of that history by other women of a younger generation. Two amongst the latter, Vasantha Kannabiran and K. Lalita have illuminated for us some of the implications of this question in their essay 'That Magic Time'.[8] The question, they say, has something common to all its variations as it occurs in the interviews: it is 'an undertone of

---

[8] Vasantha Kannabiran and K. Lalit[h]a, 'That Magic Time' in Kumkum Sangari and Suresh Vaid (eds), *Recasting Women* (Rutgers University Press, New Brunswick, New Jersey, 1990), pp. 190–223.

harassment' and 'a note of pain' which the voices of the older women carry for the younger ones to hear.[9] 'Hearing', we know, "is constitutive for discourse'.[10] To listen is already to be open to and existentially disposed towards: one inclines a little on one side in order to listen. That is why speaking and listening between generations of women are a condition of solidarity which serves, in its turn, as the ground for a critique. While solidarity corresponds to listening and inclining towards, Kannabiran and Lalita's critique addresses some of the problems arising from the privative modes of not-listening, turning a deaf ear to, turning away from. The small voice speaking in a certain undertone, as if in pain, is pitted, in this instance, against the privative mode of statist discourse, a commanding noise characteristically male in its 'inability to *hear* what the women were saying'.[11]

What was it that the women were saying in undertones of harassment and pain? They spoke, of course, of their disappointment that the movement had not lived fully upto its aim of improving the material conditions of life by making land and fair wages available for the working people of Telangana. That was a disappointment they shared with men. But the disappointment specific to them as women resulted from the leadership's failure to honour the perspective of women's liberation it had inscribed in the ideology and programme of the struggle. It was that perspective which had mobilized them *en masse*. They saw in it the promise of emancipation from an ancient thraldom which with all the diversity of its instruments and codes of subjugation was unified by a singular exercise of authority—that is, male dominance. Such dominance was, of course, parametric to Indian parliamentary politics. That it would be so for the politics of insurrection as well was what Telangana women were soon to find out from their experience as participants.

It is not difficult, therefore, to understand why the strength women added to the movement by their numbers, enthusiasm, and hope should have generated some tension within it. It was not a tension that could be solved without altering in some fundamental sense the perspective of the struggle as worked out by its leaders. Women's emancipation was for them simply a sum of equal rights—an end to be achieved by reformist measures. Emancipation by reform had indeed attracted women initially to the movement. However, as they surged forward to participate actively in it, the very impetuosity of that surge with all its buffeting, wrenching

[9] Ibid., pp. 194, 196.
[10] Martin Heidegger, *Being and Time* (Basil Blackwell, Oxford, 1987), p. 206.
[11] Kannabiran and Lalit[h]a, p. 199.

and overflowing made it impossible for the notion of emancipation to keep standing where the leadership had put it. The turbulence turned out to be the mould for a new concept of emancipation. It no longer sufficed to think it as a package of benefits conferred on women by the design and initiative of men. Henceforth, the idea of equal rights would tend to go beyond legalism to demand nothing less than the self-determination of women as its content. Emancipation would be a process rather than an end and women its agency rather than its beneficiaries.

There is no recognition at all in Sundarayya's work of women's agency either as a concept or as a matter of fact. Consider the following passage which sets the tone for his approach to this important theme in a chapter concerned entirely with women's role in the Telangana Movement. He speaks with genuine admiration about 'that tremendous revolutionary spirit and energy that is smouldering in our economically and socially oppressed womenfolk' and goes on to observe in the next sentence:

If *we* only take a little trouble *to enable* it to emerge out of its *old tradition-bound shell* and try *to channel* it in *the proper revolutionary direction*, what a mighty upheaval it will lead to.[12]

The first person plural speaks here obviously for a predominantly male leadership unaware of or indifferent to the fact that it is itself trapped in an 'old tradition-bound shell' in its attitude to women. Yet it invests itself in the triple role of the stronger condescending 'to enable' those presumed to be the weaker, the enlightened undertaking to liberate those still imprisoned by tradition, and of course the avant-garde ready 'to channel' the energies of a backward and gendered mass towards the 'proper revolutionary direction'. The élitism of this stance can hardly be overstated.

It is no wonder, therefore, that the programmatic gestures made towards emancipation were not allowed by the leadership to shift out of the groove of reform, and the authorized view of women's participation remained one of sheer instrumentality. Consequently, when the crunch came at any point of the movement and a decision had to be taken to resolve some problem or other of male dominance in a manner likely to undermine it, the solution was deferred, avoided, or simply ruled out within the party in the name of organizational discipline—a question about which Kannabiran and Lalita have much to say—and within the community at large in the name of respect for 'mass opinion'.[13] The

[12] Sundarayya, pp. 328–9. Emphasis added.
[13] 'No decision was to be given which would put mass opinion against us.' Thus Sundarayya on questions of marriage and sexuality. Ibid., p. 351.

tribune in either case was patriarchy. 'Mass opinion' was its alibi to harness expediency to its own authority, and organizational discipline its pretext to deal with questions of sexuality by a code that denounced questioning itself as subversive.

The writing of history, I regret to say, conforms fully to patriarchy in Sundarayya's narrative. The principles of selection and evaluation common to all historiography are in agreement here with a pre-fabricated statist perspective in which a hierarchized view of contradiction upholds a hierarchized view of gender relations with no acknowledgement at all of women's agency in the movement. With all its goodwill towards women and praise showered lavishly on their courage, sacrifice, ingenuity, etc. that writing remains deaf to 'what the women were saying'.

But suppose there were a historiography that regarded 'what the women were saying' as integral to its project, what kind of history would it write? The question is, for me, so complex and far-reaching that I can do no more than make some general observations at this stage. At this stage, because our critique of statist discourse cannot by itself produce an alternative historiography. For that to happen the critique must move beyond conceptualization into the next stage—that is, the practice of re-writing that history.

A re-writing of the history of the Telangana movement that is attentive to the 'undertones of harassment' and the 'note of pain' in women's voices will, in the first place, challenge the univocity of statist discourse. One of the most important consequences of the ensuing contest will be to destroy the hierarchization which privileges one particular set of contradictions as principal or dominant or central and regards the need for its solution as prior to or more urgent than that for all the others.

Secondly, a re-writing that heeds the small voice of history will put the question of agency and instrumentality back into the narrative. The latter, in its authorized version, has no room for it. The story of the insurrection is told with its agency invested exclusively in the party, the leadership, and the male, while the other active elements are all relegated to a state of instrumentality subject to no change under the impact of the developing movement. In a new historical account this metaphysical view will clash with the idea that women were agents rather than instruments of the movement which was itself constituted by their participation. This will inevitably destroy the image of women as passive beneficiaries of a struggle for 'equal rights' waged by others on their behalf. The concept of 'equal rights' will, in its turn, lose its legalistic connotation and recover its dignity as an essential aspect of the self-emancipation of women.

Thirdly, I feel that women's voice, once it is heard, will activate and make audible the other small voices as well. Those of the adivasis—the aboriginal populations of the region—for instance. They too have been marginalized and instrumentalized in the statist discourse. Here again, as in the case of women, the garland of praise for their courage and sacrifice is no compensation for the lack of an acknowledgement of their agency. What I have in mind here is not simply a revision on empirical grounds alone. I want historiography to push the logic of its revision to a point where the very idea of instrumentality, the last refuge of élitism, will be interrogated and re-assessed not only with regard to women but all participants.

Finally, a narratological point. If the small voice of history gets a hearing at all in some revised account of the Telangana struggle, it will do so only by interrupting the telling in the dominant version, breaking up its storyline and making a mess of its plot. For the authority of that version inheres in the structure of the narrative itself—a structure informed in post-Enlightenment historiography, as in the novel, by a certain order of coherence and linearity. It is that order which dictates what should be included in the story and what left out, how the plot should develop in a manner consistent with its eventual outcome, and how the diversities of character and event should be controlled according to the logic of the main action.

Insofar as the univocity of statist discourse relies on such an order, a certain disorderliness—a radical deviation from the model that has dominated the writing of history for the last three hundred years—will be an essential requirement for our revision. What precise form such disorder may assume is hard to predict. Perhaps it will force the narrative to stutter in its articulation in stead of delivering in an even flow of words; perhaps the linearity of its progress will dissolve in loops and tangles; perhaps chronology itself, the sacred cow of historiography, will be sacrificed at the altar of a capricious, quasi-Puranic time which is not ashamed of its cyclicity. All one can say at this point is that the overthrow of the regime of bourgeois narratology will be the condition of that new historiography sensitized to the undertones of despair and determination in woman's voice, the voice of a defiant subalternity committed to writing its own history.

2

Writing, Orality and Power in the Dangs, Western India, 1800s–1920s*

Ajay Skaria

I

In 1868, the *adivasis* of Panchmahals rebelled against the British and the small states in the region. A police outpost was sacked, several small places were looted. British troops were sent to quell the rebellion. The

* This chapter has benefited greatly from the comments of participants in seminars at Centre for South Asian Studies, Cambridge, and St Anthony College, Oxford, where it was presented. I am extremely grateful to Shahid Amin, Chris Bayly, and David Hardiman, whose detailed criticisms on an early draft transformed it. I am also grateful to Sunil Agnani, Peter Burke, Dipesh Chakravarty, Paul Connerton, Richard Drayton, Eva-Maria Lassen, Rosalind O'Hanlon, Sanjay Reddy, Samita Sen, Anil Sethi, Shiney Varghese, and David Washbrook for their extremely valuable comments on a later draft.

The abbreviations used in the footnotes are: BA: Bombay Archives; PD: Political Department; RD: Revenue Department; ED: Education Department; PDD: Political Department Diaries; PSD: Political and Secret Department; GR: Government Resolution; comp.: compilation; BRO: Baroda Records Office; DDR: Dangs District Records; RR: Residency Records; DN: Daftar Number; FN: File Number; DCR: District Collectorate Records, Dangs; NAI: National Archives of India, New Delhi; IOL: India Office Library; Coll.: Collector; APA: Assistant Political Agent, Khandesh; Kh.: Khandesh; Secy: Secretary; GoB: Government of Bombay; FD: Foreign Department; Pol: Political; Genl: General.

final showdown between the poorly-equipped rebels and well-trained
colonial troops occurred at a hillside where the messianic leader of the
movement was encamped along with several thousand Bhils and Naik-
das. Colonial troops had already taken up positions nearby. The scene
was set for the confrontation.[1]

It was at this stage that the British officer in command of the operation
wrote and sent by messenger a final ultimatum to the messianic leader,
Joria Bhagat, seeking his surrender. The messenger returned with the
report of Joria Bhagat's unwillingness to do so. He also brought with
him a written reply from Joria, consisting of a sheet of paper covered
with squiggles and stick drawings of human beings.[2] Colonial officials
could make no sense of it, and dismissed it as nonsensical. When in
Panchmahals district in early 1993 I showed it to persons whose ancestors
were closely associated with the movement. They were unable to interpret it either.

At the very least, Joria's reply represented a use of writing in ways so
different from conventional literate constructions of meaning that it remains opaque to us. Nor is Joria's case unique. Peasant rebels have often
both appropriated and destroyed writing. Sido, one of the leaders of the
Santhal rebellion of 1855, claimed that the decision to launch the insurrection had been prompted by divine writing on half a piece of paper that
fell on his head.[3] During the 1857 revolt in Hamirpur district of Uttar
Pradesh, crowds destroyed 'all records of every kind'.[4] Such invocations
of or confrontations with the written word were evidently fuelled by the
perception that it was enormously powerful. The notion of writing as a
weapon of the dominant is thus often a crucial element in the experience
of subaltern groups.

In the social sciences, some truisms surround our received wisdom
about how non-literate[5] communities perceive writing. The most pervasive, possibly, is that these communities see it as magical. Both Jack
Goody and David Henige, for example, explicitly set out this claim.[6] Levi

---

[1] See BA, PD, 1868, vol. 102.

[2] Reproduced from BA, PD, 1868, vol. 102.

[3] Ranajit Guha, *Elementary Aspects of Peasant Insurgency in Colonial India* (Delhi,
1983), pp. 55f.

[4] Ibid., p. 51.

[5] I prefer the term 'non-literate' to 'oral' in this context because it emphasizes
the quality of lack that such groups attributed to their orality, especially when
having to deal with colonial writing.

[6] David Henige, *The Chronology of Oral Tradition: Quest for a Chimera* (Oxford,

Strauss makes a similar point when describing in *Tristes Tropiques* the encounter of the Nambikwara with writing,[7] and Ranajit Guha, using Levi-Strauss's insights, again stresses how writing was magical in the oral culture of peasants.[8]

This emphasis in social theory on the magical nature of writing is part of a larger legacy of European mythologizing. Colonial culture had several criteria by which non-European societies were judged and ranked. One of these, as Michael Adas has shown, was constituted by machines and the perceived level of technological development.[9] Since it was a significantly literate European society that acquired colonies at an increasing pace from the sixteenth century, literacy and proficiency in writing were likely to have been other similar criteria. Certainly, the reactions of wonderment to writing amongst 'primitive'[10] colonized societies were amongst the staples of colonial portrayals, and this surfaces in colonial ethnography. In Russell and Hiralal's account of the Gonds, one of the episodes that serves to define their primitive nature concerns writing:

A Gond was sent with a basket of mangoes from Palvatsa to Bhadrachalam, and was warned not to eat any of the fruit, as it would be known if he did so from a note placed in the basket. On the way, however, the Gond and his companion were overcome by the attraction of the fruit and decided that if they buried the note it would be unable to see them eating. They accordingly did so and ate some of the mangoes, and when taxed with their dishonesty at the journey's end, could not understand how the note could have known of their eating the mangoes when it had not seen them.[11]

The emphasis on the magical nature of writing was thus part of a myth-model which glossed over conquest and domination to focus on the civilized European whose technologies bedazzled and awed the colonized primitive.

1974), pp. 97–103; Jack Goody, 'Restricted literacy in Ghana', in Jack Goody (ed.), *Literacy in Traditional Societies* (Cambridge, 1968).

[7] Claude Levi-Strauss, *Tristes Tropiques* (Harmondsworth, 1976).

[8] Guha, *Elementary Aspects*, p. 54.

[9] Michael Adas, *Machines as the Measure of Men: Science, Technology and Ideologies of Western Dominance* (Ithaca, 1989).

[10] I discuss the relationship between primitivity, tribes and castes in my paper 'Orientalism and Globalism: Conceptions of "Tribes" in Western India, 1800s–1990s'.

[11] R.V. Russell and Hira Lal, *The Tribes and Castes of the Central Provinces of India* (London, 1916), vol. III, p. 121.

That myth-model was made possible, of course, by the assumption that literacy was characteristic of 'civilized' societies. This assumption, which possibly became commonsensical with colonial domination, was systematized and formally inducted into social theory by scholars like Jack Goody, who argued that the development of logical thought (especially syllogistic reasoning and formal operations) depended upon the development of writing both in theory and in historical fact.[12] It followed that the mentality of oral societies differed fundamentally from that of literate societies. Ong provides a formidable list of the differences between the two mentalities: the oral mind is additive rather than subordinative, aggregative rather than analytic, redundant or copious rather than sparse, traditionalist rather than innovative, closer to lived experience rather than divorced from it, empathetic and participatory rather than objectively distanced, and situational rather than abstract.[13]

These distinctions have till quite recently influenced much of our understanding of the way non-literate subaltern communities perceive writing. Guha, for example, associates orality with a greater degree of immediacy, and, as in some senses, unpremeditated.[14] Such a position is formulated even more sharply in Ewald's fascinating paper on the perceptions of writing amongst the largely non-literate Taqali of Sudan. She argues that Taqali people consciously rejected written modes of communication because the Taqali polity was characterized by fluid and ambiguous relations, and 'orality fostered their political relations [while] writing was inimical to them'.[15]

But the distinctions between the mentalities of orality and literacy are increasingly being called into question. One line of attack has undermined the presuppositions that make the distinction possible. Derrida has argued that, in the Western philosophical tradition, the affirmation of the civilizational role of writing has usually gone hand in hand with the denigration of concrete writing or the actual written text. The spoken word has been considered primary and natural, while writing was seen as secondary, representational, and supplementary. This privileging of the spoken word, or 'logocentrism', as he calls it, is 'nothing but the

---

[12] Goody has arguably been the single most influential representative of this view. *See* his *The Domestication of the Savage Mind* (Cambridge, 1977) which along with his edited volume *Literacy in Traditional Societies*, set out this perspective.

[13] Walter Ong, *Orality and Literacy: The Technologising of the Word* (London, 1982).

[14] Guha, *Elementary Aspects*, pp. 257, 261.

[15] Janet Ewald, 'Speaking, Writing and Authority: Explorations in and from the Kingdom of Taqali', *Comparative Studies in Society and History*, 30 (2), 1988.

most original and powerful ethnocentrism'.[16] Criticizing Levi-Strauss's account of the deleterious effects of the introduction of writing amongst the Nambikwara, he elaborates the point:

It is, however, an ethnocentrism *thinking itself* as anti-ethnocentrism, an eth-nocentrism in the consciousness of a liberating progressivism. . . .
The traditional and fundamental ethnocentrism which, inspired by the model of phonetic writing, separates writing from speech with an ax, is thus handled and thought of as anti-ethnocentrism. It supports an ethico–political accusation: man's exploitation by man is the fact of writing cultures of the Western type. Communities of innocent and unoppressive speech are free from this accusation.[17]

I shall argue towards the end of this chapter that despite its insights, this is a deeply problematic approach; one that ignores the relations of power involved in writing.

More influential in undermining the distinction between orality and literacy, at least within anthropology, has been the explosion of empirical studies that have questioned conventional dichotomies. These have made it evident that the written and the oral should be associated with altered social and institutional practices rather than with uniquely distinctive cognitive operations or social structures.[18]

Yet this new and inoffensively correct consensus is not very satisfac-tory. For those engaged in working on the histories of oppressed or exploited groups, the similarities between the responses of Joria Bhagat, Sido, and many others are too striking to be ignored or swept under pastel carpets. We need, in other words, to develop a framework that avoids both the reification of the distinction between orality and literacy, and the

[16] Jacques Derrida, *Of Grammatology*, trans. Gayatri Chakravorty Spivak (Bal-timore, 1974), p. 3.

[17] Ibid., pp. 120–1. *See also* his *Writing and Difference*, trans. Alan Bass (London, 1978).

[18] The literature questioning the distinction between literacy and orality is large and growing rapidly. For some examples, *see* Brian Street, *Literacy in Theory and Practice* (Cambridge, 1984); Don Kulick and Christopher Strond, 'Christianity, Cargo, and Ideas of Self: Patterns of Literacy in a Papua New Guinean Village', *Man* (n.s.) 25 (2), 1990; Ruth Finnegan, *Oral Traditions and the Verbal Arts* (London, 1992); F. Niyi Akinnaso, 'Schooling, Language and Knowledge in Literate and Non-Literate Societies', *Comparative Studies in Society and History*, 34 (1), 1992. For nuanced historical perspectives, *see especially* Roger Chartier, *Cultural Uses of Print in Early Modern France* (Princeton, 1987) and his edited volume, *The Culture of Print: Power and the Uses of Print in Early Modern Europe* (Cambridge, 1992).

historicist closure of the argument with the valid but limited point that the meanings of writing varied in different contexts.

The Dangs, the region on which this chapter focuses, is a particularly apposite region for developing such a framework. The meanings of various forms of writing in the Dangs changed considerably over a century. While in the early or mid-nineteenth century (and possibly earlier), Dangis saw writing as a powerful plains technology, they did not necessarily regard written agreements as any more binding than oral ones. With the consolidation of British authority, however, the power of colonial writing came to be perceived to be greater. This was in part because of the extensive colonial use of writing, and because of their political domination and authority, which allowed them to insist on the consistent implementation of written agreements.

At the same time, contrary to the older understanding (which, as we saw, had suggested that writing introduced fixity and orality represented fluidity), it was the perceived fluidity of writing that made it appear especially powerful to non-literate subaltern groups such as the Dangis. This fluidity was a consequence of the *uncontrollable surplus of meaning* that written agreements represented in the context of colonial domination and Dangi unfamiliarity with literate practices. To the Dangis, written agreements with the British seemed an unpredictable source of new and almost always coercive meaning.

II

The Dangs, a small and densely forested 660 square mile tract in Western India, was inhabited principally by two communities, the Bhils and Koknis.[19] Both depended to varying degrees on shifting cultivation, hunting, fishing, and foraging. Koknis were ritually and economically superior, provided most of the village headmen, and practised cultivation to a greater extent than the Bhils, who were far more dependent on the other three modes of subsistence. Kokni economic superiority did not translate in the nineteenth century into political dominance because local chiefs were from Bhil lineages.

Kingship in the Dangs was far more extensive and incorporative than in the plains. The principal chiefs shared their power with numerous senior *bhauband* (co-sharers of the realm). The important *bhauband* held authority almost independently of the principal chief to whom they

[19] BA, RD, 1892, vol. 144, comp. 948.

formally owed allegiance. They controlled small, loosely defined regions within the Dangs, and some had independent relations with plains powers. Indeed, such relations were even locally a crucial dimension to maintaining authority. Ordinary Bhils were closely associated with the retinues of the local *bhauband*. Indeed the entire Bhil community was in some senses part of the *bhauband*, As officials often remarked, every Bhil thought of himself as a raja.[20] This incorporation into the authority of rajahood occurred in quite substantive ways. Bhils who cultivated, for example, did not have to pay land revenue.[21]

By the early nineteenth century, the most important plains powers were the Gaekwads to the north, and the Deshmukh of Baglan to the south-east. The Gaekwads were a Maratha successor state. The founders of the dynasty in the latter half of the eighteenth century had their earliest important base at Songadh, slightly north of the Dangs. Though they had later shifted to Baroda, Songadh fort and its surrounding regions continued to be under their control, and the local *killedar* or fort commandant dealt regularly with the Dangis.[22] The Gaekwadi fort of Salher to the east of the Dangs also provided another base for relations with the Dangi chiefs.

If Gaekwadi officials represented the new centralized state systems that were emerging in the late eighteenth century, the Deshmukh of Baglan epitomized the growing importance of small kings or chieftains located between the centralized plains powers and the plains polities. The Deshmukh, who had possibly been a hereditary Maratha official, had quite close ties with many Dangi chiefs. He was sometimes described as the 'zemindaur' of the Dangs, and his son claimed that the Dangs had been held by the family for 'hundreds' of years as their hereditary *deshmukhi* area.[23]

The Gaekwads and the Deshmukh often possessed a share in the timber dues collected along the frontiers for teak carried out of the Dangs forests. They also held several co-shared villages along the loosely defined frontiers between their territories and the Dangs. In these, the land revenue was divided equally, with the chiefs and the Gaekwads or the Deshmukh collecting their shares independently.

---

[20] Government of Bombay, *Gazetteer of the Bombay Presidency, vol. XII, Khandesh* (Bombay, 1883), p. 601.

[21] BA, RD, 1892, vol. 144, comp. 948.

[22] André Wink, *Land and Sovereignty in India: Agrarian Society and Politics under the Eighteenth Century Maratha Svarajya* (Cambridge, 1986), pp. 117–22, 189–99; BRO, DDR, DN 1, FN 2.

[23] IOL.F.4.2074, BA, PD, 1874, vol. 108, comp. 1344.

The chiefs too had several rights or *haks* in Gaekwadi and deshmukhi villages. Principal amongst these was *giras*, usually paid along with *bhet* or *sirpav*. An amount often collected in cash, *giras* was levied by chiefs on specific villages too distant to exercise consistent control over, but close enough to harass through raids. It was thus a claim to partial sovereignty over a village. Other associated payments underscored this claim. The *shela* or pagri was a marker of royal power, and the *bhet* was often a small gift in either kind or cash to a political superior.

Till the late eighteenth century, these payments often appear to have been collected by the chiefs directly from the villages from which they were due. But as a result of their role in struggles for authority amongst the chiefs, the power of the Gaekwads and the Deshmukh in the Dangs slowly increased. The upshot was that *giras* began to be paid by the *killedar* at Songadh, though most *sirpav* and *bhet* continued to be collected directly from the villages.[24] By the 1820s, the number of co-shared Dangi villages had also increased greatly because of Gaekwadi and Deshmukh dominance.[25]

Yet, while the chiefs saw the Deshmukh as a figure with superior rights in the Dangs, and similarly acknowledged the Gaekwads as a superior power, their subordination to these figures remained limited. The Dangs was densely forested, and virtually inaccessible to outside armies, enabling the chiefs to easily defy or harass Gaekwadi representatives or the Deshmukh. This interplay of subordination and independence influenced the perceptions of writing of the chiefs.

III

Not too many people in nineteenth or early twentieth-century Dangs could read or write. According to oral traditions, there were formerly semi-formalized indigenous systems of education for learning the rituals required to be a *bhagat*—a man of medicine and supernatural skills. But literacy was not a feature of these systems; only with the opening of schools on Western lines did literacy begin to be imparted. The first of these was set up by missionaries in 1904.[26] By 1915, schools had been

[24] Giberne to Newnham, 28.5.1828, BRO, DDR, DN 1, FN 2.
[25] *See* BRO, RR, DN 144, FN 719; IOL.F.4.2074; and the documents reproduced in BA, PD, 1850, vol. 30/2402, comp. 1617.
[26] Annual Administration Report, 1904–5, BA, ED, 1905, vol. 59, comp. 739.

opened in at least seven other villages attended by around 94 children.[27] Things were not all that different even by 1951, when around 5 per cent of the population was literate.[28]

For ordinary Bhils or Koknis, literacy was almost never required, nor was there much necessity for encounters with the literate world. Rights to hunting, fishing, foraging, shifting cultivation, or land revenue were organized not by written documents but around popular oral knowledge of territorial authority.[29]

So when was writing needed? Consider the case of the *jagirdars*. They were mostly Bhils: of the 128 *jagirs* noted in a list, eleven were held by Koknis, two by Marathas, one by a Bania, 81 by Bhils, and 33 jointly by various Bhil chiefs and the Baroda darbar. It is especially striking, then, that of the five *jagirdars* who possessed documents proving their grants, four were Koknis and one a Bania.[30] Koknis thus either needed grants affirming their *jagirs* more than Bhils, or were more likely to preserve written documents.

Why should this have been so? *Jagirs* were usually granted by the Bhil chiefs to their followers or other chiefs. They could represent reward for services, compensation for loss, or simply an alliance-building gesture of goodwill. But in the Dangs, as more widely in pre-colonial India, grants could also be revoked if the consensus around their continuation faded away. And the chiefs did often reclaim *jagirs* from both Bhils and Koknis in this way.[31] The principal way for a grant-holder to stave off this possibility was by constructing alliances that maintained a social consensus around the grant, and made it difficult for a chief to act against him.

Some Kokni *jagirdars* were important figures or advisers in the retinue of Bhil chiefs.[32] Most, however, were outside the circle of *bhauband*, and received *jagirs* for favours such as making a loan of grain or money to a

---

[27] Annual Report, 1914–15, BA, ED, 1916, comp. 739.

[28] Government of Gujarat, *Dangs District Gazetteer* (Ahmedabad, 1971).

[29] Annual report, 1851, BA, PD, 1852, vol. 42, comp. 1415. 'Report of a March Through the Dangs, March, 1867', BRO, DDR, DN 3, FN 12; BA, RD, 1902, vol. 107, comp. 949, pt II.

[30] 'List of *jagirdars*', 1907, BRO, DDR, DN 6, FN 34, List of *jagirdars*, 1905, DCR, DN 3, FN 4Uc.

[31] Of the 128 *jagirs*, or more precisely of the 92 held by Dangi *jagirdars*, at least sixteen were challenged in the late nineteenth and early twentieth-century. *See* the *jagiri* files in BRO, DDR, DN 6, FN 34 and DCR, DN 3, FN 4Uc for details.

[32] From oral traditions, we know that this was the case in at least three *jagiri* grants to Koknis.

chief when he was in particular need of it.[33] Even Kokni advisers, usually Patils, acquired their role through their individual abilities rather than family standing. In this sense, all Koknis were less part of the community of chiefly obligations than the Bhil *bhauband*.[34]

Their relative marginality made written deeds more important. The deeds could become a resource in maintaining the fragile consensus necessary for continuing grants. In consequence, they asked for written grants affixed with a chief's seal,[35] and preserved these documents better than the Bhils. Within the Dangs, thus, a title deed was evidence of the marginality of the land-grant and its holder in the Bhil polity.

How should we view the use of writing in this context? Here, the written deed was a *trace*. That is to say, its significance derived from the fact that it was a marker that could create fixity. But it was not unique in this. Both written and oral agreements created markers of their having been entered into, one through the document that was produced and the other through the community of listeners or participants who were involved. For the Koknis, the latter was more difficult to sustain. Their inability to maintain oral fixity—to attempt the reproduction of the community of consensus that might sustain the agreement—made the written deed more important for them.

IV

While the possession of written documents implied marginality rather than centrality *within* the Dangs, writing featured as an important element in the relations of the Bhil chiefs with plains powers. There was, first, writing—documentation and recording—by the plains bureaucracies, in which the Dangi chiefs participated only very indirectly. Second, there were written agreements or correspondence, in which Dangi chiefs were more actively involved.

[33] From oral traditions, we know that this was the case in at least six *jagiri* grants. *See also* BRO, DDR, DN 6, FN 34, and DCR, DN 3, FN 4Uc, which together confirm oral traditions in four cases.

[34] Of the four Koknis who possessed written documents, three had received their grants for loans of money or grain while a fourth, Dadaji Patil, had received it for his services with the Ghadvi chief Kerulsing. Even Dadaji Patil's grant, however, was to be contested by Kerulsing's descendants in the early twentieth-century. *See* BRO, DDR, DN 6, FN 34.

[35] Statement of Laxman Lasu, BRO, DDR, DN 6, FN 34.

Maratha bureaucracies generated extensive records in the process of administration. In the 1880s, Gaekwadi officials could produce documents dating back to 1810–11 relating to land-revenue of the co-shared villages. The Baglan Deshmukh produced documents dating back to 1767.[36] He might also have maintained a record of *giras* dues, for he provided in 1828–9 an account of how much *giras* the chiefs had been paid by Gaekwadi representatives in 1814–15.[37] This process of documenting rights was possibly accelerated by colonial domination, when records acquired a new centrality in proving claims.[38]

Possibly, this written documentation that the Gaekwads resorted to did seem powerful to the Dangis, especially since they were non-literate and the Gaekwads were politically dominant. Even so, that power is unlikely to have seemed very threatening. Gaekwadi documents provided no more than a rough index to either *giras* payments or co-shared villages. In 1865, when Gaekwadi officials listed 51 Dangi villages as co-shared, the Dangi chiefs identified fifteen additional villages in which Gaekwadi officials, unknown to themselves, possessed rights.[39] Another Gaekwadi list in 1870 again omitted three villages that the chiefs knew to be co-shared, and one of the villages in the list could not even be traced.[40]

Gaekwadi lists of co-shared villages were thus at best partial. The shifting nature of cultivation further complicated matters. A written list had either to keep track of villages being abandoned and populated, or become obsolete. Given the limited Gaekwadi control over and knowledge of the region, and the fact that 'the Gaekwar's representatives in the Dangs up to late years have been illiterate sepoys', obsolescence was routine.[41]

Similarly, *giras* payment lists could have provided no more than a rough index of the dues that were to be paid. Formally, *giras* dues were determined by *vahivat* or administrative practice, and were a continuation of what had been paid annually in the past. Yet in practice the power to claim *giras* shares had to be constantly and repeatedly demonstrated by

[36] *See* the documents reproduced in K.R. Bomanji, *The Dangs Boundary Dispute* (Bombay, 1903), vol. II, pp. 203–11 (henceforth DBD).

[37] Second Asst. Coll. to Coll., Kh., 8.7.1828, BRO, DDR, DN 1, FN 2.

[38] 'Translation of settlement', 1828, BRO, DDR, DN 5, FN 28.

[39] BA, PD, 1866, vol. 24, comp. 607, Ashburner to Rogers, 23.9.1864, BRO, RR, DN 144, FN 719.

[40] Hancock and Muller to Resident, Baroda, 20.6.1862, Ashburner to Secy, GoB, 31.3.1873, 'The Dhang Case' by T. Madhav Rao, 1883, all reproduced in DBD.

[41] Pritchard to Ashburner, 15.10.1870, DBD, I, p. 14.

the chiefs. Their raids on Gaekwadi plains villages, during which they carried away cattle, grain, and other goods, were the principal means of doing so. The raids were usually carried out just before the monsoons, when grain stocks in the Dangs were low, and when Gaekwadi retaliation would be hampered by the rains.

Gaekwadi documentation and records did not thus create fixity or fixed payments. Rather, they were part of what might be termed a *generative corpus*. That is to say, these documents recorded the transformations of customary payments, and fed into notions of custom, but did not determine these payments. Oral traditions and the political interventions of the non-literate Dangis were far more important influences. Even if Gaekwadi writing about the Dangs was an incomprehensible and potentially powerful plains technology, it was also amenable to containment.

V

In addition to this writing about the Dangi chiefs, there was also correspondence or, the writing to them and the replies from them. In 1809, for example, the Komavisdar of Valod and Buhari wrote a letter to the Ghadvi chief threatening him with dire consequences if he continued his raids on the plains.[42] Similar letters, sometimes about overdue *hak*s, were sent on other occasions. The chiefs also replied. Jararsing, for example, wrote back challenging the Komavisdar to do his worst.[43]

Given the association of writing with plains authorities, receiving such correspondence was a public demonstration of the substantive (though not necessarily cordial) nature of a chief's ties with them, and thus of his power. The fact that the letters had to be borne by a messenger, who also often carried back the Dangi chiefs' replies, further highlighted the event.[44]

The chiefs sometimes declared to these messengers that there was nobody around to read the letters to them. Such claims are best taken with a sack of salt. Silput raja of Ghadvi was sometimes afflicted by this lack of interpreters, usually when he received inconvenient letters demanding the reparation of raided goods or cattle.[45] At such times, by representing

---

[42] Komavisdar to Jararsing, 14th Magasar, Sood, 1866, BA, PDD, 351(11).

[43] Jararsing to Komavisdar, 5th Magsar Vad, 1866, BA, PDD, 351(11).

[44] *See*, for example, the correspondence in BA, PD, 1829, vol. 8/332, and BRO, DDR, DN 1, FN 3.

[45] By the late 1820s, colonial officials at Khandesh were so familiar with this

writing as a technology of the plains which was opaque to the Dangis, he and other chiefs secured the space for strategies of evasive resistance.

Also, unlike Kokni *jagir* grants or Gaekwadi writing about the Dangs, the trace left by correspondence was not seen as important. It neither sustained tenuous claims nor fed into a generative corpus. Rather, it led towards situations where trace was made. Its own content was seen as evanescent. Judging by surviving letters, most correspondence concerned arrangements for meetings, or preliminary negotiations over raids or *haks*.[46] Gaekwadi documentation of these meetings, or written arrangements made at them, were more significant as a trace.[47] In this sense, *its written nature was quite marginal to the Dangi or Gaekwadi understanding of correspondence.*

Written agreements became more common from the 1830s, when merchants obtained timber farms of the Dangs. The Dangs was a heavily forested region, with teak that was especially valuable for the construction of ships or marine craft. Merchants had extracted timber from the forests since at least the late eighteenth century. Until the early 1830s, they simply paid a fee at the chiefs' toll points along the borders.[48] From around 1836, however, merchants with the support of the British, increasingly entered into direct written leases, securing thereby a monopoly of timber in a region, and undertook to construct new pathways or passes across the hills for transporting timber.[49]

If the intention of the resort to writing was to imbue the agreements with a greater degree of fixity, the merchants did not succeed. The chiefs

---

dilatory Dangi technique that they took to sending letters with a person able to read it to the chiefs. Stevens to Hodges, 15.9.1829, BA, PD, 1829, vol. 8/332.

[46] *See* the correspondence in BRO, DDR, DN 1, FN 3, and BRO, DDR, DN 3, FN 11.

[47] When faced with growing British dominance, however, Gaekwadi officials were more aware of the danger of correspondence as trace, especially when involved in actions against colonial interests. Thus, during the build-up to the British expedition against Dangi chiefs in 1828–9, Songadh officials extended covert support to the chiefs. Fearing British reprisals, they became circumspect in their correspondence with the chiefs. They warned Ghadvi chiefs of potential British moves, and in one letter said that a man was being sent along with it to discuss orally matters which it was 'inexpedient' to write down in times of 'such difficulty'. See the correspondence in BRO, DDR, DN 1. FN 3.

[48] Nathan Crow to Committee for investigating the timber resources upon the western side of India, 31.5.1806, BA, PD, 1840–2, vol. 631/1164, comp. 669.

[49] *See* the lease agreements reproduced in BA, PD, 1847, vol. 21/1902, comp. 973, BA, PD, 1845, vol. 16/1648, comp. 444.

were to repudiate almost all the agreements that they had entered into with merchants.[50] These repudiations were not very different in principle from the annual process of renegotiation that had accompanied *giras*. Yet the use of written agreements introduced new elements into the situation. Repudiations now took a novel form: it was often alleged that a particular agreement was not genuine or had been obtained by deception.[51] This was a different tack from that adopted during the assertion of rights formerly through raids, petitions, or repudiations, where claims to having been deceived were rarely made.

The frequent recurrence of the motif of deception was the consequence of the new political situation. Involving a technology which they had little access to, written documents had always potentially excluded the Dangis. For the chiefs, such exclusion was least threatening in the case of the Kokni *jagiri* grants. Here, not only were both Koknis and Bhils equally ignorant but, more importantly, the political dominance of the chiefs was unchallenged. The writing of Gaekwadi officials was slightly more problematic. The chiefs were politically subordinate to the Gaekwadi state, and Baroda officials were often more literate than them. Yet, as a result of limited political domination, Baroda officials had treated their documents about *giras* only as major elements in a negotiable generative corpus. In contrast, the agreement with the merchants came at a time when the Gaekwads, the Deshmukh and the British had all increased their influence in the region, the merchants drawing upon the authority of all three to enforce the letter of written agreements in a way that had not been attempted before.

But why did the chiefs claim specifically that they had been *deceived*? In British legal discourse, contracts could be invalidated if one of the parties was not conscious of the implications of what he was doing, or had been forced to sign an agreement. Was this then an appeal to the necessary fictions of equality between the signatories and freely willed individual decision-making that is so central to the legal conception of the written agreement? In other words, could the chiefs have been undermining the lease agreements by appealing to a set of reasons that were acceptable in colonial discourse?

Such an explanation certainly does have a limited validity, a point to which I shall return. But in situations where non-literate subaltern communities confronted the writing of dominant groups, it is inadequate.

[50] *See* the correspondence in BA, PD, 1847, vol. 21/1902, comp. 973, BA, PD, 1845, vol. 16/1648, comp. 444, IOL, F.4.2074.

[51] Mr Boyce's memorandum, n.d., 1842.

The colonial notion of a contract that had been invalidated by deception rested on a notion of writing as a *decipherable* trace or record. That is to say, the signatory was assumed to have an *ex post facto* awareness of the undesirable implications of the contract, which he or she then contests. The principle of violation is thus premised on the sharing of codes of literate evaluation and analysis. It is inadequate to deal with the radical conceptual break represented by the perceptions of non-literate communities who, unable to share these codes, still had to engage with written agreements.

Indeed, often the chiefs were not contesting the specific implications of specific agreements—their being falsified or obtained under unfair circumstances. Consider the case of the Ghadvi chief Kerulsing, who in 1852 repudiated an agreement that he thought he had entered into with the Gaekwadi representative Bapu *killedar* on the grounds that he had been induced to get drunk and had been unaware of the import of what he was signing.[52] Later, it transpired that he had overreacted. He had signed no agreements at the meeting, barring a relatively innocuous letter to another member of the *bhauband*![53] His fear of what had been obtained from him in writing proved so great that he chose to repudiate all that he had signed.

In this sense, Dangi apprehensions sprang from a notion of writing as *surplus*. This surplus was the almost direct consequence of non-literate communities encountering writing in contexts of domination. Even after having been interpreted to the chiefs by literate codes, the written word embodied the unknown, made fearful by its increasingly close association with domination. The written text came in this sense to seen in the course of the nineteenth century as a protean fount of potentially oppressive meaning.

This influenced the finality of repudiations of written agreements with merchants, as opposed to those with Gaekwadi officials. In the latter, repudiations were part of a process of re-negotiation, where greater demands were made. In contrast, the repudiations of merchants' leases were less part of an effort by the chiefs to negotiate a better deal.[54] Often, the chiefs refused to negotiate another deal. The surplus of writing was so dangerous as to call for a much more total repudiation. That such repudiation could be successfully maintained is of course itself an

[52] Bapoo Patil to Boodya Naik and others, BRO, DDR, DN 3, FN 11.

[53] Ibid.

[54] *See* the correspondence in BA, PD, 1847, vol. 21/1902, comp. 973, BA, PD, 1845, vol. 16/1648, comp. 444.

indicator of the independence that the chiefs still retained from the merchants, despite the growing power of the British and the Gaekwads on whom the merchants depended. After the consolidation of British dominance, even such independence was to become difficult.

VI

In all the forms that writing took—grants of *jagirs*, correspondence with plains powers, or agreements with various representatives—there was one common element: the seal or *sikka*. The seals of plains authorities imparted legitimacy to their written correspondence. The Vasurna chief Anandrao claimed on one occasion that a *sipahi* had brought him a letter with 'a seal and English signature',[55] and though he could not read or have the letter interpreted, he implied, the seal persuaded him to accept the *sipahi*'s instructions.

Important chiefs in the Dangs too possessed seals. Sometimes, these were affixed on Kokni *jagiri* grants,[56] though we encounter them most often on agreements or correspondence with plains powers.[57] The principal chiefs certainly thought it very important that they possess seals and that their nominally subordinate Bhil *bhauband*, especially if they were rivals, did not.[58]

The seal was amongst the most exclusive markers. Only the really powerful amongst the *bhauband* could lay claim to it. Its seizure by a rival was a challenge to the authority of the figure who claimed the *gadi* or seat of power. This may have been because the possession of a *sikka* made two large claims: it asserted the grant-giving power within the Dangs of the possessor, and indicated that he was powerful enough to be dealing not only with powers within the *dang*, but also with powers of the *desh*.

Then there was the 'mark' or pictograph of the chiefs, which they often made on documents in addition to their seal. Unlike the exclusive seal, the pictograph was shared by ordinary *naiks* and Bhils with the chiefs.[59] The most common—almost to the degree that it was a community mark

[55] Mamlatdar, Baglan to Coll., Kh., 7.11.1842, IOL, F.4.2074.

[56] Statement of Laxman Lasu, 29.6.1923, BRO, DDR, DN 6, FN 34.

[57] *See*, for example, BRO, DDR, DN 3, FN 11, BA, PD, 1858, vol. 96, comp. 1140, for some such documents.

[58] Yad from Anandrao, n.d., 1849, BRO, DDR, DN 1, FN 2; Trial of Devising, BA, PD, 1850, vol. 38/2404, comp. 593.

[59] *See* some of the evidence in DBD.

of the Bhils—represented a bow and arrow. The pictograph was different, then, from the signature of late literate culture, or the thumb impression that colonialism imposed on non-literate groups. The identity it affirmed was principally that of a community rather than an individual one. When used together on a document, the seal made explicit the hierarchically superior position of the 'signatory' and the pictograph stressed the community of which he was part.[60]

But the seal's role in nineteenth-century Dangs as a form of authorization and a relatively independent carrier of power was limited. In many situations within and around the Dangs, such authorization was not required. When the Pimpri chief once sent one of his men, Chumbar, to another village to call a *bhagat*, the Kokni headman of a village *en route* gave Chumbar some rice simply because he was the 'rajah's man'.[61] In these relatively small territories, the chiefs men were possibly easily recognized.

Then there were other forms of authorization, other independent carriers of power. After a meeting that the Silput raja of Ghadvi had with a Havildar sent by the British for negotiations following a raid,

[60] The use of thumb-impressions as equivalent to signatures may have been closely linked to the emergence of the fingerprint as a means of identifying criminals. Fingerprinting has been one of the most 'subtle and capillary forms of [modern] control' (Carlo Ginzburg, *Myths, Emblems, Clues*, trans. John and Ann C. Tedeschi, London, 1990, p. 123), and its first systematizer, Francis Galton, proudly observed that it gave each person an individuality which could be relied on with lasting certainty. It is profoundly revealing of the constitutive role of empire in the formation of modern Europe that fingerprinting developed in the colonies specifically, in late nineteenth-century Bengal as a means of identifying natives (ibid., 121ff).

The fingerprint was of course important for identifying 'criminals'. According to Shahid Amin (personal communication), the thumb impression similarly made sense as signature only in specific contexts. It evidently would have been entirely out of place in personal correspondence. Its importance derived primarily from the need to enforce the fiction of the contract freely agreed upon. In the dealings of non-literate subaltern communities with the literate and powerful, it created an imaginary equality that made the contract possible.

For the powerful, it is likely that not being literate increasingly began to carry its own stigma as colonial rule consolidated itself. Illiterate *zamindars* in Northern India would often authorize an estate functionary to sign the papers on their behalf rather than affix their thumb impressions, which would have been demeaning. Besides, they possibly thumb-marked the power-of-attorney paper, which was a legal and not a public document. I am grateful to Shahid Amin for his comments on these points.

[61] Case II, BA, PD, 1859, vol. 92, comp. 584.

he regretted that he could not send a suitable present to the Circar as a fire had destroyed all his cloth turbans &c. but says he, drawing an arrow from the well-filled quiver at his back 'Take this and give it to the people of my village of Kehl and demand 9 rupees'. To the companion of the Havildar he gave another arrow telling him to demand five rupees at another of his villages. They delivered the arrows as described and instantly received the money, the villagers said they knew too well to refuse, but that the arrows being shown at Jummabundy [tax-collection] the sum given upon them was always brought to their credit.[62]

Here the arrow had become, quite like the seal, a form of authorization.

So while the seal was powerful, it was but one in a whole complex of markers of authority. Amongst the others were not only arrows but *nagaras* or drums, funerary rituals, *shelas* and *pagdis* (shawls and turbans) appropriate to the rank of the chiefs.[63] Indeed, none of these markers really mattered as much as the alliances a chief built within and outside the Dangs. Without these, markers could create only simulacra of authority. In this sense, control over the seal remained a subordinate feature of early nineteenth-century Dangi polity.

There remains one crucial question: did the importance of the seal for Dangi chiefs derive from the fact that it represented writing, a powerful technology of the plains? Such an association is potentially an instance of what Mudimbe has described as epistemological ethnocentrism.[64] That is to say, it runs the risk of presuming that the valorization of writing in non-literate societies must necessarily be a consequence of incomprehension and wonderment in the face of an external stimulus.

We fall back on such presumptions, which after all form our common sense, all the time. Consider this example. In Panchmahals, as in the Dangs, some *bhagats* would during divination look into the leaf of a *khakra* tree, 'waving the leaf now and then backwards and forwards as when a man finds it difficult to decipher bad writing'. Finally they would read the leaf, and determine the causes of an illness or misfortune.[65] Persons who divined illness in this way were known as *panfodya bhagats*.[66]

---

[62] Giberne to Newnham, 16.10.1828, BA, PSD, 1828, vol. 29/230.

[63] For a more detailed discussion of these, *see* 'A Forest Polity in Western India: The Dangs: 1808–1920s' (University of Cambridge, 1992), pp. 233–43.

[64] V.Y. Mudimbe, *The Invention of Africa: Gnosis, Philosophy and the Order of Knowledge* (Bloomington, 1988), pp. 13–22.

[65] H.J. Antia, 'A Few Notes on the Aborigines of Chhota Udepur State in the Rewa Kantha Political Agency', *Journal of the Anthropological Society of Bombay*, vol. XI, no. 7, p. 873.

[66] D.P. Khanpurkar, 'The Aborigines of South Gujarat' (Ph.D. thesis, University

Now this could easily be interpreted as the infusion of incomprehensibly powerful writing with magical power, which is then appropriated to social goals. Lacking the material to historicize the phenomenon, such an interpretation implicitly relies on a nineteenth-century tradition of originary speculation. It posits an origin to the phenomenon by drawing on a distinction between magic and science, and placing the colonized Other firmly on the side of magic. Though originary speculation of this sort went out of fashion in both anthropology and the social sciences in general in the early twentieth century, we have never really engaged with its legacy. As a result, many of its Frazerian premises survive as subliminal common sense, affecting both our research programmes and our paradigms.

Seen in this light, the analysis of the *panfodya bhagat* (or similar figures in other societies) reveals more about the selective and blinkered nature of our organizing criteria than about the perception of writing within these societies. There were at least three other kinds of *bhagat*s in the Dangs: those who divined using winnowing fans or *supchalyam bhagat*s, those who used water or *kalasya bhagat*s and, highest of all, those who used stones for divination.[67] But water, stones, and winnowing fans remain invisible and unimportant to us. Our focus on writing because of its presumed association with the encounter with modernity do not allow them to be constituted as relevant facts.

Once the privileging of writing is abandoned, it is easier to admit that we do not know the original reasons (if there are such creatures) for the adoption of the seal or the *bhagat*s' reading of leaves. Whatever these might have been, the seal had by the nineteenth century been integrated into a symbolic hierarchy to the point where its power was derivative not from its association with writing, but from its role as a marker in the symbolic hierarchy of chiefly power. Such inscription is best described as *monumental writing*, or writing where the written text is subordinated to the process of the construction of a powerful symbol.[68] This was a phenomenon quite distinct from writing as either trace or surplus, where meanings derived centrally from the character of writing itself.

---

of Bombay, 1944), p. 64.

[67] Ibid., p. 64. Current oral traditions mention several other means of divination by *bhagat*s. Maybe Khanapurkar's attempt to classify *bhagat*s into four types on the basis of the means of divination was quite misplaced.

[68] I borrow the term from Rosalind Thomas, *Literacy and Orality in Ancient Greece* (Cambridge, 1992), pp. 85–8, though it is used here in quite different ways.

VII

By the latter half of the nineteenth century, the significance and role of
writing in the Dangi polity had changed. These transformations, which
had already commenced with the consolidation of colonial rule in the
early decades of the century, are best understood in the context of the
reconstruction of the Dangi polity as a consequence of British domination.
In 1818, the British took over Khandesh, a region adjoining the Dangs,
from the Peshwas.[69] Soon after, colonial officials arrived at agreements
with the Dangi chiefs that they would not raid British Khandesh.[70] But
the agreements soon broke down, as did those with others.

Through the 1820s, halting these raids was an obsessive colonial concern. Initially, Khandesh officials thought that irregular Gaekwadi *giras*
payments were the principal cause for the raids. And once assembled for
a raid on Gaekwadi territory, it was argued, the Bhils did not think twice
about also raiding British territory.[71] Persuaded by this neat piece of logic,
the British rode roughshod over Gaekwadi protests and implemented by
1829 what they thought would be the solution. *Giras* was now paid from
the Khandesh treasury to the Dangi chiefs at an annual meeting, and the
amount was charged to Baroda.[72] The new system did not achieve the
desired results: the Dangi chiefs raided Khandesh less than two months
after the first *giras* payments.

Other measures, such as the military expeditions into the Dangs, secured better results. These expeditions demonstrated the ability of the
British to reach into the Dangs and led to the British *sirkar* being perceived
as immensely powerful. As a result, there were virtually no raids from
the 1830s. The only one that took place was in 1839. But so deep was the
fear of the British *sirkar* by then that when a retaliatory expedition was
threatened, the chiefs who had raided surrendered themselves, rather
than resist as they had formerly.[73]

The ensuing decades saw increasing British control over the region.
The Dangs produced some of the best teak in India for shipbuilding, and

---

[69] For an account of the takeover, *see* Arvind Deshpande, *John Briggs in Maharashtra: A Study of District Administration Under Early British Rule* (New Delhi, 1987),
pp. 8–9, 21–7.

[70] Briggs to Resident, Baroda, 14.7.1821, BA, PSD, 1820–1, vol. 4/8.

[71] BRO, DDR, DN 1. FN 1.

[72] Coll., Kh., to Comm. in Deccan, 30.7.1825, Rigby to Bax, 27.3.1826, BRO, DDR,
DN 1, FN 2, 'A Forest Polity', pp. 84–90.

[73] *See* the extensive correspondence in BRO, DDR, DN 1, FN 3.

by the 1840s many colonial officials thought it essential to control this timber, even if it meant setting aside the leases they had earlier helped merchants to obtain.[74] By 1843, the British had leased almost the entire Dangs from the chiefs. Other steps followed. Amongst these were the appointment of a Diwan to look after the area, and the institution of an annual meeting or darbar to distribute lease payments.[75]

These developments also led to the freezing of patterns of authority, since the resources necessary to transform them were no longer available. If a *giras* payment had formerly been fluid and shifting, this was because it had been, amongst other things, a barometer of shifting relations of power. In transforming *giras* into a regularly paid fixed amount, its political context was rendered superfluous. No longer connected to the assertion of authority, it was now merely a payment that affirmed the relations of power existing at the time when the dues had been settled. Similarly, the cessation of raids resulted in the atrophy of one of the major instruments through which chiefs had built up their authority or generated resources to distribute amongst followers.

After the leases, the relative immutability of patterns of authority took on a new dimension because of what we may call the emergence of a list of chiefs. Formerly, authority was so widely shared that it was difficult to speak of distinctive chiefdoms. Loosely, the Ghadvi chief was recognized as the principal one, but others were effectively independent. This web of overlapping authority could not be easily grasped by the notions of singular sovereignty which colonial officials brought to bear on understanding the Dangs. Their notions assumed the existence of distinctive chiefdoms. Such a view was also convenient. It fitted in well, for instance, with the need to identify persons with whom agreements could be signed, or who could be held responsible for offences. Proceeding from this understanding, the British came up over the decades with a list of fourteen principal chiefs within the Dangs, each seen as holding singular authority over a separate tract of the Dangs. Somewhat arbitrary, the list treated several important chiefs as feudatories of the fourteen. These officially recognized chiefs also became more powerful, since *giras* and lease amounts were in the main distributed through them. Even more importantly, the British supported these fourteen lineages against their rivals.

Also, members from rival lineages had formerly often laid a claim to

---

[74] *See* the correspondence in IOL, F.4.2074.

[75] Coll., Kh., to Secy., GoB, 24.7.1855, BA, PD, 1855, vol. 36, comp. 1242. I deal with the darbar in my paper 'Hegemony, Ritual and Resistance in Western India: the Dangs Darbar, 1840s–1990s'.

succession to the *gadi* if they could build up adequate alliances within and outside the Dangs. Such claims were usually supported by assertions that the ruling family had secured its authority illegitimately, and rightful authority belonged to the rivals. But the British supported a system of male primogeniture, and with their support descendants of ruling families easily put down challenges by rivals. In this sense, not only was the power of the fourteen chiefs enhanced and consolidated, but that of their rivals was seriously whittled down.

At the same time, the British feared that the principal chiefs' rivals would obstruct the colonial working of the forests if the lease and *giras* amounts were not distributed amongst the *bhauband* by the fourteen recognized chiefs. They therefore acted against principal chiefs on complaints by rival *bhauband* of inequitable distribution. Quite apart from this, even the fourteen chiefs did not wish to halt the distribution of resources, save to especially hostile rivals. After all, it was through the distribution of resources that alliances were created and authority was demonstrated. Thus, by a logic of the Dangi polity which colonial intervention did not entirely subvert, the fourteen chiefs consolidated their authority but did not completely exclude other lineages.

British domination also led to the exclusion of other plains powers from the Dangs. In the long run, the Gaekwads could not hold out against the active efforts of colonial officials to exclude them from the region. By the late nineteenth century, ties between the chiefs and Gaekwadi representatives had been almost completely eviscerated. The upshot of all these developments was that the British emerged by then as the principal fount for conferring legitimacy and authority on the chiefs.

VIII

In the process of the consolidation of colonial power, the meanings of writing also changed dramatically. While both the Mughal and Maratha regimes in the region had produced extensive documentation, the British were far more obsessive about recording grants, landholdings, or revenue in writing. Even more importantly, writing was used and perceived differently by the British, leading to transformations in the way colonized, non-literate subaltern groups experienced it.[76] This is a crucial dimension to colonial rule that histories of subaltern groups must engage with.

[76] *See* Bernard Cohn, 'The Census, Social Structure and Objectification in South Asia', in *An Anthropologist Amongst Historians and other Essays* (New Delhi, 1987).

The use of writing played a crucial role in the colonial subordination of the Dangs. Written agreements figured all along. There was the agreement in 1818 against raiding, that in 1829–30 to collect a fixed *giras* amount from the British, and those between 1842–3 that leased out the forests. From the 1830s, the seemingly unchallengeable nature of colonial domination also made it difficult to repudiate agreements.

Similarly, lists and written genealogies quite evidently helped the official recognition of fourteen chiefs and the shift to succession by male primogeniture. The takeover and conversion of *giras* into a fixed annual payment took place through the means of writing. Gaekwadi representatives submitted a written schedule of their annual payments. The chiefs, it is noted in the records, could not produce any documents to back their claims. This means that they must at least have been asked about such documents, which could have left a deep impression about the novel colonial valorization of the written word.[77]

Writing played a role also in the halting of raids. The most important measure in achieving this was the expedition of 1830 led by the founder of the Khandesh Bhil Corps, James Outram. The expedition led to the capture of several chiefs, including the Silput raja of Ghadvi. They were then taken to the Khandesh plains, where Outram summoned them and 'went through the form of making a list of them and their villages in front of them and informing them that they are now known and can be easily apprehended'.[78] The expedition was thus an occasion for the creation of an archive that would enable closer control of the Dangi chiefs. The written archive that the British created was here a trace or record, an immutable and enumerative reality that could be used to inflict retribution on named individuals.

Also, as the emphasis on going 'through the form' indicates, Outram drew consciously on the chiefs' perception of writing as a powerful tool in the hands of the dominant. Pre-emptive control was a matter not only of possessing knowledge but demonstrating it; it was about the aggressive visibility of the archive as knowledge.[79] By drawing up the list publicly, he emphasized simultaneously the collective and individuated subordination of the chiefs to the knowledge of the British.

It would be mistaken to assume that only chiefs were affected by the

---

[77] *See* the correspondence in BRO, DDR, DN 1, FN 2.

[78] Outram to Boyd, 24.5.1830, BRO, DDR, DN 1, FN 3.

[79] The ubiquity of the metaphor of the archive as both knowledge and empire is pointed out by Thomas Richards, *Imperial Archive: Knowledge and Fantasy of Empire* (London, 1993).

colonial use of writing. Given the close ties of kinship amongst the extensive *bhauband*, the chiefs' encounter with writing possibly affected and
was visible to other Bhils too. Besides, colonial officials also used writing
to remake modes of subsistence, and its role in this context would certainly
have been visible to ordinary Dangis.

Dangi shifting cultivation involved lopping and occasionally felling
the trees, as well as burning patches of fields to enable them to sow their
seeds; their hunting involved burning down the undergrowth to provide
a clear view of game; their collection of *mahua* flowers while foraging
involved clearing by fire the area around the base of trees.

While such practices did not usually kill trees, they resulted in many
not growing to a large size, or having crooked boles. This was of little
consequence to the Dangis, who had little use for large timber. But it did
matter to forest officials, since large and straight boles were the most
valuable commercially. After the leases, they made repeated efforts to
curb and reshape Dangi use of teak and timber, but met with little success.[80] By the late 1870s, it was felt that the only way to succeed was to
completely revamp forest rules. Officials proposed forest demarcation,
dividing the Dangs (an entirely forested region) into two tracts: the reserved and protected forests. In the reserved forests, which included the
densest portions, it was planned that Dangis would not be allowed to
cultivate or use fire at all. In the protected forests, it was proposed that
they be permitted to cultivate or hunt, but only using techniques that
would minimize damage to production of large timber.[81]

The demarcation was about a specific form of writing: surveying and
mapping the Dangs. As Brian Harley has argued in his seminal essay,
maps are not neutral objects but are designed to serve specific interests.[82]
In this case, mapping was part of the attempt to control the region.

---

[80] For a detailed discussion of Dangi subsistence practices and their conflict with
British forest management in the nineteenth-century, *see* chs 5 and 7 of 'A Forest
Polity'.

[81] For greater details of other arguments developed in earlier and subsequent
sections *see* 'A Forest Polity', esp. pp. 59–62, 84–97, 102–14, 132–8, 307. 'Timber
Conservancy, Dessicationism, and Scientific Forestry: The Dangs, 1840s–1920s',
forthcoming in Richard Grove (ed.), *Environmental History in South and Southeast
Asia* (New Delhi).

[82] J.B. Harley, 'Maps, Knowledge and Power', *in* D. Cosgrove and S. Daniels
(eds), *The Iconography of Landscape: Essays on the Symbolic Representation, Design and
Use of Past Environments* (Cambridge, 1988). *See also* Denis Wood, *The Power of Maps*
(London, 1992). I thank William Sherman for introducing me to the literature on
maps.

Dietritch Brandis, the Inspector General of Forests for India, pointed out that maps were needed 'to guide the Forest Department in the selection of these reserves'.[83] One official argued for more detailed maps than Brandis had allowed for. These would help 'to determine what Rajah or chief to hold responsible when unauthorized Dullee [shifting cultivation] is made in the forests and when illicit cuttings take place'.[84] Thus, maps helped to create a new geography for the Dangs, where people were denied access to nearly half the area, and the most densely forested portions at that, in order that they be reserved for British timber extraction.

But writing was not just a technology that the British used. There was an ideology surrounding the written word that valorized it far above the oral in administrative practices. This could be called the *rhetoric of fixity*, or the notion that meanings, once inscribed in writing, were more stable and less arbitrary than those embodied in oral traditions or pre-colonial forms of writing. From this perspective, the inscription of colonial laws, for example, substituted a regular and ordered world for a personal, tyrannical, and arbitrary one.[85]

This understanding extended to the necessary fictions surrounding the contract or the written agreement. The principle of inviolability of the written agreement, the assertion that it bound both parties to stipulated and unchangeable rights and obligations, was the cornerstone of the written agreement. If signatories failed to adhere to the stipulations of the agreement, they left themselves open, within the terms of colonial ideology, to legal measures, punitive sanctions, and delegitimization.

All the same, fixed interpretations of written texts, even if produced by the British themselves, would hardly have helped them maintain dominance. Indeed, the rhetoric of fixity and the principle of inviolability were accompanied by sophisticated colonial reading strategies as part of the politics of reading. Such interpretation subverted the binding nature and unilinear implications of the written word in formal ideology, and made possible the derivation from it of diverse courses of action. There seem to have been at least three strategies of this sort available to the British.

[83] Brandis to Chief Secy, GoB, 13.6.1870, BRO, DDR, DN 3, FN 18.

[84] Shuttleworth to Chief Secy, 6.4.1871, BA, RD, 1871, vol. 18, comp. 552.

[85] For a similar point, *see* Brinkley Messick, *The Calligraphic State* (Berkeley, 1993). Maybe the colonial disparagement of traditional legal systems, or of what came to be known as Oriental despotism, also drew on the association between colonial writing and a desirable fixity.

First, an inconvenient written document could be overruled, marginalized, or even rendered invisible. During the build-up to the demarcation, for example, the 1840s leases were set aside on the grounds that colonial rule in the Dangs was based 'more upon might than right', and on the basis of appeals to 'practice'.[86] Second, a new written consensus could be created that formally overrode the previous one—as when colonial officials in 1889 secured, after nearly a decade's efforts, the written consent of the chiefs to the demarcation. The third, and possibly the most important colonial strategy, involved the reinterpretation of the written agreement—the discovery of the desired new meanings in the inviolable text itself. Thus, forest officials justified an ever-increasing set of restrictions on Dangis by reference to the terms of the leases.[87]

This politics of reading was obviously dependent on there being a narrowly defined interpretive community.[88] Within this community, which consisted primarily of the British officials authorized to undertake such reading, there was often a considerable diversity of interpretation. But this was often occluded from the view of even the community by the rhetoric of fixity, which stressed the continuities between interpretation and text more than the disjunctures. Indeed, interpretations drew their legitimacy from appearing 'literal' or 'true', from claiming to *be* the text.

All these points indicate that the politics of reading was, contrary to what De Certeau has implied,[89] more than a matter of providing authorized interpretations to the subordinated. Given colonialism's skewed relations of power, the constitution of any interpretive community was not an aesthetic or mildly social act. In the very act of constituting a colonial interpretive community—an act founded, after all, on the exclusion of the colonized—domination was asserted. It was also one of the ways in which domination remained supple and was reproduced: new circumstances were met with new interpretations. Given the centrality of the rhetoric of fixity in colonial ideology, textual derivations for actions were of seminal importance.

[86] Memorandum of Mr Naylor, Legal Remembrancer, BA, RD, 1879, vol. 90, comp. 947; Note by Ashburner, n.d., BA, RD, 1879. vol. 90, comp. 947.

[87] *See*, for example, Roberts to Elphinston, 22.7.1848, BA, RD, 1848, vol. 95, comp. 1088; Memo from Dr Gibson, 16.5.1849, BA, RD, 1852, vol. 51, comp. 851; Rules for the Forests of Dangs, BA, RD.1856, vol. 48, comp. 1104.

[88] My use of the phrase is similar to that of Stanley Fish. *See* his *Is There a Text in This Class: The Authority of Interpretive Communities* (Cambridge, Mass., 1980).

[89] Michel De Certeau, *The Practice of Everyday Life* (Berkeley, 1984).

IX

The changed nature of writing in the colonial context had dramatic consequences for perceptions of writing and the role of writing within Dangi society. Most striking was the transformation of written agreements. Formerly, as we saw, written agreements were quite like oral ones, in that they could be easily repudiated. By the time the leases to the merchants were concluded, the increasing power of the British and the traders had made such repudiation more difficult, though still possible. In the course of the nineteenth century, such repudiations became increasingly difficult, and finally impossible as a consequence of colonial dominance.

This transformation was already visible during the negotiation of the forest leases between 1841 and 1844, a process that repays detailed examination because it is one of the few well-documented instances we have of chiefs' attitudes towards written agreements with powerful forces. The initial leases were finalized in 1842 by the British Timber Agent at Surat, W. Boyce. Boyce made two trips from Surat into the Dangs, signing an agreement with the Ghadvi chief during the first trip in January. During his second trip in April, he met the Vasurna chief Anandrao and the Pimpri chief Dalpat Vagoo, and signed agreements with both of them.[90] The leases provided that the chiefs would be paid an annual sum, in return for which the British would acquire exclusive and complete rights to the timber in the region.[91]

Problems commenced in November, when Anandrao repudiated the agreements. Initially, he refused to accept the lease-payment that Boyce sent him.[92] Timber-cutters sent into the forests by Boyce were later turned back and warned indirectly that they would be attacked if they returned. He also refused to allow timber that had been felled to be removed from the forests till fees were paid by the cutters directly to him.[93] Within a few months, the agreements with almost all the chiefs had collapsed. I have examined elsewhere the reasons for and the processes of repudiation. Here, I shall focus only on Anandrao's four wildly contradictory petitions and letters, in which he sought to delegitimize his written agreement.

Four themes are discernible in his repudiations. First, there was the

---

[90] Mr Boyce's memorandum, n.d., 1842, IOL, F.4.2074.

[91] *See* IOL, F.4.2074 and BA, RD, 1844, vol. 63.

[92] Boyce to Arbuthnot, 19.1.1843, BA, PD, 1846, vol. 16/1781, comp. 222; Boyce to Arbuthnot, 3.2.1843, IOL, F.4.2074.

[93] Boyce to Arbuthnot, 3.2.1843.

consistent undercutting in all representations of his own authority to enter into leases. In one letter to Boyce, he claimed that:

I have no power to grant you a lease as I told you at Kerjaee and now again. I state that if government insist upon the treaty I cannot restrain my cosharers from breaking it and I shall receive the blame—to prevent this the Government must consider that they have not received a lease from me.[94]

By professing lack of authority to lease the forests, Anandrao possibly invoked the necessary legal fiction of the written agreement as one signed between persons authorized to do so. Both the Deshmukh of Baglan and the local diwans were involved in drafting at least some of the petitions.[95] The foregrounding of that theme may have been part of their attempt to help him engage with colonial concerns.

Second, there was the portrayal of Boyce, the person with whom the agreement had been signed. While in one letter he acknowledged Boyce's presence, he remarked in another that 'some Saheb was there [at the meeting] whom I did not know but he detained me and asked me for a lease of my territory'.[96] In two other letters, he described Boyce as a Parsi, a community in the region that ran liquor shops and engaged in timber trade:

there was no Gentleman there, a Parsee and a person in black dress and a dozen or so Mussalman sepoys were there, without any badges. The Raja asked where the saheb was. The Parsee said he is gone but give me a lease of your territory.[97]

Maybe Anandrao actually suspected Boyce of being a Parsi, since Parsis were known to often have fair complexions like sahibs. Even so, he was not simply drawing a harmless homology between Parsis and sahibs. He was engaged in delegitimizing the agreement, for the lease obviously had less force if it had been obtained by a Parsi or even an unknown sahib than if it had been obtained by a known sahib. Besides the *sirkar* would not think it a very hostile act if he denied leases to vagrant sahibs or mere Parsis.

Third, there was the delegitimation of the written document itself: 'What was obtained from me in writing I did not understand and *whilst the writing was in progress* I told him he had the power of forcing me but

---

[94] Anandrao to Boyce, n.d. (after 12 Nov. 1842), IOL, F.4.2074.

[95] Reeves to Willoughby, 1.7.1843.

[96] Anandrao to Boyce, 8.1.1843.

[97] Mamlatdar, Baglan, to Pringle, 7.11.1842.

that I did not agree of my own free will.'[98] Again, then, Anandrao depicted the process of securing the leases as a violation of the key fictions of the freely willed contract: not only did he not know what he had signed, but he had been coerced into signing, protesting even 'whilst the writing was in progress'.

Fourth, there was an impugning of the occasion at which the agreement had been secured. There were insinuations of deception and impropriety in a Parsi having been at Karzai instead of a sahib, and in the *sipahis* being without badges. Anandrao was improperly equipped too: he did not have with him his seal or his *karkun*.[99] As for the unknown sahib, he, 'taking me by the hand took me from one place to another and threatened to take me to Surat. Seeing he was determined to use compulsion I said if you will force me I must submit.'

In Anandrao's account of the signing of the leases, then, everything that could possibly invalidate the written agreement had happened: he did not have the authority to sign leases, Boyce was not really a sahib, the paper had not been signed legitimately, and the occasion itself was improper.

For the colonial mind, with its emphasis on the 'what really happened', the four starkly varying accounts must have seemed to be, quite simply, a tangle of 'false allegation[s]',[100] and a rather poorly-constructed, self-contradictory one at that. Quite evidently, this is not an adequate answer. A closer look is necessary at what appears on first patronizing sight to be the deployment of a delightful subaltern mendacity as a means of resistance.

One point must not be overlooked. Many of the claims in the letters were plausible perceptions or speculations for Anandrao. Boyce was, after all, an unknown figure whose association with the *sirkar* was none too clear to the Dangis; many Parsis were, like Europeans, fair persons; Boyce possibly had to work quite hard to persuade the *bhauband* to sign the leases in the first place;[101] cajolery from a sahib, even if unknown, could be coercive.

The second point is more important: the use of consistency as a criterion to evaluate Anandrao's petitions may be profoundly misleading. This is not because of any difference, fundamental or otherwise, between

[98] Anandrao to Boyce, 8.1.1843, IOL, F.4.2074, italics added.

[99] Mamlatdar, Baglan, to Pringle, 7.11.1842.

[100] This was how Boyce described them. *See* Anandrao to Boyce, 8.1.1843.

[101] We do not have the details of how the leases were secured from Anandrao. However, we do know that Boyce had quite a difficult time persuading the Ghadvi *bhauband* to sign the leases. *See* Mr Boyce's memorandum, n.d., 1842, ibid.

orality and literacy. Rather, it had to do with the nature of colonial writing and domination. Anandrao was unhappy about the way the leases had been obtained, the restrictions that followed, and the minuscule lease payments.[102] But his representations mentioned these specific grievances only as a tactical filigree, an attempt to relate to colonial concerns. They concentrated principally on delegitimizing the agreements as a whole. If he did not limit himself to specifying complaints and negotiating a better deal, this had to do with the *surplus* of written agreements with dominant groups. Already worrisome when dealing with the merchants, the surplus was even more fearful when dealing with the much more clearly dominant British.

Given the dominance of the British, agreements also had be repudiated cautiously. Earlier, in 1809, when Jararsing raja was warned by a Valod official after a raid, he replied: 'If your Company Bahadur wish to fight with me I will even advance a few paces to meet you. There is no fear.'[103] By the 1840s, there was enough and more fear to go around. Anandrao's repudiations were accompanied by appeals—that the *chowkies* established to check felling be removed,[104] or that no restrictions on felling be introduced,[105]—rather than by defiance. Even his protests about being unfairly treated emphasized the overall rightness of British justice. 'The English Sirkar never oppresses anyone and to the present time have never taken a lease of any forest by force and I have never heard of such a thing.'[106] And his petitions repeatedly affirmed his subordination to British rule. He had, he said, never disobeyed the British *sirkar* and would follow its orders. 'There is not much timber in my forests and from it I and my relatives obtain a livelihood therefore the Sirkar must not take this from us, however this is as the Sirkar pleases, what can I state more.'[107]

It is indicative of the limited British control over the region in the 1840s that the repudiation by Anandrao did not lead to retaliation or to their

[102] *See*, for example, Anandrao to Mamlatdar, n.d., Anandrao to Mamlatdar, Baglan, n.d., Anandrao to Boyce.

[103] Jararsing to Komavisdar, Valod, 5th Magsur, Vad. 1866, PDD, 351(11).

[104] Anandrao to Boyce, n.d. (after 12 Nov. 1842), IOL.F.4.2074.

[105] Anandrao to Mamlatdar, Baglan, n.d.

[106] Anandrao to Boyce, 8.1.1843. Anandrao's professions should not of course be taken at face value: as I show in my thesis, he was much more hostile to the British in contexts where he did not fear retaliation. The point I wish to make is simply that British domination had made the use of colonial rhetoric a strategic necessity for the Dangis.

[107] Anandrao to Boyce, 8.1.1843.

protests being overridden. The British attitude during the demarcation around four decades later was much more intransigent. Officials were, as we saw, keen on obtaining the raja's consent. But ever since the idea had been put to them in 1881, the rajas had been hostile to the demarcation. It was only by 1889 that the chiefs finally signed an agreement authorizing the demarcation. The document gave forest officials what they wanted. It specified that once the demarcation was completed, 'no one would be allowed to enter [the reserved forests] without permission of the forest officer'.[108]

The chiefs' assent had been reluctant. An official remarked:

A good deal of difficulty was experienced in inducing the chiefs to agree to the demarcation; they are very suspicious of change and very tenacious of their rights over the land, and I doubt if I would have been successful had it not been for the influence possessed over the chiefs by the Dangs Diwan [a government official], Kutubuddin, and for the patience and tact he displayed in explaining matters to them.

But since the agreement had been obtained, he added, there would not be 'any difficulty with the chiefs, for a Bhil will keep a promise once made'.[109]

Such a stereotypical prognosis was belied three years later in 1892 when the rajas submitted a petition demanding that the agreement be set aside. That year, the consequences of demarcation had become clearer, with the Department ordering the evacuation of fifty villages from the newly designated Reserved Forest.[110] Another petition from the rajas two years later reiterated the same points.[111] Both petitions claimed that the agreement had been obtained unfairly. The first appears to have been drafted with professional help, though we do not know who the rajas approached for this. Cast in legalese, it charged that the Collector had 'brought forward a certain paper in the Durbar and obtained the signatures of our Dewans to that document'. The rajas 'did not know what the document contained or that it was intended . . . to coerce us and our . . . cultivators to forsake our lands and villages'. Building on these claims, it went to describe the written agreement as 'nullum pactum', or a void

[108] Agreement to Demarcation, BA, RD, 1889, vol. 164, comp. 948. The agreement finally gave forest officials what they wanted. It specified that once the demarcation was completed, 'no one would be allowed to enter [the forests] without permission of the forest officer'.

[109] Loch to Secy, GoB, 25.7.1889.

[110] Petition from rajas to Coll., Kh., 26.6.1892, BRO, DDR, DN 4, FN 24.

[111] Op. cit., n.d., 1894, BRO, DDR, DN 5, FN 25.

agreement.[112] This time round, then, the fiction of the freely willed contract had been invoked explicitly, with some legal assistance, and put through its paces to repudiate the agreement.

Repeatedly in the petitions of the chiefs, it was their ignorance that was portrayed as nullifying the contract. One petition charged that the Collector, 'finding that we are ignorant and illiterate men', had secured their signatures,[113] and the other maintained that the Collector had taken advantage of the fact that they were 'poor, illiterate and jungly people'.[114] In the Dangs, as in many other places around the world, non-literate groups were certainly deceived in this manner.[115] We should not however hobble ourselves to the question of whether charges of deception were true in this or that specific context. There is a more basic matter at issue here. What did the claim to having been deceived, or of being ignorant, mean?

Sometimes, the Dangis resorted to what might be called *strategic illiteracy*, where the claim to be ignorant became a means of resistance.[116] The anthropologist D.P. Khanapurkar reported: 'They have a peculiar way of expressing themselves when taken to task by officers. Their reply is "Amhi anadi loka, bimjat nahi"' (We are ignorant people. We do not understand).[117] Silput raja was of course, never able to muster the services of an interpreter when in receipt of letters ordering him to restore raided cattle! Anandrao too was plagued by similar disappearances of seals, *karkuns*, and interpreters when he had to negotiate a lease with Boyce.

Yet while the image of confident manipulation by subaltern groups of stereotypes about them may occasionally be inspiring, it is not always particularly convincing. Quite apart from the point that subaltern groups manipulating dominant ones were usually apprehensive rather than confident,[118] the claim to be ignorant was not only deployed strategically but was part of their self-perception.

[112] Op. cit., Coll., Kh., 26.6.1892, BRO, DDR, DN 4, FN 24.

[113] Ibid.

[114] Op. cit., n.d., 1894, BRO, DDR, DN 5, FN 25.

[115] For studies of how this happened with the Maori in New Zealand, *see* D.F. McKenzie, 'The Sociology of a Text: Oral Culture, Literacy and Print in Early New Zealand', *in* Peter Burke and Roy Porter (eds), *The Social History of Language* (Cambridge, 1987); Sahlins, *Islands of History*, pp. 67–71.

[116] I thank Sunil Agnani for suggesting the phrase as a way of describing the phenomenon.

[117] 'The Aborigines of South Gujarat' (Ph.D. thesis, University of Bombay, 1944), pp. 77f.

[118] For a remarkable and moving document that combines subaltern apprehension with confidence, *see* Dugmore Boetie *Familiarity is the Kingdom of the Lost*

By this I mean that it was an acknowledgement by the Dangis that they were *radically outside* the community of interpreters of the written text. The interpretive community, as we noted earlier, consisted primarily of colonial officials. From within their welter of interpretations emerged those that were constituted as policy. In this sense, colonial officials not only read meanings into written texts, but made these meanings real.

Then, at the margins of this official British community, there were some native figures. Usually lacking the power to make meanings real, their readings often diverged from the authorized interpretation. In his brilliant essay, Michel de Certeau has compared such reading to poaching, arguing that the reader surreptitiously finds meanings other than the authorized ones in texts.[119] This is a mild characterization in our context. The frequently oppositional readings of British texts and ideologies by a plethora of figures from the chiefs' petition-writers to liberal nineteenth-century nationalists were, by virtue of their public nature, acts of defiance. Maybe the metaphor should be that of highway robbery rather than poaching.

But the point I am getting at is slightly different. It is this: the Dangis belonged to neither the umbral or penumbral interpretive community. Even the strategies of poaching or confrontation were not available to non-literate subordinate groups like them. This was one sense in which they remained radically outside the discourse of the literate and powerful; it was why they persistently described themselves as ignorant.

The other sense in which they were radically outside that discourse was the result of colonial dominance, not of illiteracy. In the case of Gaekwadi officials, exclusion from the interpretive community through illiteracy did not matter so much because the Dangi chiefs possessed the authority and power to participate in or influence that community through other means, such as raids. What had changed since then was the fact of overwhelming colonial domination, which made this means of entry into the interpretive community impossible.

This double exclusion from the interpretive community also throws a different sort of light on the surplus which was so marked in Dangi perceptions of colonial writing. One might say that the surplus was in some senses created by this exclusion. It was a consequence of the fact that the actions of the British interpretive community directly influenced the life of ordinary Dangis, who however had no access to that community.

(London, 1969), where a small-time black South African conman tells his story.

[119] Michel De Certeau, 'Reading as Poaching', pp. 165–76, *The Practice of Everyday Life* (Berkeley, 1984).

The claim to be ignorant, then, was a claim that they were speechless when faced with the surplus of the colonial text; that this text made them fall silent. Silence, in this case, was a sort of powerlessness.

The dual nature of their exclusion also explains why most Bhils remained unwilling to acquire literacy skills. Outside the Dangs, in relations with the British, literacy alone meant little given that it was political subordination too which kept them out of the interpretive community. Navlu raja of Dherbhavti, who was persuaded to attend school at Malligaum in Khandesh in the 1850s, remained unconvinced about its merits. He lost his father and two brothers to cholera while he was away at Malligaum, and 'attributes his misfortune to the fact of his having been detained there'.[120] In oral traditions too, there is a repeated emphasis on the hostility of ancestral figures to *seekhel bhanel lok*, or literate persons, who they did not want in the Dangs.

In social relations within the Dangs, the Bhils and their chiefs did not need the skills of literacy because of their continuing social dominance. Similarly, the relative political powerlessness of the Koknis might explain why, when schools commenced in the Dangs in the early twentieth century, many more of them enrolled their children, usually sons. Given their marginality, literacy as a resource seemed to them far more important than it did to the Bhils.

But to return, after this long excursus, to the 1889 agreement. It is quite likely that the chiefs did broadly realize the implications of what they were signing, despite their claims to having been ignorant. Quite apart from the Collector's claim that the document had been explained to them, the resistance they put up to signing it indicates that they broadly understood its contents.

How, then, should we treat the petitions? Surely, not as simply as the Collector did, dismissing it as 'untrue'. Nor is it adequate to close the issue by invoking strategic illiteracy. Even if not factually accurate, the petitions were true representations of the coercive context within which the agreement had been obtained. As we saw, the chiefs' reluctance to sign the agreement had been overwhelmed by the Diwan's ragbag assortment of sterling qualities. In the chiefs' perception, possibly, the Diwan's very attempt at persuasion was coercive, pushing them into signing the agreement. For, in the final analysis, the powerful British *sirkar* could not be denied something it wanted as badly as it obviously did the demarcation agreement. Their repudiations, combined with extensive resistance by

---

[120] Fenner to Coll., Kh., 30.8.1858, BA, PD, 1858, vol. 95, comp. 734.

Dangis in other spheres, did stave off the demarcation for some time. But in 1902, as we saw, it was finally imposed, with the Bombay government resolving that the rajas had violated the agreement of 1889 by clearing and cultivation in the forests.

X

In this new context, it is quite possible that there was an increasing emphasis on the possession of written documents to confirm contested rights. Cases like that of the late nineteenth or early twentieth-century Kokni *patil*, Lasu, may have become more common. Lasu purchased the *jagiri* of Sumadha village from Govinda *naik*, one of the Amala *bhauband*. Ratansing raja, the principal chief, told Lasu that he could have the deed on the seal of Govinda *naik*, if he had one. Otherwise, Ratansing said, Lasu could pay Rs 100 to him and have his seal affixed on the deed, a course of action to which Lasu Patil agreed.[121] This purported incident may not actually have taken place. We learn the story from Lasu's son Laxman in the 1920s, and he never actually produced the deed. He claimed that it had been destroyed during the 1907 rebellion, and that when he had approached Ratansing raja for another copy, he had been told that none would be needed. Laxman's claim is similar to those narrated now by several Dangis in support of their rights—that their written documents have been destroyed in fires, consumed by insects, or that their father had died without telling them of the bamboo culm in the forest in which he had hidden the document.

Narratives such as that attempted by Laxman could be looked at simply as a strategic manœuvre to conform to colonial norms of proof, in which written documents played an important role. In many cases, they were indubitably no more than that. Yet even this simple attempt to conform to colonial norms of proof signalled a change in attitudes towards the writing of the *sirkar*. Impossible to slough off, potentially coercive in its implications, writing was now seen as very powerful.

The shift in attitudes is most evident in the emergence of *fetishized writing* by around the early twentieth century. In some ways it was quite like monumental writing, in that the written word figured as part of a powerful symbol. Yet the written word had in monumental writing been subordinate to the larger symbols of which it was part. Its presence had

---

[121] Statement of Laxman Lasu, Kokni, 29.6.1923, BRO, DDR, DN 6. FN 34.

little to do with writing as either the trace or surplus created by the
dominance of plains powers; rather, it normalized writing as just one more
marker and symbol. In contrast, the new fetish hypostatized the power
of writing and saw it as the basic source of the power of symbols.

In a discussion of commodity fetishism in nineteenth-century capitalist
societies, Marx pointed out that the 'mysterious character of the commodity form consists . . . simply in the fact that the commodity reflects
the social characteristics of men's own labour as objective circumstances
of the products of labour themselves, as the socio–natural properties of
these things'.[122] Taussig has pointed to the continuing relevance of commodity fetishism in contemporary advanced capitalist societies.[123] The
emergence of fetishized writing can be conceptualized in similar terms.
As colonial writing seemed increasingly powerful and able to determine
developments in the Dangs, such writing itself came to be imbued with
power, and the social relations which gave power to writing became
invisible.

The emergence of powerful writing was visible in the Bhil polity from
the mid-nineteenth century. During this period, there was a fundamental
transformation in the sources of power of the Bhil chiefs. Markers of
authority, especially those bestowed by the British, came to be seen as very
important. Amongst these were the turbans or shawls received at dar-
bars.[124] These markers also sometimes took written form, as for example
the armbands worn by the two or three *sipahis* or attendants in important
bhauband retinues. Supplied by the British, and engraved with the name of
that particular member of the *bhauband* and his *dang*, the armbands were
treated as an affirmation of the authority of the local chiefs.

Even more important was the *sikka-daftar*.[125] The *sikka*, as we noted,
had already been important in the Dangi polity as a form of monumental
writing since at least the late eighteenth century. Yet, given British

---

[122] Karl Marx, *Capital: A Critique of Political Economy* (London, 1976), pp. 164f.

[123] Michael Taussig, *The Devil and Commodity Fetishism in South America* (Chapel
Hill, 1980).

[124] I look at the the construction of authority through markers at the darbar in
'Rethinking hegemony: Ritual and Resistance in India: the Dangs Darbar, 1840s–
1990s'.

[125] There is little archival evidence for the constitution of the *sikka-daftar* as a
conceptual category. The category however exists in the Dangs today. Several
conversations with older men have however suggested that it existed as a category
by the early twentieth century. I discuss these oral traditions, and the radically
different perspective from colonial records that they often offer on Dangi history,
and the methodology needed to use them as sources in 'Hybrid Histories'.

dominance, the *sikka* by itself was evidently inadequate. The legitimacy of the *sikka* was greatest when it was conjoined with the *daftar*, a word used in oral accounts to refer to records. The *daftar* is the epitome of the writing of the *sirkar*, and in oral traditions this imbues it with special power. As a new marker that emerged in the early twentieth century, the *sikka-daftar* indexed the colonial domination of the Dangs, for it made explicit the point that the *daftar* was now necessary to affirm and sustain the authority already displayed in the *sikka*.

The *sikka-daftar* is attributed with great centrality in determining the course of events in oral traditions now. In the nineteenth century, for example, the *gadi* of Ghadvi was held by Rajhans raja. Rajhans was killed by his uncle Udesing, who seized the *gadi*. Rajhans' brother, Devising, made several unsuccessful efforts to claim back the *gadi* from Udesing's son Kerulsing. In oral traditions narrated by his descendants now, however, his failure is ascribed to Udesing having taken away his *sikka-daftar*, leaving him with no means to prove his claims to the *sirkar*.[126]

In the perceptions of Devising's descendants and many other Dangis, then, the writing of the *sirkar* directly determines the actions of the *sirkar*. How should we treat this centrality? At one level, it is a sensitive barometer of the extent to which the writing of the *sirkar* has shaped Dangi reality for well over a century. The written genealogies prepared by colonial officials provided the guiding principles in settling questions of succession to the *gadi*. After the 1900s, claims to *jagirs* or shares of lease allowances were granted or denied in keeping with what the *daftars* or records indicated.[127] The trace created by the colonial written word stretches out from the past to determine the present.

At another level, the centrality is indicative of the fetishization of the *daftar*. In seeing the inscriptions in the *daftar* as almost entirely determining the *sirkar's* actions, the rhetoric of fixity and iconic centrality accorded to the *daftar* in colonial discourse was taken at face value by many Dangis. This was in part because of the *radical unknowability* of the *daftar*, caused by the limited Dangi access both to the *daftar* and the means of interpreting it. As a result, the colonial politics of interpretation

---

[126] We saw above how Devising had around 1849 handed over the seal to Kerulsing, Udesing's son. The claim is often made in oral traditions that chiefs like Rajhans possessed not only a *sikka* but also *daftar*. While the *daftar* is firmly associated in the present with the *sirkar*, the association of the *daftar* with some chiefs of the past is a way of emphasizing their authority.

[127] *See*, for instance, the proceedings of various disputes in BRO, DDR, DN 6, FN 34.

that fundamentally modified the rhetoric of fixity remained invisible (as it was indeed to most British officials for different reasons). Combined with the enormous power that records did possess in determining social change within the Dangs, this seemingly ineradicable fixity of the *daftar* led to its fetishization.

Paradoxically, a second and equally important cause of fetishization was the *surplus* of meaning of the *daftar*. Written agreements were, as we saw, often invoked by the colonial state to legitimate coercive agendas that in Dangi perception had no precisely delineated genealogy within it. Radically unknowable, the epitome of state writing, the daftar was thus the source from which coercive agendas inexplicably sprang. It had a frighteningly protean quality to it.

Consider, for instance, the case of the 1843 lease agreements, which provided in their text for the leasing of the entire Dang's forests.[128] The specifics were possibly soon forgotten by the rajas. Their understanding of the lease was organized around customary usage, and since the British initially cut only teak, *tiwas*, and *sisu*, they believed that the British had rented only these.[129] But the British, too powerful to be defied openly by the chiefs, kept increasing restrictions, always with reference to the leases. In a non-literate Dangs, where the only producers and purveyors of meanings from the leases were colonial officials, that set of documents must have seemed a frighteningly protean fount of meaning.

This novel perception of colonial writing in non-literate subaltern thought can also throw light on how and why British records became targets during rebellions. In 1907, when Bhil rebels reached the British administrative headquarters in the Dangs at Ahwa, they ransacked the office and destroyed the files.[130] In doing so, they treated the *daftar*, first, as a metonym for colonial power, a linkage entirely justified by the centrality of writing in the consolidation of British authority. Second, they destroyed the information that was used in their oppression. Finally, their act lay simultaneously at the fringes of this rational calculus, for they attacked the *daftar* as a fetishized entity that was oppressive partially because it was, like the *sirkar* with which it was associated, unpredictable and capricious in its meanings.

In fetishizing writing, the Dangis and the rebels were not that radically different from people in contemporary western culture. Writing, especially

[128] For the text of the leases, *see* Government of Gujarat, *The Dangs District Gazetteer* (Ahmedabad, 1971), pp. 138–41.
[129] Annual Report, 1850, BA, PD, 1852, vol. 42, comp. 1415.
[130] Coll., Surat, to Secy, GoB, 23.9.1907, NAI, FD, Intl.-B.Proc., March 1908.

in its printed form, is of course very central to the emergence of modernity, and to a whole range of technologies associated with it. But writing is also more than that. It is part of the myth-models of European culture. It epitomizes learning, civilization, and all that distinguishes the West from the Rest. As Michel De Certeau observes, writing defines modern Western culture:

The 'oral' is that which does not contribute to progress; reciprocally, the 'scriptural' is that which separates itself out from the magical world of voices and traditions. A frontier (and a front) of Western culture is established by that separation. Thus one can read above the portals of modernity such inscriptions as 'Here, to work is to write', or 'Here, only what is written is understood'. Such is the internal law of that which has constituted itself as 'Western'.[131]

This formula—writing equals modernity—is in part the consequence of its historical role in the consolidation of state power and domination,[132] and leads to the fetishization of writing in contemporary Western culture. Severed from its possible social contexts, it is ascribed immense determining power. Even De Certeau and Derrida, the two analysts who have provided the most incisive analyses of the discourse around writing and modernity, often accept the claims of that discourse at face value. In one sense, this occurs literally, in their occasional ascription of a fundamental, autonomous, and determining role to writing. More seriously, it happens when they use writing as not just a metaphor but almost a metonym for some of the most central developments and processes of modernity. Both, for example, often extend it to refer to virtually any form of inscription, and De Certeau develops the notion of a 'scriptural economy', which he extends to understand medicine as a system of inscription on the body.[133] The persuasiveness of this metaphor–metonym, I suggest, derives not only from its remarkable insight *but also from the fetishization of writing*, which makes us espy it everywhere.

The differences between the concepts of magical writing and fetishized writing, so similar at first glance, are also clearer now. Unlike magical

[131] Michel De Certeau, *The Practice of Everyday Life* (Berkeley, 1984), p. 134. *See also* Richards, *Imperial Archive*.

[132] The role of writing in the consolidation of state power is evident from Michael Mann, *The Sources of Social Power: Volume I: A History of Power from the Beginning to 1760* (Cambridge, 1986). *See also* M.T. Clanchy, *From Memory to Written Record: England 1066–1307* (2nd edn, London, 1993).

[133] Michel De Certeau, *The Practice of Everyday Life* (Berkeley, 1984); *Of Grammatology; Writing and Difference*.

writing, fetishized writing is not a characteristic of the non-Western Other, but is a pervasive feature of both Western and non-Western societies. In this sense, it belongs, like commodity fetishism, to a class of concepts which have global, though varying, contemporary relevance. Second, if writing is fetishized, it is not because of any characteristics inherent to it, but because of the power associated with it and experienced in everyday life. Domination and some forms of writing are, thus, closely linked.

But a curious silence surrounds the link between the two in Derrida's otherwise exemplary analysis of logocentrism. The association between writing and domination does make some fugitive appearances in his analysis, principally through the potentially robust notion of ethnocentrism. *Of Grammatology* begins, as we saw, with a ferocious, almost programmatic positing of a nexus between logocentrism and ethnocentrism. Later, analysing Rousseau and Levi-Strauss, Derrida again focuses briefly on the theme, pointing to how this ethnocentrism masquerades as progressivism. Yet, that is all, or almost all. Despite the crucial importance he ascribes to it, despite the fact that his first remark in *Of Grammatology* about logocentrism is that it is 'nothing but the most original and powerful ethnocentrism', ethnocentrism itself remains a marginal concern through the book.

It is displaced by another theme, that of authenticity. Derrida demonstrates how logocentrism is closely connected with the privileging of the spoken word, which is seen in the Western philosophical tradition as authentic. He locates in that tradition a series of contrasts between speech and writing, where speech stands for liberty, natural goodness, and spontaneity, and writing for servitude, articulation and death.

Still, one crucial dimension of authenticity remains unexplored—that of the noble savage, a concept almost identified with Rousseau in popular understanding today, and pivotal to Levi-Strauss's discussion of the Nambikwara. It is a pivot, moreover, which swivels us back to the theme of ethnocentrism, of writing as potential domination. After all, in Rousseau and Levi-Strauss' framework, the savage is the epitome of speech. The savage is not only without writing, but before writing. The savage is debased, corrupted and made servile by writing. Speech and writing stand in for savagery and civilization; the defeat of the former is inevitable but passionately regretted. Yet the savage, omnipresent in Rousseau and Levi-Strauss, remains a powerful absence in Derrida, and the foreshadowed unpackaging of ethnocentrism never does take place.

The reconnection of ethnocentrism and logocentrism, severed in Derrida because of his decoupling of philosophical concerns from social and political developments, can begin with a focus on authenticity. The search for authenticity in western culture since the sixteenth century has focused repeatedly on the theme of natural man, usually the noble savage. The noble savage blended in with the earthier aspects of naturalness. Like nature, he could be red in tooth and claw, or generous and of simple pleasures.[134]

By privileging natural man as ineradicably different, it reified the distinction between 'civilization' and those real societies associated with the natural man. This was the sense in which the distinction contributed to the emergence of modern ethnocentrism.[135] Yet one crucial dimension of this natural and noble man was about equality and egalitarianism. If being civilized was about being unequal, this was a hearkening back to a society without power relations amongst men.[136] In a paradoxical sense, then, this was 'an ethnocentrism *thinking itself* as anti-ethnocentrism; an ethnocentrism in the consciousness of a liberating progressivism'. It was often those who wished to attempt a radical critique of their society who drew most on the contrastive power of the image of natural man.[137]

In this world of natural man, the flotsam of civilization would have not just been unauthentic, but a corruption. All the same, one bit of flotsam was quite distinctive from another. Contrast money and writing. There was a well-developed discourse around money. Producing first only for subsistence, natural man started to produce later for barter, and then for sale. But this was contrary to nature, and destroyed the bonds between households or solidary communities. Marx picked up and elaborated this pervasive theme in European thought, arguing how money drove a wedge

[134] For discussions of the noble savage, *see* E. Dudley and M.E. Novak, *The Wild Man Within: An Image in Western Thought from the Renaissance to Romanticism* (Pitsburgh, 1972).

[135] On the links between racist culture and modernity, *see* David Goldberg, *Racist Culture: Philosophy and the Politics of Meaning* (Oxford, 1993).

[136] While inequality between men was not seen as natural, that between men and women was treated as natural. For a forceful and persuasive analysis of the patriarchial basis of social contract theory, *see* Carole Pateman, *The Sexual Contract* (Cambridge, 1988).

[137] On this point, *see* Hayden White, 'The Noble Savage as Fetish', in his *Tropics of Discourse: Essays in Cultural Criticism* (Baltimore, 1978). The invocation of the noble savage could also be part of a more conservative perspective. *See* Harry Liebersohn, 'Discovering Indigenous Nobility: Tocqueville, Chamisso and Romantic Travel Writing', *American Historical Review*, vol. 99, no. 3, 1994.

between the producer and his product. The worker has no access to the means
of production and is paid a wage for his labour. As a result his product is held
to belong to somebody else, and is alienated on the market in an absolute way
as if it had no connection with him.[138]

In this sense, the non-monetary and the monetary can be and often are
collapsed into the traditional and the modern.

But there was a crucial difference in the modernity of writing and that
of money. *While money debased, differentiated, and alienated, writing was
associated not with such a general fall but with subordination.* This possibly
had to do with the perceived difference between the two in the colonies—a
formative influence on post-Renaissance European thought. Money in
most forms could be made part of colonized societies quite quickly. In
this sense, it corrupted. In contrast, writing and literacy could not be
quickly absorbed. It remained far more clearly an instrument of the colonizers: it subordinated. If anything, hostility to money was more explicitly
about a search for the authentic and natural than hostility to writing.

One can see now how progressive ethnocentrism and logocentrism
are akin, how logocentrism is in some senses a strand of progressive
ethnocentrism. The former privileges natural man to critique inequality,
the latter privileges one presumed trait of natural man to question domination. Logocentrism is often *a ferocious critique of contemporary society,
which it contrasts to a prelapsarian past or Other; one without subordination.*
Because he glosses over the ferociousness of the critique, Derrida misses
the motivation that informs Levi-Strauss's analysis. *Tristes Tropiques* remains a profoundly passionate, though problematic, attempt to engage
with writing and domination; with the fact that writing 'favoured the
exploitation of human beings rather than their enlightenment'.[139] For
Levi-Strauss, the primitive-without-writing is a 'sign and a stopping place'
which he recognizes as arbitrary and fictional, but which still serves as a
conceptual point from which to launch a critique of contemporary culture.
In this sense, as in the others that Torgovnick has pointed out, his 'vulnerability to the kind of critique Derrida mounts is, absolutely, willed'.[140]

Logocentrism in the broader sense, by which I mean the privileging
of or a focus on the oral, remains closely associated with radical critiques.
Surely it is not accidental that the concern for oral history began amongst

[138] Jonathan Parry and Maurice Bloch, 'Introduction', in Parry and Bloch (eds)
Money and the Morality of Exchange (Cambridge, 1989).
[139] *Tristes Tropiques*, p. 392. *See also* Marianna Torgovnick, *Gone Primitive: Savag
Intellects, Modern Lives* (Chicago, 1990), p. 220.
[140] *Gone Primitive*, p. 222.

the more radical historians, and that conservative scholars continue to be less enthusiastic about it. In subaltern popular cultures too, a privileging of the oral over the written occurs. In the fiction of Juan Rulfo, where 'popular culture intervenes structurally', the popular manifests itself

not as a voice expressed (the voice of the peasants, the people, and so on). . . . Rather than the illusory pretension of a direct transcription of orality, Rulfo opts for tracing the contours of an oral world through its clashes with the written. . . . [he] shows how the dominant historical process moves in the opposite direction: the silencing of oral culture through the power of the written word. Some peasants have been allocated land under the Revolutionary Government's agrarian reform programme. When they complained that the land is so arid as to be useless, the bureaucrat in charge answers, 'Put it in writing and now go away.' . . . What this means for the peasants is 'they did let us say our things'. Speech here has to be understood as action, and power.[141]

This popular logocentrism, then, was *not about authenticity but about subordination, subalternity, and empowerment.* To challenge the dominance of the written word, to refuse to give it primacy, often was to resist dominant historical processes rather than to hearken back to an authentic core.

In analysing the science of writing, grammatology, Derrida also points to the privileging of phonetic writing in it. The emergence of phonetic writing[142] is often posited as the 'natural "outcome"' of social development.[143] It is this privileging, he argues, which is ethnocentric and has made the forms of writing of other societies invisible. Questioning this privileging, he undertakes a sustained deconstruction of some of the distinctions drawn between phonetic and other forms of writing.[144] 'Actually, the peoples said to be "without writing" lack only a certain type of writing'. Drawing on Leroi-Guhan's insights, he points out that phonetic writing is based on the linearity of the symbol. Yet '[w]riting in the narrow sense—and phonetic writing above all—is rooted in a past of non-linear writing. It had to be defeated . . . A war was declared, and a suppression of all that resisted linearization was installed.'[145] If inscription

[141] William Rowe and Vivian Schelling, *Memory and Modernity: Popular Culture in Latin America* (London, 1991), p. 209.

[142] Briefly, unlike other systems that represent objects through symbols (hieroglyphics, for example), phonetic writing represents objects through symbols of their sounds. For a preliminary contextualization of phonetic writing, *see* Ong, *Orality and Literacy*, pp. 83–93.

[143] *Of Grammatology*, p. 91.

[144] Ibid., p. 83.

[145] Ibid., p. 85.

is more broadly looked at as writing, he seems to imply, then all societies can be seen as possessing forms of writing.

There is a parallel to this manœuvre in Latin American popular culture. In Andean oral narratives today, there is often a focus on the civilizing figure of Inkarri, 'who is destroyed by Spaniards and whose return will bring a new historical age'. One of these narratives claims explicitly that after the defeat of Inkarri, '*quipus*, the system of knotted strings used by the Incas, were a form of writing denigrated and disqualified by the Spanish'.[146]

Does Derrida's argument, then, by some remarkable leap of empathy, prefigure or run parallel to one strand of subaltern popular culture? Matters are slightly more complex than that. I suggest that the claim about *quipus* in Andean oral traditions is itself a consequence of the dominance and power of phonetic writing. For the privileging of phonetic writing globally in popular and élite culture is not mere accident. It has historically been the most closely associated with the consolidation of authority and power. The claim that knotted strings are like phonetic writing is an attempt by subaltern groups to imbue their past with the power of phonetic writing.

Derrida's argument is evidently quite distinct from this. His suggestion that all inscriptions are forms of writing is meant, amongst other things, to neutralize the ethnocentrism inherent in the narrower understanding. By doing so he powerfully deconstructs the evolutionist foregrounding of phonetic writing. But there are some unintended casualties in the process, for he glosses over the close links between writing and political domination.

In this sense, Derrida's emphasis on the commonality between various forms of writing is quite similar to the claim that speech is prior to writing. Just as the latter separated speech from phonetic writing with an axe, so does the former fuse all writing to phonetic writing. Just as the latter treated speech as natural and original and before power, so does the former treat all writing as being devoid of power. Just as the latter insists that writing is only a supplement of speech, so does the former insist that phonetic writing is only a supplement of writing in general. Maybe one could even say that phonetic writing remains in Derrida (as he has said of writing in Rosseau's framework) 'a debased, lateralized, repressed, displaced theme, yet exercising a permanent and obsessive pressure from the place where it is held in check'.[147]

[146] *Memory and Modernity*, pp. 54ff.
[147] *Of Grammatology*, p. 270.

Also, unlike subaltern attempts to appropriate the phonetic writing of the dominant, Derrida's fusing of all forms of writing is noi part of a politics of resistance to such domination. That politics imparts, always, a slipperiness and ambiguity to subaltern fusions of various forms of writing, for they seek simultaneously to denigrate and appropriate phonetic writing. In the absence of this tension, Derrida's catch-all notion of writing threatens to envelop not just ethnocentrism but also hostility to it within an anodyne sameness.

Obeisances, absolutions, and jeremiads over, one can move from the Dangs to nearby Panchmahals, and return to Joria Bhagat's appropriation of writing, with which I commenced this chapter. Why did Joria Bhagat squiggle on the paper and send it back? The writing in which the British commandant encoded his message to Joria was not just a transparent carrier. *Historical developments*—not, note, any characteristics inherent to writing—had transformed it into both a tool of colonial domination and an independent, protean source of oppression. On that mild winter morning in February, these two meanings, congealed into a fetish, confronted Joria. But Joria was a rebel. Not for him the claim to be ignorant, to be outside the community of interpreters. Maybe we can read his response as angry caricature, as sardonic inversion. Maybe there was black humour involved. By replying as he did, in terms nonsensical to the British, he turned their signs against them. He placed himself at the centre of the interpretive community, and *them* at its uncomprehending margins. He created, however fleetingly, however momentarily, an *alternative interpretive community*. By replying as he did, dare one say in these epistemologically turbulent days, he arrogated voice, speech, and writing to subaltern rebels, and refused to fall silent when faced with the colonially authored text. This became one of his last acts of defiance. In the confrontation that followed, he was captured, summarily tried, and hanged.[148]

The power of writing continues to be enormous in both non-literate and literate societies in India today. Shiney Varghese and I are currently studying the Satipati movement, very popular amongst the Adivasis of Maharashtra and Gujarat, including the Dangs, since the fifties. Followers of the movement, whose numbers may be as high as 100,000, refuse to recognize the Indian Government and claim that the leader of the movement, Keshrising Kuver, is the real government. In the past, they have sometimes refused to pay revenue to the government or obey Forest Department laws, questioning the legitimacy of the government to impose laws or demand taxes. They are also very hostile to non-adivasi outsiders,

[148] BA, PD, 1868, vol. 102.

who have emerged during the last century as an exploitative and oppressive dominant group.

Keshrising Kuver, or Dada as he is called, is a strikingly charismatic adivasi in his eighties or early nineties. The arguments advanced by him and his followers constitute a remarkably elaborate and complex cosmology and ideology of subalternity. Dada is prolific in his writings, and these form a central element of the movement. From the village where he is based, some printed books by him together with others consisting of photocopies of his various handwritten reflections, may be bought. A significant number of his followers have copies of these books.

But there are profound paradoxes involved here. First, the bulk of the followers who buy the books are non-literate. So we are confronted with the question of why they buy it, and what they do with it. Second, almost like Joria Bhagat's document, his writings seem at first sight to be nonsensical. By this, I mean that the writing is not used to convey ideas in the way we are taught to in the process of being made literate. Having stayed with him for some time, we have learnt to recognize some specific words or symbols, used in ways novel to those unfamiliar with the vocabulary of the movement. Read in this way, some documents now make sense. Others still don't, and some possibly never will. This will not only be because of a failure of comprehension on our part, but also because his books, as embodiments of fetishized writing, are simply assertions of the subaltern right to write. Such an invocation of writing is both a trivialization inspired by a puckish sense of humour and a magnificently defiant gesture of appropriation. It picks up where Joria Bhagat left off and restates, in the baldest and most moving terms, the subaltern perception of writing as a desirable, dangerous instrument of élite domination, one that has to be both challenged and incorporated.

3

Science between the Lines

GYAN PRAKASH

> ... all translation is only a somewhat provisional way of coming
> to terms with the foreignness of languages.
>
> Walter Benjamin.[1]

Sometime during the nineteenth century, it is said, modernity seized
control of India and subjected it to a 'second colonization'. Emerging
as an instrument of the British 'civilizing mission', modernity's power,
authorized by science, cast its long shadow on India's history. Darkness
fell upon the country as modernity eclipsed 'little knowledges' and empowered an élite that enunciated the discourse of science.

There is much to support this narrative. Who can deny that the 'idea
of a brave new world was first tried out in the colonies'?[2] It is certainly
true that the beginnings of science's cultural authority in India and the
authorization of its middle-class élite lie in the early nineteenth-century
civilizing mission. It was then that the British inaugurated new forms
of rule, and created a milieu for the reformulation of colonial knowledge
and subjects. Formed in this milieu and functioning under the shadow
of the modern West, the newly-emergent Western-educated Bengali élite
began to increasingly invoke the name of reason to produce biting
critiques of the 'irrationality' in Hindu religious and social practices. By

[1] Walter Benjamin, *Illuminations*, Hanna Arendt (ed.) (Schocken Books, New
York, 1969), p. 75.
[2] Ashis Nandy, *The Intimate Enemy: Loss and Recovery of Self Under Colonialism*
(Oxford University Press, Delhi, 1983), p. x

the late nineteenth century, such critiques acquired a different edge as
scientific reason became the organizing metaphor in the discourse of the
western-educated élite. Impressed and stimulated by scientific and industrial progress in the West, the élite began to scrutinize indigenous
religions and society in the light of scientific reason, not just rationality.
Cultural traditions and social identities were realigned as the élite,
infused and licensed by the sign of science, put science's authority to
work as a grammar of transformation to achieve the rearrangement of
knowledges and subjects. It was thus that the cultural authority of science
and the authorization of the élite as agents of modernity and progress
achieved an enduring dominance in India during the second half of the
nineteenth century.

It is against such dominance that Ashis Nandy has written movingly
and compellingly. Arguing that 'colonialism won its great victories not
so much through its military and technological prowess as through its
ability to create secular hierarchies incompatible with the traditional
order',[3] he suggests that colonial rule produced an enduring dominance
of the ideology of modern science. The ascendance of this ideology
signalled an intensely coercive and deeply hierarchical transformation
of society and culture. Traditional cultural practices and social structures
had to either justify and transform themselves in accord with the stand-
ards of reason and science set by the discourse of colonial modernity or
face extinction. Cultural genocide, therefore, according to Nandy, constitutes the real meaning of the myth of modernity.

We have, then, ranged against the all too familiar narrative of progress,
the powerful critique that the insidious will to dominate inspired the
enduring myths of modernity. This criticism is not wrong, but it remains
captive to the object of its criticism. It imparts a dark meaning to the
'civilizing mission', but concedes the triumph of that ideology; it renders
modernity into a grim tale of oppression, but does not unravel the narrative.
India becomes 'modern' in this telling, just as the nineteenth-century vision
predicted, though modernity appears as the relentless reign of domination
and instrumentality. So intent is this criticism on disclosing domination as
the secret of science's life in the colonies that it overlooks the process and
implications of securing an existence nourished by the life-blood of subordinated subjects and knowledges. So great is the concern to reveal modernity's colonizing impulse that what escapes examination is the effect on

[3] Nandy, *The Intimate Enemy*, p. ix. *See also* the essays his edited volume, *Science,
Hegemony, and Violence: A Requiem for Modernity* (Oxford University Press, Delhi,
1988).

its position as it works upon, and expresses its authority in, the language of the colonized.

This essay seeks to offer another understanding of modernity's history in colonial India. Locating science's authorization as a sign of modernity in contingency and contention, it suggests that we recast 'second colonization' as a process of negotiating and realigning incommensurate positions, as translation. Such an approach can be read also in the writings of Rajendralal Mitra, the prominent nineteenth century Bengali Orientalist and intellectual, who treated the question of the diffusion of Western science in British India as an issue of translation. Confronting the problem of rendering Western science into Indian languages, Mitra wrote in 1877 that the proposed translation could not be a 'system of servile verbatim translation, like a Chinese copy, with patch and all'.[4] Not a 'Chinese copy' indeed, for Mitra recognized that translation was a process of aligning and realigning non-equivalent languages; of transforming one into another. This process exposed science to the contagion of the subordinated, indigenous culture in which its authority was represented. There ensued, then, the dissemination, not dialectic, of western science and indigenous culture from which neither one nor the other could reappear in its 'original' position. The 'evaporation' of a culture's 'intransmissable' and 'undefinable' essence in translation was inevitable, Mitra acknowledged. To achieve precise translation, not a 'Chinese copy', therefore, it was necessary to incorporate western scientific terms into vernacular textbooks. But this system too was 'evil', Mitra admitted immediately, because it created a 'new language foreign to people at large', and furnished an 'exclusiveness to the professors of science not much unlike the Cabalists and Gnostics'.

There is an intimation here of another history. It is a history that emerges from science's authorization in the language of the other; and it consists of a process of cultural appropriation that bears the marks of an 'inappropriate' negotiation between incommensurable knowledges and subjects. This history finds expression in Mitra's recognition that the translation of western science, subjected to the subaltern presence and agency of the 'people at large', could only produce an 'evil' system with the obscure authority of 'Cabalists and Gnostics'.

Mitra's perspective urges another reading of the enunciation of the

---

[4] Rajendralal Mitra, *A Scheme for the Rendering of European Scientific Terms in India* (Thacker, Spink & Co., Calcutta, 1877), p. 18. Mitra wrote this originally as a submission to a committee established by the Bengal government to study and develop proposals on vernacular textbooks for the medical college.

discourse of science by a middle-class élite; it exhorts us to step beyond the cultural binarism of the 'second colonization' and place the discourse of science in what Walter Benjamin called an interlinear, or between the lines, translation.[5] For, understood as translation, the enunciation of discourse of science becomes a far more complicated matter than the colonizer's victory over the colonized. Translation turns our attention to the undoing of binaries and borders entailed in the authorization of the discourse, and it highlights them as those productive in-between strategies and spaces in which an authoritative discourse takes shape. As an interlinear translation, the discourse of science appears as an outcome of the negotiation of incommensurable positions, involving the dislocation and relocation of unequal subjects and knowledges. It is in this history between the lines that we can witness both the powerful authorization of an élite discourse of science, and the rearrangement of colonial power and knowledge. Emerging in the twists and turns of the discourse, produced by dislocating movements and estranging appropriations, this is a history of science's functioning as a sign of modernity that sits oddly beside both the heady celebration of the phenomenon as progress and its stinging denunciation as 'the colonization of the mind'. The purpose of this essay is to sketch this history, to outline those 'evaporations' in which an authoritative discourse was materialized; to trace those alienating encounters in which modernity was established as a form of 'evil' translation. Quite simply, my aim is to reveal that the in-between translation of modernity produced a ghostly double of the 'original'.

THE INSTITUTION AND ALIENATION OF SCIENCE'S AUTHORITY

There is no doubt that the modern West permeated the discourse of the Western-educated intellectuals as they opted for modern science to authorize their reform projects. But if the activities of the élite, inspired by the association of the modern West and science, enacted colonial power, this enactment was performed on the alienating stage of difference. There, the discourse was compelled to confront and contain the menace of difference, plunge into and transform religious dispositions and literary writings of the 'natives', in order to enunciate its authority. Only then could there be an indigenization of science's authority, the imperceptible exercise of colonial domination. In these complex strategies of hybridization and

[5] *Illuminations*, p. 82.

negotiation of difference and discrimination, science's status as a sign of Western power was instituted and came undone.

An early example of the alienating installation of the narrative of progress can be seen in a Hindi text, *Bhugolsār* (1841).[6] The origin of this text lies in an 'interesting experiment' conducted in 1839 by a colonial official, L. Wilkinson.[7] He organized a school for Hindu and Muslim boys who were taught, among other subjects, Hindu mathematics and astronomy from the Siddhantas, 'which are wholly free from the fables of the Poorans, and which carry the student just to the point to which the Science of Astronomy had been carried in Europe when Copernicus, Newton, and Galileo, appeared to point out and to establish that the sun and not the earth was the centre of our system'. Wilkinson reported that the first effect of his attempt to expose the 'absurd ideas, usually prevalent among the Hindoos from the authority of the Poorans, was to rouse a very keen and general opposition among the Bramins in many parts of India'. Very few were convinced, although opinion ranged from an outright and total defence of the Puranas to acceptance of certain classical Sanskrit texts as scientific. *Bhugolsār* was written in response to this debate. Its author was Omkar Bhatt, identified as a '*jyotish*' (astronomer), and it compared the Copernican system with the systems described in the Puranas (epics collected and compiled between 500 BC and AD 500), and in the *Siddhānta Shiromani*, a twelfth-century text of an astronomer–mathematician, Bhaskaracharya. The text asserts the superiority of Western knowledge through a dialogue between a guru and his disciple:

Disciple: 'Revered guru, how is the earth defined?'

Guru: 'The earth is defined in many ways; the Jains call it an infinite unity; and revered Vyasa in his Bhagwat calls the earth an expanse of 500 million *yojanās* and like a lotus leaf; and Bhaskaracharya calls the earth small and round in his *Siddhānta Shiromani*; the British also judge it to be round.'

Disciple: 'The earth is one, then why many opinions?'

Guru: 'There are many kinds of men, and everyone says as he believes.'

Disciple: 'Which one is true?'

Guru: 'The truth is that the earth is round.'

Disciple: 'What method establishes the truth that the earth is round?'

Guru: 'There are many ways, but the chapter on calculations of the sphere in *Siddhānta Shiromani* establishes it in the following way. . . . If the

---

[6] Omkar Bhatt, *Bhugolsār* (Agra School Book Society, Agra, 1841).

[7] 'Note', in *Minute by the Right Honourable the Governor-General* [Lord Auckland] (n.p., Delhi, 1840), pp. lxx–lxxii.

earth was a mirror, and if the sun went around the earth, then we
would have only days, no nights; the fact that this does not happen
proves that the earth is round.'[8]

The text presents itself as an examination of scientific truth that is
indifferent to colonial difference. Thus, Bhaskaracharya and the British,
the Jains and the Puranas, appear as competing claimants to truth. The
Puranas, narrated by the sage Vyasa, in Bhatt's view, consist of great
poetry and wonderful descriptions of god's play but not science. Bhaskaracharya's definition of the earth, on the other hand, is scientific not only
because it converges with the British view, but also because the origin
of the Siddhantas goes back to Surya, the sun god, who narrated the
Surya Siddhānta to Mayasur, a Puranic artisan–demon. Bhaskaracharya's
Siddhānta Shiromani improved on the earlier Siddhantas, corrected its
imperfections, just as its knowledge has been rendered more accurate
by the Sahibs.[9]

But how could the Sahibs' knowledge be more accurate; what accounted
for the greater accuracy of western calculations of the earth's revolutions
when western astronomy developed later than Hindu knowledge?

Disciple: 'While Hindu astronomy is ancient, the Sahibs' knowledge is more
accurate, even though they acquired it recently and from several
different countries; why is this so?'

Guru: 'Because the Sahibs, after observing the entire earth, travelling
through and living in every country, have measured their latitude
and longitude accurately. Because those who work hard are also
right, their knowledge is more accurate. Cotton grows in India; the
Sahibs take it across to their own country, yarn and weave it into
cloth, then sell it in India, arousing everyone's appreciation; their
cloth sells more than indigenous cloth. In the same way, the Sahibs
have taken knowledge from the Arabs, Greece, and India, and like
cotton, they have woven the thread of knowledge gained from these
very books into a better fabric of astronomy.'[10]

Colonial exploitation as the model for the progress of science, capitalist
colonialism as the accumulation of knowledge—such was the representation of history in discourse. The normalizing myth of colonialism as the
accumulation and distribution of knowledge, however, is produced under
conditions of questioning and contention. The authority of the Sahibs'

[8] *Bhugolsār*, pp. 2–3.
[9] Ibid., pp. 85–6.
[10] Ibid., p. 20.

science cannot be simply asserted, but emerges after its subjection to interrogation by the pupil. Why Bhaskaracharya? Why not Vyasa? How can the Sahibs' science be more accurate? Under the pupil's insistent questioning, the seamless narrative of the progress of knowledge unravels. In its place, the teacher patches together a text of science from the astronomy of Bhaskaracharya, the divine speech of Surya, and the information gathered by the Sahibs. Such a process of hybridization and differentiation empowers the discourse; it enables the guru to defend and assert the superiority of the West's 'observations' and 'proofs' over the mere 'description' and 'poetry' of Hindu texts.

The denial of the content of the subordinated's knowledge, however, could not erase the effect of the position given it in discourse; the subordinated, speaking sometimes through the divine speech of gods, and at other times in the archaic voice of ancestors and tradition, exercises a constant pressure on authoritative representations.

Disciple: 'The disrespect of tradition is improper because everyone accepts its testimony, but you violate the brilliant and boundless *Bhāgwat* [one of the Puranas] and some of the siddhants to establish new principles. Explain why.'

Guru: 'The error of the old and the truth of the new should be acknowledged when that is the case. Revered Bhaskaracharya followed this method too. . . . I have followed his direction, to the best of my understanding, in determining errors; besides, because the Hindu Puranic treatises on geography do not deal with proofs and have been written by poets, we should overlook their descriptions and set our sights on demonstrable proofs alone as astronomy recognizes observable demonstration only . . . the geography of the *Bhāgwat* is mere description, and not all geographical knowledge has been produced by the Hindus. The siddhants do not even describe travels south of the equator. . . . The westerners have seen the entire globe; in 1497, Vasco de Gama Sahib of Portugal discovered the route around the Cape of Good Hope for his journey to India and circled Africa.'[11]

Here, the narrative of progress goes awry as the use of the pupil's insistent questioning to demonstrate that the Hindu traditions cannot equal western astronomy produces a profound disturbance in the discourse. The text, confronted with the weight of traditions that it has invoked itself to achieve the authority of Copernican astronomy, encounters the troubling question: What justifies the violation of 'the brilliant and boundless

[11] Ibid., pp. 101–2.

Bhāgwat'? This was a critical moment where the discourse's strength, its very production of an indigenized authority, turned against itself. The text was brought face to face with the colonial institution of science's authority. The narrative of progress was compelled to acknowledge western power—Vasco de Gama, Captain Cook, the British explorations of Africa—as the basis for the authority of western knowledge.[12] Here, the representation of science as a progressive accumulation of knowledge unconnected with the exercise of power was called into question.

Bhugolsār was not an isolated case. The alienation of the narrative of progress was a general phenomenon that shadowed its most explicit statements. Such statements were quite common during the early nineteenth century. Intellectuals of the 'Bengal renaissance' like Rammohun Roy diagnosed the root of India's afflictions in its social and religious practices and, overlooking colonial oppression, portrayed the institution of British rule as the revival of the era of reason.[13] This formulation was not uncommon even in the late nineteenth century when political nationalism began to make its appearance. Thus, Mahendra Lal Sircar, the prominent Bengali champion of science and the founder of the Indian Association for the Cultivation of Science (IACS), condemned the 'despotism of traditional opinions', that is, Hindu beliefs, and lauded British rule for having established liberty and free inquiry.[14] In much the same vein, Gosto Behary Mullick, the secretary of the Burra Bazar Literary Club in 1874, spoke of reviving

the days of Elphinstones and Malcolms, Thomasons and Metcalfs, of Joneses and Wilsons and Bethunes . . . who came to India not for its rice or cotton, indigo or jute, shell-lac or lac-dye, sugar or saltpetre, but to raise from the depths of ignorance and superstition—fruits of years of foreign [Muslim] domination—a race whose venerable relics of literature and science play fantastically like the dazzling coruscations of a polar winter athwart the mysterious gloom that shrouds the dark night of ages.[15]

---

[12] Ibid., p. 103.

[13] Sumit Sarkar, 'Rammohun Roy and the Break with the Past', in *Rammohun Roy and the Process of Modernization in India*, V.C. Joshi (ed.) (Vikas, Delhi, 1975), pp. 46–68.

[14] 'On the Desirability of a National Institution for the Cultivation of the Science', in his *The Projected Science Association for the Natives of India* (Anglo-Sanskrit Press, Calcutta, 1872), pp. 4–7.

[15] *The Seventeenth Anniversary Report of the Burra Bazar Family Literary Club, Established in 1857, with the Abstracts of Anniversary Address and other Lectures* (Calcutta Press, Calcutta, 1874), pp. 17–18.

Obviously, the small Bengali Muslim élite, gathered in the Mahomedan Literary Society, could not share the belief that the 'years of foreign domination' had produced 'ignorance and superstition', but it, too, sang praises of British rule and claimed that the 'new world of thought' had calmed the minds of the 'ignorant and bigoted co-religionists'.[16]

These celebrations of British rule were not blind to the colonial divide; instead, they restaged the British rule of India as an instrument of new knowledge. Crucial to this restaging was the idea that the truth of science did not depend on power. Father Lafont expressed this idea well when, in addressing the meeting of the Burra Bazar Family Literary Club, he stated that he had chosen to speak on a scientific topic because 'it was the safest topic to be discussed in meetings like this'.[17] Science was 'safe' because it was thought to be nature's self-evident truth, contained in its working, and, unlike faith, free from power. Yet, Mullick claimed that 'Joneses and Wilsons and Bethunes' had been necessary to raise India from 'the depths of ignorance and superstition'.

How could science's authority emerge from colonial power and yet remain insulated from it? There is something odd in the celebration of modern science as deliverance from despotism, as a sign of free inquiry, at the very time when its institution is acknowledged to lie in colonial domination. This was no self-contradiction but a deep division in the discourse produced by its functioning. The narrative of progress courted difference to demonstrate the necessity of reimplanting modern knowledge. Thus, Mullick spoke of the 'depths of ignorance and superstition' to represent the British Orientalists motivated not by saltpetre but scientific knowledge; and Abdool Luteef Khan cited the agitation of the 'ignorant and bigoted co-religionists' to demonstrate the calming powers of the 'new world of thought'. Similarly, Sircar prefaced his plea for the establishment of IACS by detailing the lapse of the Hindus into speculation and superstition; the error of their beliefs. Science was expected to conquer their false beliefs and institute the true knowledge of the laws of nature that would place devotion to the almighty on a new basis. But having normalized difference as superstition, the mocked traditions returned as menace. Sircar claimed that the very success of science had bred lethargy and complacency, making people indifferent to the methods of

[16] *A Quarter Century of the Mahomedan Literary Society of Calcutta: A Resumé of its Work from 1863 to 1889 for the Jubilee of the Twenty-Fifth Year* (Stanhope Press, Calcutta, 1889), p. 12.
[17] *The Seventeenth Anniversary Report*, p. 11.

science.[18] Condemned to achieve progress and recognition slowly, science faced the overwhelming power of complacency, superstition, and error. How could this power be controlled so that the authority of science could emerge? It is at this point that the discourse's attempt to contain and exclude the difference in which science was authorized ended up alienating the colonial ideal of science as free inquiry.

The narrative of progress, therefore, was not 'safe' from the contagion of colonial difference. As the narrative's enunciation thrust science into intimacy with those sunk into 'the depths of ignorance and superstition', there emerged, along with the myths of 'Joneses and Wilsons', another story; perched beside the heroic tales of Copernicus and the Sahib's science, there appeared a troubled acknowledgement of the deep-seated incompatibility between modern science and its colonial institution.

DISPLACEMENT AND RENEGOTIATION

In the displacement of the colonial ideal of science as free from power, we have a story of the emergence of a division in the functioning of science in the élite discourse. On the one hand, it was projected as a sign of modernity and progress, indifferent to difference. On the other, the menace of cultural/colonial difference was the media of the production of science's authority. To recognize this division of science's position in the process of its institution is not to celebrate the boundless play of the signifier. If the creation of difference or division is, as Homi Bhabha argues, 'the sign of the productivity of colonial power, its shifting forces and fixities'; and if 'the effect of colonial power is seen to be the *production* of hybridization rather than the noisy command of colonialist authority or the silent repression of native traditions, then an important change in perspective occurs'.[19] In the changed angle of vision, the dissemination of science's identity in the divine speech of Surya does not position difference as the truth that exposes colonial science's myths of autonomy and originality; instead, difference and dissemination displace the status, the position from which the authority of science's truth is asserted. The truths of western astronomy are rendered dependent on and shown to

[18] 'On the Necessity of National Support to an Institution for the Cultivation of the Physical Sciences', in *The Projected Science Association for the Natives of India*, pp. iv–ix.

[19] 'Signs Taken for Wonders: Questions of Ambivalence and Authority under a Tree Outside Delhi, May 1817', *Critical Inquiry*, 12 (Autumn 1985), p. 154.

reside in their transferability and transformability; the Sahibs' knowledge becomes one that is 'acquired recently and from several countries', and developed from the 'knowledge taken from the Arabs, Greece, and India'. Western astronomy acquires the status of truth as it travels, changes its shape, and loses its 'origin'.

The dissemination of the narrative of science, then, was a charged event. As it was split open and lost its autonomy and originality in the indigenization of its authority, a space opened for the renegotiation of science's status as truth. Such a space emerges in *Bhugolsār* where the strategy to situate western astronomy in traditions produces the demand that the text justify its transgression of traditional authorities. Faced with this demand, the text cites colonial explorations and conquests as the basis for the West's superior knowledge. This produces a breach in the narration of science as a free accumulation of knowledge; as a matter of the replacement of error with truth. If the truths of western science were gained in the exercise of western power, then why should Hindu traditions give way to Copernican astronomy? It is remarkable that the text gives voice to these demands in its effort to authorize science. Thus the pupil, acknowledging western power but questioning its cultural authority, asks: 'How can you consider western treatises true and doubt our own?'[20] The text steps into the breach opened by its own question to offer another basis for the cultural pre-eminence of western astronomy.

Disciple: 'Revered Guru, explain what are the fruits of instruction in geography and astronomy?'

Guru: 'The knowledge of geography and astronomy offers many benefits in this world as also in the other world. First, let me tell you about its use in this world; it is certain that the Brahmins who study geography and astronomy will command greater respect than other astronomers. As people become aware astronomy is the best of all knowledges, their doubts will disappear. Deeply-held false beliefs— that there exists a country of one-legged people, and that Rahu [the Puranic name for one of the nine planets] devours the moon at the time of the eclipse—will vanish. Now listen to how this knowledge makes god's greatness visible. The understanding of the movement of sun and other planets, the difference between seasons, the marvellous movement of meteors will reveal god's greatness and help place our hearts at god's feet. This will free us from desire, anger, greed, and illusion, and make the heaven attainable.'[21]

[20] *Bhugolsār*, p. 104.
[21] Ibid., pp. 121–2.

The intrusion of theology in science, or vice versa, remarkable though it may appear today, was neither novel nor unique; indeed, such inter-penetration can be observed also, for example, as early as the twelfth century in the European naturalist texts.[22] Remarkable, however, was the mechanism of natural philosophy's utterance in the colonial context. On the one hand, natural philosophy licensed the text to mark the Hindus as people with 'false beliefs', who were yet to realize, unlike the Europeans who knew already, the superiority of astronomy as a form of knowledge. On the other hand, it returned to inscribe the Hindus as people whose capacity to recognize that 'astronomy is the best of all knowledges' rendered them fit to see god's greatness. Thus, natural philosophy appeared in discourse neither as a lingering survival of an old idea, nor as the adaptation of science to the cultural heritage of India. Its specific meaning was produced in the double inscription of the Hindu, in between the mark that smeared the Hindus as given to false beliefs and the remark that conferred on them the capacity to understand 'the marvellous movement of meteors'. The text renegotiated science's signification in between the double inscription of the Hindu, relocating its cultural force in its 'use in this world' and benefits 'in the other world'.

The authorization of science in its functionality—its 'use in this world' —was a manifestation and mechanism of its cultural relocation. This structure comes into view clearly in a lecture delivered to the Bethune Society in 1868 by Rev. K.M. Banerjea. Banerjea was one of the firebrand followers of Henry Derozio's 'Young Bengal' movement, who, feeling 'persecuted' by Hinduism, had converted to Christianity, and was one of the most prominent *bhadralok* intellectuals. He wrote and delivered lectures frequently on a subject dear to Bengali intellectuals—the reform of culture. On this occasion, too, he spoke of reform. Inevitably, he turned to science, arguing that it must 'supplement' the instruction in Oriental classics: 'the one for introducing, the other for naturalizing the enlighten-ment of Europe in Asia'.[23] Neither was complete in itself: the Occidental was a 'supplement', and the Oriental needed introduction to the European enlightenment. What emptied cultures of their purported wholeness *and* offered another basis for their reformed existence was their function in the discourse of reform. Thus, Occidental knowledge, dispersed as

[22] David C. Lindberg, *The Beginnings of Western Science: The European Scientific Tradition in Philosophical, Religious, and Institutional Context, 600 BC to AD 1450* (University of Chicago Press, Chicago and London, 1992), pp. 197–201.

[23] Rev. K.M. Banerjea, *A Lecture Read Before the Bethune Society on February 13, 1868* (Thacker, Spink & Co., Calcutta, 1868), pp. 6, 23.

'supplement' so that it could be 'naturalized' in India, came to swiftly acquire the creative power to 'introduce' enlightenment. Likewise, Oriental classics, rendered incomplete without the 'supplement', became, in a flash, the fecund ground of 'naturalization'.

Such dispersals and reformulations of culture constituted the life of science's functioning as a grammar of reform in élite discourse. Thus, two years after Rev. Banerjea's address, the Bethune Society's deliberations at a meeting in 1870 witnessed the élites engaged, once again, in the same process. Like many of its meetings, this one also included a lecture–demonstration on a scientific subject. On this occasion, the lecture–demonstration was on respiration. Following its conclusion, Kali Kumar Das, an enthusiast of phrenology, rose to thank the speaker for having shown how the ignorance of common principles of ventilation were ignored in the construction of native houses, but disagreed that respiration was an involuntary act. He cited the practice of Yoga to argue that the ancient Hindu devotees of the practice had controlled respiration through will power, and went on to refer to an account published several years earlier of a fakir (religious mendicant) who presented himself at the court of Maharaja Ranjit Singh of Punjab and had himself buried on one occasion for forty days, and on another for ten months, but was alive when disinterred.[24]

A somewhat similar expression of science in translation and transaction of cultures occurred also at the meeting of the Burra Bazar Literary Club. The meeting featured a lecture–demonstration by Father Lafont on heat, electricity, and magnetism. Ashutosh Dhar, a lawyer, enthused by the lecture, responded that it had demonstrated the unity of forces, and called for an abolition of the distinction between the organic and the inorganic. Father Lafont angrily rejected Dhar's demand that the mind's functioning be attributed to the action of physical forces and chemical reactions: 'no amount of phosphorous ever made or will make a single thought; let us be sincerely and frankly spiritualists and rest satisfied with the noble use of *mind* to study and scrutinize *matter*, without confusion of two widely different departments of science'.[25]

The call went unheeded. The 'confusion' of categories permeated the discourse of the predominantly Hindu élite as it commissioned the cultural force of science to revive Hinduism. All over India, there ensued reassessments of the Vedic texts, the Puranas, and a variety of textual commentaries and religious sects. As this Hindu 'revivalism' gathered force during the last few decades of the nineteenth century, the crossing

[24] *Minutes of Proceedings of the Bethune Society*, pp. 17–18.
[25] *The Seventeenth Anniversary*, pp. 19–20.

of boundaries became increasingly common. Texts like *Bhugolsār* and discussions like the Bethune Society's discussions on yoga and science proliferated. The close of the nineteenth and the beginning of the twentieth centuries witnessed a vast explosion of pamphleteering and organization-al activity that assumed and deployed science's authority to achieve a syntactical rearrangement of religion.

The most striking element in these reshapings of Hinduism was the attempt to produce a rigorously monotheistic vision. This attempt was not new, of course. In the early nineteenth century, Rammohun Roy had declared that monism was the true essence of Hinduism and its classical texts. Later religious reform had also invoked these texts to place popular Hindu practices under intense scrutiny. The belief in the worship of multiple deities, the practice of a variety of rituals, the caste system, the status of Puranic myths—all had come into question. What was new, however, to the closing decades of the century, was the force of the language of science. Under its influence, earlier formulations of mono-theistic Hinduism acquired a new dimension.

Hindu intellectuals across India advanced the idea of a monotheistic Hinduism by asserting a fundamental indivisibility of science and re-ligion. The influence of positivism was palpable in this idea, and positivist philosophers were often cited to legitimate 'dispositions' that, according to Hindu intellectuals, Hinduism itself contained.[26] These 'dispositions' were defined increasingly, with citations from Herbert Spencer and Thomas Henry Huxley, as the belief in the oneness of all phenomena, and in the existence of one supreme power; just as science had one truth, so did 'essential religion', not superstition masquerading as religion.[27] Hinduism, as this 'essential religion', it was argued, did not reside in its symbols and rituals but in the recognition of the laws of nature in which the almighty manifested itself.

The belief in the indivisibility of science and religion pervaded power-ful movements of Hindu reform. The Arya Samaj is the best known of such movements in north India. Established in the 1870s by the charis-matic preacher Swami Dayananda Saraswati, it quickly won a large fol-lowing among the educated élite in Punjab for its vision of a pristine Vedic

[26] Jogendra Chandra Ghosh, *The Hindu Theocracy: How to Further its Ends* (S.K. Lahiri & Co., Calcutta, 1897), p. 1. This was the text of speech before the meeting of the Indo-Positivists held on the anniversary of Auguste Comte's death.

[27] *See*, for example, Lala Ruchi Ram Sahni, *Science and Religion: Being the Substance of a Lecture Given at the 32nd Anniversary of the Punjab Bramho Samaj, Lahore* (n.p., Lahore, 1895), pp. 1–3, 9–14.

Hinduism, shorn of 'superstitions'.[28] It was premised on the belief that the Vedas contained and were based on the laws of nature, and it summoned the authority of science in advancing its project of reforming Hinduism, eradicating it of 'superstitious' ideas and practices. So widespread was the notion in the milieu of religious reform that Hinduism and science were inextricable, that it showed up in the views of even as bitter an opponent of Swami Dayananda and the Arya Samaj as Pandit Shiv Narayan Agnihotri. Beginning as a Bramho Samaj activist in Punjab, Pandit Agnihotri clashed with Dayananda and the Arya Samaj, and finally established his own organization called the Dev Samaj in 1887. It propagated a religion named Dev Dharma, defined as a doctrine 'in Harmony with Facts and Laws of Nature and based on the Evolution or Dissolution of Man's Life-Power'.[29] Dev Samaj, like the Arya Samaj, advocated radical social reform, but developed a distinctive 'science-grounded religion' that combined positivist ideas of the evolution of society and knowledge in stages with a deep veneration and worship of Pandit Agnihotri.

The notion, then, that Hinduism embodied the truth of the indivisibility of science and religion was common to the movements of Hindu revival and reform and was produced by combining the languages of science, positivism, and classical texts. No movement better illustrates that Hindu monism was 'rediscovered' in the 'confusion' of categories than the Theosophical movement.

Theosophy, which became the most prominent vehicle for transmitting the belief in the indivisibility of science and Hinduism in south India, was different in tone and emphasis from the Hindu revivalism of the Arya Samaj. But it too assumed the authenticity of an archaic Hinduism authorized by science. Originating in the spiritualist movement in the United States, Theosophy was developed by Madam Helena Petrovna Blavatsky and Colonel Henry Olcott. It was formulated at the intersection of ancient religions and modern science, containing a heady mix of clairvoyance, mesmerism, and hypnotism, and was presented as

[28] For a history of the Arya Samaj, see Kenneth W. Jones, *Arya Dharm: Hindu Consciousness in 19th-Century Punjab* (Berkeley and Los Angeles, 1976); and J.F.T. Jordens, *Dayananda Sarasvati: His Life and Ideas* (Oxford University Press, Delhi, 1978).

[29] Shriman Amar Singh, *The Advent of a Science-Grounded Religion for All Mankind* (Dev Ashram, Lahore, 1913), p. 1. *See also Religion of the Age* (Dev Samaj, Lahore, 1914), rpt. from the journal *Science-Grounded Religion*, for the philosophy of the Dev Samaj.

a form of knowledge, or an occult science, that surpassed the understanding offered by modern science. The Theosophists claimed that their
doctrine penetrated beyond the material substance to reveal underlying
principles and consciousness.[30] Convinced that the origins of their occult
science lay in Indian religions, particularly Buddhism and Vedic Hinduism, they brought Theosophy to India in 1878, travelling widely,
delivering lectures, receiving great respect and response, and forming
alliances with men like Swami Dayananda Saraswati. In Dayananda's
Arya Samaj, these Theosophists saw a mission very similar to their own,
namely the reappropriation of ancient religions as a key to a rational
and scientific understanding and restructuring of modern societies. While
their plan to incorporate the Arya Samaj in the Theosophical movement
did not succeed because Dayananda resisted and denounced their pluralism, Theosophy began to gather impressive support after 1882 when
Madam Blavatsky and Colonel Olcott turned their Adyar estate in
Madras into the headquarters of their movement.[31]

Established in the Adyar estate, Blavatsky edited the *The Theosophist*
in which she presented the turn to the Vedas as the return of modern
science to its ancient roots. Or, as she wrote in an article, whatever explanations and hypotheses that scientists may offer, 'modern phenomena
are fast *cycling* back for their true explanation, to the archaic *Vedas*, and
other "Sacred Books of the East"'.[32] While Blavatsky concentrated on
developing the philosophical doctrine, Olcott worked as a tireless organizer, promoter, and practitioner of occultism. Travelling tirelessly in
India and Ceylon (Sri Lanka), Olcott campaigned relentlessly for this
combination of ancient wisdom and scientism, and practised mesmerism
to cure patients suffering from such ailments as facial paralysis, glaucoma,
deafness, and hysteria.[33] Olcott's tour of south India in 1883 to establish

[30] The most comprehensive statement of Theosophy is contained in H.P. Blavatsky, *The Secret Doctrine; the Synthesis of Science, Religion, and Philosophy* (5th edn.,
Theosophical Press, Wheaton, Illinois, 1945), 6 vols. Originally published in 1893–7,
this magnum opus became the canonical text of Theosophy.

[31] J.N. Farquhar, *Modern Religious Movements in India* (Macmillan, New York,
1915), pp. 208–91 gives an account of Theosophy in India. *See also* Kenneth W. Jones,
Socio–Religious Reform Movements in India (The New Cambridge History of India,
III.1) (Cambridge University Press, Cambridge, 1989), pp. 167–79.

[32] 'Occult or Exact Science?' *Theosophist* (April–May, 1886), rptd. in H.P. Blavatsky, *Occult or Exact Science* (H.P. Blavatsky Series No: 19, Theosophical Company, Bangalore, 1984), p. 11.

[33] Henry Steel Olcott, *Old Diary Leaves: The History of the Theosophical Society*, II
(1900; rpt. The Theosophical Publishing House, Madras, 1974), pp. 395–404.

branches of the Theosophical Society was successful beyond his expectations. He was received by huge crowds, carried in open palanquins in torch-lit processions led by temple elephants, bell-bearing camels, and bands of musicians, addressed packed audiences in town halls and temples.[34] 'I knew perfectly well that not one man in perhaps a dozen there could understand English or really know anything more about me than the fact that I was a friend and defender of their religion, and had a way of curing the sick that people called miraculous'.[35] Theosophy's defence of Hinduism against missionary attacks added force to and drew strength from the movement for Hindu renewal championed by the educated élite. As the Theosophists promoted Vedic authority and Sanskritic knowledge, they both advanced and expressed the élite's move from religious scepticism and suspicion of inherited cultural practices to a critical revival of Hindu religion and culture.[36]

The Tamil Brahmin and high-caste non-Brahmin élites, caught in between the languages of science, positivism, and Vedic philosophy, were drawn to Theosophy. They flocked to meetings and discussions conducted by Olcott and, after 1892, Annie Besant, appreciative of Hinduism's western champions. Thus began the enduring alliance between Theosophy and the 'Mylapore élite' of Madras that proved to be of crucial importance in the 1910s when Annie Besant turned the local branches of the Society into instruments of nationalist mobilization.[37] These local branches were formed in the 1880s and the 1890s when Olcott's tours sparked a great deal of interest in Theosophy among the small-town élite intellectuals.

N.K. Ramaswami Aiya was one such Brahmin intellectual who attended a discussion chaired by Olcott in 1898 in Chittoor. His autobiography offers a rich portrait of the discursive milieu in which Theosophy was thrust and prospered.[38] Aiya came from a deeply religious family whose grandfather was a *sanyasin*, a Hindu ascetic, and whose uncle was a follower of Vedantic and Yoga philosophy. Growing up in Tanjore where his father was a deputy collector, Aiya was first attracted to Vedanta, then to the views of the eighth-century Hindu philosopher, Sankara,

---

[34] *Old Diary Leaves*, II, pp. 453–61.

[35] Ibid., p. 453.

[36] R. Suntharalingam, *Politics and Nationalist Awakening in South India, 1852–91* (University of Arizona Press, Tucson, 1974), pp. 301–2, 304–8.

[37] D.A. Washbrook, *The Emergence of Provincial Politics: The Madras Presidency 870–1920* (Cambridge University Press, Cambridge, 1976), pp. 288–90.

[38] *The Strange Story of My Spiritual Evolution* (Theosophist Office, Madras, 1910).

and finally to Herbert Spencer whose writings he read in college. In 1886, the year he graduated from college, he 'gave up religion and accepted Herbert Spencer's Monism'.[39] Later, he read Charles Bradlaugh and Annie Besant, published his first philosophical work, *Multum in Parvo*,[40] in which he 'attacked Religion and advocated Monism', and in 1896 he began publishing a journal, *The Awakener of India* to advocate monism and demolish Theosophy and Vedanta.[41] A chance meeting with Swami Vivekananda in 1897 convinced him that Vedanta and Theosophy accepted scientific monism, prompting him to reorient his journal. He began to study Vedanta and Theosophy, but this did not deter him from attacking Theosophy when Colonel Olcott visited Chittoor in 1898.[42] However, he became convinced in 1903 that Vedanta and Theosophy were scientific, and joined the Theosophical Society. He continued to lecture and write on science and religion,[43] and kept having mystical experiences that had begun in his youth; only now not only Sri Sankara but Masters M and K (the spiritual Mahatmas who, according to the Theosophical legend, lived in Tibet) also appeared in his dreams.[44]

Aiya's frenetic movement between different bodies of thought and his

[39] N.K. Ramaswami Aiya, *The Strange Story*, p. 2.

[40] *Multum in Parvo or Morality, Religion, Sociology and Science* (Indian Press & South Indian Times, Chingleput and Trichinopoly, 1894). The author is cited as 'Bachelor of Arts and Laws (Madras).'

[41] N.K. Ramaswami Aiya, *The Strange Story*, p. 3.

[42] Olcott also mentions the incident, writing that 'Among the questioners was a blatant, coarse-voiced infidel who roared at my companion, until he had driven her into a state of nervous agitation.' The editor's footnote identifies this 'infidel' as N.K. Ramaswami Aiya 'who later joined our Society and did some good work'. *Old Diary Leaves*, VI (1935; rpt. The Theosophical Publishing House, Madras, 1975), p. 378.

[43] The other writings that I have been able to locate are the following. *Vedanta— The Philosophy of Science* (Victoria Jubilee Press, Chittur, 1903), argued for the truth of the Advaita Vedantic philosophy, that is, of strict monism of the Vedanta. Aiya says in the text (pp. 5–6) that the study of Sankara convinced him of the accuracy of monism he had gained from western philosophy. *Godward Ho!* (V. Govindan & Brothers, Tanjore, 1909), was 'a comparative study of Science, Philosophy and Religion', drawn from the writings of Herbert Spencer and Annie Besant. He mentions here that he had sent a pamphlet, *Religion of Science*, to Herbert Spencer who in reply wrote that he was pleased to know that Indian philosophy resembled his ideas (p. iii). Perhaps this pamphlet was *Religio–Scientific Philosophy or Religion of Science and Science of Religion* (Kalyansundaran Pown Press, Tanjore, 1910), a tract arguing that both science and religion taught the unity of nature.

[44] N.K. Ramaswami Aiya, *The Strange Story*, pp. 3–13 *passim*.

mystical experiences make him a rather special case—indeed so special that the Theosophist leaders asked him to pen them down in an autobiography. But the volatility of his shifts and movements should not distract us from recognizing that the combination of science and religion characterized Hindu revival extending from Punjab to Madras. Powerful social movements and prominent reformists like Swami Dayananda, as well as little-known intellectuals like N.K. Ramaswami Aiya, blended positivism, classical Hindu texts, and modern science to authenticate a monotheistic Hinduism.

The significance of the rise of monism in Hindu revival was that it permitted the discourse of reform to invade every area of thought and practice. Formed in the 'confusion' of knowledges, and linking the condition of the human soul to the moral state of the social body, the belief in the indivisibility of science and religion authorized an invasive programme of reform. Swami Dayananda's programme, for example, ranged from the elimination of idolatry to the eradication of the influence of astrology in the daily lives of Hindus.[45] Pandit Guru Datta Vidyarthi, a leader of the militant wing of the Arya Samaj in the 1880s, prepared the philosophical ground for the programme of total reform by offering a 'scientific' explanation for a 'central conscious being' called ātmā, or the human spirit.[46] Such a scientific explanation then enabled him to offer 'expanded intellect, and not prayer', as the cure for the afflictions in the 'inner life'.[47]

Arguments upholding natural laws and physiology as the basis for the understanding of mental phenomena and religious life had become quite common in élite discourse.[48] Indeed, even Mahendra Lal Sircar, no

[45] This is laid out in his seminal text, *Satyārth Prakāsh* [in Hindi] (1882, 2nd edn.; rpt. Dehati Pustak Bhandar, Delhi, 1952). According to Kenneth W. Jones (*Arya Dharm*, p. 35), 'First published in 1875, this book, more than any other, was to influence Hindu thinking in Punjab and much of northwestern India'.
[46] *Wisdom of the Rishis or Complete Works of Pandita Guru Datta Vidyarthi* Swami Vedananda Tirtha (ed.) (Arya Pustakalaya, Lahore, n.d.), p. 243. The chapter, entitled 'Evidences of the Human Spirit' is an argument against the designation of spirit as a human delusion. It develops its argument by first citing western scientists and philosophers (Thomas Henry Huxley, among others), and then Vedic texts.
[47] *Wisdom of the Rishis*, p. 259.
[48] 'Poor India! O thou self-lost soul, why seekest thou an astrologer, when Nature is the greatest and the most sapient astrologer?', wrote Sangit (Babulji Sadashiv), *An Essay in English Read at the Pāthāre Prabhū Social Samaj Hall on Sunday 20th August 1905, Mr. Balaram Krishnanath Dhurandhar B.A., L.L.B., being in the chair* (Published by the Author, Bombay, 1906).

78   GYAN PRAKASH

religious reformer himself, had argued in 1869, citing phrenological
science, that physiology could place morality and religion on 'stabler
foundations'.[49] About three decades later, the renowned physicist and
hero of the Bengali *bhadralok*, J.C. Bose, addressing a literary conference,
argued for the unity of knowledge. Stating that while the West was known
to compartmentalize knowledge, the 'Eastern aim has been the opposite,
namely that in the multiplicity of phenomena, we never miss their underlying unity'.[50]

The insistence on the unity of forces, the oneness of phenomena, had
a powerful effect when deployed in the realm of religion. Because it
enabled a critique of a variety of existing religious and social customs in
the name of science, the 'orthodox' reaction was also compelled to invoke
science. Thus, U.P. Krishnamachari, who represented himself as a pro-
ponent of 'Aryan orthodoxy' and published a fortnightly journal called
The Orthodox Dynamo, delivered a series of fourteen lectures published as
The Tribunal of Science Over Reformation vs. Orthodoxy.[51] He reviewed the
charges that orthodoxy caused physical and moral degeneration by en-
joining early marriage, created disunity through the caste system, produced moral decay by telling obscene Puranic stories, and was responsible
for intellectual decline by breeding superstition and idolatry. In reviewing
these charges, he cited Darwin, Spencer, Malthus, Adam Smith, Max
Müller, and Huxley, among others, as authorities whose opinions supported his refutation of the reformist charges.[52] The text ended with the
'Judgement of the Tribunal of Science' that acquitted orthodoxy of all
charges. Orthodox Hindu practices were adjudged as beneficial, practical,
and in conformity with scientific laws.[53]

It was in these 'confusions' of categories that the élites conducted the
debate over the reform of Hinduism. Their transgressions of cultural
borderlines empowered them to forge an invasive discourse. Both re-
formers and the defenders of 'orthodoxy' required Hinduism to accommodate the laws of nature, and placed the Hindu soul and Hindu practices

[49] *On the Physiological Basis of Psychology*, p. 4.

[50] *Literature and Science: the Substance of the Presidential Address Given in Bengali
by Prof. J.C. Bose to the Literary Conference at Mymensing, April 14, 1911* (n.p., Calcutta,
1911).

[51] ([Published by the Author], Benaras, 1916).

[52] *The Tribunal of Science*, p. vi.

[53] Ibid., pp. 57–61. A somewhat similar defence of idol worship, arguing that
mass ignorance dictated that Postive Science could only be communicated through
the religion of the sense, was offered by V. Mutukumaraswami, *Symbolic Worship
in India* (Mercantile Press, Rangoon, 1904), p. 7.

at the service of modern science. If this colonized the indigenous culture, then it must also be admitted that colonization required the renegotiation of knowledge and power. The authority of science as a sign of western power was lost as it was compelled to express itself in the Hindu *ātmā*. There, the signification of science as a sign of modernity was renegotiated as it was articulated with the archaic, the other. Father Lafont recoiled in horror when recognizing the loss of science's western provenance to the other; to the Muslim fakir and the Hindu yogi; to willed respiration, and the unity of phosphorous and human thought. Then, with science's western identity and originality imploded by indigenization, the renegotiated/ translated science appeared to Lafont as the production of an alien, grotesque difference. 'Confusion' expressed and normalized the fear of this loss to grotesque difference caused by the breach of cultural boundaries. Yet, it was precisely in such boundary-crossings that the discourse of science achieved its enduring insertion in the élite culture.

CULTURAL TRANSFORMATION ON THE BORDERS

Towards the end of the nineteenth century, a debate broke out among the western-educated élite over the adoption of European habits and ideas by young Indian men. Many felt that the educated youth were following European fashions blindly. They had taken to tea and coffee, for example, with a zest that disregarded the ill-effects of these beverages in the hot Indian climate. The *Calcutta Monthly*, a journal of the Mohammedan Sporting Club, published an article in 1896, criticizing the imitation of European practices:

Now a word or two about the hard and fast rules which our ancestors (I mean the hardy Arabs and the primitive Aryans) observed. . . . Plain living and high thinking was their motto. . . . Our ancestors discarded all luxury and artificiality. The great benefit they derived by never drinking anything but water and milk cannot be estimated by the unthinking and the sceptic. It is only when one takes into account the prostrating influence of the sherbet (which produces languor and lassitude), the unnatural stimulating effect of tea and coffee and the various diseases brought on by intoxicating liquids (especially in a hot country like India), that the great scientific value of never drinking anything but water and milk becomes obvious.

  Again, take for example, the habit of our ancestors of wearing nothing but white apparel. . . . Of course, if you asked them why they did so, they would reply that because our ancestors did so, or because coloured clothes look childish. But look at the thing from a scientific point of view. White coloured substances reflect all radiant light and heat. Cotton is a bad conductor of heat. Such clothing is scientifically the best for both winter and summer.[54]

Evident here is a shift in perspective that reveals the 'scientific value' of drinking milk and water, that discovers a modern 'scientific point of view' secreted in the ancient faith of 'hardy Arabs and the primitive Aryans'. This shift registers the extent of the distribution of science's authority: even the ancestral practice of drinking nothing but milk and water is now justified by its 'scientific value' and the contemporary habit of consuming tea and coffee is criticized for its 'unnatural stimulating effect'.

But also registered is another subtle move: the authority of modern science emerges in the startling language of ancestral reason and as an effect of discrete strategies to reform daily habits.

Encapsulated here is both the story of the powerful transformation of the élite culture and an account of the renegotiation of science's authority as it activated and authorized the élite discourse. It would be a mistake to characterize science's divided, hybrid authorization as a story of the cultural adaptation of western knowledge to Indian conditions. 'Adaptation' does not capture the contention and contingency of translation; it fails to recognize the renegotiation of knowledge and power forced upon western science in its authorization. This renegotiation ensued because western knowledge could not achieve dominance through imposition. It was compelled to seek the media of the Hindu *ātmā* to express its authority, imploding prior conceptions of 'Western' and 'Indian' identities. Remarkable in what followed was not the strange content of the science of respiration that emanated from the breath of the buried fakir but the estranged position of hybridity and liminality from which the authority of modern knowledge was enunciated.

Hybridity refers to the implosion of identities, to the dispersal of their cultural wholeness into liminality and undecidability. Such a notion of hybrid, non-originary mode of authority is profoundly agnostic, and must be distinguished from the concept and celebration of hybridity as cultural syncretism, mixtures, and pluralism. Hybridity, in the sense I have used it here, refers to the dissemination, dislocation, and undoing of founding oppositions entailed in their very establishment; and it seeks to highlight cracks and fissures as necessary features of the image of authority. Recall, for instance, Mahendra Lal Sircar's dispersal of western science's identity

---

[54] 'On the Health of the Body', *Calcutta Monthly*, 1: 4 (Oct. 1896), pp. 33–6.

as free inquiry when he linked its position to its enunciation in colonial conquest; recollect also Father Lafont's recognition of the loss of science's 'safety' to the contagion of 'confusion'. There, one can witness the seamless narrative of progress unravel in the process of its narration. One can almost hear the 'original' Hindu tradition crackle as the science of Bhaskaracharya is wrenched free from the fable of the Puranas and spliced with the Sahib's knowledge. Formed in this hybridity, the Hindu élite relocated science's authority in its 'use in this world', not in its signification as a mark of western superiority. The knowledge of modern astronomy could bring greater respect to those Brahmins who possessed it; geography was capable of rendering god's greatness visible; and Occidental knowledge could function as a 'supplement' to Oriental classics. Authorized in its functionality, the rule of science came to penetrate the depths of the élite culture. By the turn of this century, fields ranging from literature to religion were opened to science's functioning as a grammar of reform. Constituted in these transformations, the élite came to occupy the centre stage of colonial India, even though it was limited by size, by its use of exclusive linguistic mediums (including English), and by its reliance on the printed word.

To view the transformation of élites as the 'colonization of the mind' is to concede the triumph of the 'civilizing mission', albeit in an inverse form. Such a view overstates the capacity of the discourse of science to remain unchanged, to preserve its 'originality', when put into operation. But more importantly, it fails to appreciate that the colonized élite's reach for hegemony could not but alienate colonial representations; that the estrangement of the West and the production of hybridity were necessary strategies and effects of the modern élite's dominance. Modernity became an authoritative force in India by alienating itself between the lines, by losing itself in the otherness it sought to appropriate. Such a mode of authorization could not but divide the signification of science between the 'original' and the 'copy'.

If science in the colonies was obliged to appear in the reclamation of the ancestral 'hard and fast rules', then the 'second colonization' functioned as renegotiation, as a form of translation between the lines. Renegotiation did not separate science from colonial power; rather, it constituted power's dynamic and divided exercise; and it occurred in those fleeting moments when the tyrannical authority of science staggered before traditions it represented and sought to master. At those moments, repressed knowledges and subjects returned, not as timeless traditional entities, but as figures of subalternity to reclaim some ground, to force a translation and transformation of power. It is in forcing such a transformation that an élite staked its claim to represent subaltern forms of culture and staged itself as a force that would guide India's march to modernity.

4

Small Speeches, Subaltern Gender: Nationalist Ideology and Its Historiography*

KAMALA VISWESWARAN

She came to my house and spoke. So well she spoke . . . and with conviction. I thought, why should I not also speak like that?

['N.T. Mary' upon meeting Captain Lakshmi in Burma (interview, 1988)]

My tongue is really tied.[1]

[Gayatri Spivak, interview, 1990]

* Research for this article was completed in 1988 under a Fulbright–Hayes Fellowship. I am grateful to Shahid Amin, Dipesh Chakrabarty, Partha Chatterjee, and Gyan Prakash for their extended comments on this article. Members of the 1994 Columbia University South Asia Seminar on 'Gender and the Politics of Agency' also provided helpful readings. I also thank Lata Mani and Rajeshwari Sunder Rajan for their comments on earlier versions of this essay, Meera Velayudan for pointing me to the right records, and finally, the staff at the Tamil Nadu State Archives, Madras for their assistance.
[1] 'Gayatri Spivak on the Politics of the Subaltern', interview by Howard Winant, *Socialist Review*, 1990, pp. 81–97.

There is, of course, an overwrought irony in contrasting the (heroically decisive) words of a Burmese Tamil woman who fought with the Indian National Army in the last years of the nationalist movement, and the (halting, indecisive) words of a well-known feminist critic who has written extensively on the perils of subject retrieval. In juxtaposing the two, however, I mean to throw into stark relief the problematics of voice, subject retrieval, and agency raised by Gayatri Spivak's essay 'Can the Subaltern Speak?' Spivak has of course, answered this question with an unequivocal 'No'. Yet while one might concur with her analysis of the ways in which all representation is overdetermined by a structure of interests, this should not stop us from asking the crucial questions of *how* it is overdetermined. What are the places subaltern speech is denied; the ways in which it is contained; the moments when an act of speech might puncture, even rupture, official discourse?

Mary's words emphatically suggest a sense of what it might have meant for women to 'speak' during a particular period of the nationalist movement in India. Yet, however important it might be to explore the range of meanings imbued in women's speech for women themselves, this chapter takes as its starting point the problematics of retrieving speech, and of constituting certain gendered subjects as subaltern. It is not, therefore, directly concerned with questions of subaltern consciousness, the awareness of, and opposition to, patriarchal or class structures of domination.[2] Thus, I am concerned here not with the meaning of women's speech, or the reasons and motivations for women's entry into the nationalist movement, but rather with their rendition as discursive subjects. I am concerned with what women's speech (or, more precisely, its suppression), might have signified for the deployment of nationalist ideology and its (counter-) historiography. I ask how it is that subalternity is inflected by gender.

Recent studies of 'Women in the Indian Nationalist Movement'[3] have

[2] The distinction is, an artificial one. The normative description of humanism, which this essay works against, is of a subject possessing sovereign consciousness. But several subaltern studies writers also use the terms subaltern consciousness and subaltern subject interchangeably.

[3] *See* Manmohan Kaur, *The Role of Women in the Freedom Movement* (Sterling, Delhi, 1968); Vijay Agnew, *Elite Women in Indian Politics* (Vikas, Delhi, 1979); Aparna Basu, 'The Role of Women in the Indian Struggle for Freedom', in B.R. Nanda (ed.), *Indian Women from Purdah to Modernity* (Vikas, Delhi, 1984); S. Alexander, 'Participation and Perceptions: Women and the Indian Independence Movement', *Samya Shakti* (Delhi, 1986), vol. 1, no. 2; Radha Kumar, *The History of Doing* (Verso, London, 1993).

performed the much-needed task of enumerating and naming the women involved in nationalist politics from various regions. I attempt to take the next step from such compensatory history by 'reading' the records from one particular region, the Madras Presidency, for what they can tell us about the attitudes of male nationalists and colonial officials toward women activists in the nationalist movement.

It would not be unfair to say that while the praxis of *Subaltern Studies* has originated in the central assumption of subaltern agency, it has been less successful in demonstrating how such agency is constituted by gender. The occasional Subaltern Studies theorist, when he has ventured to comment on the role gender has played in nationalist ideology, has also been strangely content to point to the absence of women from nationalist registers.[4] Is then the silence on the subject of women within the parameters of *Subaltern Studies*, somehow related to the simultaneous creation of nation and (counter-) narration? Let me answer with a brief overview of Partha Chatterjee's essay, 'The Nationalist Resolution of the Women's Question', which bears heavily on my argument.

GENDER AND SUBALTERNITY, GENDERED SUBALTERNITY

Chatterjee has made a crucial contribution to the debates on Indian nationalist ideology by revealing its gendered inception, and while it is possible to contest parts of his argument, it remains useful at the level of a model. He begins with the puzzle of why the 'Woman Question' ceases to become an issue for nationalist discourse by the end of the nineteenth century and argues that it is in fact 'resolved' by a necessary kind of silence; a nationalist refusal to make the issue of women an item of negotiation with the colonial state. The 'home' then, becomes the discursive site of nationalist victory when the 'world' has been ceded to the colonial state. The male nationalist turns inward, reifying the home, and women's place within it, as a spiritualized 'inner space' that contests colonial hegemony.

Extending Chatterjee's argument, it is possible to see a kind of logic at work: if the family or home is the site of nationalist silence, and women's subjectivities are located in the home, women's agency is itself subject to

[4] Partha Chatterjee, 'The Nationalist Resolution of the Women's Question', in *Recasting Women*, Kumkum Sangari and Sudesh Vaid (eds) (Kali for Women, Delhi, 1989).

a kind of silencing.[5] It is but a short step to contend that such logic actually forecloses upon the question of women's agency, excluding it from nationalist discourse or its (counter-) historiography.

Thus, the nationalist resolution of the woman question, must be seen not only as a strategy for contesting colonial hegemony, but as a strategy for the containment of women's agency, carrying within it the seeds of colonial assumptions about gender. Colonial attitudes toward nationalist women depicted them as beings dependent upon their husband's agency, and this idea of the 'dependent subject' was replicated in the way nationalist ideology rendered women as domestic(ated), and not political subjects.[6] I suggest it is the failure of the Subaltern Studies historian to break from the discourse he analyses, which results in an inability to adequately theorize a gendered subaltern subject.

One of the strengths of the notion of 'subalternity' thus far advanced by *Subaltern Studies* is its contingent or relational nature.[7] By this I mean the assertion of autonomy that conceives of domination itself as a relation of power. It is the assertion of subaltern autonomy as relational that allows us to move away from the idea of originary autonomy at the heart of a self-constituting sovereign subject of consciousness. One possible strategy of the Subaltern Studies historian then, is to resist essentialism by recovering the presence of the subordinate constituted and refracted through a series of discursive relations, no less 'real' for not containing its own origins within itself.[8] It is particularly important to mark strategies of containment (points at which the subaltern are contained by dominant

[5] This formulation does not alter when women enter the nationalist public sphere, and is indeed the very basis for their participation in Indian civil society, women are seen to embody the virtues of domesticity and cannot then be contaminated by the public activity. *See* the larger argument in my 'Modesty of the Modern: Women's Participation in the Public Sphere of late Colonial India', in 'Family Subjects: An Ethnography of the "Women Question", in Indian Nationalism' (Ph.D) and Chatterjee, p. 243.

[6] *See also* Kumkum Sangari and Sudesh Vaid, 'Recasting Women: An Introduction', in Sangari and Vaid (eds), *Recasting Women* (Kali for Women, Delhi, 1989), p. 9, for another analysis of the domesticization of women under cultural nationalism.

[7] *See* Gyan Prakash, 'Writing Post-Orientalist Histories of the Third World: Perspectives from Indian Historiography', in *Comparative Studies in Society and History*, 1990, p. 399, for a discussion of the relational aspect of post-foundational history.

[8] I am paraphrasing Rosalind O'Hanlon here in a more discriminating evaluation of Subaltern Studies than appears in her later work. *See* 'Recovering the Subject: Subaltern Studies and Histories of Resistance in Colonial South Asia', *Modern Asian Studies*, 22,1 (1988), p. 202.

ideology) as sites of power and the assertion of subaltern autonomy. I want to argue however, that the constitution of the subaltern in, and as series of relations of power, requires some revision when gender is concerned.

To consider the gendering of subalternity, one must distinguish between the figure of 'Woman' as subaltern and the question of subaltern women. ('Woman' here, is the universalizing term; 'women' the non-essentialized one). It is the former that Gayatri Spivak takes up in her essay 'Deconstructing Historiography',[9] but it is with regard to the latter that I want to address the (im)possibilities of feminist analysis.[10]

The first question demands we understand that if subaltern and élite appear as opposed terms, this opposition is itself fractured by the introduction of a third term, the figure of 'Woman'. In so far as subaltern and élite are produced as masculinized terms, their opposition is derived not only from one another, but from 'Woman' (or rather élite women and subaltern women). That is to say that subaltern and élite men become men in relation to women as well as in opposition to one another. (This is what I think Spivak means by the tendency of Subaltern Studies historians, 'not to ignore, but to rename the semiosis of sexual difference "class" or "caste solidarity."')[11] Of course, the reverse is also true: for women become women not only in relation to men, but also in opposition to other women. Thus the subject position of the middle-class or élite nationalist 'woman' must be counterposed to that of subaltern women. The gendered relation of subalternity means that with regard to the nominal male subject of nationalist ideology, the figure of woman is subaltern; with regard to subaltern women, the recuperated middle-class woman as nationalist subject certainly is not.

What I want to notice and forgo at the same moment is the discursive conflation in nationalist and colonialist ideologies of 'women and the

[9] *See* Gayatri Spivak, 'Subaltern Studies: Deconstructing Historiography', in *In Other Worlds* (Methuen, New York, 1987); originally published in *Subaltern Studies IV* (Oxford University Press, Delhi, 1985).

[10] I find myself quite at odds with defences of the deployment of woman as a universal category found (among other places) in Rosalind O'Hanlon and David Washbrook's recent essay, 'After Orientalism: Culture, Criticism, and Politics in the Third World', *Comparative Studies in Society and History*, 34: 1 (January 1992), p. 154, and as they are based on such serious misreadings of feminist theory, cannot take them up here. *See*, however, Gyan Prakash's response in 'Can the Subaltern Ride?', *Comparative Studies in Society and History*, 1992, pp. 182–3.

[11] Spivak, op. cit., p. 218.

poor', 'women and the lower castes', which excludes the term 'poor women', or 'lower-caste women'[12] and produces the idea that gender is a separate category equivalent (but ultimately marginal) to caste and class, rather than a structuring principle of nationalism and its (counter-) historiography. Subaltern Studies historians echo this discursive conflation when they speak of 'women and the subaltern'. Spivak thus underscores the complicity between the subaltern studies group and subalternity in observing, 'Male subaltern and historian are . . . united in the common assumption that the procreative sex is a species apart, scarcely if at all to be considered a part of civil society'.[13]

In summary then, two distinct problems mark the theorization of gender by the Subaltern Studies group. Either gender is subsumed under the categories of caste and class, or gender is seen to mark a social group apart from other subalterns, (which is symptomatic of the formulation 'women and the subaltern'). But even where recent work by Subaltern Studies historians such as Partha Chatterjee and Dipesh Chakrabarty situates gender as a structuring principle of nationalist and colonial relations, deftly accounting for how ideals of wifely domesticity mark the formation of (male) nationalist subjectivity,[14] their own complicities in identifying the domesticization of women, prevent them from seeing such as a strategy for the containment of women's agency, of asking what it is that makes women subaltern. The question of *subaltern* women then, must be framed first by the recovery of a non-originary or 'dependent' subject in the understanding of subaltern autonomy as relational. Exposing strategies of containment (points at which the subaltern are contained by dominant ideology), thus reveals both the relational aspect of power and the assertion of subaltern autonomy. The question of subaltern *women*, however, requires that we understand how such subjects are rendered dependent by the gendering of nationalist ideology and its (counter-) historiography.

[12] This formulation in turn equates 'poor' with 'lower-caste', making it difficult to distinguish poor lower-caste women from middle-class lower-caste women . . .

[13] Spivak, op. cit., p. 217. Feminist historians may make the same mistake, as when Rosalind O'Hanlon, in an otherwise perceptive essay, argues that the recuperation of subalterns and women operate from parallel cases of dispossession from civil society. *See* O'Hanlon, op. cit., pp. 220–1.

[14] *See* Partha Chatterjee, *The Nation and its Fragments* (Princeton University Press, New Jersey, 1993); *also*, Dipesh Chakrabarty, 'Who Speaks for Indian Pasts?: Postcoloniality and the Artifice of History', *Representations* 37 (Winter 1992), and 'The Difference–Deferral of [a] Colonial Modernity: Public Debates on Domesticity in British Bengal', *History Workshop* (Autumn 1993), 36: 1–34.

It is at this point that this chapter properly begins, but not without some further cautions. Since we are operating in the field of nationalist ideology and its critique, vigilance is necessary. In an analysis such as this one, where the voices of some women do emerge, recuperation of a nationalist middle-class or élite subject is inevitable. Not so paradoxically then, the point of intervention for the feminist historian often rests uneasily upon the retrieval of middle-class subjects. Every discourse operates through powers of selective inclusion and exclusion; nationalist discourse is no exception.[15] Thus, I am aware that advancing a middle-class woman's 'counter-subjectivity' displaces lower-class subjects in the same way that the masculinized male subjectivity of nationalism displaces female subjects. The very anonymity of lower-class women is in some sense only possible through the entry of middle-class women into nationalist historiography through the class-selected acts of writing and speech.

This analysis, however, focuses primarily on colonial strategies for the containment of women's agency: the refusal to take women seriously as political actors, or when their agency cannot be denied, to impute it to domestic influence. Elsewhere, I have also described in detail, nationalist strategies for containing women's agency.[16] As I cannot reproduce that analysis here, I want only to note important junctures where the two narratives converge in their gendered descriptions of agency.

The containment of nationalist women's agency can be most clearly identified with the discursive process of domesticization that seeks less to limit women's agency to the physical space of the home, as to impute its effects to domestic influence. For example, women satyagrahis were not seen to share a common set of motives which led them to undertake satyagraha. Rather, married women arrested for such activities were considered respectable, especially if they could affirm their social status in the home with evidence of servants to perform their domestic chores.[17] Their political motives, therefore, remained unquestioned. Unmarried women, lower-class women, or women who could not otherwise establish respectability—that their lives were 'no better than other women attending to household duties themselves, without assistance of servants'[18] —might have the labels 'prostitute' or 'paramour' attached to them, and their political motives were suspect. Indeed, colonial officials often

[15] As Uma Chakravarti reminds us, 'Vast sections of women did not exist for 19th century nationalists'. *See her* 'What Ever Happened to the Vedic Dasi?', in *Recasting Women*, op. cit., p. 79.

[16] Visweswaran, 'Family Subjects'.

[17] *See* Government Orders (G.O.) 1671: 2.4.41.

[18] *See* G.O. 1196: 23.3.32.

assumed that because such women could not prove respectability, they were undertaking satyagraha to gain respectability. This logic resulted in the deliberate selection of middle-class and élite women as nationalist actors.

However, since speech was often equated with agency, a second means of containing women's agency was to dismiss the power of their speech by arguing for the influence of male relatives. But again, respectability and social status were key, for if a woman's husband was unimportant, she must also be unimportant, and so, therefore, her speech. Thus, the second moment of convergence between nationalist and colonial narratives is the conscription of women's agency to various forms of silencing. On this point, the relationship between the introduction and the body of this chapter, underscores the further convergence of Subaltern Studies counter-nationalist historiography with nationalist and colonial narratives. As I have indicated, these processes of silencing and selection are not so much contradictory as complementary.

ON SPEECH AND AGENCY

Women's subjectivities are often refracted through third person accounts of how they spoke (noting the effects a speech produced: the drawing of a crowd, creating 'excitement' or 'disturbance'), and less frequently through accounts of what they said. Even where a woman's words might be reported as direct speech, they appear as fragments. Thus middle-class women themselves are often rendered 'speechless' by the records.

Colonial records rarely tell us *what* women said, but rather emphasize *how* women spoke. Indeed, they often seek to denigrate or deny the impact of women's speech by implying that even within the élite nationalist mobilizational genres of 'speech-making' or 'speechifying', they did not speak at all, but rather 'made noise', 'shouted slogans', or 'read from prepared statements'.[19] The colonial state equally used similar strategies for describing many nationalist activities. For example, when Kamaladevi and her husband Subramanya Ayyar led a Congress procession through the streets of Madras on 19 January 1932, officials said:

. . . there was a large crowd in front of the Congress office obstructing the public and causing annoyance to the passers by in the Big Bazaar Street. . . . The first accused was holding the national flag. There were about 2,000

. . [19] I thank Shahid Amin for reminding me of this point.

persons gathered at that time. A big noise, 'Mahatma Gandhi [ki] jai' was made.[20]

Thus the terms colonial officials might use to describe a nationalist rally, a demonstration by poor people, or a woman's individual act of protest were often deployed interchangeably: the drawing of a crowd, and therefore 'obstruction of public traffic and cause of public annoyance' or nuisance. In this sense, 'women and the masses', 'women and the poor' are continually deployed as interchangeable terms within colonial discourse which work to exclude the identity of 'poor women'.

This splitting of the lower-class woman's identity into two categories ('women' and the 'poor') is part of the same process by which her subjectivity becomes an excluded term in colonial (and in nationalist) discourse, while élite or middle-class women come to signify 'women', and poor men come to signify the 'poor'. Indeed, the latter two terms might be considered the oppositionally invoked identities against which the bourgeois male subject is constituted. This subject in turn functions through a dual strategy of evocation and repression of the identities of middle-class women and subaltern men, revealing that 'the subaltern cannot exist without the thought of the élite'.[21] The normative operation of this subject, however, disguises its dependency upon relations with others by claiming for itself a self-authorizing and autonomous agency.

The 'autonomous' subject seeks to authorize itself through speech. Thus in problematizing the relationship between speech and agency, I mean to put into relief the very production of bourgeois (–nationalist) subjectivity. The idea of a 'speaking subject' is of course central to the philosophies of humanism. Speech as agency, invokes the idea of self-originating presence, so that conversely, lack of speech is seen as absence.

In denying or downgrading the speech of nationalist women, however, colonial ideology sets into play a project of subject retrieval that can only complement or complete the formation of a sovereign nationalist subjectivity. To recuperate a subject is of course to invest it with rights and duties, but also to make it do the work of its authorizing project. The demonstration that subaltern women speak, then, is an act this analysis strains against, but which is inevitable given the terms of subject retrieval deployed in a nationalist field. Any feminist history that relies on retrieval as a partial method must therefore register a series of postponements or run the risk of

[20] G.O. 600: 16.2.32. *See also* descriptions of women-led 'flag processions', and the 'crying of Congress slogans, "Inquilab Zindabad"', etc. G.O. 721: 17.2.31 and G.O. 5100: 15.1.43.
[21] Spivak, op. cit., p. 203.

universalizing the standpoint of a certain class of women; of again making élite or middle-class women stand for all women (exactly the discursive manoeuvre that nationalist and colonial discourses perform).

For example, activists might prove themselves strong or weak speakers, but it was their social status or standing rather than elocutionary skill that made their speech worthy of notice. Thus, élite women such as Sarojini Naidu made 'strong and impressive' speeches with 'telling effects';[22] and while the speeches of C. Rajagopalachari (or Rajaji) during the Vedaranayam Salt March in April of 1930 might have been less than rousing, his stature made him worthier of arrest than more powerful but unknown orators:

Rajaji is usually the only speaker at his meetings. His speeches are mild. It is not likely that he will give occasion for the employment of section 108 CPC. On the other hand, some of the local orators from Kumbakonam and Manargudi who go about to work up enthusiasm in advance are violent. Some of their speeches have been distinctly seditious; but the orators themselves are negligible men.[23]

For colonial officials, a speech was only important if the speaker was important. In arguing that some women speak, then, my aim is to underscore precisely that model of agency which both nationalist and colonialist discourses authorize, for speech as agency is also a strategy of dominance produced in the process of silencing women.[24] The result is actually a two-pronged strategy of containment: one which locates agency in speech and then denies speech to most women, setting in motion feminist attempts to recover lost enunciatory positions. I must therefore mark my own complicity at every turn.

I am aware that I have sacrificed a chronologically textured analysis of the activities of Indian women during various phases of the nationalist movement in order to highlight the similarities between nationalist and colonial views of women. While my analysis occupies the broad historical ground between the turn of the century and the moment of Indian Independence in 1947, I see this chapter as a step toward confronting some of the difficulties in theorizing about subaltern agency in the hope that it will strengthen rather than undermine, the critical project begun by the Subaltern Studies group.

[22] History of the Freedom Movement (HFM) File no. 65: 17.3.19, 'Madras Beach Meeting: Anti-Rowlett Committee'.

[23] Undersecretary Safe (USS) File 687, 'Civil Disobedience, Tanjore District: Vedaranayam Salt March', letter from J.A. Thorne to Cotton, 21.4.30.

[24] I am indebted to Gyan Prakash for these observations.

THE RECORDS

Although contemporary historical accounts assert that women participated in the nationalist movement by the thousands, there are no statistics or even estimates available on the number of women who participated in India's nationalist movement across regions. There do exist directories of 'Freedom Fighters' published by state and district that enumerate those who have received official recognition for their contributions to the nationalist movement. Of course, receiving such a designation required proof of conviction or time served in jail for nationalist activity, but was as often the result of individual political manoeuvering, or official connections. Of the approximately 12,000 entries in the three volumes of the Tamil Nadu *Who's Who* only 236 (or 2 per cent of the total) were women.[25] Since the *Who's Who* is also based largely on a record of convictions, the total number reported is much lower than the actual number of women who participated.

Not surprisingly, the records reveal a similar skewing, as they are the basis of the *Who's Who*. We can, however, in spite of the incompleteness of records, gain a more thorough appreciation of the proportions of women convicted in connection with the nationalist movement in the Madras Presidency if we break down the numbers by years.[26]

In the years preceding 1930 the number of political prisoners in the Madras Presidency began to climb steadily. There were 464 reported in March 1927;[27] by 25 August 1930 the total number of prisoners convicted in connection with the Civil Disobedience movement was 4,147, 45 of whom were sent to the women's jail in Vellore. Nineteen each were held in B and C class jail conditions respectively, with 7 women held in A class.[28] On 15 November 1930 the Government of India disclosed a total figure of 29,054 political prisoners for the country. Of these, 359 were women.[29] In November 1930 the number of women satyagrahis (or

[25] The exact number of entries is 11,793. The total number of entries including members of the Indian National Army is 16,158. Numbers for Andhra Pradesh are similar: of 12,558 listed in the *Who's Who*, only 361 or 2.9 per cent are women. *See* Indira Devi, 'Women and Indian Nationalism: A Case Study of Andhra Pradesh', Indian Association of Women's Studies, Papers of the Third Annual Conference (Delhi, 1986), vol. III, p. 2.

[26] Unless otherwise specified, all G.O.s cited are from the Law General Index in the Tamil Nadu State Archives, Egmore, Madras.

[27] G.O. 7: 4.1.28.

[28] G.O. 3606: 28.8.30.

[29] Sumit Sarkar, *Modern India: 1885–1947* (MacMillan, Delhi, 1984), p. 290.

political prisoners) in Madras Presidency had dropped to 42.[30] However in March 1931 satyagrahis with less than 3 months to serve had their sentences commuted due to overcrowding at the women's prison. Thirty-eight women were released out of a total of 1,583 satyagrahis under provisions of a 6 April 1931 general amnesty.[31] This lowered the prison population's total from 261 to 205, although the official capacity was given as only 184.[32]

The total given for prisoners convicted for offences connected with the Civil Disobedience movement was 4,168 from March through October 1930, and 4,059 on 2 February 1931. Of these, 86 were given A class, 42 B class, and 3,552 put in C class.[33] As we shall see, while the vast majority of Civil Disobedience prisoners were assigned to C class, the largest number of available records is for prisoners in A or B classes (or for those negotiating a transfer from C to B class).

Arrests dropped to 523 by February of 1932.[34] By June 1933 the number of Civil Disobedience prisoners was listed as 480;[35] in February 1934, it had dropped to 77.[36] A Legislative Council Question of 2 February 1935 put the number of Civil Disobedience prisoners still in jail at the end of July 1934 as 10 men and one woman.[37]

By all accounts, women entered the Indian nationalist movement in large numbers only in the Civil Disobedience movement of the 1930s. This is reflected in the available historical records: very few of the women in Tamil Nadu *Who's Who* went to jail for offences committed in the 1920s, and then only in the latter half of the decade, well after the Non-Cooperation movement of 1919–21 had ebbed.

Thus when women satyagrahis started to flood the jails in the 1930s, the British had no policy to deal with women political prisoners. The archives reveal a great deal of how British views of Indian womanhood were constructed during this time period.

[30] G.O. 795: 23.2.31.

[31] G.O. 1981: 7.5.31; G.O. 2012: 9.5.31.

[32] G.O. 3833: 10.10.31; G.O. 1162: 13.3.31.

[33] G.O. 1164: 13.3.31.

[34] Totals given by district were: Trichinopoly 22; Madras 28 (of those 9 were women); Chittoor 8; South Arcot 24; Tanjore 82; North Arcot 55; Salem 93; Ramnad 49; Tinnevelley 32; Chingleput 3; Madurai 73; Coimbatore 54. *See* G.O. 1562: 16.4.32.

[35] G.O. 2809: 25.8.33.

[36] G.O. 1349: 1.5.34.

[37] G.O. 408: 2.2.35.

ARRESTING WOMEN

Records from the early years of the Civil Disobedience movement reveal the distinct reluctance of colonial administrators to arrest women agitators. For example, in an episode from the 1930 Vedaranayam Salt March in Tamil Nadu, inspector J.A. Thorne, reporting to Georgetown on the progress of the state-wide satyagraha, writes of a 'scuffle', in which 'Mrs. [Rukmani] Lakshmipathi took an *active part* . . . dashing about to prevent the cordon from being broken (emphasis in original). He adds, 'Mrs. Lakshmipathi has had the impudence to haunt the salt lines and the quarters of the police to distribute pamphlets purporting to be issued by Rajaji . . . which are designed to undermine the loyalty of the constables and salt peons'.

In a report that fastidiously details Thorne's dealings with the prominent Tamil Congressman, Rajaji, Thorne's irritation at Rukmani Lakshmipathi's intervention is instructive. First, her encounter with the colonial authorities is described as a 'scuffle', not as a dignified surrender, (as when Rajaji is arrested). Second, she 'dashes about' and 'haunts' the salt lines (that is, she does not hold her ground as a man would). Third, she has had the 'impudence' to assume a role that was more properly Rajaji's before he was arrested, distributing pamphlets 'purportedly' issued in his name. Thorne clearly saw Rajaji as a worthy adversary; Rukmani Lakshmipathi was merely unworthy of arrest.[38] On being detained, Rajaji himself is said to have 'complained mildly that the government are not playing the game in refraining from arresting the rank and file'.[39] Yet Rukmani, as one of the leaders of the campaign, was not arrested until two weeks after Rajaji.[40]

Almost two years later, in January 1932, the Public Department of the Government of Madras issued a confidential report on the treatment of women involved in 'satyagraha activities'. The letter urged that the use of force, especially with lathis (bamboo staves) used to disperse crowds, was to be avoided when dealing with large gatherings of women. The

[38] *See* Thorne's discussion of whether to arrest Rukmani in the letter to his superior on 5 May 1930, USS File no. 687.

[39] USS File no. 687, 'Civil Disobedience in Tanjore District: Vedaranayam Salt March', 2.5.30, letter from J.A. Thorne to Cotton, describing Rajaji's arrest on 1 May 1930.

[40] *See* HFM File no. 65, 'Civil Disobedience, General Salt File', S.F. 699 (d), vol. IV, which gives her date of arrest as 13.5.30, and G.O. 2229: 21.5.30 for her sentencing date.

government recommended the use of water-hoses, which had been used in Madras City 'with some success'.[41] These attempts to disperse women without excessive use of force, underlined the colonial view of women as essentially weak. And because many judges were reluctant to jail women, the letter went on to advise the full prosecution of women convicted for Civil Disobedience offences. Although the government felt that there was no reason why women should not serve prison sentences, it did hope that fines would serve as a 'sufficient deterrent'.[42] The imposition of fines may also have been part of the British strategy for limiting arrests of women for lack of jail accommodation.

It became common to impose fines with prison sentences, on the understanding that if the fines were paid, the second half of a sentence, or time remaining to be served, would be annulled. Thus, when Allammal and her stepdaughter Thayammal were arrested in 1933 for picketing a foreign cloth shop in Coimbatore, the remainder of Allammal's sentence was annulled after she paid her fine of Rs 200.[43] In practice however, many women did not pay their fines, and 'distress warrants' might be issued for their collection.[44] That same year, Parvathavarthani Ammal was given the choice of paying a fine of Rs 1,000 or serving rigorous imprisonment for 6 weeks. When she did not pay her fine however, 'the jewels which she wore at the time of her arrest were distrained and sold in public auction', but as the balance of Rs 834 could not be collected, Parvathavarthani Ammal served her entire sentence anyway.[45]

Initially, convictions and sentencing of women were minimal. They were rarely given more than two or three months of 'simple imprisonment' (incarceration without labour), although six months was typical for serious offences such as seditious speech (comparable sentences for men ran from one to two years). Records show that when men and women were arrested together, men were given heavier sentences for the same offences. Even women who were repeat offenders usually

[41] Women I interviewed also confirmed the use of water-hoses to spray sewage into the faces of demonstrators. They also spoke of being picked up from demonstrations in vans and being driven to the outskirts of town late at night so that they would be forced to walk the long distance home in the dark.

[42] HFM File no. 65: 12.1.33.

[43] See G.O. 752: 3.3.33, G.O. 2825: 26.8.33, and G.O. 6000: 10.12.41.

[44] See G.O. 721: 17.2.31, G.O. 1475: 27.4.33, G.O. 3050: 18.8.32, G.O. 4301: 26.9.41.

[45] G.O. 2531: 31.7.33. Later records establish that Civil Disobedience prisoners with unpaid fines whose sentences had expired or were suspended, were written off by the government. See G.O. 294: 29.1.34.

received sentences of no more than a year. It was extremely rare for women to be sentenced to 'rigorous imprisonment' (incarceration with labour).

There were complex reasons for colonial leniency toward women satyagrahis. Indian magistrates like Abbas Ali, who were sympathetic to the nationalist movement (but nevertheless owed their livelihood to the British), often sought to downplay women's contributions to the movement in order to justify more lenient sentences. In February of 1941, Abbas Ali sentenced women such as Tirupusundari Ammal and Jayalakshmi Ammal who had spoken before crowds of 600 and 1,000 people to three months simple imprisonment. For each woman he noted, 'Taking into consideration her sex, and the fact that she is not a conspicuous member of the Congress, but only a 4 anna member, I do not wish to deal with her severely'.[46] Such logic could however reach the heights of absurdity. Rajam Bharati who was also convicted of making an anti-war speech to 300 people was also sentenced to three months simple imprisonment plus a Rs 250 fine. The judge noted, 'I have dealt with the accused leniently as she is a middle-aged lady and had not taken an active part, except that she was once secretary of the District Congress Committee. She has not taken any prominent part in the movement. She has offered only symbolical satyagraha'.[47] Here, the judge conveniently overlooked the fact that *all* satyagrahas were symbolic in nature, no more so than during the period of 'individual satyagraha' in 1941. Besides, how could the former secretary of the Madras District Congress Committee fail to be considered a prominent member of the Congress Movement?

However, colonial attitudes toward women nationalists, while dismissive or scornful, could also be quite harsh. Two years later, a report in the *Hindu* of 24 February 1943 deplored the sentencing of two 'Kshatriya ladies' to two years' rigorous imprisonment each for disrupting a judge's courtroom by marching through the trial in progress and demanding that he resign and 'work for the country instead'. They argued that Gandhi was on his deathbed and that the judge was contributing to his murder by upholding the Raj. Sentencing the women, the subdivisional magistrate I.V. Seshagiri Rao admonished,

These two young ladies have taken a wicked idea into their heads to paralyse administration established by law by such acts of interference of the duties of

---

[46] G.O. 604: 4.2.41; and G.O. 914: 22.2.41. *See also* G.O. 587: 4.2.41 for exactly the same formulation in Balammal's sentencing.

[47] G.O. 495: 31.1.41.

public servants. This would appear to be a prelude for an organized attempt of the fair sex at this kind of lawless acts. If such acts are not nipped in the bud with an iron hand now, there will be a recrudescence of trouble and it will spread like wildfire. These ladies deserve a deterrent punishment. They are able-bodied and can do such labour as entrusted to them. If they are made to sit without work, their idle brains will be the devil's workshop.[48]

The women's sentences were later reduced to three months' rigorous imprisonment, so it is not possible to conclude that colonial policy toward the 'fair sex' became stricter as officials were forced to recognize women as political agents. It is worth noting, however, that after more than 20 years' of women's mass participation in the nationalist movement, and with only four years remaining until India was to gain Independence, 1943 was a fairly late date to assert 'deterrent punishment'.

Although the need for a separate women's prison was noted as early as 1920, The Madras Presidency Jail for Women in Vellore was not completed until 1927 due to lack of funds.[49] Until that time women were held in district sub-jails, and jail wardens often worried about their inability to fully segregate women from male prisoners.[50] Thus, nationalists viewed the transfer of women Satyagrahis out of the women's jail as a convenient excuse by the British to punish wilful women. For example, when the well-known leader Durgabai Ammal was moved from Vellore to the Madurai district jail in March 1932, charges were levelled by the Women's India Association and members of the Madras Legislative Assembly that she had been placed in solitary confinement when the government admitted she had been transferred for her role in instigating other prisoners to break prison rules.[51] It was also alleged that 'Durga Bai who was transferred . . . with no companion except ordinary criminals . . . suffered from fever and it is feared there might be some mental derangement', from the effects of being sent to an all-male prison. The government later denied this allegation, maintaining that two women had been transferred with Durgabai to keep her company because of overcrowding at the women's jail, thus reversing its earlier admission that she had been transferred for causing trouble.[52]

[48] G.O. 768: 5.4.43.
[49] See G.O. 3302: 22.11.24 and G.O. 1989: 6.5.29.
[50] Ibid.
[51] See WIA letter, G.O. 1552: 16.4.32, and G.O. 1714: 28.4.32, LCQ 'Transfer of Durga Bai from Vellore to Madurai', G.O. 587: 4.2.41.
[52] G.O. 4313: 1.12.32.

ON THE GENDERING OF JAIL ATTIRE

Sexual segregation in jail was just one marker of nationalist debate that increasingly focused on women as symbols. Indeed it can be argued that the degree of legislative elaboration regarding the treatment of women satyagrahis exemplified the extent to which women's bodies became nationalist signifiers.[53] Occasionally this was expressed in displays of unity between Hindu and Muslim legislators.[54] One Legislative Council Question (LCQ) moved by Basheer Ahmed Sayeed entitled, 'Alleged Compulsion in the Matter of the Wearing Apparel of Durga Bai', enquired whether Congress leader Durgabai Ammal was forced to wear white saris by jail authorities and asked 'whether the government had received any representations that Hindu married women of the Brahmin caste do not wear white saris'.[55] In spite of Gandhi's urging that women wear homespun saris of white khadi (and a 1929 budget motion moved in the Legislative Council by S. Satyamurthi to supply khadi clothing to prisoners),[56] Sayeed also asked whether the government was unaware, 'that it is against the custom of the Brahmin community even so of the Muslims to wear white saris in the married state or maidenhood.'

The government was forced to acknowledge that it had indeed supplied white saris to high class prisoners as well as casual offenders. Revisions were made in the jail manual regarding clothing specifications. Cloth with a green border was supplied to married women of all classes, blue bordered cloth was given to habituals and red bordered cloth to 'lifers'. In closing, however, the government noted caustically that 'the LCQ seems to have referred to the higher class female prisoners. So far as "C" class women prisoners are concerned, there is no complaint about the supply of the white cloth to them'.[57] Concern over women's dress in jail was indeed, a long-standing nationalist concern. In 1913, two stanzas in a satirical poem published in the *Indian Patriot* alleged women prisoners were kept blouseless and improperly clad in too-short saris, sparking a series of investigations by colonial authorities on whether blouses should

---

[53] *See* G.O. 2121: 28.5.32.

[54] This was particularly striking as differing political agendas between two communities had already emerged in the 1920s—the Khilafat movement for one. *See* Gail Minault, *The Khilafat Movement* (Columbia University Press, New York, 1982).

[55] G.O. 2563: 7.7.32.

[56] G.O. 3952: 14.10.29.

[57] G.O. 3676: 7.10.32.

be provided to women of all castes, and the proper length and width of the jail sari.[58]

Another LCQ moved by M.B. Rangaswami Reddi on the 'Treatment of Women in the Madras Presidency Jail' sought information on whether *kumkum* had been forcibly removed from women, and whether only two meals a day (from 12–1 p.m. and from 4–5 p.m.) were given to C class prisoners, with the result that children staying with women in jail were not fed until noon. A reply of 'negative on both counts' was issued by the government.[59] Evidently nationalists were not satisfied with this response, for another LCQ based on reports from the 3 March 1932 issue of the *Swarajya*, 'Women Prisoners in Vellore: Complaints About Diet, Kumkum and Bangles Tabooed',[60] again revealed Hindu and Muslim consensus that both *kumkum* and bangles were to be considered sacred symbols of all Indian married women. The LCQ's sponsor, V.C. Subramanya Bhatt contended:

In view of the fact that even among the Mohammedans, glass bangles on the person of the ladies are broken intentionally only on the death of the husband,

---

[58] *See* (Judicial) G.O. 495: 12.3.13, 'Clothing of Female Prisoners' establishing six yards as the normal length of the prison sari. The complete extract from the *Indian Patriot*, 24 Feb. 1913 reads as follows:

'Dress in Jail'

> The sun is set, the daily work is o'er
> The warder drives his willing flock to bath
> Like burden dragging cattle, sick and sore,
> They plunge or pour and then pursue their path
> No clothes have they to dry the water,—none.
> Stinking and stitched, their dress is all they own,
> Bathing, they sink into the dirt again,
> the cell walls catch and kill their weary groan.
> Their anxious eyes fall on their other dress
> On which no impure hands be laid until
> Inspection time—and Government does confess
> This meets Native humanity not ill.
> No jacket for the breast, no cloth so broad
> That it covers the limbs, half naked, lo,
> A Government keeps its female convicts—God!
> And newspapers make mock at human woe!
>
> S.K.N.

[59] G.O. 3219: 9.1.32.

[60] G.O. 1911: 11.5.32; *see also* G.O. 3219: 1.9.32, 'Treatment of women in Madras Presidency Jail'.

may I know whether the Law Member will issue instruction immediately to prevent women being treated as widows during the lifetime of their husbands?

The government's reply to this LCQ is informative. It held that while the caste threads of Brahmins and the *tali* (marriage necklace) or wedding rings of women should be not removed,[61] glass bangles came under the category of 'other jewelry', that if broken could be used as weapons— hence the rationale for their removal. The government, in a quasi-anthropological mode, concluded that it could not subscribe to the view that glass bangles were 'sacred symbols of every lady having her husband', and that their removal should be construed as forcing women to 'appear as widows'. Rather, glass bangles were not 'sacred symbols, but conventional symbols'.[62]

Such judgements followed reports of a more serious incident of a woman's gold tali being forcibly removed by jail authorities on order to realize the fine imposed on her for participation in Civil Disobedience activities. The 'Mrs Prabhu case', as it came to be called, later generated much outraged discussion transcribed in the pages of *Stri Dharma*, the Women's India Association journal.[63]

It is possible to read nationalist debates about women's sartorial status in jail as expressive of ideas about how women should be treated in public life, or as an extension of the contest over women signifying nationalism's 'inner space'.[64] This part of the analysis could thus be seen as broadly in line with Chatterjee's arguments about the gendering of nationalist ideology.

However, I want to emphasize the points at which colonial discourse affirms or denies the gendering of the nationalist subject. Therefore, the signs of symbolic widowhood in jail: white saris, snatched *talis*, lack of *kumkum* or broken bangles, also point to an active site of contestation, not merely over public representation of the inner space of Indian nationalism, but about the construction of the masculine subject of nationalism itself. Colonial attempts to enjoin symbols of widowhood in jail may have been seen less as an attack on Indian womanhood, than as an attack on Indian

[61] Jail Manual Amendment, G.O. 735: 28.2.35.

[62] *See also* David Arnold's discussion of caste symbols and prison dress in 'The Colonial Prison: Power Knowledge and Penology in 19th Century India', *Subaltern Studies VIII* (Oxford University Press, Delhi, 1994).

[63] *See* the February 1932 issue, pp. 237, 240, 266, 297, 301.

[64] Dipesh Chakrabarty, personal communication, 12 April 1991; and Partha Chatterjee, personal communication, 18 April 1991.

manhood, since an appeal to stop the practice was not made on the basis of the affective stigma women might feel as widows, but on preventing women being treated as widows ' . . . *during the lifetime of their husbands'* (emphasis added).

This material can thus be seen as a challenge to Chatterjee's central thesis that the 'woman question' ceases to be an item of negotiation with the colonial state. While the 'woman question' might focus less on the reform of women, than on operational definitions of women's status, the discursive effects of the woman question are still in play: an appeal to sovereignty through a demonstration of women's status. Of course, the terms are reversed, for it is now the colonial state that is unfit to rule because it degrades women by forcing them to live as widows—an important nationalist inversion of the social reform debates on widowhood.[65]

COLONIAL CONSTRUCTIONS OF
CLASS AND GENDER

It has become commonplace in Indian historiography to argue that British presence in India actually consolidated the caste system.[66] Yet little attention has been paid to the ways in which the British also set in motion certain notions of class.[67] The negotiation and construction of class in British India can be seen clearly in jail records of nationalists jailed in the thirties and forties. Jails became the sites for the struggle over definitions of class and caste. The contested definitions of class privilege in jails at that time tells us much about the treatment of Civil Disobedience prisoners in general, and women satyagrahis as a subset of that group, in particular.

In 1922, non-cooperators raised questions about the definition of 'political prisoner' and of special privileges for dissenters in the Madras Presidency. Among other things, they asked to be separated from other

[65] I have argued the question of widowhood in greater detail in 'Family Subjects'. *See also* Rosalind O'Hanlon, 'Issues of Widowhood: Gender and Resistance in Colonial Western India', in D. Haynes and G. Prakash (eds), *Contesting Power* (Oxford University Press, Delhi, 1991) for a discussion of the social reform debates on widowhood.

[66] *See* Bernard Cohn, *An Anthropologist Among the Historians* (Oxford University Press, Delhi, 1987). Nicholas Dirks, 'The Invention of Caste: Civil Society in Colonial India', *Social Analysis* (1989), 25: 42–52, and 'Castes of Mind', *Representations* (Winter 1992), no. 37.

[67] *See* Richard Fox, *Lions of the Punjab* (University of Carolina Press, Berkeley, 1984).

prisoners. They pointed out that the governments of Bengal and Punjab had allowed political prisoners special clothing, separate latrines, personal bedding, rights to write and receive letters once a month, and to keep lights on until 10 p.m.[68] The government's response to a Legislative Council Question[69] on the subject was that it did not 'understand' what was meant by the term 'political prisoner'. As late as 1931, the colonial state reaffirmed this non-definition:[70]

The government of India consider it desirable to avoid the use of the term 'political prisoner', especially in formal documents such as rules and official orders. The more correct phrase, 'prisoners convicted of offences connected with political movements' should be used to describe such prisoners.[71]

Such a circumvention followed an earlier unsuccessful petition from satyagrahis that all political prisoners (if not charged with '"violence, moral turpitude or personal greed"') be considered at least B class'.[72] Yet by 1932, another G.O. acknowledged that 'every effort was made to separate Civil Disobedience prisoners from the ordinary jail population'.[73] Nationalist concern over the treatment of political prisoners who had been assigned to C class can be seen as an attempt to contest the alleged criminality of their protest, but in attempting to separate themselves from 'common criminals', nationalists also left unchallenged colonial definitions of 'criminality'.

Nationalists however, also attempted to assert gender as a category of classification. Legislative Council Question no. 109 challenged the placement of women in C class and questioned whether C class women were receiving proper treatment in jail. The government's response was that the classification criteria did not 'contemplate any special classification of women prisoners'.[74] Yet it was clear that women prisoners were seen to

[68] G.O. 662: 13.3.22.

[69] G.O. 2787: 13.11.22.

[70] Ranajit Guha describes the central intervention of Indian nationalism as the articulation of a subject with rights, even as the colonial state properly denied subjects extended rights. See 'Dominance Without Hegemony', in Subaltern Studies VI (Oxford University Press, Delhi, 1990). The threat of an emerging nationalist subject can be seen in the refusal of the colonial state to legitimize the category 'political prisoner' or to standardize attendant privileges.

[71] G.O. 3180: 25.8.31.

[72] G.O. 3302: 6.8.30. Interestingly, 'persons convicted of cruelty or acts of premeditated violence' were apparently eligible for B class. See G.O. 1001: 1934.

[73] G.O. 3767: 15.10.32.

[74] G.O. 463: 2.2.31.

have special needs, and were treated differently from men. The year 1932
also saw LCQs regarding women political prisoner's access to doctors,
and establishment of rights for women to keep small children with them
in prison.[75] A Women's India Association resolution also requested that
female political prisoners be escorted to jail only by female wardens,[76]
while another suggestive government order from the superintendent of
the Presidency Jail for Women in Vellore queried whether provisions in
the jail manual should stipulate a scale of bedding since 'Indian female
prisoners of B class who do not adopt the European mode of dressing are
in many cases accustomed to the use of mattresses, pillows, towels, san-
dals, etc.'[77]

A letter from Muthulakshmi Reddy, then secretary of the Women's
India Association on 3 March 1932 justified better treatment for women
C class prisoners as they had not committed any 'acts of moral turpitude'.
It also charged that:

1) 'C class political prisoners who are not used to the rice from boiled paddy
are given that rice with the result that many of them do not like the smell, 2)
they are not getting buttermilk, 3) The married women are not allowed to use
kumkum and also coconut oil was not given to the C class prisoners for the
use of their hair daily, 4) Bottles containing toddy were hurled at the lady
picketers who were picketing a toddy shop, 5) Two or three old ladies above
the age of 60 in the C class . . . are [un]able to stand the rigours of C class life
and food [and] should be transferred into the B class.'

The government responded only to the first two points and stated that
the supply of 'raw rice and buttermilk' was too costly, and further that:

There is no reason why C class prisoners connected with the Civil Disobedience movement should be treated differently from other C class prisoners, nor
is there any special reason why women prisoners should be treated in a
manner different from male prisoners in the matter of diet. There is no case
for relaxing the rules in the jail manual.[78]

In the tripartite prison class scheme of that episode, 'A' class consisted
largely of the upper-class élite, who were entitled to wear their own
clothes, cook food from home supplies, and were allowed reading materials and writing privileges. 'B' class prisoners received similar treatment but were limited to fewer letters and food supplies from home. 'C'

[75] G.O. 3435: 10.9.32; see also G.O. 3526: 22.8.30.
[76] G.O. 423: 4.2.32.
[77] G.O. 439: 5.2.32.
[78] G.O. 1552: 16.4.32.

class prisoners, because they were considered 'common criminals' were often presumed illiterate, and struggled to gain reading and writing privileges.[79] They were restricted to prison clothes and diet, and as their diet consisted largely of rice and a few poorly cooked vegetables, the lack of buttermilk or ghee in their diet was a common issue of protest.[80]

Since the British refused to standardize criteria for classification and allocation of privileges, they were easily revoked. For instance, when Durgabai Ammal requested permission to hold a Hindi exam for nine women in the Vellore jail, precedents for other Civil Disobedience prisoners to sit for university examinations outside the jail had already been established.[81] While one official argued, 'She gave us a lot of trouble in North Arcot, I would refuse it', another official countered, 'Durgabai, it is true gave us much trouble when at large, but she is reported to be well behaved in jail—and I don't think we should do anything that savours of petty persecution'. Finally, citing the idea that Durgabai's appeal smacked of a 'political stunt', officials turned down the request.[82] Similar views were involved in the suspension of privileges like sleeping outside for those convicted in connection with the 'Quit India' movement of 1942.[83]

However, some jail requests were also seen to be nationalist symbols, and the colonial administration was only too happy to allow them if it could profit from such 'privileging'. Those who were committed to Gandhi's

[79] 'A' class prisoners were allowed to see people three times a month, could write and receive letters twice a month; were allowed up to 12 books at their own cost and access to uncensored newspapers. 'B' class prisoners were allowed one letter and one meeting a month, and up to six books at their own cost. 'C' class prisoners were only granted one meeting and one letter every two months, and allowed to see only books and periodicals kept in the jail library. They were not permitted to read any newspapers. See G.O. 215: 25.1.44.

[80] Prison protests about the making and manner of serving food were common in the nineteenth century. See Anand Yang, 'Disciplining Natives: Prisons and Prisoners in Early 19th Century India', South Asia, 10: 29–45, and David Arnold, Colonizing the Body (University of Carolina Press, Berkeley, 1993). Women I interviewed told me that during the Civil Disobedience movement, more privileged prisoners shared their food across class lines.

[81] See G.O. 3531: 22.8.30 and G.O. 446: 31.1.31.

[82] G.O. 1043: 6.3.31. Of the nine women, six were Brahmins, and three were from cultivating or 'trade' castes (one woman's caste was not specified). It is worth noting that with the exception of Rukmani Lakshmipathi, all the Brahmin women were serving sentences of six months simple imprisonment or less; the lower caste women were all serving sentences of one year's simple imprisonment.

[83] G.O. 733: 31.3.43; G.O. 3031: 23.8.42.

constructive programme could always spin in jail. An LCQ established as early as 1922 that prisoners undergoing 'simple imprisonment' could spin (although they had to provide their own materials),[84] while spinning and weaving were already considered two acceptable forms of jail labour for prisoners undergoing 'rigorous imprisonment'. In 1941, a Government Order stipulated that prisoners arrested under the 'Defense of India' rules and incarcerated in the central Jail in Trichinopoly were allowed to use their own *charkhas* (spinning wheels). Of the 183 'Defense of India' prisoners in A and B classes, 124 were undergoing RI, and 59 were undergoing SI, of which 41 had elected to work. Forty-two men were already working with their own *charkhas*, and an additional 38 prisoners were willing to purchase their own spinning wheels if permitted. Noting that '82 charkhas will have to be purchased at government cost for those who are unable to get their own charkhas', A-class prisoner Rajaji, who was consulted in the matter, suggested that 'he would make necessary arrangements to supply the prisoners with charkhas and cotton slivers from private sources'. According to the Home Department, which approved the request, 'SI prisoners who work to the satisfaction of the [jail] Superintendent are allowed the higher scale of diet provided for convicts sentenced to RI and are allowed to earn remission'. Those undergoing simple imprisonment were thus allowed to keep the yarn as labour was not mandatory for them. Those undergoing rigorous imprisonment, however, had to 'contribute something to their maintenance by way of their labour', and though they might provide their own cotton and charkhas at a savings to the government, their labour would be unremunerative if they were allowed to keep the results of it. Thus they were not allowed to keep the yarn they spun unless they brought it back at the end of their prison term.[85]

However, spinning and weaving for those in the Madras Presidency Jail for Women was not allowed until 1939 after a spinning teacher had been hired at Rs 5 per month, and a prolonged trial period was began on 20 April 1938.[86] Then it was noted, 'output good and cost effective [double the return]'.[87]

On the one hand, British accommodation to nationalist jail demands appears almost incredible. On the other, in accommodating the nationalists, the colonial regime appropriated one of the primary symbols of resistance to the Raj to its own ends. In an ironic reversal of its previous

[84] G.O. 2780: 13.11.22.
[85] G.O. 1984: 24.4.41.
[86] *See* G.O. 2671: 26.5.38.
[87] G.O. 835: 15.2.39.

position disallowing khadi in jails,[88] the cloth woven from the cotton yarn the prisoners spun was used to make jail uniforms.

Gandhi's Non-Cooperation and Civil Disobedience campaigns are credited with bringing about the end of 'petition politics' in Indian nationalism. Yet the onset of these two movements might more properly be called a 'continuation of petition politics by other means', even though nationalists sought precisely to leave these forms of protest behind in their pursuit of mobilizational politics. Although the government of India refused to alter its prison classification scheme to accommodate political prisoners generally, or women in particular, as separate categories, the amount of lobbying for special privileges and reclassification suggests that neither class nor gender were stable categories, and more than material conditions were at stake. I explore this in greater detail by looking at the location of middle-class and lower-class women in colonial discourse.

JAIL NEGOTIATIONS

If we were to study only records of women's convictions for political activity, we might arrive too quickly at the conclusion that colonial officials treated all women equally. However, by looking also at Legislative Council Questions about jail conditions and petitions for jail reclassification, we can see that these sources actually reinscribe the existence of middle-class or élite subjects by establishing their 'status'. It is therefore not surprising that most surviving jail records are those of A and B class prisoners. Even so, the jail classification of women nationalists, like the practice of lenient sentencing, can be seen as a strategy for the containment of élite women's agency.

While many activists attempted to follow Gandhi's lead and did not request transfers out of C or B class, this did not stop a flood of petitions from concerned friends and relatives, highlighting that while activists might be equal in a satyagraha campaign, jail negotiations baldly centered upon notions of privilege drew from and reinforced already existing social inequalities. Although the British specified criteria for determining what class prisoners should be designated in the jail manual, the actual practices involved in classifying prisoners were highly variable. Records took note

[88] Satyamurti's budget motion, while passed by the council, was refused by the Government of Madras which held that khadi was more expensive, less durable, and 'as a symbol of a certain school of political thought . . . inadvisable for disciplinary reasons', G.O. 3952: 14.10.29.

of land revenues paid to the government, or the extent and worth of property owned. However, this alone was insufficient to determine classification. Education and culture, or 'mode of living' had to be considered. Thus, when Sunderambal, a non-Brahmin woman, was sentenced in January 1943, the judge noted that although she had some education and came from a 'tolerably rich' family (her husband owned properties worth Rs 30,000), there was 'nothing to indicate that she is accustomed to a high style of life'.[89] Still, Sunderambal was granted B class, an improvement over her first time in jail in 1941, when she had been placed in C class.

The case of two *devadasis*[90] illustrates the construction of class over caste, and raises other questions about the determination of women's status. The two *devadasis*, Thyammal and Sitalakshmi, are aunt and niece respectively. Their petitioner is C. Natesan, Thyammal's brother, who describes their economic assets in some detail: properties worth nearly one lakh rupees, extensive wet and dry agricultural lands, jewellery and movable properties valued at Rs 15,000 and Rs 20,000 respectively, and a 'motor car'. Sitalakshmi is also described as having 'studied up to the 10th form', and as a 'stongstress of renown', with 'His Master's Voice Gramophone Co. who have [sic] broadcast several of her masterpieces . . .' Natesan's point in his petition is that the women's standard of living rather than their caste should be considered when deciding upon their jail classification. By both British and Indian definitions, the property and status of these women exceeded that of many placed in 'B' class. Thus Natesan argues that his sister and niece are entitled to 'A' class treatment:

. . . by birth, breeding, habits and upbringing, the said ladies have always been used to a high standard of life. By their own wealth and social position, they were used to amenities and comforts of an elegant, cultured life. To be now suddenly deprived of all these, would unduly depress them in both body and mind. They were convicted of only technical political offence, of picketing foreign cloth shops, which they did in an absolutely non-violent fashion, and the moment they were arrested, they submitted quietly.

 . . . . Probably the authorities seem to have been influenced by the fact that the two ladies belong to Devadasi community and as such are not entitled to

[89] G.O. 5081: 12.1.43.

[90] A caste of temple dancers often erroneously described as prostitutes. *See* Amrit Srinivasan, 'Reform and Revival: The Devadasi and Her Dance', *Economic and Political Weekly*, vol. XX, no. 40 (2 Nov. 1985) and 'Reform or Conformity? Temple Prostitution and the Devadasi Community in the Madras Presidency', in Bina Aggarwal (ed.), *Structures or Patriarchy* (Kali for Women, Delhi, 1988), for analyses of the social life of *devadasis*.

an elegant and high standard of life. The petitioner submits that the said distinction is invidious and quite opposed to the times and can in no event be urged against just and legitimate claims of individuals who have always led an honourable, decent, respectable life, and caste can never be a ground of disqualification. The first mentioned Thyammal is a member of the Madura Ratepayer's Association organized by Rao Sahib R. Narasimha Iyengar, a jail visitor, having been elected member by the General Body of the Association. This is eloquent proof to show her status in society and how [the] Madura public have recognized her services and in what high esteem and respects she is held by them. She was also a member of the Tamil Nadu Province Congress Committee and of the Madura District Congress Committee. She is president of the Bharata Sevika Samithi; and the second mentioned Seethalaksmi is the secretary of that association.[91]

Originally placed in 'C' class, the District Magistrate (D.M.) defends his judgement on moral grounds by arguing:

It may be that these prostitutes were accustomed to a certain amount of what may be termed 'luxury' at the expense of their patrons; but they are certainly women of no social status and are not fit associates for the persons of respectability who are supposed to constitute the 'B' class of convicts.

Here it is acknowledged that while these women might have money, they lacked respectability. The Madurai D.M. is in the last instance however, overruled by two of his colleagues who decide in favour of 'B' class, concluding that 'the fact remains that several women of this class have a high standard of living and of culture and are not "prostitutes" in the bad sense of the term'. More important than the seeming liberalism of this judgment, is the pronounced confusion over economic status or social standing as the definitive category for prison classification. Natesan argues that his sister and niece have both, and later officials reviewing the case agree. Questions of caste, and dubious morality are subverted by class considerations, as the concluding comment on the case indicates:

. . . that they are prostitutes cannot influence the question of classification. The two ladies, according to the D.M.'s report, possess properties of their own. The D.M. himself admits that one lady was getting a fairly decent living by her music. The fact remains, whether at their own expense, or at the expense if their patrons, the ladies have been living in a style superior to that of an ordinary 'C' class prisoner, and as such, under the classification rules they deserve a higher class.

The D.M. raises an interesting point. He says that the ladies are not fit

[91] G.O. 1539: 15.4.32.

associates for the persons of respectability who are supposed to constitute the
'B' class of convicts. This point of view based on the morals of a convict has
not been referred to in the classification rules. The question of segregation in
jails of prisoners is a matter which may well be left to the Inspector General
of the prisons.

The case of the two *devadasis* also represents colonial attempts to come
to terms with women as autonomous individuals or property holders,
and in their roles as prominent members of the community. In another
case, Pitchaimuthammal, a doctor, is a woman of independent means.
Although she has no property and does not earn as much money (Rs
300–400 per month), the fact that she was educated in London for six
years, and that she came from a respected Indian Christian family is
enough to ensure her 'B' class. The text of her judgement says, ' . . . the
prisoner by social status, education, and habit of life has been accustomed
to a superior mode of living. She is an England returned lady doctor of
28 years standing'.[92]

Unmarried women, then, had to prove respectability in conjunction
with independent financial means, but this was not always easy, as 19
year-old Ratnamal's petition to be transferred from C class to B class
reveals:

As regards my status before conviction, I beg to say that I am the daughter of
the late Mr Muthu Pillai, who was then manager of a bank drawing a pay of
Rs 300 per month and that I have been living a superior mode of living with
my father's property worth Rs 7,000 saved before his death. As regards my
qualifications, I beg to add that I am a passed school final student. My mother
is at present practising midwifery for the last 11 years and earning a salary of
Rs 35 with good income. As I am the only daughter I have been brought up
well.

Colonial officials did not agree, and her petition was denied by noting:
'It has transpired that the convict was being kept by one Nityanandan of
Bodi, now undergoing imprisonment in the Central Jail, Trichinopoly
. . . and that she had little or no means other than what her paramour was
giving her . . . there is no reason for any class higher than C'.[93]

While the colonial state was obliged to reckon with unmarried,
well-established women like Pichaimuthammal or the two *devadasis* as
self-supporting individuals, married women, when they demonstrated

---

[92] G.O. 598: 5.2.32. *See also* G.O. 598: 16.2.32, G.O. 1389: 5.4.32, and G.O. 4735:
10.11.30.
[93] G.O. 2253: 8.6.32.

independent means, were still evaluated on the basis of their husbands' status and income. In the case of Saraswati Pandarangam, a non-Brahmin woman, her refusal to pay a Rs 100 fine and her husband's standing led to her status being downgraded to C class when she was imprisoned the second time in 1932. The magistrate complained, 'If her status were good, I do not see why her fine should still remain unpaid. . . . It is not known on what grounds she was placed in B class before. Her father's status may perhaps entitle her to B class but not hers or her husband's'.[94]

In yet another case, the wives of the two prominent Congress men, Akilandammal (a Brahmin woman), and Lakshmi Ammal, (a non-Brahmin woman), were given B class in spite of their husbands' protests. The official reviewing their husband's petition did not see 'sufficient reason for placing these ladies, who have not their husbands' educational qualifications or the same concern with public life, in A class,' and supported the City Magistrate's classification'.[95] However, this provisional decision was overruled by yet another official who did 'not consider that differential in "education" and/or "concern with public life" should be relied on to justify a departure from the policy hitherto pursued of giving the same classification to husband and wife unless other circumstances supervene', deciding 'A class may be given'.[96] Later, in 1941, when Lakshmi Ammal was rearrested, she was a prominent Member of the Legislative Assembly, which prompted colonial officials to note, 'Her status in life is that of an MLA, but her mode of living is definitely not very expensive and superior. She may however, be placed in the A class'.[97]

As we can see, there was a tendency to treat women as beings dependent upon their husbands' social and economic position for status. This was true even if a married woman could demonstrate financial independence. For example, on the sentencing of Lakshmiammal, a 'dictator' of the Tamil Nadu Congress Committee, it was noted that 'Mrs Sankara Ayyar knows English and has been trained in midwifery. She attends delivery cases and patients in the wards her husband maintains in a private hospital', but it was decided to place her in 'B' class 'in consideration of the status of her husband . . .'[98] In the case of V.M. Kothanayagi

[94] G.O. 3050: 18.8.32; *see also* G.O. 3935: 2.9.41.

[95] G.O. 521: 11.2.32.

[96] *See* G.O. 1031: 15.3.32, G.O. 2237: 6.6.32, G.O. 3496: 23.3.32, and G.O. 2665: 16.7.32.

[97] G.O. 1671: 2.4.41. One Anjalaiammal's status similarly improved when she went to jail a second time after being elected an MLA. See G.O.s 3196: 17.7.41 and 326: 4.2.44.

[98] G.O. 918: 7.3.32.

Ammal, editor of the Tamil journal *Jaganmohini*, it was noted that 'She writes books and sells [sic] and they are in good circulation. Herself edits a paper . . .', but again it was on the basis of her husband's property and because 'She has relations in high posts and belongs to a respectable family' that she was assigned 'A' class.[99]

Occasionally women who were MLAs like Lakshmi Bharathi, might be assigned a higher class than their husbands' who were also in jail for Civil Disobedience activities. When this was discovered, however, the wife's classification would not exceed her husband's.[100] Similarly, women who owned property of their own and might be entitled to higher classification, could be hampered by their husband's low status. When Govindammal, a Gounder woman, petitioned for reclassification, her substantial property qualifications were ignored, the first consideration being that her husband, Ayya Muthu Gounder, had been placed in C class when arrested in 1931. And while her husband was the manager of a local khadi store, a writer who contributed to Tamil journals and said to be a 'person of some culture', he owned no property, and hence Govindammal's petition for B class was denied.[101]

SEDITION AND SPEECH

During the 1920s Gandhi attempted to draw women into his constructive programme by asking then to spin and wear khadi. During the Civil Disobedience movement of the 1930s he encouraged them to picket liquor and cloth shops, although many women also took part in Salt March satyagrahas around the country. In the final phase of Gandhian politics, activists were to undertake individual satyagrahas, pledging to fill the jails by violating the laws of the colonial state. One way of doing this was to announce in a public place that the speaker refused to help the British war effort. For example, when Jayalakshmi Ammal, a Mudaliar woman, and 'four anna member of the Congress' offered satyagraha:

At 10: 45 p.m. . . . the accused came and standing on a table in front of Chinnakesavaperumal Koil, she shouted before an audience of 1,000 people

[99] G.O. 984: 10.3.32. *See also* C.S. Lakshmi's study, *The Face Behind the Mask, Women in Tamil Literature* (Vikas, Delhi, 1984), for more on Kothanayagi's role in the burgeoning women's literary movement of that time.

[100] *See* G.O. 4: 3.1.41 where the original recommendation of 'A' class for Lakshmi Bharathi was refused as her husband had been assigned 'B' class.

[101] C.O. 1196: 23.3.32.

NATIONALIST IDEOLOGY AND ITS HISTORIOGRAPHY 113

the anti-war slogan in Tamil, 'The British government have dragged India into the present war without our consent, and are using our men and money for the same. We should not contribute to the war effort'.[102]

Such descriptions were common enough, and the British often attempted to reduce women's statements to formulaic utterances ('Don't help the war with men or with money'.)[103] Yet even when portions of women's speeches are transcribed, substantive differences emerge. Like Jaya-lakshmi Ammal, N.S. Rukmani held that 'The British government have dragged India in the present war without our consent'.[104] But Neelavathi Ammal, who 'shouted anti-war' slogans opposite to khaddar stores in Pondy Bazaar, Thyagarayanagar (Madras), emphasized not the issue of consent, but that 'All wars are wrong and should be resisted non-violently', and like Balammal and Lalitha Annaji, argued for non-violent resistance.[105]

On the other hand, Rukmani Lakshmipathi or students like Maya Joseph, Sakuntala, P. Sushila, M. Lalitha Rao, T. Anusaya, and Maha-lakshmi Bharathi might argue against the war by shouting for the resig-nation of government servants,[106] while Kamladevi Arya's address, trans-cribed from Hindi, urged soldiers to find other work:

Dear Brothern [sic].
Mahatma Gandhi has been arrested. Therefore desert the military. Join the Congress. Leave off slavish job. Cruel Britishers, yesterday fired rounds on brethern [sic] in Bombay. Murder is committed yesterday; lathi charge was done on one of our brothers in Madras. Therefore military job is a sin. Work for your country.[107]

Although the period of individual satyagraha was surpassed by the mass-based 'Quit India' movement of 1942, the archival records are equally split between the numbers of women who went to jail for Civil Disobedience and individual satyagraha activities. But we would be wrong to assume that the movement of the 1930s relied more heavily upon women's silent activities than did the individual satyagraha move-ment. Groups of women who picketed during the Civil Disobedience

---

[102] G.O. 914: 22.2.41.
[103] See G.O. 587: 4.2.41.
[104] G.O. 592: 4.2.41.
[105] G.O. 6000: 10.12.41, G.O. 4301: 26.9.41, and G.O. 587: 4.2.41.
[106] See G.O. 4941: 7.12.40 and G.O. 5534: 31.3.43.
[107] G.O. 3129: 29.8.42; See also HFM File no. 98, 'Madras District Civil Dis-obedience, Aug.–Dec. 1942'.

period like Ambujammal, Kamalambal, and Muthulakshmiammal; or Akilandammal, Lakshmi Ammal, Jayalakshmi, and Meenambal, might simply have distributed nationalist pamphlets, and 'loitered with the intent of obstructing purchasers from entering a shop',[108] or like Savitri Ammal and Janaki Ammal, they might have 'exhorted the people not to bid at the arrack sales'.[109] Like Kamalam, Kalyani Ammal, Padmavathi Ammal, and Sivabogammal, they might actively have 'dissuaded intending purchasers from entering into and dealing with [foreign cloth] shops'[110] or with Krishna Bai and Kamala Bai 'preach[ed] to the shopkeepers to stop selling foreign cloth'.[111] Thus, in both movements, a premium was placed upon a woman's speech.

Middle-class women who were convicted during these two movements also used the occasions of their sentencing to reassert their speaker status on the margins of official accounts with a variety of strategies. For example, they might attempt at their hearings 'to read out a long written statement in Tamil about matters unconnected with the case'.[112] They might also plead not guilty and attempt to explain why their actions should not be considered illegal: ' . . . the accused states that the assembly was not unlawful, that they were peacefully picketing the shop and that if any breach of the peace was apprehended it was more due to the inhumane action of the police in beating the volunteers than to their picketing'.[113] Or again, 'Accused says she has assisted the operations of these [regional and national Congress] committees, but adds that though the government have declared them unlawful they are not really unlawful'.[114]

Pursuing another strategy, women might plead guilty as a means of reaffirming their original statements, 'I have no statement to make except to . . . emphatically reassert . . . my appeal to Mr Basu Dev, Sir Mohamed Oosman and others not to participate in the effective conduct of the war',[115] or again, while not refuting the charges, might legitimize action by appeals to conscience: ' . . . shout[ing] various slogans, one of them being an appeal to government servants to resign their jobs. . . . The

[108] See G.O. 304: 28.1.32, G.O. 3685: 10.10.32 and G.O. 30.8.33.
[109] G.O. 1080: 17.3.32.
[110] See G.O. 937: 8.3.32 and G.O. 663: 18.2.32.
[111] G.O. 64: 13.2.31.
[112] Neelavathi Ammal, G.O. 6000: 10.12.41.
[113] G.O. 64: 13.2.31.
[114] G.O. 1144: 21.3.32.
[115] G.O. 4941: 7.12.40; see also G.O. 914: 22.2.41.

accused does not dispute the facts but pleads . . . that according to her conscience what she did was right'.[116]

SUBALTERN SPEAKERS?

Much nationalist historiography would have us believe that only an élite group of women became leaders. However, the archives provide 'telling' evidence that women of the rank and file proved themselves able and provocative adversaries to the British, as when one Sarla Devi 'lectured the villagers and dwelt on the actions of the government and incited them to break the Salt Act by boiling sea water fearlessly'.[117] Here I quote from fragments of three other letters that illustrate the agency generated by 'objectionable' and 'inflammatory' speeches middle-class women made during the salt satyagraha campaigns of 1930. For example, one letter began:

District Magistrate's Office
Camp Calingapatam
May 22, 1930

My Dear Mr Cotton,

I have had unfortunately, to order the arrest of a woman, Kamaladevi, the wife of a Cocanada doctor. She had broken the Salt Act before, and made objectionable speeches in this district. She came to Danpade on the 20th night and would undoubtedly have put fresh spirit into the 'volunteers'. I gather that she has been a nuisance in other districts. She was arrested on the 20th while making a speech, and should be by now in Vellore.[118]

Here Kamaladevi's capacity as a political agent ('She would have put fresh spirit into the volunteers') is undercut by the narratorial voice describing her as a 'nuisance' and expressing dismay over having to arrest a woman.

Durgabai's speeches, however, produce direct results that need not be inferred. In her case, 'all the present troubles' in the District stem from her inflammatory speeches.

[116] See G.O. 5534: 31.3.43 regarding the sentencing of T. Anusaya, student, age 19.
[117] G.O. 2482: 12.6.30.
[118] HFM File no. 65, S.F. File no. 699(d), vol. IV, 'Civil Disobedience General Salt File'.

N. Arcot Collector's Office
Vellore 27/5/30

Dear Mr Cotterell,

My district was perfectly calm till Durgabai came here on the 21st. She delivered very violent and inflammatory speeches at Gudiyattam, Vellore, Arni,
and Arcot on the 21st, 22nd, and 25th instants and openly incited the masses
to disobey all order and authority. All the present troubles are the direct result
of her speeches in the District.[119]

In another case, Varahalu Ammal's influence on the public also remains uncontested when she addresses an audience of 50 people in Conjeevaram:

In the course of the speech she is alleged to [have] characterized the salt tax
as an unjust levy by the British government, which has impoverished India
to the extent of 20 crores annually (the accused challenges that she said 7
crores, not 20 as deposed to); that the sister provinces have defied and broken
the salt laws with impunity while the people of this Presidency have been
slow to follow their lead in this respect. The accused is further reported to
have told the audience that she has brought salt earth from Mahabalipuram
on purpose to demonstrate to the people of Conjeevaram the process of
converting it into salt. She concluded by exhorting the audience to congregate
in large numbers at about 3 p.m. the next day, at the entrance to the Devarajas-
wamy temple so that they might start in a procession therefrom along the
public streets to Sankusapet Maidan where she would teach them practically
how to manufacture salt from the salt earth. This course would enable the
processionists to learn and prepare salt for themselves and refuse to pay the
tax levied by the government.

The place where Varahalu Ammal is able to puncture official discourse (by challenging that she said 7 crores and not 20) can be read as
a sign of her defiance and an assertion of her speaker status. When the
charge is reread to her, she again asserts that 'what she has said and
done will not amount to an offence, that the salt tax is an unjust import
unknown to any other government, that she had made it her life mission
to educate her brothers all over India on the above lines and to induce
them not to pay this tax any more'. The judge notes when sentencing
her, that 'Although she is a young woman, her case does not merit the
leniency which I would otherwise be inclined to show towards her, as
she refuses to offer any apology and persists in defending her action. . . . Having regard to her youth and sex, I sentence her to undergo

[119] Ibid.

simple imprisonment for six months'.[120] Of course, since sentencing for women was in any case more lenient than for men, Varahalu's punishment was far from severe.

Colonial discourse registers the speech of Jayalakshmi Ammal and Kamaladevi as a nuisance or the mere shouting of slogans. The speech of Durgabai and Varahalu Ammal however, is registered as 'violent', 'inflammatory', 'inciting', and defiant (for lack of apology), pointing to a discursive oscillation between women as powerless and insignificant or women as powerful and threatening. We would, however, be wrong to assume that recognition of the power of middle-class women's speech meant that they were seen as autonomous political subjects. Thus the case of Padmasani Ammal, which follows, is not very different from the women considered above, in spite of the remaining evidence of her 'speech acts'. Rather, the intensity of her speeches call forth different strategies of containment: colonial discourse and nationalist discourses converge to recognize her only as a wife or woman.

Padmasani's entry in the Tamil Nadu's *Who's Who* states that she was arrested in 1920 and sentenced to six months in jail. Beginning in 1932, she also served 18 months in prison. We also know that she was a member of the Madurai Town Congress Committee[121] and the Tamil Nadu Youth Conference.[122] Padmasani delivered several seditious speeches, often justifying the use of violence to overthrow the Raj. For example, in a speech on 9 September 1929 she argued, 'The Congress dictated non-violence. Even if we are beaten by bureaucracy, we should submit to it. But Tilak said, before we get beaten, we should beat ten men. The days of non-violence are gone, the days of violence are approaching'. As a result, Padmasani's speeches were held classified in the Undersecretary's Safe at Georgetown (then seat of the Madras Presidency government). Her speeches are some of the few that have survived the moment of production. Although the original Tamil transcriptions have been lost, the English translation, however mangled, bears testimony to the power of her speeches. What follows are extracts of a speech given by Padmasani Ammal on 23 February 1929:

About 150 or 180 years ago these foreigners were uncivilized, they were not able to distinguish their country from other countries. They were using leaves as clothes and lived upon the flesh of other brutes. In those times what was the state of our country? Our country was full of gold. All kind of grains and

[120] G.O. 3428: 15.8.30.
[121] G.O. 3204–C: 31.10.30.
[122] USS File no. 737: 23.5.31.

gems were in our country only. They [British] feasted on the product of this country, became fat and preached all kinds of gospels.

We sold away our rights, our sisters and mothers for our own maintenance. . . . We have sold away our honour to foreign bureaucracy. Owing to their haughtiness they forgot that they were once uncivilized, feasted upon raw flesh, that they begged for a piece of land from us and started to trade. They want now to make us civilized. They call us uncivilized . . .

When our Indian women emigrate to foreign places [out of poverty] to eke their livelihood, each white man takes 10 women [to satisfy his lust] and 10 white men keep one woman. Thus they undergo a lot of difficulties.[123]

In her speech Padmasani parodically turns colonial images of India back upon the British. She uses ridicule, derision, and mockery to argue that it is the British who are uncivilized, eat meat, and keep women the captives of lust. However, we would be mistaken to think that Padmasani was not also an acute political observer. Interspersed in her speeches are references to the Jalianwalla Bagh massacre, the Mapilla 'rebellions', the Minto–Morely reforms, the controversial visit of the Simon Commission and the coming world war. Supporting a recent strike by railway workers, Padmasani argues that it was the Raj which 'created this friction between Hindus and Mohammedans as a weapon to rule over us', and uses the occasion to remind her audience of 150 people of the uses to which the railways are put:

Look into a railway carriage. There is breathing space at least for gunny sack, but not for man. It was in this train that Mapillas died of suffocation.[124] If they made these 'conveyances' it is only to destroy us. Supposing a riot takes place here. Immediately a telegram will be sent to the nearest military station. Ammunition, guns, etc. will be transported. We will all be crushed and our blood will be sucked off. They plunder us of our money and make us living corpses. They have degraded us and pushed us into an abyss.

Padmasani continues to deploy vampiric images when she complains of high taxes:

If we get an income of Rs 100 from lands, we have to pay Rs 50 as taxes. Formerly 1/6 of the produce in kind was given in taxes, which would be stored and distributed during famine. But. . . . British Raj, they impose taxes for everything. What are these taxes? Is it to suck out our life blood, to make us cowards and to carry away our wealth day by day?

[123] USS File no. 651, 1929.
[124] In Podanur on 20 November 1921, the bodies of 66 Mapilla prisoners who had died of asphyxiation were found in the railway compartment where they had been held. See Sarkar, op. cit., p. 217.

She also criticizes the 'bureaucracy which is the pillar of the government', by pointing to the inadequacy of legislative reforms and urging the boycott of the Simon Commission:

They are expecting a world war. If there is a great war, this foreign government will be annihilated and drowned. As we are unfortunate, they are prolonging their stay here for some time more. They came here to give us Minto–Morely reforms. There was no limit to their atrocities after these reforms. They launched all sorts of repressive measures.

She is a powerful speaker, often taking recourse to typically male subject positions, referring to herself as a property-owner when she complains of taxes, then later drawing the analogy of the householder facing a trespasser to describe imperialism:

The decision of Gandhi is, 'I will wait until the midnight of December 1929, if Dominion status is not given by that time, I will start a campaign for complete Independence'. What I say to you is this: There is no necessity to wait till then. We want complete Independence at once . . .

Suppose a stranger or a thief trespasses into my house, I would drive him away by beating of sticks, would stab him and raise hue and cry. Similarly, if foreigners trespass into our country consisting of 33 crores of population, if these people [the Indians] raise a hue and cry, one will take up a knife, the other will have recourse to stones and strangers will run away.

Pencilled along the margins of the reports of Padmasani's speeches are the comments of British administrators: 'Someone must be helping her. If not her husband, whoever it is . . . send for him and warn him that [she will be arrested] if she does not curb her tongue'. 'CID think she must have been primed by her husband'. Such observations were to be formulated as an official warning:

My dear Cobbald,

The government desire that you should send for her husband or other relative or person under whose protection she is at present living, and warn him that you will consider the institution of proceedings under section 108 C. Pl. against his wife if she makes another speech of such a nature.

Here, as with the case of Lakshmi and Akilandammal, colonial discourse postulates a woman's dependence upon her husband in order to contain her agency by undercutting the basis for an independent subject position. It is important to note that Srinivasa Varada Iyengar's own testimony about his wife colludes with the colonial view in describing her first acts of Civil Disobedience as signs of loyalty to him:

My wife, Padmasani, took charge of the [Bharata] Ashram [founded in 1921 by Subramania Siva]. She refused to wear jewelry till her husband was released from jail and gave up one meal daily. She used to spin daily and enrolled more than 500 ladies in the Congress. She addressed meetings and made fiery speeches, carried on a campaign of khadi sales from house to house, and was mainly responsible for the political awakening of women in Tamil Nadu.[125]

Srinivasa Varada's description of his wife is itself a strategy of containment. Her activities are depicted as 'women's work': spinning, selling khadi, and organizing women. And by citing Padmasani as being responsible for 'the political awakening of women in Tamil Nadu', Srinivasa Varada by implication, also asserts that she had nothing to do with the political awakening of the general public in Tamil Nadu.

Colonial officials, of course, do regard Padmasani's speechmaking as inciting the public at large, but they seek to undercut her agency by attributing her speeches to her husband's influence. And while her husband acknowledges her 'fiery speeches', he restricts their influence to the women's sphere. Yet in spite of the way in which Padmasani's agency is contained by the narratives of her husband and those of colonial administrators, she is one of three women (Pichaimuthammal and Rukmani Lakshmipathi being the other two) who appear in a special Inspector General's Report of 1930 about Congress leaders in the Tamil Districts whose activities should be watched because of their influence over 'the public in general'.[126]

Implicit in many officials' response to women like Padmasani or Rukmani Lakshmipathi is a kind of incredulity that a woman would be capable of formulating or expressing her own thoughts and actions. British policy towards women in the nationalist movement is alternately tolerant, irritated, and then threatened, but women's words do not make them nationalist subjects.

---

[125] HFM File no. 108, 'Personal Statements of Political Personalities'. Interview with R. Srinivasavaradaran, 8.6.55.

[126] 'Attached is a list of Congress workers in the Tamil Districts of this Presidency who either [have] been released from jail on the expiry of their sentences, or will be released in the process of time. All unimportant people have been omitted and everyone on the list has some influence over the Congress rank and file, while some of them are definitely known as "leaders" who may be expected to influence the public in general, should they decide to take part in the anti-government campaign again'. See G.O. 3204–C: 31.10.30.

SMALL SPEECHES

The archives provide only scant information about the participation of lower-class women in the nationalist movement. They usually appear only at the margins of bureaucratic accounts, and are often coded as observers rather than participants.[127] For example, a report about 'Satyagraha Day', 6 April 1919 (the day before the Jalianwallah Bagh massacre), tells of the largest gathering of Hindus and Muslims at Marina Beach in Madras till that date.[128] Although the report's authors note that it was mostly the middle-classes and a few well-to-do who were present, 'The poorer classes were also numerous. There were about 200 women present and they were provided with an enclosure on the fifth platform, but they were mostly illiterate people of the working class who had come merely to see what took place'. There we see again the identity of poor women split into two categories: women and working-class.

Poor women are also deployed strategically by the British as markers of (élite) nationalist oppression. For example, a report from the District Magistrate of Tanjore to the president of the District Congress Committee alleged that 'vegetable' market dealers in Tanjore had been influenced not to employ Adi-Dravida women as coolies unless they secured a written undertaking from their husbands not to visit toddy shops.[129] In this way, the report argued, lower-class people, and particularly women, were pressured into committing acts of Civil Disobedience.

The erasure of lower-class activists by colonial authorities is underscored by the case of two low-caste women arrested on 4 April 1932 for picketing in Tuticorin (a medium-sized town in Madras Presidency). The text of the judgement is worth citing in full:[130]

This is a petty case against two insignificant 'Congress women' both illiterate and penniless, one a goldsmith's wife, the other a coolie in the salt pans. The witness . . . says they were picketing the shop of Palavesa Pulvar and making small speeches. They do not deny the fact of being opposite the shop but say there was no 'big' crowd. The head constable swore they attracted a big crowd which obstructed traffic and caused annoyance to the public.

It is plain to me that these two women are out to achieve a cheap martyrdom. They look 'bold and bad', the common street-walking-type; and I don't think the public can take them seriously Their speeches are a nuisance—a literal nuisance—nothing more.

[127] I thank Lata Mani for this point.
[128] HFM File no. 65, 24.4.19.
[129] USS File no. 748, p. 72.
[130] G.O. 1671–3(s): 23.4.32.

Kanthiamathi Ammal, the 7th dictator of the Tuticorin Taluk Congress Committee, is a person of no consequence, and is said to be a concubine of the man whom she calls her husband. Perianachi Ammal is a coolie. . . . Both are illiterate and poor, and there is really no room for a charge under any of the ordinances because the public can never take these insignificant persons seriously . . . I am convinced that one day's RI in the local sub-jail is a more deterrent punishment than a year's RI in the Vellore Jail for Women. As a matter of fact, they were courting arrest so that they may go to the Vellore Jail.

As we noted earlier in the case of Rajam Bharati, there is a contradiction in the description of Kanthiamathi Ammal. She is described in a single sentence as the 7th dictator of the Tuticorin Taluk Committee and as a 'person of no consequence'. Kanthiamathi Ammal and Perianachi Ammal are then pressured to apologize. Their thumb imprints appear after a statement written in English, 'I am sorry for having joined Congress and picketed cloth shops and for having been convicted. Therefore I request that I might be pardoned. I declare that under no circumstances whatever shall I join the Congress and picket foreign cloth shops or take part in activity connected with the Congress'.

Unlike the effects which middle-class women's speech produces, lower-class women are described as insignificant and illiterate 'street-walkers' whose acts of resistance are scorned as 'making small speeches'. The women's sentencing to an unsegregated prison and their apologies can only be seen as moves to denigrate and humiliate them, especially when we consider the outcry over Durgabai Ammal's transfer to an all-male prison.

The extraction of apologies from lower-class women needs to be underlined, however. Unlike middle-class women who usually refused to apologize,[131] and therefore asserted their speaker status by refusing to have words put in their mouths, the direct speech reported for lower-class women is literally of words put into their mouths. There is, besides, a striking irony in having illiterate women sign written statements (be they in English or vernacular). Thus, when an elderly lady named Ramakka was arrested for participation in a Congress procession, she was released on signing a written apology in Telegu to the effect that 'I am very old and am not in good health. Hence I hereby give an understanding that I will not take part against the government again'.[132]

[131] See G.O. 2482: 12.6.30, G.O. 3428: 15.8.30, G.O. 325: 26.1.31, G.O. 937: 8.3.32, G.O. 4941: 7.12.40, G.O. 5534: 31.3.43.
[132] G.O. 5100: 15.1.43.

The dismissal of agency coupled with exemplary punishment also demarcates the acts of lower-class women from their middle-class counterparts.[133] For example, when lower-class women did not apologize, they faced more stringent sentences than those from the middle-class. In another Tuticorin case, Subammal and Lakshmi, two young Marava women, cited as dictators of the Tuticorin Taluk Congress Committee, were arrested for picketing foreign cloth shops, and faced fines of Rs 100 in addition to lengthy sentences of, respectively, 15 and 18 months of rigorous imprisonment. Only Rs 8 had been collected of Subammal's fine, and Rs 9 of Lakshmi's, but they had their sentences suspended after spending a year in prison when the District Magistrate wrote, 'Neither of these convicts is a person of any importance, and the offences committed by them were unconnected with violence. I recommend that they may be ordered to be released and the uncollected fine remitted'.[134] Again, like Kanthiamathi and Perianachi, Subammal and Lakshmi are noted as leaders of the local Congress Committee, but dismissed as people of no importance in the same breath.

Nationalists, however, showed no less complicity in the selection of middle-class 'respectable' women as political actors. For example, Muthulakshmi Reddy's response in a 1931 issue of the *Stri Dharma* to an article entitled, 'Adi-Dravida Women Beaten and Molested; Innocent' is revealing. She argued,

It is simply horrifying to read about [the treatment of] women satyagrahis in Bombay by the police staff. The majority of women who take part in the Civil Disobedience Movement are not illiterate; they are patriotic women of the finest and best type, who have come out of their happy and comfortable homes at the call of the greatest man now living. Still the police had behaved most brutally to the best and noblest women of the land.[135]

Reddy's defence of the women satyagrahis rests upon an exclusionary logic (and might seem surprising given her well-known campaigns against the *devadasi* system and in favour of Harijan temple entry). Yet *devadasis* and Harijans were seen as objects of reform, and not as subjects of their own histories, for she does not argue that women are entitled to equal treatment under the law regardless of their caste or class; rather, she is at pains to show that the majority of women who were arrested in the Civil Disobedience campaigns were not 'Adi-Dravidas' and therefore 'not illiterate', but were 'patriotic women of the finest and best type, who

[133] I thank Shahid Amin for this point.
[134] G.O. 1475: 27.4.33.
[135] *See* the July 1931 issue of *Stri Dharma*, p. 92.

have come out of their happy and comfortable homes'. In this way, élite nationalists and colonial administrators shared similar attitudes towards lower caste, poor women. Such women were not considered appropriate representatives of the nationalist movement, either by the British or Indian nationalists.

While middle-class women received jail privileges that lower-class women did not, we can still see the points where nationalist and colonist discourses registers the speech of some middle-class and lower-class women similarly. That is, they shouted slogans, preached, attracted and exhorted crowds, or caused public annoyance. But middle-class women such as Durgabai Ammal and Padmasani Ammal were also known for their elocutionary power and 'inflammatory speeches'; whereas Kanthiamathi Ammal and Perianachi Ammal make small speeches, and their motives are denigrated for seeking 'cheap martyrdom'. Except in the case of the two *devadasis*, the moral character of middle-class women activists was never called into question, but Kanthiamathi and Perianachi are called 'bold and bad', 'the common streetwalking type', 'poor', 'illiterate', 'insignificant persons' and 'people of no consequence'.

We must then ask why the bourgeois subject resorts to the subterfuge of attempting to contain agency through the projection of stereotypes: on the one hand, shouting women, and women who make seditious speeches; and on the other, silent illiterate women who 'came to see', were 'pressured' into Civil Disobedience activity; or bold and bad women who make small speeches.[136] Women are not admitted as proper subjects by the discourse, but it does register and seek to contain their agency.

What then, is the agency that inflammatory and small speeches alike threaten to ignite? This is an agency without originary autonomy; it is the underside of the subject which seeks to contain it. As subaltern agency it is registered not so much in speech as presence, but in the effects of 'crowds', hence the care with which records transcribe a woman's incitement or drawing of a crowd. But we can read these dual strategies of containment of women's agency (women must speak; women don't speak) alternately as moments of evocation ('inflammatory speeches') and repression ('small speeches'). If we agree that the point of retrieval marks the subaltern's silencing in history, and that it is at the point of erasure where the emergence of the subaltern is possible,[137] then this analysis

[136] I thank Gyan Prakash for this observation.
[137] Prakash, 'Postcolonial Criticism and Indian Historiography', p. 12. Spivak's original formulation is, 'subaltern consciousness . . . is effaced even as it is disclosed', *see* 'Deconstructing Historiography', p. 203.

transits the lines of enfranchisement and disenfranchisement, oscillating between nationalist agency and subaltern agency. It is in this tension, this moment of oscillation, I would argue, that we recognize the effect where the gendered 'subaltern' is felt. Woman as subaltern; subaltern women.

5

Speech, Silence and the Making of Partition Violence in Mewat

SHAIL MAYARAM

This account investigates the making, experience, and representation of the violence that accompanied the partition of the Indian subcontinent in the Mewat region in north-east Rajasthan.[1] It is a twofold

[1] This chapter is derived from my doctoral dissertation on State and Society in twentieth-century Mewat. I am particularly grateful to my supervisors, Profs Ashis Nandy and Rama Kant for their support; to Pankaj Chaturvedi for his assistance in the course of field-work; for critical readings and comments to Profs Gyanendra Pandey, Shahid Amin, Partha Chatterjee, Dipesh Chakrabarti, Susie Tharu, and others at the Subaltern Studies Conference to whom this work was first presented; and to feedback from audiences at the Universities of Chicago and Syracuse. The hospitality and warmth of my Meo and non-Meo friends of Mewat, Sulaiman, Islami, Fateh Singh, and many others, underlies this work, as also the working ambience at the Institute of Development Studies where I was based when this chapter was researched and written. Shubh, Arvind and Drs Rima Hooja and Varsha Joshi have been frequent sounding boards. Dr Binda, Praveen, and Rajan have helped with the map and printouts.

Abbreviations used are AICC = All India Congress Committee; ASR = Alwar State Records; BSR = Bharatpur State Records; Confd. = Confidential; Ch = Chaudhari; DO = Demi-official letter; DM = District Magistrate; ERSA = Eastern Rajputana States Agency; FIR = First Information Report; FPF = Foreign and Political files of the Government of India; FR = Fortnightly Intelligence Report; GOI = Government of India; HH = His Highness; HT = *Hindustan Times*; IGP = Inspector General of

exploration of the organization and legitimation of violence by its perpetrators, on the one hand, and the phenomenological experience of and
modes of articulation of violence by the victim community, on the other.
I have attempted to understand the ideological formation presupposed
by violence and the altered mode of consciousness of the aggressor's self
that involves the objectification of the other; and conversely, to explore
the inner life of the victims, modes of resistance to victimhood, and the
resulting transformation of the self and of community.

The issue problematized is the relation between speech and silence.
At one level, there is an obvious association between both speech and
silence and the construction of truth. Speech is generally viewed as the
other of silence, the absence of voice. Paradoxically, as we shall see, both
language and speech do not preclude silence. Memory, however, makes
it possible to counter the erasure involved at the level of speech and
inscription.[2]

From the perspective of the victim, a distinction has been drawn between consensual and non-consensual forms of violence.[3] Contemporary

---

Police; M = Maulana; MLA = Member of Legislative Assembly; MOS = Ministry of
States; NAI = National Archives of India, New Delhi; NMML = Nehru Memorial
Museum and Library, New Delhi; PA = Political Agent; Pol = Political; RAO = Files
of the Rajputana Agency Office, National Archives of India; RC = Regional Com-
missioner; Rep = Report; RSAB = Rajasthan State Archives, Bikaner; RSAA =
Rajasthan State Archives, Alwar; RSS = Rashtriya Swayam Sevak Sangh; Sec. =
Secret; Secy = Secretary; teh. = tehsil; v = village; VS = Vikram Samvat.

[2] The issue has also been raised by Lyotard in his analysis of the holocaust. As
the victim of an event such as Auschwitz is reduced to silence, he argues that silence
surrounds the phrases and silence itself is a phrase. Jean-François Lyotard, *The
Differend: Phrases in Dispute*, trans. from the French by Georges Van Den Abbeele
(University of Minnesota Press, Minneapolis, 1988 (1983)), pp. 10, 44, 56–7. The
stark nature of the silence brought home to me during the course of researching
partition violence deeply affected me personally. For one, it cleaved my academic
sensibility: I had been researching the Meos for a few years before I realized the
enormity of the experience (as a political anthropologist I had presumed the silence
to be an absence). As I investigated the 'record', its silences and what is deliberately
silenced, the problematic character of 'history writing' was exposed. At a personal
level, this work has shaken to the core of my being premises and beliefs I have
grown with and to which I know some members of my family adhere. Time and
again, I was confronted with my own positionality: an inner struggle to rent a
silence, a repeated refusal to recognize oral testimony until it had been 'verified'
by 'authoritative' sources. I write this account with the growing realization of how
we are all participants in the making of silences.

[3] Veena Das and Ashis Nandy suggest that the sacrifice and the feud represent

ethnic violence can be seen as a form of non-consensual violence. As it is grounded in the absence of the consent of the victim, it requires other sources of legitimation and the creation of a moral ideology. This ideology, firstly, constitutes the self (victimizer) as victim. That is, violence is represented as counter-violence, in reaction to initial aggression and/or necessary for survival. It thereby becomes an act of reason and the moral becomes the rational. Secondly, what has been described as the objectification of the subject takes place with regard to the constitution of otherness. All aspects of subjectivity and history are obliterated in the totalizing construction. Thirdly, a notion of the social good, is articulated so that violence becomes a moral act and the only alternative to the victory of evil. Experiential violence is thereby concealed by an alternative narrative and conceptual structure.[4] Lifton describes the process as one of 'psychic numbing'.[5]

Mewat is a region named after its Meo inhabitants. In the early twentieth century it was spread over the princely states of Alwar and Bharatpur in north-eastern Rajputana, the Gurgaon district of Punjab, and a part of Mathura in the United Provinces (*see* map).[6] In the decades preceding Independence a strong peasant movement had developed in the area that questioned the legitimacy of princely rule. Partition served

---

consensual forms as violence is legitimated through cultural forms and institutional structures. Consensual violence also occurs in forms of implicit or disguised violence in the social order in which individual subjectivity is completely denied in the scientific world-view; in the doctor–patient relation in modern medicine, or in gender relations grounded in patriarchy. *See* 'Violence, Victimhood, and the Language of Silence', in V. Das (ed.), *The Word and the World: Fantasy, Symbol and Record* (Sage, New Delhi, 1983), pp. 177–80.

[4] On the legitimation by the performer and the contested legitimacy of the victim or witness, *see* David Riches, 'The Phenomenon of Violence', in D. Riches (ed.) *The Anthropology of Violence* (Basil Blackwell, Oxford, 1986), pp. 1–26.

[5] Robert J. Lifton, *Death in Life: Survivors of Hiroshima* (Random House, New York, 1967), p. 171.

[6] The voices I present are of over fifty persons belonging to a cross-section of castes and communities from the Alwar and Bharatpur states. They were recorded approximately forty-five years after the partition of the Indian subcontinent in the course of field-work in the region between January 1990 and May 1993. Their identity is frequently not disclosed or disguised. The extremely heterogeneous nature of the experience of violence needs to be emphasized. I have tried as far as possible to represent this varied experience in the *qasba*s and villages of the region. In Bharatpur district, besides Bharatpur city, I spoke to persons in Sinsini, Dig, Kaman, Karmooka, Naugaon, Bilang, Garh Ajan, Ubhaka, and Nagar, and Semla Kalan. In Alwar, persons in Jiwana, Tijara, Pata, Ramgarh, Kaulani, Govindgarh, Lachmangarh, Rayabka, and Alwar city were interviewed.

as an occasion to launch a reign of terror on the Meo Muslim population and rupture the movement along communal lines. Thirty thousand Meos were slaughtered, according to one estimate, in Bharatpur state alone, over thirteen thousand were converted, and over one hundred thousand fled to British India.

1.1 POLITICS IN THE PRINCELY STATES OF BHARATPUR AND ALWAR

The Meo population of 809,903 was concentrated in Alwar and Bharatpur states.[7] Bharatpur state had a total population of 486,954 persons, including 389,723 Hindus and 94,054 Muslims. Of the ten *tehsils* the Jat population of 72,383 owned much of the land in the *tehsils* of Bharatpur, Dig, Kumher, and Nadbai; the Chamar (Jatav) population of 79,181 persons, among the highest in Rajasthan, was concentrated in the Rupbas and Weir *tehsils*; and the Meo population of 46,475 persons held much of the land in the northern *tehsils* of Pahari, Nagar, and Kaman. In Mewat, land was equally distributed between Jats and Meos. Ahirs and Gujars also had some landholding. In Alwar the total population of 823,055 persons consisted of 539,369 Hindus and 220,324 Muslims.[8] The Meos comprised 167,530 persons (60 per cent) of the Muslim population, and were a dominant caste possessing a third of the state's land and concentrated in the Mewat *nizamat*s of Tijara, Kishangarh, Alwar and Ramgarh. The Rajputs held much of the land in the *jāgirdārī* area.

The social mosaic of Muslims in the two princely states suggested patterns of internal differentiation with Meos, Gaddi Muslims, and Shia Muslims in Paharsal; Rebari Muslims in Hasanpur; Kunjras in Alwar; Khanzadas in Tijara and Rangad Rajputs concentrated in Mandawar; and Muslim service castes such as Julahas, Kasais, Sakkas, Bhadgunjas, Darzis, Musalman Jogis, Qazis, Mirasis, and others. The Meos of Kaman are still deeply immersed in the culture of Krishna's land, Brajbhumi. Men from the rural areas of Bharatpur still flock to the *mela* held at the Govardhan–Girraj temple and take the *'parkarmā'* of 14 *kos* (circumambulatory route) and participate in the *kushtī dangal* (wrestling matches). As one Meo explained

[7] B.L. Cole, *Census of India, 1931: Rajputana Agency,* vol. 2, table 18 (Manohar, Delhi, 1992; rpt. of 1932 edn), pp. 550–1.

[8] *Alwar State Administration Report 1943–44* (Alwar State Press, Alwar, 1944–5); and *Census of India, 1941,* vol. 24, Rajputana and Ajmer–Merwara Tables, Provincial Table 2, pp. 170–1.

their participation in the festivities associated with the Krishna myth, *'ham to hain jādū pāl kai, pānch jādū, pānch tūmar aur do rāmchandarjī kai'* (we are from the Jadu or Yadav *pāl*s, five Jadu, five Tomar and two from Rama).[9] As a major peasant group they were the *jajman* to a large number of Hindu castes. Chamar women, for instance, detailed the heavy embroidery on the *lhāsī* (skirt) of Meo women. In Mewati, Meos continue to distinguish themselves from other Muslims with statements such as *'mev to miān nāy hain'* (Meos are not Muslims). Participants in the mob violence against them also referred to them as 'half Hindu, half Musalman'.

Alwar and Bharatpur were Rajput and Jat ruled states, respectively. Colonel H.H. Maharaja Brijendra Sawai Shri Brijendra Singh Sahib Bahadur Jung (1918–1995) acceded to the throne in 1929.[10] As Colonel-in-chief, he was commander of the army and President of the State Council, and his brother, Girraj Saran Singh (popularly known as Bacchu Singh) was Military Secretary. Tej Singh of the Naruka sublineage of the Rajput Kachwahas was ruler of Alwar. Both states had undertaken considerable military expansion and upgradation of weapons systems.

The nationalist movement led by the Praja Mandal (rechristened Praja Parishad in 1939) at Bharatpur was among the most intense in Rajputana. Dominated by an upper caste, Brahman and Baniya, leadership its major hold was in the urban areas of towns and *qasba*s and obtained strong support from traders and shopkeepers. Linkages with the Kisan Sabha enabled it to form a broad coalition of agrarian and urban interests. The Alwar Praja Mandal was likewise spearheading a movement demanding responsible government and other reforms. It also organized meetings of peasants and labour but, on the whole, was far more representative of the *jāgirdārī* peasantry.[11]

In the post-war period, communist activity in Mewat had gained substantial momentum under the leadership of the activist and historian, Kunwar Mohammad Ashraf. Ashraf was the leader of an inner nuclei of Communists working within the Congress. As General Secretary of the AICC, which had Nehru as President, he had helped organize a vigorous Muslim mass contact campaign within the Congress party in the 1930s

[9] Based on interviews at Ajangarh and Kaman, 18–19 May 1993. Isab Khan is a Meo wrestler who chairs the Committee for Wrestlers at Kama. He learnt his skill from a Hindu Brahman, has a large number of Hindu followers, and is supported by the Hindu community of Kaman.

[10] *Memoranda on the Indian States* (Government of India Press, 1938), pp. 246–7.

[11] FR of the Police Adviser to the Resident for Rajputana, ERSA (Confd.) 9–P/46, 1946.

that claimed a membership of over 100,000 persons. He was assisted by Syed Ahmed Barelvi and Dr Kachru, Syed Mutalabi Faridabadi in Mewat (then General Secretary of the District Congress Committee in Gurgaon), and others. There was a resolute attempt by Ashraf and his colleagues to combat Jinnah and the Muslim League and to capture (and subvert) Muslim League organizations.[12] It was Ashraf's close working with Sheikh Abdullah that led to the reformulation of the Jammu & Kashmir Muslim Conference as the National Conference which then enabled Hindus, Muslims, and Sikhs to join it. It is significant that Ashraf came from the community of Malkana Rajputs situated around the Mathura area. Regarded as neither Hindu nor Muslim in a theologically purist sense and subject to contests of identity akin to the Meos, he could perhaps perceive their special problems.

Following the closing of the Muslim Mass Contact Cell, Ashraf and his colleagues had shifted their attention to the organization of the peasant movement in the Mewat region. Like their work at inter-communal mobilization in Kashmir, the organization of the peasantry was attempted across caste and religious lines. The communists' work among the Meos, Gujars, and Jats, to begin with, countered the Arya Samaj led alliance between upper castes and Chamars, and the Jat ruler's attempt at promoting an exclusivist Jat identity. Several leaders such as Syed Mutalabi, Mahadeo Narain Tandon, Kishan Lal Joshi, Abdul Haye, and others, joined the Kisan Sabha. As it acquired increasingly anti-state overtones, active Jat leaders such as Deshraj left it. But Meo *chaudharis* such as Dundhal, Shafat Khan, Imrat Khan, Kunwal Khan, Pratap Khan and Kale Khan, helped the leadership organize the Bharatpur Meos and Jats in a 'no rent' campaign. In Alwar, Maulvi Abdul Qaddus worked among the Kishangarh Meos against the payment of tobacco duty. His arrest was reacted to with a raid on the District Magistrate's camp by 300 Meos armed with lathis, swords, and guns.

The Bharatpur Muslim League was established as late as May 1946 with Hafiz Maula Bux as President and Mohammad Shafi as Secretary. According to Abdul Haye, it was set up at the instance of the Bharatpur ruler in order to counterbalance the influence of the Praja Parishad.[13] The

---

[12] AICC papers G–68, 869–F, 1937–8, NMML. See also Mushirul Hasan, 'The Muslim Mass Contacts Campaign: Analysis of a Strategy of Political Mobilization', in M. Hasan (ed.), *India's Partition: Process, Strategy and Mobilization* (Oxford University Press, New Delhi, 1993), pp. 132–58.

[13] Abdul Haye, 'The Freedom Movement in Mewat and Dr K.M. Ashraf', in Horst Kruger (ed.), *Mohammad Ashraf: An Indian Scholar and Revolutionary* (People's

Muslim League, however, commanded only a fraction of Meo allegiance. Several Meos I interviewed had not even heard of the Muslim League or of Jinnah. The Muslim Conference continued to hold joint meetings with the Praja Parishad and the Kisan Sabha.

Meo memory carries a strong impress of their anti-colonial past.[14] In Gurgaon in 1922, when the newly formed Congress committee had been severely repressed by the British regime, the Meos of the Baghora pal, active participants in Meo peasant revolts in the nineteenth and the early twentieth centuries, had attacked a police station and freed the Congressmen.[15] The Meo leader, Yasin Khan, belonged to the Unionist party. His associates such as Syed Mutalabi, Abdul Haye, and Chaudhari Kamal Khan joined the Congress and worked towards activating Congress organization through committees in the large villages of Mewat. Dr Ashraf and his colleagues were active in the Congress organizations of Gurgaon, Bharatpur, Mathura, and Agra. On the whole, it was quite clearly the Meo panchayat that was the spokesman for the Meos, not the Muslim League, as was alleged.

What made the totalization of Meos as Muslims in Hindu consciousness possible? There was certainly the context of national politics, the role of the Muslim League and its slogan of 'Islam in danger', and the movement towards vivisection abhorred by large numbers of Hindus.[16] This was however matched by the growth and ideological dissemination of Hindu chauvinist organizations. The Hindu Sangh had been active in Alwar since the 1930s, encouraged by the Hindu Mahasabha. N.B. Khare, expelled from the Congress for indiscipline, and member (and later President) of the Hindu Mahasabha, had taken over as Prime Minister.[17] Mauli Chand

---

Publishing House, Delhi, 1969). The file 'Framing of charges against the Maharaja of Bharatpur', discusses state sponsorship of the Muslim League.

[14] This is manifest at the level of both collective and individual representations. The Meo (oral) cultural performance tradition highlights the anti-English saliences of the Meos, and writings by Meo authors tend to do the same. For instance, a monograph by Chaudhari Rahim Khan, President of the All India Meo Sabha, entitled *The Meo Martyrs of 1857* and pays homage to those 'who valiantly sacrificed their lives for the freedom of the motherland . . . '

[15] Haye, 'The Freedom Movement in Mewat and Dr K.M. Ashraf', pp. 295, 302.

[16] For an account of the Muslim League see Lance Brennan, 'The Illusion of Security: The Background to Muslim Separatism in the United Provinces', *Modern Asian Studies* 18 (1984): 237–72; David Page, *Prelude to Partition: The Indian Muslims and the Imperial System of Control 1920–1932* (Oxford University Press, New Delhi, 1982).

[17] See Craig Baxter, *The Jana Sangh: A Biography of an Indian Political Party* (University of Pennsylvania Press, 1969), p. 22.

Sharma, later President of the Jan Sangh, Hindu Mahasabha ideologues such as T.J. Kedar, Girdhar Sharma Sidh, and Ramchandra Vyas were active in Alwar.[18] Following the Praja Mandal agitation for a public representative, Vyas was inducted as Minister in the Rajput- dominated Council.

Local organizations at Alwar and Bharatpur, as in Gurgaon, became nodal points that brought in larger networks of activity organized under the aegis of the Mahasabha and RSS.[19] The post-war period had witnessed a considerable growth of the Sangh and the Mahasabha in the two princely states.[20] Upper castes and Rajputs provided the mainstay of its support, although it appealed strongly to the young educated as well. Ideologically, the Sangh was antithetical to the Congress and the Praja Parishads of the Rajputana states. It was supported, however, by the Bharatpur police, and military and state assistance to it, financial and otherwise, was given.[21] The weekly intelligence report stated that exhibition grounds were used for Sangh parades; weekend camps were held in its forests (in July 1947 Golwalkar took the salute at a large camp); that the government itself was manufacturing arms and ammunition; and that its membership in the state had grown to 1,500. Of its leaders the schoolmaster Keshav Deo and Choteylal were also active in the Sanatan Dharma Sabha and its school, suggesting the horizontal links between the Sangh and the Sanatan Dharma organizations.[22] In November 1946 the RSS was reported to have been

[18] Mauli Chand Sharma, General Secretary of the Civil Liberties Union, was mediator between Patel and Golwalkar to lift the ban on the RSS after it had been acquitted of involvement in the Gandhi assassination. L.K. Advani, present chief of the Bhartiya Janata Party, was also an RSS *Pracharak* at Alwar. Acharya Girraj Kishore, presently part of the national executive of the Vishwa Hindu Parishad, was at Bharatpur. Acharya Dharmendra's father was active in regional politics and the cow protection movement.

[19] Alwar FR for the second half of June 1946 reported a meeting of the Hindu Sabha on 16 June under the presidentship of the lawyer, Ram Chandra Vyas. Speeches emphasizing *hindu sangathan* (organization) were delivered by several persons. Intelligence Rep (from IGP to Police Adviser), Prime Minister's Office, BKN 6/45–6 and 6/46–7, RSAA.

[20] *See* DO no 77–S.B./42, 10 June 1943, in which the Pol Assistant to the Rajputana Resident reports that the RSS attempts to entrench itself in the Hindu states 'to perfect its organization' and proceed with training unhindered are underway. Pol and communal organizations in Indian states, ERSA 9–P/1945 Sec. *Bharat Vir* suggests the expansion of the Mahasabha through *shakhas*, *sabhas*, and *akharas*, 20 Dec. 1927.

[21] Bharatpur affairs, RAO 83–P/48, 1948.

[22] Weekly Intelligence Rep., 195–8, RC, Abu II, Bharatpur Weekly Intelligence Rep., and Special Rep. of 30 Jan. 1948. RAO 114–P/48.

behind the destruction of a *pir*'s tomb.[23] There were also isolated instances of conversion.[24] According to a participant of a 'mob':

The Jat ruler supported the RSS that had been established in 1942. Brajendra Singh had good relations with its Sarvasanghchalak, M.S. Golwalkar. He called an all India conference of Sanghchalaks of the RSS in 1946 at the military headquarter of Kanjori line at which Golwalkar presided.[25]

The district Sanghchalaks, in turn, organized the physical training of volunteers.

Independence meant different things to different people. To the RSS it meant a project of transforming social space and relocating individual Muslim bodies, implied by their spatio–temporal construction as 'foreigners'. At a meeting at Didwana, Hindus were exhorted 'to drive out Muslims', and the speaker foretold of bloodshed 'in the country not seen for the last 2,000 years'.[26] The ideology of violence was to be articulated in its performance: both Bharatpur and Alwar had become bases for military and political training. Persons were rushed through intensive courses and sent to 'theatres' in Delhi, Punjab, Bihar, and other states. Arms and ammunition manufactured in at least two factories were supplied to the RSS.[27] From all accounts, there was substantial popular support for the RSS.[28]

The Bharatpur ruler was of the view that the Congress was 'weak and anti-Hindu', and that the Indian Cabinet should have only included staunch Hindus like Vallabhbhai Patel, Shyama Prasad Mukherjee, and no Muslim. But it was not merely, as an official report stated, that the Bharatpur Maharaja was 'a very staunch Hindu and a determined patron of the Hindu Mahasabha movement and the Rashtriya Swayam Sevak Sangh [and] a great advocate of the movement to raise a strong Hindu militia to be able to fight successfully the forces working against Hindu culture and civilization and to establish a domination of Hindus in India.'[29] Indeed, the RSS world-view cohered with the ruler's own ambitions. Brajendra Singh's self-image was as a rightful claimant to Jat allegiance. As one Jat leader put it, 'Kishan Singh, the raja of Bharatpur,

[23] *See* Pol Activities of the Bharatpur State, ERSA (Confd.) 2–P/42, 1942.

[24] Sec. from district officers, IGP regarding Hindu–Muslim riots or other occurrences, 10C HH Govt. (Confd.), 1939, ASR, Alwar.

[25] Government official, interview, Bharatpur, 9 Dec. 1992.

[26] *See* FR of the Rajputana States, RC's Office, Abu, RAO 18–P/48, 1948, p. 43.

[27] Framing of charges against the Maharaja of Bharatpur.

[28] Khemchand Mathur, interview, Jaipur, 14 Jan. 1992.

[29] Framing of charges.

was the prophet of the Jats. . . . We said that we will not join either
Hindus or Muslims but have an independent state of Jats. But Jatistan
is a rumour spread by persons who are against us.'[30] He did not see
the self-contradictory nature of his statement!

The notion of 'an independent state of Jats' created a political imaginary of territorial conflict. The reclamation of space in the Bharatpur state
was made possible by an emergent sense of Jat subnational identity. The
Jats were the largest peasant community in India. Bharatpur and Dholpur
were the two Jat regimes, but Jats were spread over Shekhawati and up
to Nagaur in western Rajputana. Jat identity was fairly well pronounced
by the beginning of the century. The Jat Mahasabha of Bharatpur, of which
every Jat was a member, had emerged out of the Jat Sabhas. This, in turn,
was part of a larger formation, the All India Jat Mahasabha.

Jathood was a complex of multiple identities, Hindu and subaltern.
Jats had been made strongly aware of their subalternity in Rajput-ruled
states such as Jaipur. Stigmatized as low caste by Rajputs, they were not
allowed to carry weapons, ride elephants or horses. The Jat reaction had
led to a major movement in Sikar spearheaded by the Jat Kisan Sabha.[31]
Bharatpur's Jats distinguished themselves from the Jat Sikhs of the Punjab.
The sense of Hindu identity had become pronounced in the twentieth
century with the Jat ruling family and Jat leaders' role in larger movements
such as the Arya Samaj's *shuddhi* movement and the Hindi movement in
the 1920s. The experiment in eliciting subject positions through an exercise
in domination had already been undertaken. For a large number of Jats,
violence held the promise of swift possession of land.

There was also the disappointment of smaller imagined nationalities
with the possibility of being subsumed under the category 'Bharat'. The
Bharatpur regime was palpably unhappy with the post-Independence
Indian government. There was no celebration of Independence; instead
the national flag was pulled down. It was reported that the regime spared
no effort to criticize the Praja Parishad and the Congress, and to bolster
Jatistan. At a rally in April 1947 the slogan was, '*hāth main bīrī munh main
pān banā ke rahenge jātistān*'. This was an obvious response to the Muslim
League as the Alwar Muslims had celebrated the All India Muslim League
Election Victory Day with a similar imagery of bravado and non-chalance
as though Pakistan was a trophy for *bīrī* smoking and *betel* chewing males.

[30] Satyadev Chima, Punjabi Jat, Assistant President of the All India Jat Mahasabha, interview, Bharatpur, 5 Dec. 1992.
[31] *See* Barnett R. Rubin, *Feudal Revolt and State Building: The 1938 Sikar Agitation
in Jaipur State* (South Asia Books, New Delhi, 1983).

Maps of a proposed Jatistan were reported to have been found.[32] Brahmans and Baniyas were mocked as being incapable of rule, and it was suggested that they should be replaced by the Jats.[33] 'Jai Hind' was substituted by 'Jai Brijendra': the logic was that as the leader of the seven million Jats and President of the Jat Mahasabha, he was the legitimate successor to the English.[34] The ruler cemented alliances with the Maharajas of Alwar and Patiala who were both patrons of the Jat Mahasabha.[35]

Since the communist-led movement in Mewat was bitterly contested, it is necessary to examine the stated objectives of the Left leaders. The communist vision involved support to a system of regional self-governance grounded in the Meo *pāl* system which was conceived of as a 'democratic' system as well as a bulwark against Hindu–Muslim conflict.[36] Abdul Haye points out the distance between the Left and 'Muslim' leadership, and of how Yasin Khan and Syed Mutalabi Faridabadi (Yasin's political advisor) were suspicious of all Muslim leaders from Delhi and the Punjab, including Haji Rahimbaksh of Karnal, Syed Ghulam Bhik Narang of Ambala, M. Daud Ghaznavi of Punjab, and others. After Ashraf took over the movement from Yasin Khan, with the latter's own encouragement, it entered a new phase with the organization of Alwar's villages for the eventuality of an armed struggle if the demands of the Meo peasantry *vis-à-vis* the state were not conceded.

As the peasant movement gained in strength, the communist leadership formulated, in a pamphlet issued under the name of Abdul Haye, its proposal for a Pal Pradesh, i.e. 'a local provincial government to be set

[32] Rep. for first week of Oct., FR on political situation in Rajput States for the year 1947. Pol. and MOS 10 (11)–PR/1947 Sec.

[33] As another Jat put it, 'we said only Jats and no Brahmins and Baniyas will rule'. Neither did we want Malis or Gujars, he added. Interview, Bharatpur, 18 May 1947.

[34] The proposed charge-sheet refers to talks in the Bharatpur military to the effect that in case of a conflict between India and Pakistan, the Jats (led by their ruler) would launch an attack on Delhi. *See* 'Framing of Charges'.

[35] Congressmen alleged that the ultimate objective was to overthrow the Nehru government and instal a Jat–Kshatriya state.

[36] The *pāl* is the territorial unit of Meo self-governance. Mewat is divided into 13 *pāls*, each of which has a *pāl panchayat* that arbitrates disputes of all castes living within in its territorial jurisdiction. Ashraf and his colleagues saw the *pāl* system as a 'natural' entity and one in which feuds were not fought along lines of religious division. In Haye's construction of the Meo *qaum* the Meos are defined as both anti-Mughal and as kshatriya, suggesting the bilingual aspects of Meo identity. Haye, 'The Freedom Movement in Mewat and Dr K.M. Ashraf'.

up in Mewat [and adjoining areas] . . . which would form a unit within independent India.' At the first *panchayat* to be held at Naugaon (Gurgaon), both Jat and Meo *chaudhari*s of the Mewat *pals* and persons from Mathura, Alwar and Bharatpur participated. As section 144, prohibiting assembly of over five people, was declared, the *panchayat* was held at Teengaon just within Bharatpur state. But the conception involved both anti-colonial and anti-princely saliences. It's emphasis on community collaboration and autonomy, thereby proscribing and limiting the role of the state, was presumably too radical.

Ashraf was declared a second Jinnah, the author of a second Pakistan called Meoistan. He was under fire from sections of the Congress and from the Jamiat ulama-i-Hind. The proposal was also opposed by the Muslim League and the Jats affiliated to the Unionist Party, for both of whom the conception undercut the proposed Muslim and Jat states respectively.[37] To both the Bharatpur and the Alwar regimes, for whom Meo and Muslim politics were identical, Ashraf's vision was a territorial and a political challenge. The Alwar state reaction in its Order in Council that the 'HH's government holds that the present move is political and intended to deprive the Alwar state of the Mewat area', speaks volumes of its sense of threat. It quickly condemned the attempt to establish 'Mevistan' or another Pakistan.[38] The human tragedy was the mass extermination campaign; but there was, in addition, a conceptual tragedy —the marginalization, by deliberate refraction of information, of a movement that challenged the very conception of exclusivist ethnic states, whether Muslim or Jat. The Meo alternative, in contrast to the Rajput and Jat nationalist models, was both traditional and radical. It was based on a vision of intercommunal solidarity. What it elicited was a mass extermination campaign.

[37] A Congress leader of Alwar recollects, 'Mutalabi Faridabad was a Congress worker with me. He was also a communist. He showed me the maps of the Pal Pradesh. It included the district Bulandshahr, Gurgaon's Firozpur, Nuh, Palwal, Alwar, and Bharatpur's Tijara, Nagar, Kaman, Dig and a tract towards Mathura. It was not a 'small Pakistan'. It was not based on Hindu–Muslim prejudice, but a cultural idea'. Shanti Swarup Data, interview, Alwar, 28 Jan. 1993.

[38] It was not that the Alwar state was not aware of the nature of the Mewat movement. In one file that refers to the *HT* report of 1 May that the Gurgaon Muslim League has proposed 'Direct Action' to create a 'Mewat Province' from the territories of Alwar, Bharatpur, and Gurgaon, the note on the margin comments that it is the Meo Panchayat and not the Muslim League that is behind this movement. *See* Final Rep. on the situation of the Tapukra *ilaqa*, Rep.: Disturbances in Tapukra, Law 65 L/P/47, RSAA.

1.2 REPRESENTATIONS OF VIOLENCE

The administrative record masks the creation of terror with terms such as 'communal strife' and 'disturbances'.[39] Aggression is instead attributed to 'provocative actions and attacks by Meos on Hindu towns [which have been] beaten off'. The state itself assumes a mantle of innocence in contrast to civil society which is rendered the site of disorder. Files of the Alwar state report Hindus fleeing under an onslaught of Meo attacks; Meos collecting at various villages such as Khori, Tapukra, and Naugaonwa; and Meo attacks on the Ahir village of Tikri. But it is completely unable to explain why Meo refugees from Bharatpur begin pouring into Alwar on 25 June 1947, and why Meos with thousands of cattle come into Kishangarh from the Bharatpur, Lachmangarh, Ramgarh, and Alwar *teh-sils*. The official record fails to mask the first incident at Hodal on 23 March in which a one-sided massacre of ten Muslims by Hindus occurred.[40]

To begin with, the violence was confined to Gurgaon as Meos, Jats, Ahirs, and Gujars participated in a reciprocal burning of villages. The *Statesman* reported that by 18 June over 106 villages involving a population of 212,000 had been affected around the areas of Nuh, Taoru, and Mathura.

What is the nature of the silent record? The senior military official, Francis Tucker, cites Bharatpur state officials as stating that the Meos had burnt their own houses and villages to bring discredit on Hindus. But even Tucker's own account reflects an extraordinary gap of information in the claim that the state troops of Bharatpur had remained 'neutral' and that 'there was no direct evidence that they attacked the Meos'.[41] Virtually no official reports were registered of the killings, the abduction and rape of women; the wounded were not even admitted into hospitals; there was no post-mortem of the dead.[42]

---

[39] Disturbances in Alwar and Bharatpur State, Pol and MOS 2(36)–PR/1947; Disturbances in Bharatpur, Pol and MOS 2(52)–PR/1947 and 2(55)–RR/1947; and Report about disturbances in Indian States, Pol and MOS 15(6)/1947. Needless to say, all these files are 'not transferred' or secret.

[40] A wild rumour that a Hindu boy had been stabbed had led to panic and an attack on Muslims in nearby Rewari. *See* Francis Tucker, *While Memory Serves* (Cassell, London, 1950), pp. 315–16.

[41] Tucker, p. 327.

[42] With reference to the *thana* record of Lachmangarh for the incident of 21 May 1929, 135 persons were arrested under section 295 and 395. In another episode in 1940 an FIR is filed under section 295. The violence of 1947 is, however, completely

The question that arises is why and how was the feud transformed by the state into genocide? Obviously the 'communal riot' narrative that dominated media reports fails as a description of the organization of violence in Alwar and Bharatpur, the intervention of the state's overwhelming power to facilitate re-territorialization and annihilation. The following account of a captain in the Alwar army who was deputed for 'operations' to the Tijara 'sector' provides some clues:

I was the ADC to HH Tej Singh. We were with the RSS. It had been decided to clear the state of Muslims. The orders came from Sardar Patel. He spoke to HH on the hot line. The killings of Hindus at Noakhali and Punjab had to be avenged. We called it the 'Clearing Up campaign' (*safāyā*). All the Meos from Firozpur Jhirka down were to be cleared and sent to Pakistan, their lands taken over.

Horror stories were coming in with the refugees from Pakistan, he said. 'We did whatever was happening there, like parading women naked on the streets in Tijara and Naugaonwa after their families had been killed.' The performative display suggests the mimetic nature of violence, a common language shared by right wing organizations, whether Hindu or Islamic.

The ground had already been prepared by the training of RSS volunteers by the Rajput state. The army organized camps where thousands were trained in the use of arms. 'Like Godse who killed Gandhi', added the captain. But when 'the CBI Inquiry was held we did not tell anything'. The trouble with the Meos went back to 1942 when Maulvi Abdul Qaddus organized the Kishangarh Meos against payment of land revenue. A *patwari* sent to collect it was tied with ropes to a tree and the guns of the police party were also taken. When Tijara, Govindgarh, and other areas also revolted, the Maharaja sent in the army. The violence of 1947 was not the outcome of an idiosyncratic ruler and a right wing organization: it had to do with demographic rationality for the post-colonial Indian state. 'Governmentality'[43] required an ethnically conducive subject population. The reading of the Meo peasant movement by the state suggested how revenue and demographic rationality were entwined. 'Disorderly' groups were problematic and eroded the fiscal base of the state.

---

ignored in the village *jarāyam dahi* or crime notebook, with no entry against section 295.

[43] The idea of 'governmentality' is Foucault's. *See* Michel Foucault, 'Governmentality' *in* Graham Burchell, Colin Gordon, and Peter Miller (eds), *The Foucault Effect: Studies in Governmentality* (University of Chicago Press, Chicago, 1991), pp. 87–104 [Ed.].

In 1947 Alwar was divided into four sectors under different army officers to clear the state of Muslims. The captain detailed the account of the Clearing Up (*safāyā*) and Cleaning Operations:

I was sent on Special Duty to Tijara. The Hindu–Muslim riots had started. The Alwar state had run out of ammunition. We did not have such sophisticated arms. Sardar Patel supplied us with reinforcements from the Second Lancers who were returning to England [names an elaborate stockpile of weaponry]. In Tijara the Hindus–Jats, Ahirs, Gujars joined us.

About 10,000 Meos led by Ayyub Khan and Maulvi Qaddus fought the battle at Tijara. The army won after reinforcements arrived on the second day.

I went ahead and posted the force on a hill—below was the valley through which they were to pass. We killed every man, all of them. The next four days we had to do the 'Clearing Up' operation. My men and the villagers dug men's graves, threw their bodies in—there was such a stench and then a danger of disease from the dead cattle and men.

My gunner was a Muslim—the skin of his hands had peeled off because of the heat of the gun, but still he kept firing. Wherever he is, Abdul Hamid, '*khudā usko jannat bakshe*' (may God grant him heaven). He could have killed me while I was driving the jeep.

The calculated planning occasionally took cognizance of exceptions: Muslims such as Abdul Hamid who were part of the state apparatus or who were suitable candidates for 'subjecthood', having already proved their loyalty.

Intelligence reports and the drums beating in the hillside brought the captain to villages such as Mubarakpur:

When we entered we announced, 'either be killed or show a white flag and convert, become Hindus'. If they did we would enter the village and call all the people who lived there. The *shuddhi* squad from Delhi always used to accompany us. Right away they would shave the men, make them eat a piece of pork. The women—if they were of marriageable age—were all taken. They were *shuddh* after drinking *gangā jal* and could be taken. No, the Meos were not Muslims, they were half-Hindu. In their marriages they had both *pherās* and the *nikah*. They were not with the Muslim League. They did not want to go to Pakistan. But we had orders to clear them. Not a single Muslim was left in Alwar. Alwar was the first state to clear all the Muslims. Bharatpur followed. The rulers used to consult each other. Yes, Bharatpur also supported the RSS—Bachu Singh organized it.

The act of domination was signified by a range of activities: by military control over women, who were raped or absorbed into families after a perfunctory purification with *gangā jal* (sacred Ganga water); by the Arya Samaj *shuddhi* squads that accompanied the armed attacks; and by giving the 'half Hindu' Meo males the choice of becoming fully 'Hindu' or being killed. The 'Hindu' was constituted not by criteria of inclusion, that is, absorbed into the Hindu fold, but by exclusion from Islam signified by the eating of pork. Later, when the task of recovering abducted women was initiated, officials were only taken to villages where there were few women and villages with large numbers of such women (many of whom had by then given birth to children) were avoided.

The army had been sent to the 'Tijara sector' for the coercive reclamation of territory. The culmination of the operation was the massacre at the Kala Pahar:

Naugaonwa was a large Meo stronghold. We butchered them. That was the last battle of Mewat. Their resistance was over. After Naugaonwa they went to Sohna, Taoru. Upto Dharuhera is the Kala Pahar. That was their objective— all the Muslims fled there. . . . We thought that till they remained there they would keep coming [back]. We made a three pronged attack from both sides and the air, using the police and army. It took us more than two months, July, August, during the rains to clear the whole bloody area. Then they flooded Delhi and it was a problem to evacuate them to Pakistan. A book was written for me in which I was described as Alha Udal [the heroes of Bundelkhand whose fight with the Muslim invader is celebrated in *Alhā khand*].[44]

In the enactment of annihilation the state as spectacle enabled its reproduction through performance.

In the official discourse the reworking of social space takes place based on the dislocation of body space and a simultaneous relocation. Self-legitimation is inherent in a narrative in which the Meos are projected as a further source of vivisection, as a representative account suggests:

Later when Pakistan was made they asked for Mevistan and a six mile wide corridor to Pakistan. Dr Narayan Bhaskar Khare and Kanvar Raghubir Singh of Jaoli, who was the Home Minister, suppressed them. They did great service. In Tej Singh's rule not a single mosque remained. I wrote:

hinduon re pūjo pāo
tej singh dūjo rāj singh mahārānā nā bhao
shane shane vilaj mlechh mandal ravāna bhao

[44] Interview, ex-Alwar army officer, Alwar, 23 May 1993. He was interviewed in English, hence, the language is not subject to translation.

> There has been no ruler
> like Tej Singh.
> Hindus be happy you rule,
> Now that the *mlechha* leaves.

In the Felicitation volume for Khare I wrote [as he had thrown out by the Wylie regime]:

> khāskar alvar mlech sam trāskar
> narāyan bhāskar nāsh kar rahyo hai
> Specially the Alwar *mlechha*
> were turned out.
> Narayan Bhaskar
> destroyed them all.[45]

Muslims are both stigmatized and totalized as the ritually impure *mlech-has*, inherently separatist. Hence, the valorization of the incomparable Tej Singh and of Narayan Bhaskar Khare of the Hindu Mahasabha. They demolish mosques, but their agency is deleted in the semantic selection of the Meos who leave.[46] The exodus, then, is rendered a voluntarist act rather than an outcome of coercive collective action.

State officials from both Alwar and Bharatpur such as the Home Minister of Alwar replicate the account:

The Meos were creating disorder. From Alwar to Gurgaon are all Meo villages. And on this side from Bharatpur to Dig, there is only Mewat, very few other castes. The Meos and Muslims wanted a state—a mini Pakistan. . . . Yes, the Meos and the Hindus fought. The Meos killed a cow. The Bharatpur state began, it pressed from that side and we from this side. We threw them out. Yes, we thought they should go to Pakistan. The people here exploded when they saw a special train from Hyderabad, Sind, full of bloody corpses. They killed the Muslims then. The people got excited. What could we do? Why should Muslims stay here? Another country, Pakistan was made. So go there. It was in the air, send them there. Why are they sitting on our land? The *dhāṛ* came from the villages, they wanted to loot and kill the Muslims. We finished the Muslim League.[47]

In the Home Minister's account of the Meo movement, the killing of a

---

[45] Charan, poet and Hindi Reader, Home Ministry, Alwar state, interview, Jaipur, 29 Nov. 1992. Narayan Bhaskar were the first and middle names of Khare.

[46] Narration in the passive voice completely deletes agency. Similarly, Acharya Dharmendra described the Meo exodus as '*mev to chale gaye*' (the Meos left). Interview, Jaipur, 26 Sept. 1993.

[47] Interview, Alwar, 28 Jan. 1992.

single cow by the Meos became an additional pretext for slaughter. The notion of 'criminality' suggests the penetration of the colonial world-view. 'Criminality' as a cluster concept suggests a doctrine of collective guilt; a conception of 'martial' races *vis-à-vis* the 'primitive' tribes and castes who are liable to disorder (*uddaṇḍ, upadrav*); a coalescence of time as the explanation of present behaviour is by means of an assumed past. It involves an essentialist formulation, of a community defined by a single attribute of criminality (*jarāyam / chorī peshā*). Not only do the Meos stand defined, so are Muslims collectively responsible for the train of corpses—a notion reproduced by their corresponding Hindu aggressors.[48]

1.3 THE ORGANIZATION OF VIOLENCE

Partition violence was a departure in terms of form from the 'feud', the traditional mode of dispute and settlement between groups and between group and state. Violence had already been multiplied by forms of bureaucratic rationality and the spread of economically extractive technologies. What obtained now was a modern form of political violence in which the mutuality of exchange of the feud was rendered obsolete. Logistics of scale were made possible by modern forms of transport and weapons. Forms of communication, such as the press and pamphlet, image reproduction through photographs,[49] and speech as mobilizing spectacle in public meetings, enabled the rapid multiplication of sites of tension. It helped override both caste and class conflict and equipped the military and crowd with a shared narrative structure in which Meo resistance was presented as the originary cause of counter-attack. All prior aspects of history, and

---

[48] *See* V.P. Menon for a similar explanation of violence in terms of Meo disorder. *The Story of the Integration of the Indian States* (Orient Longmans, Bombay, 1955), pp. 240–1. Patel refers to the one lakh Meos who have left and are 'not penitent'. Khare wrote that he was

very busy quelling the rebellion of the Muslims against the Alwar State. Practically war is going on and I am doing my best to maintain law and order with equal fairness and justice to all communities. The trouble flared up by an incident of a cow in a Hindu temple and the murder of the priest. Naturally the Hindus got inflamed and followed and exceeded Bihar. It is said that the Shuddhi Sangathan-walas have converted about 10 to 12 thousand Muslims to Hinduism.

Khare Papers, NAI, nos 165 and 140, 13 and 7 August 1947.

[49] There is large-scale evidence of the circulation of photographs in Alwar supposedly detailing what the Muslims had done to Hindus in Pakistan.

the reasons why a community resorted to resistance, were obliterated. The states constituted a regional configuration in which information was shared, strategies planned. The rulers of Bharatpur, Alwar, and Dholpur, for instance, frequently consulted one another.

The Meo conflict with the Jat state dated to the 1932 peasant movement. It did not, however, imply a conflict with the Jats.[50] Indeed, Jat and Meo villagers participated in peasant protest in 1927, in 1932, and in the Kisan Sabha's activities in the 1940s. A Jat ex-MLA of the Congress from Bharatpur described the conflict and indicated his own participation in the *dhārs* that abducted Muslim women:

In 1946 the Meos began supporting the Muslim League and the latter began to grow stronger. Shafat Khan, the son of Dundhal, the *zaildār*, supported the Pakistan proposal in May 1947. The League proposed a 'corridor' from Mewat [to Pakistan]. But it had been recently formed and did not play much of a role in partition.

In the 1947 riots the leadership of the *dhārs* was in the hands of Thakur Dhruv Singh of Pathena who was the next leader after Deshraj. He was most active. He joined hands with Bachu Singh and his military and they took the Hindu *dhār* to Mewat and killed people there. The Jats had gone to assist the castes who were being troubled by the Meos. This is why Nagar, Pahari, Kaman were abandoned. The Brahman–Baniya residents, who were well off felt threatened by the Meos. The Jats went at their invitation and they looked after the food and drink of the Jats. The *dhārs* had weapons like the *lathī* [staff], *vallam* [spear], *talwār* [sword], and *pharsā* [axe]. The Meos had *barchīs* [javelins], *ranchangī bandūks* [guns]. . . . [51] Jats were the main caste in the *dhār* but the Gujars of Nagar also joined. . . . The Meos began to leave in *bhādon* [July]. No one stopped them. The refugees, mainly Jat Sikhs, had started coming earlier.

Bharatpur's first conflict began on Janamashtami with the looting of the train to Agra which was on the metre gauge. It was stopped a kilometre and a half ahead of Bharatpur. All trains were stopped and people killed. . . . Many mosques were broken. . . . Had it not been for Bacchu Singh, Hindus would not have remained alive in Bharatpur. When he stood for election he said, 'I don't want Muslim votes only Hindu ones'. His symbol was the *murgā* [cock] because he would eat a chicken every day, indicating that Muslims were domesticated cocks. He won the election of 1952, because Hindu feeling was in his favour.[52]

---

[50] Sinsini Jats stated that although the Maharaja was their 'brother' (by virtue of belonging to the same village) they did not hesitate to oppose him. Interviews, Sinsini, 18 May 1993.

[51] Locally manufactured gun into which gunpowder is stuffed before use.

[52] Interview, Bharatpur, 9 Dec. 1992.

Congress narratives are sometimes hard to distinguish from those of the 'mob'. The MLA's narrative is typical of Jat accounts in its ambivalence regarding the religious status of the Meos. They are 'half Hindu' having only recently become 'clear cut' Muslims.

Mainstream nationalism seems to have offered scant resistance to the dominant anti-Muslim ideology in the region. Some Congressmen were active participants, some others were sympathetic bystanders to the violence. Tucker reports the unhelpful attitude of members of the Provincial Legislative Assembly and nationalist stalwarts such as Purshottamdas Tandon.[53] Nehru went on record stating, 'what I am really afraid of is the enemy who is being born right inside our own ranks'. The role of collective silence has been repeatedly pointed out with respect to Argentina, Ireland, wartime Germany, and contemporary Israel. Feldman refers to it as the 'backgrounding of violence' in the informal ideologies of everyday life.[54] From all indications there was considerable anti-Muslim feeling in both Alwar and Bharatpur. A former Congress Minister from Alwar commented on the shared

Hindu feeling in everyone that what is happening in Pakistan should be avenged. The Maharaja was involved, otherwise how would the military have moved? The Prime Minister was involved and also the state government. If the Muslims are not going, get the military to turn them out.[55]

Institutionalized ideology frequently constitutes social action. The princely state produced an institutional authorization of violence and its further actions were sustained by the widespread legitimation of violence, including from sections of the Congress.[56]

Narratives of participants in the *dhāṛs* on the whole authorize domination and legitimize violence. The imagined community of Pakistan projected by the Muslim League as the 'homeland' of the Muslims enters popular discourse and deterritorializes the Meo notion of their 'homeland' (*hamārī bhūmī*). The sense of a shared regional culture in terms of origin myths, ritual, and kinship practices, caste and *jajmani* relations and the common memory of peasant protest against the state is obliterated by an

[53] Tandon, Speaker of the United Province Legislative Assembly, addressed a Congress volunteers training camp saying non-violence is out of date and people must take up arms to fight against gangsterism. Cited in Tucker, p. 314.

[54] Allen Feldman, *Formations of Violence: The Narrative of the Body and Political Terror in Northern Ireland* (University of Chicago Press, Chicago and London, 1991), p. 110.

[55] Badri Prasad, interview, Alwar, 30 Jan. 1992.

[56] Interview, Bharatpur, 9 Dec. 1992.

alternate re-territorialization for the 'Muslims'. Ironically the name of Krishna invoked in the slogan, 'Girraj Maharaj *kī jai*', was used to kill those who regard themselves as his descendants. A Brahman described the experience that effaced the memory of long enduring relationships with Meo *jajman*s at whose households he performed death rites or the *gānth jornā* (tying of the nuptial knot) at weddings:

We knew the Meos were making Pakistan, this was well known.... My entire *thok* went in the *dhāṛ*. Thakurs from U.P. had also come, Gujars too—all Hindu castes.... Some were in the jeep like Bacchu Singh, others walked. People from villages joined it on the way. We burnt Firozpur Agrawali which is one *kos* away. Bilang is four miles further ahead. Some people would go ahead on horses to see that there was no enemy ahead. The fight lasted 2–3 days. Samay Singh [Meo] was the *zaildār*. We had worked closely together. He used to collect the revenue (*vasūlī*) and maintain order. Each *pattī* of a village had a *lambardār* and there could be 4–5 *lambardār*s in a village. We fought during the day. Women came to our support, brought water and food to the *morchā*, Brahmanis and Mainis. The fighting would stop while we ate. The bugle would play. We went after worshipping Thakurji or the *devi* shouting, 'Bhagwan Ram, Kishan *kī jai*.' We had devised signals, if a Meo was running we would shout, '*uttar ko*' [towards the north]. We besieged it for 3–4 days. Bacchu Singh had to leave. Then the Gujars and Brahmans of Bolkhera came to our help. We burnt the village. The dead could not be counted. Samay Singh went to Haryana.[57]

Both *dhāṛ* and *morchā* constituted exhibits of a colonizing power. The role of women suggests that gender was not necessarily a significant category that might have created fissures among the victimizers.

Ritual was an important aspect of violence. Jats at Sinsini first offered the ritual sacrifice of goat to their deity, Sinsini. The mythic memory associated with the deity is of its beheading following an attack of Turks. The iconic representation of the deity inscribed an initial act of violence that must be avenged. Ritual consecrated the totalized memory of Muslim aggression. In Alwar the sacred thread (*kalāyā*) was tied around the wrists of members of the crowd preceding an attack.

The *dhāṛ* itself became a performative spectacle, a masculinization of violence:

A panda from Sancholi was a renowned wrestler who held wrestling shows in Punjab and Delhi. The Jats made him the *dūlhā* (bridegroom) and leader of the procession, of the *dhāṛ*. In the first week of June they went around fighting and injuring and killing people. He had a fight with his student, Parwal Meo,

[57] Interview, Kaman, 21 May 1993.

in which the latter was killed. The Meos reacted by surrounding and killing him. The Jat–Meo conflict now became a Hindu–Muslim one. Wherever the *dhāṛ* went people from the village joined it. Eventually the people outnumbered the military. Most of the people were Jats, also some Gujars (they did not do the killing and only came afterwards for the loot like of silver and gold guineas, the mustard crop, cattle and other animals, ornaments. They benefited the most although the Jats got the land). There was much killing in Kakra Bedam in Dig *tehsil*. The Gujars and Jats of Panhori, Kurken, and Januthar villages did this.[58]

Violence was imaged by the masculine wrestler *qua* bridegroom leading a bridal procession. The spectacle itself became a gendered, phallic metaphor and victimhood was defined in terms of claiming the feminine and underlining the subordination of bridegivers.

The confessional ideology of *shuddhi* was inscribed onto the bodies of Meo men and women in a collective ritualization of violence. At Alwar the *shuddhi* conducted by Mauli Chand Sharma was done with a combination of Sanatan Dharma and Arya Samaj rites. It involved the *yajño pavīt* (sacrifice with fire oblations), the wearing of the *janeū* or sacred thread, headshaving, keeping the *choti* or tuft of hair at the crown of the head, as the following accounts suggest:

There were 5–10 of us Rajputs like Sultan Singh of Palwa (he was a minister), the *vakil* of the Hindu Sabha, Ram Chandra (later he went away to Jaipur). . . . The Arya Samaj and the Sanatana Dharma both were active in bringing our *bhai* [brothers] back. Yes, some Meos came back but most left for Pakistan. Only those remained who became *shuddh*.

There was, thus, an exchange of political rites between Hindu organizations.

A former official at Kaman describes the Bharatpur state's organization of *shuddhi*:

The Arya Samaj was more popular than the Sanatan Dharma here. In 1947 the Arya Samaj did *makkārī* [cheating] in the name of *shuddhi*. We did it at the Vimal *kund* (temple tank) in Kaman to Garhe Gujars, Malkana Thakurs, and Meos and reconverted them. Raghuvir Singh Dhau, a Jat, got it [*shuddhi*] done at the instructions of the Maharaja. All of us Brahmans were called and told to join in, to eat the food cooked by the Muslims and to feed them. We told him, 'we'll do this, but first you marry their daughter and give yours to them'. Dhau got his daughter engaged to a Gujar from Weir.

The Meos who did not run away became Hindus. They were made to recite

[58] Interview, Bharatpur, 10 Dec. 1992.

the Gayatri *mantra*, swear on the Ganga and drink a mixture called *panch gab* that included *gaū mūtra, gaū gobar, gaū dūdh, gaū ghī*, and *gaū dahī* [the five cow products comprising cow urine, cowdung, milk, clarified butter, and curd]. The Quran had to be put into the flames. Then they took a dip in the *tīrth rāj* and were made to keep a *choti* [braid worn at the crown] and wear a *janeū* [sacred thread]. We would sing songs like, '*pat hojā hindū phir pakegī khīr*' [a wife addresses her husband, 'become Hindu then we'll cook rice in thickened milk]; "*Īd, Bakr Īd nā Subhrāt pyārī, tīno kī aisī taisī sankrānt ne mārī*" [Id, Bakr Id nor Subhrat are dear, all three have been taken over by Sankrant, i.e. the Hindu festival]; "*kahe amīran bāt karīman suṇ bahnā, 'korān sharīf kī koī rakāyat āyegī nā āṛī*"' [Amiran says to Kariman, 'listen my sister, no *āyāt* of the Koran *sharīf* will help you now']; '*nabbā ke abbā kī main bhī mundvā dūngī dāṛhī jumme tak suṇ lenā*' [listen, by Friday I will get the beard of Nabba's father shaved]. We renamed a Muslim *rangrez* (dyer), Nazir, and called him Narottam. He would bathe everyday at Vimal *kund* and do *darshan* at the temple, but when there was peace he ran away to Pakistan.[59]

Shuddhi served its purpose of reversing the ritual status of the stigmatized *mlechha*. In the case of abducted women, after the sprinkling of *gangā jal* they could be absorbed in the Hindu families of their abductors. Although there was evidence of the considerable abbreviating of *shuddhi* ritual in contrast to the *shuddhi* of the early decades of the century that involved far more persuasion, the folklore of partition details the continuity of some compositions, ritual, and symbols.

The abduction of women was a policy of terror; an exercise in which the state transgressed domestic space and invaded the formerly inviolate women's bodies. One victimizer put it:

The Jats of Bharatpur reacted to the Muslim League and what was happening to Hindus in Punjab. There was Hindu feeling among them too. This was a time of communal frenzy and passion when people forgot humanity [*insāniyat*]. We took away women. That was the system. Women do not have any religion. Subsequently, there was an exchange of women and a large number of Muslim women went to Pakistan. Some did not want to go back.[60]

The perception of women as property enabled mass abduction, and another account described it:

Meonis were made *shuddh* and kept in Gujar and Jat homes, the Meos also took our women. We took hundreds, they took ten–twenty. Any man who did not have a woman took her and kept her, even if he was fifty years old.

---

[59] Interview, Kaman, 6 Dec. 1992.
[60] Interview, Kaman, 6 Dec. 1992.

Any woman was taken, even as she was walking or cutting grass she was lifted, carried over the shoulder. She would not say anything for fear. After a while she would walk by herself, they were so scared. No-one wants to die, they would come themselves. The gun was shown and they would walk away. Marriage? There was no question of marriage with a *barāt* [bridal procession]. After children are born it is like marriage. After *shuddhi* she became a Hindu, kept fasts and festivals. Gujars and Jats had no problem with Muslim women, eating food cooked by her.[61]

The enactment of violence targets the whole through the part; a few or more victims become substitutes for the community.[62] Its organization in public places and during the daytime signified command re-ter-ritorialization in compressed time. The image of bloody Hindu corpses in trains, that participants of Hindu *dhāṛ*s frequently expressed, repre-sented an inversion of what happened in the area. In Bharatpur a large number of attacks on trains carrying Muslims and the army were organized in which, in most cases, the assailants were from the Bharatpur army led by Bacchu Singh. The attacks on trains, thus, became moving signs that would prevent the other from returning. Public spaces, such as railway stations, streets, and wells where larger visibility is ensured had maximal effect. The dead thereby become signals to the living of the construction of ethnic boundaries. The sites were carefully selected. A train was attacked near Jagina, the large Jat–Brahman village of Thakur Deshraj. It had long been the site of work by the Arya Samaj, Praja Parishad, the Kisan Sabha, and the Jat Maha Sabha. Large Meo villages such as Titpuri, Kaimasa, Bichur, and others, were specially targeted in order to have a ripple effect on the consciousness of the other. These are described as the sites of *bhārī kattī* (heavy slaughter), following which survivors fled.

The file 'Framing of Charges' reports, 'The object is rapidly becoming loot and not only communal revenge'. The Chief Commissioner com-ments, 'Bharatpur has apparently run completely amok. They have got rid of all the Muslims and consider all those in traffic as legitimate prey'. 'I saw corpses all around. . . ' '30,000 were killed, a thousand converted and the rest driven out. The property of Muslims was taken over by the State and auctioned, the sale time proceeds being credited to the State Treasury. The Maharaja is reported to have expressed delight that no

[61] Interview, Kaman, 22 May 1993.
[62] To my question regarding how many persons he killed, a participant in crowd violence responded cryptically, 'in the killings people are not counted by ones and twos'.

Muslim was left in the State.'[63] The violence, lifting of women and cattle, raiding and killing continued till October.[64] Despite being on records the charges were never filed or pursued: no one was ready to stand witness. But a discursive inversion was reproduced in official discourse. *Tej Pratap*, Alwar's official newspaper, reported on 8 August that the Meos were *'offering themselves* for conversion' (emphasis added). In most Jat accounts, likewise, the notion that *'they* attacked first' is widespread.[65] The comment 'had the Muslims not been cleaned they would have captured Alwar', also inverted the *safāyā* operation which became reconstructed as a pre-emptive strike.

1.4 VIOLENCE AND THE COMMUNITY: REPRESENTATIONS OF VICTIMHOOD AND RESISTANCE

Partition had created a total of twelve million refugees, of whom about two million died. Half of the Meo population is estimated to have migrated to Pakistan. According to the Census of 10 July 1948 there were 60,000 Meos in Gurgaon out of whom 25,000 were from Alwar and 35,000 were from Bharatpur. Many Meos later returned to Alwar. To begin with only 18,000 Meos went back to Bharatpur.[66]

To recover the speech of victims is, in a sense, to reinvest the victim community with subjectivity. I have tried to suggest how the memory of exodus, slaughter, and violence is inscribed, retained, transmitted, and reproduced; that the signification of violence is culturally regulated and mediated; and that it has do with aspects of speech, language, and silence. Occasions of exceptional trauma and holocaust, it has been pointed out, are witnessed by a rupture of language. In Meo accounts, what is particularly noticeable is not only the fractured quality of individual speech but also of the traditional forms of mythic history through which the community transmitted collective memory and reproduced itself culturally. Both speech and silence indicate also the strategies of renegotiation of

[63] Chief Commissioner's Office, Misc DO (Sec.), Ajmer, 16 Oct. 1947. 'Framing of Charges'.

[64] According to Hiralal Shastri's report, raids were carried by the army into the British dominion as well and the Jats of Rohtak and Gurgaon were also active. 'Framing of Charges'.

[65] Interviews, Sinsini Jats, 18 May 1993.

[66] Resettlement of Meos in Alwar and Bharatpur, RAO (Pol) 179–8/49, 1949.

community identity, the attempt at restoration of signification to inter-community relations, thereby remaking ethnic fissures.

A large number of accounts suggest the overwriting of the time of the nation onto community time. Whereas the peasant movement and other events are computed in Vikram Samvat, *saintālīs* or 1947 is the referent for partition and violence, rather than for freedom from colonial rule. Much of the victim's testimony is characterized by short, abbreviated, condensed descriptions: almost all pronouns are deleted in the process. In most accounts, time is engraved as the time of eviction, a wrenching from roots, as it were. The journey or life in the camp is hardly referred to at all, although in actual terms it took far longer than eviction which was often sudden.

For Mehtabi, time is figured by both the public event (*saintālīs*) and by familial time marked by the birth of her child who was fifteen days old when she had to flee. *Batwārā* (vivisection) rather than *āzādī* (freedom) constitutes a marker of Meo consciousness. The division was not only of countries but also of extended families. Mehtabi said, 'of my eight homes six fled [to Pakistan], two remained here. My husband went also and stayed with his sister.' Mehti told me in Tijara:

My first child was born in the *chaurā* [open] during the *bhagā bhagī* [exodus]. We left everything. The *dhāṛ* of Gujars, Chamars, Malis, Kolis, Ahirs and Jats had come. We fled to the Pahar, my husband and this child in my womb. I was all alone when my child was born, just me and my husband. No cloth, only an iron grain strainer in which he cooked the *rotīs* when the child was born. Then the firing began on the Pahar. They used the *ganj machine* [Bren gun] and the *chīlgāṛī* [aeroplane]. But we were sheltered by a rock. People were killed like in *lāvnī* [the operation of cutting fodder generally done by women]. We stayed for two years in Punhana. . . . Many people went to Pakistan in *kafilā*s. But they told me, don't come with us or your child will die on the way.[67]

Partition signified for her a dual pain, of dislocation and of labour that brought with it birth, yet meant a wrenching from her affinal kin. It was an event in which her 'normal' world collapsed with its male–female division of labour, demolishing also the boundaries between inside–outside. The private event of childbirth, thus, took place exposed. The exposure was not just a personal one but one that underlined the vulnerability of her family, her *birādarī*, her *jātī*, and rendered them vulnerable to military violence imaged in the human onslaught on nature (*lāvnī*).

[67] Interviews, 29 Jan. 1992.

In a large number of Meo accounts, the *chīlgārī* is rendered the flying panoptic presence, the state plane's surveillance marking out places of hiding prior to swooping down low and opening fire. In Chand Khan's narrative the dead are measured by corpses spread over a distance of *kos* (as the enumerative measurement that dominates the early part of his account fails). Then the *chīlgārī* gives way to the *chīl* (kites)—the human, the mechanical, and the natural, signifying the act of prey. A disconsolate Chand Khan treks through loot and murder for almost a week with a bullock cart, carrying grain and joins a large camp of two to four lakhs of people congregated from all over the Alwar *riyāsat* at the Kala Pahar:

> In the morning our *baṛo līdar* [major leader], Chaudhari Yasin, came and told us that tomorrow there will be firing. Bacchu Singh's *chīlgārī* came low and closely surveyed the camp. At around 12 the next morning a huge *dhāṛ* came. People were killed for two *kos*. All the persons who could be seen were killed. My *chāchā*, Dhan Singh, and I were saved because we hid behind a rock. The *ganj machīne* left none alive. . . . I saw a child suckling at a dead woman, children were howling. . . . When the military came they cut women's arms for the jewelry. We kept hiding, the *chīl* [vultures] screeching.

Tundal's account evokes the sounds and the *rolā* [noise] associated with violence, the uncertainty of the route and possibilities of being looted and killed. His wife Sarupi's concerns were with the everyday of survival—water, children, hunger, food, on the hostile (in terms of both nature and man) landscape of the Kala Pahar. She refers only in passing to the trauma for herself and the now continuous pain that she has in her head:

> These children were small, three boys and two girls were with us, the youngest were one and two and a half years old. What did we have to eat? They went hungry. I left everything when I ran away, could not even take grain. We ran to Khanpur Ghasoli. We stopped at the *kheṛā* [village]. And the *duniyā* [the rest] was climbing the hill. Who had the time to eat when we left? I had a few *rotīs* in my *khāṛī* [basket]. I had told the children to eat them but there was such a big, black scorpion. When my son told me about it I told him to throw away the *rotīs*, 'If you eat them there won't even be any water for you'. Then we went to the Kala Pahar. We climbed straight up and came down along the Dhond-lond pass. The children's feet had blisters from the walking and so I tied the *akhoṛā* leaf on them and forced them to walk. We had to walk and walk, the people went through Ghoda ka thana, and the people were running, running with all the belongings they could carry. We had no food, all were hungry. Some were falling in the *nālā*, some by the hillside. What could they carry? A few utensils, some clothes for the children—nothing else. Those who

hid in the crevices of the Kala Pahar survived, others were rained bullets by the machine . . .

I stayed in *angreji* [British India] with my sister. She also left, her whole village left. When the route closed at the border they could go to neither side. Later some came here, others went there, those who got permits. I got no land until a few *bighās* much later. I had to work hard as a labourer. I worked at Roshan Lal's house for fifteen years, pounding pulses. For three–four years I looked after his buffaloes. I chopped the fodder for the buffaloes, milked them and got 30 rupees in a month. One rupee for a day. I made three buffaloes from one buffalo, I stayed so many days. When I churned the curds I could bring back one bucket for my children. Then those poor ones had something to drink. Then I came back to Alwar. I don't know what has happened in my head, I have been so ill I feel I am crazy . . . [68]

Several accounts hint at the reinforcement of kinship and community through the *kafilā*, strategies of survival and refuge (though no descriptions of experience with their kin which are assumed as 'natural', are provided). Undeniably there were also fissures: with the old and the infirm who were left behind; between those who chose to leave and others who preferred to become *shuddh*. Jamil Khan of Saimlakhurd in Lachmangarh tehsil said:

Bacchu Singh had come with his platoon and some Ahirs, Gujars and Jats. From Naivado, Pahatvado and Singalvati about 500–1000 Meos came with *lathis*. They had heard a rumour that Maujpur had been surrounded and came to save us. We stayed in Maujpur for 5–10 days, then went to my *phuphi's* [father's sister] house in Ranota, *tehsil* Punhana. We met people from Maujpur, refugees at Ghat Khuteta. They had *lathis* and one gun. The Sakkas came with water for us. We stayed here for six months. . . . My father ran to Maujpur to our relatives, to Chand Khan's father who is our *māmā* [mother's brother].[69]

Islami's concerns derived from sacred notions of a uterine space that was invaded by violence: affecting children and women's bodies, their homes and religious practices:

Bacchu Singh came with a *dhār* of thousands and surrounded the villages. When the *dhār* moved shouts could be heard from all sides, '*bajrang bali ki jai*' [victory to Hanuman]. All the Meos had come here. There was hardly a village that was not burnt. All the *batevrās* were set on fire. These Kir, Bhangi and Chamars really killed people. I saw a child being flung in the air and then caught at spear point. One woman was hit so on her neck, I saw her body somersaulting. So many were sent to Titpuri and from there they went to

[68] Interview, Alwar, 2 Feb. 1992.
[69] Interview, Lachmangarh, 30 Jan. 1992.

Lachmangarh for *shuddhi*. There were thousands and thousands of cattle in the Itarana and Dautana *rūndh*s. The committee then got them auctioned.[70]

Batevṛās are beautifully crafted stacks of cowdung cakes. Regarded as women's inviolable space, even Meo men are not permitted to touch them.

A series of choices were thrust upon the community: between getting killed and becoming *shuddh*, and as Tundal's account brings out, between going to Pakistan (taking the *gail* or route) or staying on in India. Hurmat Mev refers to the choice of his village:

In 1947 we went to Gurgaon. The Maharaja turned us out by using the military. Captain Sadiq came and warned us to leave the village. He said, 'we are also going. Better go yourself. If you stay here either you will be killed or have to become *shuddh*.' Everyone left the area except for one Meo, Sagipar Khan, who died. None became *shuddh*. Only some persons from villages near Maujpur and near Alwar became *shuddh*. We went to Doha Raoli on the Gurgaon border beyond Naugaonwa through the Jalalpur Pahar. The village was burnt and looted after we left. I saw the *dhār* in Kaimasa. There I saw Bacchu Singh raja, and with him 2–3000 men. They had guns, spears, axes, staffs, swords. They were shouting, '*māro inko, lūto, nikāl do*' [hit them, loot them, throw them out]. We didn't have any guns except for the *topīdār* guns that kill pigs. The entire village left with my dada Mev Khan.[71]

Fateh Singh of Samola and his *pāl* made an alternative choice and he describes the experience of *shuddhi* for persons of his village:

I was converted with four other Meos. They took us to Titpuri, Lachmangarh. They told us, 'you belong to the [ruling] Naruka lineage'. My father, Khairati Meo, was named Khadag Singh. Water was filled at the well and Sidhji was called who is the father of the BJP leader, Dharamvir Sidh. The pandits were called. My head was shaved and a *chotī* left. I was given new clothes and made *shuddh* [pure] with *gangā jal*. All the Hindu villages from Rupbas had also come. The police fired at the crowd. The Pundlot *gotra* has always been close to the Maharaja. He was misguided by Dr Khare. Other people were also involved: the IG, Richpal Singh, the Collector, Mulchand Badhavar, the Thakur of Garhi, Bhavani Singh, and an SP called Bakhtavar Lal. Mulchand Badhavar was the Collector of Rajgarh and he gave the order to kill. Richpal Singh also said 'kill' and so the DSP ordered, 'kill the Meos'. We were saved because we became *shuddh*.[72]

Mandawar had about 300–400 homes of Rangad Rajputs. Although they

[70] Interview, Tijara, 6 Dec. 1992.
[71] Interview, Govindgarh, 4 Dec. 1991.
[72] Interview, Alwar, 23 May 1993.

had been converted, their customs were Rajput. After their *shuddhi*, their daughters were taken in marriage, but Hindu Rajput daughters were not given to them. Thus, though the former Muslims had been sanctified as 'pure,' nonetheless, they continued to be regarded within Hindu communities as sources of pollution.

Ramjani's father underwent *shuddhi* after his elder son was killed. Bacchu Singh had arrived with 500 men all armed with spears and swords. She saw about a hundred people slain on the Ratnaki, Govindgarh road:

Then *shuddhi* took place, my father was shaved, he was made to keep a *chuttī* and was sprinkled with *gangā jal*. Nathu came from Thekda ka bas and Bhairu was installed with vermilion, a lamp and food offering. He is the *panī kā rakhvālā* [protector of water]. They call him Bhairuji, we call him Khyajakhedar, an *auliyā*. It is the first thing to be done before a well is dug.[73]

In Ramjani's account there was a bewilderment as to why Bhairuji, whom the Meos worship anyway, was thrust on them. It suggests the distance between the totalized binary construction of ethnic ideologies and her lifeworld constituted of ritual objects. But strategies of resistance were part of the underlife of the collectivized ritual. Several persons got their *choti*s cut after a few months. In the '*shuddh*' persons view the ritual of purification was inverted as defilement.

Violence and victimhood were not passively encountered by the Meos. We have numerous indications of the organization of resistance. Following the state-led attacks of armed mobs numbering up to 10,000–20,000 on such villages as Mandawar and Harsauli, Meo refugees from Bharatpur and Alwar attacked Hindu villages. Meo villages organized their defence although spears, axes, swords, staffs, and *topīdar*s could hardly match the .303, Bren guns and mortars. Nonetheless, other groups remember the panic and fear associated with Meo *dhāṛ*s. Fanon suggests that victims objectify the aggressors and exorcize them to affirm their humanity and constitute themselves into a moral community.[74] At Naugaon, Bharatpur, the capture of Bacchu Singh's cannon (according to villagers, it has an inscription of the Mughal Emperor Alamgir on it and was looted at the time of the Jat attack on Red Fort) was a sign of defiance. Hidden in a pond, it became a symbol of heroic Meo resistance and was not

---

[73] A reference to Khwaja Khizr, a well-known patron saint of boatmen and otherwise connected with water. Ramjani, interview, Lachmangarh, 30 Jan. 1992.

[74] Frantz Fanon argues that violence as exorcism is the only way in which victims can recover their subjectivity through 'objectifying' the perpetrators of violence. *The Wretched of the Earth* (Penguin Books, Harmondsworth, 1967).

recovered even after the entire village was burnt and its inhabitants fled
to the Gurgaon border that runs along the horizon of low-lying hills visible
from the village. Abdul Haye's account informs us of the 'sudden encircle-
ment of soldiers' when Ashraf and he had come for a meeting and their
organization of Meo resistance:

The news of the arrival of the troops quickly spread to the villages round
Naugaon. . . . By midnight positions had been taken up facing the Maharaja's
forces on the border of Teengaon, which is in Gurgaon district. . . . Soon after
dusk the army started to mount their old-fashioned, indigenous cannon in
order to bombard the village next day. The attack was to begin the following
morning. Dr Ashraf advised a full-scale onslaught on the military camp before
the enemy forces could organize themselves and launch their attack. The camp
was to be set on fire. . . . After midnight the young Meos went to attack the
Maharaja's camp. The attack was successful although a few Meo youths were
killed. The Maharaja's out-of-date cannon was captured. Meanwhile the men
of Teengaon also arrived. In less than no time the military camp was abandoned. By midday the Maharaja's forces were wiped out.

A few days later Bacchu Singh led the massacre in Bharatpur.

Resistance rather than victimhood has a strong narrative presence in
the oral tradition, although contrasted with the peasant movement where
resistance generated extraordinary poetico–mythic creativity, for Partition
we have but a fragmentary account called *hullaṛ ke dohe*:[75]

> rājā kahe rānī sūn,
> rājā sapnā main ādho jido main bhūl gaī ausān
> tero taṛkai toṛaigo bharatpur nahīn moy pahūnchā dai mursānd

> mormal hai sūrmā rāhai rab kī aut
> dhaingalvātī nāharpur mall huo jākai hāth sajai bījlot
> toto namī top chī jānai roshan kīnī kot
> naugāvān hai bhārtī rākh lī bachū singh kī top
> āndhā kā bhālā kī dhonkār sūn terī kānp rahī bījrot

> rānī sūn rājā kahe:
> suniyo rānī bāt bāt mat bolai kacchī
> terī ī supna kī bāt kadai nā hovai sacchī
> pakṛūn mev supāt jīvto nā vākūn choṛū
> merī gaddī sadāmadā sūrmā lākh din unko moṛu
> tīnū līdar pakaṛ kai chothū pakṛūngo dhānā ko partāp
> inkī khāl kāt kar bhūs bharūn choṛūngo dūr angrejī kai pār

75 Recorded from Mirasi Abdul, Alwar, 23 May 1993.

The rani tells the raja:
Raja, I argued with Andho[76] in my dream
when I lost all consciousness.
He will destroy your Bharatpur in the morning
so send me to Mudsand.[77]
Mormal is very brave
with the protection of the Lord.
In Naharpur in Dhaingalvati
there was Mall with a weapon adorning his hand.
Toto is a well-known cannon-firer
who has made Kot famous.[78]
Bharti of Naugaon
has taken Bacchu Singh's cannon.[79]
With the noise of the mace of Andha
your Bijrot trembles.[80]

The raja says:
Listen rani
do not speak from weakness.
The matter of your dream
can never come true.
I will catch the Meo, Sapat,
I will not leave him alive.
My throne has always been brave,
they may try a lakh times.
I will catch all three leaders and the fourth, Dhana's Pratap.[81]
I will cut open their skin, stuff them with hay
and leave them in British India.

At one level, the heroic verse captures defiance but inverts the utter desolation and slaughter in its celebration of the valour of Andha, Sapat, and others. At a deeper level, the fragmentary *dohas* metaphor the state policy of ethnic cauterization and carnage in the raja's threats to the heroes. The heroes' actions described by the rani similarly indicate Meo resistance.

[76] Meo of Shorpur, *tehsil* Pahari.

[77] The rani's natal home.

[78] Abdul tells the story of Tota Meo of Kot who fired at a drunken elephant and injured its eye. In agony the elephant who was meant to kill the Meos trampled all over the Jats instead.

[79] Naugaon which had taken the Jat cannon was one of the first places to be attacked by Bachu Singh on 5 June 1947.

[80] Bijrot is a Gujar village that played a major role in looting.

[81] The three leaders, according to Abdul, are Sapat Khan of Mandalka, Ismail Khan of Khandelwa, and Imrat of Mallhaka.

Stories of Bacchu Singh suggest the personifying imagery of the source of violence. One account tells of the arrival of Bacchu Singh in a jeep disguised in Meo clothes at Kaithwara. He eavesdrops on the deliberations of the Meo meeting for a while and then opens machine-gun fire and kills 500–1000 persons. A song that Pankaj recorded from women is a fragment account of the terror Bacchu Singh symbolized:

> top chalai bandūk chalai aur golī chalai ishārai tai
> abkai jān bachā dai allā jāt bharatpur vārai tai
> kaise kaise jān bachaigī yā bacchū hatyārai tai
> abkai jān bachā dai allā jāt bharatpur vārai tai

> The cannon and the gun
> fire at a signal.
> Oh Allah, save our life just this time
> from the Jat of Bharatpur.

> How can we save our lives
> from the killer, Bacchu.
> Oh Allah, save our life just this time
> from the Jat of Bharatpur.

The state had planned its attack on villages that were the critical nodal points of the peasant–state conflict such as Ismail's Khandewla, Ajmat, and Dundhal's Mallhaka, Jullan Khan's Saisan, Samay Singh's Bilang, Juhrera, and Naugaon. A resident of Bilang described the violence:

First the *dhāṛ* came from Kaman. They laid a *morchā* but we fought back, then they came from the Bolkhera side. There were Jats and Chamars. We have *bhāī bandī* with the people of Bolkhera. Gujars and Jats are in the [Pahat] *pāl* panchayat. We go to their weddings and they came to ours. We still give each other *bhent* [contribution towards marriage expenses]. The fight started at the Ganga ghat. Then travelled here. . . . They were on the hill, we were in the village below. But it was no use. They had the *do mīl bandūk* (two mile gun). We only had the *topīdar*, the *toṛedars* (muzzle loaders)—not like them. We ran to Firozpur, to our relatives. We did not want to go to Pakistan. We did not go. Those who stayed in the camp went to Pakistan.[82]

The *dhāṛ* ruptured a shared political and ritual space, the *bhāī bandī* of the *pāl* and the worship of the *pir* in which large numbers of Hindus participated along with Meos.

Following the exodus, camps became the domain of the contest over

[82] Interview, Paltu Khan, Garh Ajan, 19 May 1993. Interestingly, Pakistani Meos still continue to maintain their Mewati identity. They follow the *pal* system and marry according to *gotra*s.

Meo identity, re-territorialization, and the future. They were opened at Sohna, Gurgaon, Jama Masjid and Idgah, Delhi, to process the onward journey to Pakistan. According to Abdul Haye, the 'nominal Muslims' of Alwar had virtually nothing in common with Pakistani Muslims except the nomenclature of Muslim. Their security already in jeopardy, their future seemed bleak. On the other hand, was the possibility of being uprooted from their land, homes, and especially people as Meos did not intermarry with other Muslims. The Left leadership had brought complaints of the involvement of Congress leaders in the violence to Gandhi. Gandhi's tour of Mewat was organized by Dr Ashraf and P.C. Joshi to prevent the Meos from going to Pakistan. Nuh's Sardar Mohammad wanted to send them all to Pakistan and is reported to have said, '*pakistan jāo nahīn to chuttī rakh denge*' (go to Pakistan or they will make you grow a Hindu tuft of hair). But Chaudhari Yasin didn't want them to go. Ironically, the Communist Party decided to send both Dr Ashraf and Syed Mutalabi to Pakistan to organize the Communist movement there. The field was left virtually open for an alternative leadership to take over the traumatized Meos and reappropriate Meo identity.

What was the nature of the territorial passage? Large numbers of Meos who returned to Alwar and Bharatpur stated that they had done so because of Yasin and Gandhi. According to a Bharatpur Congressmen, 'there was popular anger against Gandhi because he stopped their *kafilā*. Sardar Patel wanted them to go and would say, "*jāo tumhārī jannat hai pākistān*" (go, Pakistan is your heaven) although Nehruji, Satyam bhai, a follower of Gandhi, and others persuaded them to stay.' The Congress undertook the responsibility for their resettlement. A list was made of those Meos who had left for Gurgaon and Uttar Pradesh, a total of 18,000 families who had to be resettled. Vinoba Bhave was sent to live in Alwar and Bharatpur. Satyam bhai and Gandhi were locally blamed for undoing the work of *shuddhi*.

Mehti captures her return to nothingness:

When we came back we found not even doors, not even their frames. I got very less land, only 30 *bīghās* of *barani* [non-irrigated] land. It is not so good, it doesn't even have a well. I grow wheat and *sarson* now; just enough for my subsistence. Our house had been taken over by Sikhs. But we said nothing to them, the Meos are afraid of them.

Curiously, it was the Baniyas of Govindgarh who called them back.[83]

---

[83] Mehtabi had told me that it was the Chamars who comprised the *dhāṛ*, not the Baniyas.

Villagers of Naugaon remember that the Jats of their twelve hamlets
had come to call them back.[84] In some instances, the violence also had
an implicit healing process, inscribed in individual memory, such as of
a Gujar who came to return a buffalo to a Meo family. The marriage of
an Ahir girl who was left behind when her family fled the Meo area,
to an Ahir at Taoru (Sohna), was organized by her 'Meo family'. Chand
Khan remembers that his village was protected from a *dhāṛ* of 5,000–6,000
Rajputs, Minas, Gujars, and Chamars.[85] His grandfather Abdulla's family
remained, but its protection was contingent on his undergoing *shuddhi*
that the Thakur of Chimraoli had organized at the instance of the
Maharaja. After *shuddhi* his family got back all their land of about 150
bīghās. Persons of the Pundlot *pāl* were similarly rewarded.

Dalpat's account is particularly telling as an analysis of the nature of
the violence. 'Seventy-five per cent Meos went to Pakistan. But a large
number thought what is Pakistan to us? This was our land and that of
our ancestors. The conflict was not a religious one. The fight had been
caused by those who didn't have land.'[86] In Pakistan, he said, he met a
large number of Meos who were very troubled for they had become a
māngne khāne vālī kaum (group of beggars). Only after several years were
the *patwari* records of ownership copied and sent to the land records
department of Pakistan. The association of land and identity emerges in
this account: that territory is far more than a mere material factor. Bereft
of it and prior to the rehabilitation and land allotment, their perceived
status was that of beggars.

It is now time to tie the multiple strands of this essay together. I have
argued that the organization of violence in Mewat recounts a fourfold
onslaught for the community: by the state, by other social groups, by
sections of the press, and by the modern bureaucracy of the post-colonial
state.[87] Writing is the clue to both the representation and obliteration of
violence. This is accomplished through the selection of particular categories such as those of Meo aggression and 'criminality' and, therefore,

[84] Interviews, Naugaon, 19 May 1993.
[85] Interview, Lachmangarh, 30 Jan. 1992.
[86] '*Hamāre buzurg, hamāri bhūmī to yahān hai. ye to koī mazhabi laṛāī se nahin huā.
jhagṛā unne karāyā jinke pās bhūmī nahin thī.*'
[87] For reasons of space sections on the role of the press and the problems the
Meos had to face with regard to their re-territorialization by the post-colonial state
have been omitted. Despite claims of having rehabilitated 'evacuees', it was the
'refugees' or 'displaced persons' (read Hindus and Sikhs from Pakistan) who were
given precedence.

the need for 'counter-violence' (by the state); 'communal riot' (by the press); 'Musalman' rather than 'Meo', (by the 'mob'); 'shuddhi' or purification by the Hindu leadership; and 'displaced persons' versus 'refugees' (by the post-colonial state). It is counterposed by the lexical reordering in the speech of victims that uses phrases such as 'bhagā bhagī' (referring to the exodus), 'mārā mārī' (to the violence), katī (to the slaughter); and of 'genocide', by a marginal voice coming from the Left leadership, articulated in the communist party's press.

The issue of speech as ripping silence is, however, not quite as straightforward. Layers of silence mask both inscription and speech, and obliterate annihilatory practice. Even the Meo performing art tradition that ensures the cultural reproduction of collective memory is marked by a substantial silence. It is not only that there is a breakdown of the traditional forms of mythic history, but that the poetic language of Pingal verse fails to communicate pain and suffering. Further, communities themselves impose silences on the transmission of memory as a strategy enabling the remaking of inter-subjective existence.

The new found secular state concerned with the work of 'Rehabilitation' saw this as implying also the cessation of the memory of conflict. The 'disappearance of files', the screening of the Alwar state's involvement in hearings of the Gandhi Murder trial, and the concealment of the territorial inscription of violence was to ensure that transmission of the experience would cease, and thereby create the conditions for 'governmentality'.[88] The development of sanitized categories such as 'displaced persons' suggested that the post-colonial state preferred a neatly segmented world that would enable both knowledge and control.

There was no room for liminal categories such as the Meos represented, a people in-between Hinduism and Islam. The blurring of the margins defies knowledge (as intelligence) and corrodes control. Silence continues to mark the speech of victimizers with a narrative framed by, 'they started it . . . . then we retaliated'. Significantly, it also denotes the speech of victims concerned with the everyday activity of living once again with the aggressors of 1947.

The history of Partition then is one that can only be written in fragments: provided by splintered accounts such as the exodus of refugees to Ajmer, Agra, Delhi, and Jaipur, and the near complete evacuation of the

---

[88] The new Executive Engineer of the 'Public Works' Department was deputed to cover up the well full of corpses at the Nagli crossing in the Civil Lines area of Alwar city. Family interview, Jaipur, 26 March 1993.

Alwar and Bharatpur princely states;[89] the files on the abduction and later recovery of women from eastern Rajputana;[90] the request from the princely states to be provided with additional arms; the massive enterprise of resettlement. . . . It is a history that must take cognizance of both speech/inscription, on the one hand, and of the levels of silence. What emerges is the extraordinary capacity of the subaltern for violence as they participate in the state-sponsored campaign of *safāyā*, epitomizing the ideology of cleansing and cauterization that Lifton refers to in another context.[91]

For the Meos, Partition meant a significant renegotiation of group identity. Refugee camps became fertile ground for the work of the Tablighi jama'ats who told them that their fate was the expression of the wrath of God incurred because they were not good Muslims. A Rajput's account of what a Meo once told him brings out the sense of despair and the corresponding shift in identity,

'*mev to miyā nahīn. ham to thākar-mīnon main se hain. lekin kyā karte, tum ne bhī nā apnāyā, to ham ek taraf to rahe* [Meos are not Muslims. We are from Rajputs and Minas. But what can we do? You "Hindus" did not accept us. So we might as well be on one side].' Similarly, Dalpat said, 'In 1947 they called us "Muslim" when all along we'd been saying that we were Jadubanshis from Kishanji's *khāndān*. We realized there is no point in riding two horses. Yes, everything is fine now, but the bitterness remains in the heart.' It is interesting to note the dialogical aspects of Meo identity. Dalpat's statement poignantly expresses how the self was reconstituted after the experience of violence.

For the community, occasions of exceptional trauma are reproduced at the level of dreams and everyday life and constitute ever-present possibilities of the lived present. And so is the case with Partition violence. Lifton refers to the death anxiety that marked Hiroshima victims.[92] As the Ramajanmabhumi movement gained strength in the countryside, the re-enactment of the trauma of Partition was a live and present possibility for the Meos. The tremor was not a visible one, but one that was apparent in the rapid frequency of visits of the Tablighi jama'at; the bonding

[89] FR on Pol situation in Rajputana States for the year 1947. Pol and MOS 10 (11)–PR/47 (Sec.).

[90] *See* Statement of recovery between 6 Dec 1947 and 15 Aug. 1949, Recovery of abducted women and maintenance of children born to them, MOS 1–R/49, vol. 1.

[91] Robert Jay Lifton, *The Nazi Doctors: Medical Killing and the Psychology of Genocide* (Basic Books, Inc., New York, 1986).

[92] Lifton, *Death in Life*, p. 136.

together of the community as parties to intra-Meo disputes were persuaded to compromise (*rājī nāmā*); and the social pressure to perform regular *namāz* and exclusively (Tabligh) sanctioned ritual was intensified. Communal violence in its annihilatory form can be conceived of as a rite of political and territorial passage for the community as it is followed by a major renegotiation of individual life-worlds, of the dissolution and remaking of community identity and networks with the larger world.

MEWAT AND SURROUNDING AREAS IN 1947

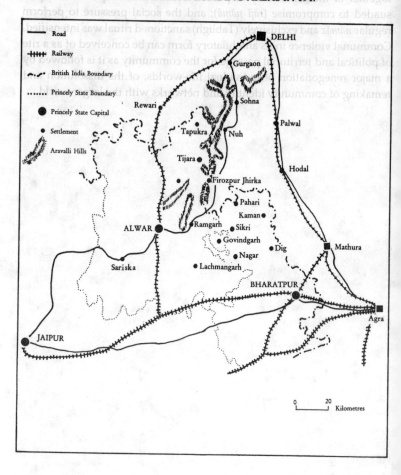

6

Productive Labour, Consciousness and History: The Dalitbahujan Alternative[*]

KANCHA ILAIH

INTRODUCTION

Mainstream historiography has done nothing to incorporate the Dalitbahujan perspective in the writing of Indian history: *Subaltern Studies* is no exception to this. To make matters worse, recent Hindu politics—and its historiography—has sought to wipe out the possibility of a Dalitbahujan perspective and a Dalitbahujan history by simply declaring that the Dalitbahujan are (fallen) Hindus. This essay seeks to challenge that Brahminical historiography by pointing to the contrariness—and differentness—of Dalitbahujan perspective and history.

* Although the principal themes of this chapter are drawn from my book *Why I am Not a Hindu?*, it was reworked after I joined the Nehru Memorial Museum and Library, New Delhi, as a Fellow. I thank the members of the staff of the NMML. I am grateful to Susie Tharu, Duggirala Vasanta, Manohar Reddy, S. Simhadri, Veena Shatrugna, K. Lalitha, Rama Melkote, R. Srivastan, Paroma Deb, Shahid Amin, Dipesh Chakrabarty, and Gyan Pandey for their valuable comments on this chapter at various stages of its writing.

I also thank G. Ramalingam, K. Bharathi, K. Kattaiah, K. Rama Devi and other members of my family who helped me in various ways when I was working on it.

Particularly since the 1990s Hindu politicians, writers, sadhus, and *sanyasis*, using all the communicational means at their command, have drummed it into our ears day in and day out that everyone in India, who is not a Muslim, a Christian, or a Sikh, is a Hindu. We, the Dalitbahujan—a concept that has come to be used to designate a united whole of Scheduled Castes, Scheduled Tribes, and the Other Backward Classes—are now being told that we are Hindus. We are now told that our parents, our relatives and the castes and communities in which we are born and brought up, are Hindu. These efforts to co-opt us into their Hinduism are violent and virulent, and bombard our consciousness which, for centuries, was carefully and violently kept separate and defined as different from theirs. Earlier, treating us as the 'other' and arresting our beings in the cages of our caste was the sacred duty of their religion—Hinduism. Now co-opting us into their Hinduism is undertaken as a political programme. Both their earlier acts of keeping us unequal, and their present attempt to co-opt us into their fold clearly indicates that they consider us as Beings whose culture, consciousness and ideology have no identity. At a time when we craved to be part of 'them' they decisively thrust us aside; kept us away from them; treated us as the vulgar 'working mass' having no dignity, no self-respect. Our history, our language, our philosophy, our skills, our knowledge of science and technology were all rendered invisible. The reason for this is the institution of caste. On the one hand, our beings and our consciousness were arrested within caste, and on the other, they saw to it that the very idea of caste negated the idea of history. Our history, therefore, became non-history.

Fortunately, however, our history is a book of blank pages to fill with whatever letters—language—we wish to write. Just as we are becoming conscious that our history is a book of blank pages and are acquiring the new skills—in addition to our existing skills of production—of writing our history as we would want to write it, they are turning round and proclaiming that there is no difference between 'you and us'; and that too not by assimilating us into their total beings, into their self (through marriage, etc.). Their only desire is to keep us in their fold as political elements who have now acquired a right to vote. At the same time, socially, culturally, and even physically, they want us to remain their 'other', while acting politically as 'homogeneous Hindus' who can be their tools against Muslims or Christians (in their language 'minorities'). In the arena of education and jobs—as the Mandal Yuga (era of Mandal) has come about they abuse us as meritless creatures, but in their Ramarajya we are again defined as Hindus.

I therefore feel quite strongly that the time has come when we must make our statement as to what we really are and how we really differ from them. Not as different in the way they had shown us to be; meak, meritless, unskilled, foolish 'others'. We differ from them because we are skilled producers, productive instrument-makers, creative builders of the material basis of the society. We must also show that today we are determined to prove that Hinduism and Brahminism represent the world-views of the atrocious 'others' who have been parasites and whose role has never been positive and constructive. To do that we must search for our own methodology, understand how we know ourselves. What is our epistemology? It is an epistemology that is built brick by brick, based on our long experience in production and distribution of material goods and commodities for centuries. We are now prepared to convert that experience into a framework of knowledge. This knowledge has its own historicity. The first premise of our epistemology is the affirmation of the potential of 'our own selfhood' and the comparison of this self with the self of the other. In this process we will lay the foundations for a transformation of the caste–cultural consciousness that is the very source of inequality in India. The aim is to negate all factors of negation—Hinduism, Brahminism, Feudalism, and Capitalism. While the need for a critique of Brahminical epistemology from the point of view of Dalitbahujan epistemology is pressing and immediate, in the face of our non-history it is not an easy task. Brahminism has built up the whole body of literature, from the Vedic period to the present, and permeated all layers of Dalit-bahujan society. The entirety of Dalitbahujan existence is encapsulated in the notion of karma and made to appear unreal—maya. However, the task of Dalitbahujan organic intellectuals is to show to the world the real face of Hindu Brahminism.

As feminist friends have suggested, the personal must be made political. In other words, our experiences and our aspirations must be taken as the framework of the new knowledge. It is the Dalitbahujan who must now begin to set the agenda of the society. Throughout history—their written history, our unwritten history—our voices have been silenced and muted, while our hands and bodies have been working. We never compared our wisdom, our skills, and our productive and reproductive processes with those of others. What I propose to do in this essay is to state what we are in our own words; to compare ourselves with the others in the minutiae of everyday life and in every other respect. To do that we must construct our narratives and create our own texts. These, no doubt, will be new narratives and new texts. The language of such narratives and texts will be our own, and it will naturally differ from the language of others. It must be remembered that we have our own language, our own idioms, and our own proverbs. For example, some popularly used Telugu Dalitbahujan proverbs express the difference between our culture and their culture thus: *Maadi panipata samscruti* (Ours is a culture of work and songs), *vaalladi chaduvu sandhya samscruti* (theirs is a culture of learning and worship). Their learning alienated them from our culture of work and songs, and by keeping us away from their *chaduvu* (learning) they ensured that our *panipata* (culture) would not get on to the printed page. While they desired to remain alienated from *pani* (work), they subverted our songs by creating their *mantras* (divine chants). Gradually our productive work-culture was depicted by them as mean and vulgar, as *chandalam* (human excreta), while their culture of worship was projected as *goppa* (sacred).

The methodology and epistemology that I use in this essay being what they are, this discussion might appear 'unbelievable', 'unacceptable', or 'untruthful' to those 'scholars and thinkers' who are born and brought up in Hindu families. Further, I deliberately do not want to take precautions, qualify my statements, footnote my material, nuance my claims, for the simple reason that my statements are not meant to be nuanced in the first place. They are meant to raise Dalitbahujan consciousness and to show the 'other' in our mirror in such a way that their hegemony is jeopardized and our hegemony begins to be established.

I strongly believe that unless the oppressed learn to hegemonize their own self, unless the culture and consciousness of the oppressed is put forward visibly in public debate, unless this culture is prepared to clash with the culture and consciousness of the enemy in public, a society of equals will remain an illusion. At a time when the enemy is attacking us, day in and day out, the gesture of taking precautions or nuancing our statements will only 'devalue' our historiographical energy.

I am writing principally to conscientize the Dalitbahujan. Instead of looking at our weaknesses it is important to look at our strength. I have also been subject to 'friendly' upper caste suggestions that in the process of highlighting Dalitbahujan strength, there is no need to attack the other (in their language, 'abuse the other'). They say 'make out your case strongly, name the exclusion and claim the space you need but do not abuse the others'. In other words we are being asked to submit a statement of our sorrows and seek remedies. It also means that we should not abuse the abuser. The Dalitbahujan experience—a long experience of 3,000 years at that—tells us that no abuser stops abusing unless there is retaliation.

An atmosphere of calm, an atmosphere of respect for one another in which contradictions may be democratically resolved is never possible unless the abuser is abused as a matter of shock treatment. Indeed, there is no other way to break the culture of silence of the 'historical object of abuse'.

Secondly, there are millions in this world who, though they do not suffer from the casteism of Hinduism (as caste oppression is a phenomenon specific to Hinduism), suffer from discrimination of colour and class. Africans, whose beauty the Dalitbahujan of India share, have taught us that 'black is beautiful', but what we learnt from our own experience is that unless we also say that 'white is ugly', at least till the beauty of all human colours is universally recognized, no white person is going to listen to what we say. Since beauty and ugliness are both culturally constructed notions that gradually transform our consciousness, it is important that these notions be recast to change the hegemonic relations that have been brought into force in the process. Until this painful phase of inequalities has passed, and the consciousness that only the dominating groups are beautiful and others are ugly, the condemned must learn to condemn the others. So I appeal to the blacks of the world to read this essay with sympathy, compassion, and camaraderie.

Thirdly, women are of the sky and they have many things in common with the Dalitbahujan and blacks. In many respects the experiences of upper-caste women allow them to relate themselves to Dalitbahujan and black experiences. I hope they too will find this essay useful. The religious 'minorities' who have become an object of attack by the Hindus are no 'others' but are in reality Dalitbahujan who converted. I therefore, appeal to them to read this essay with sympathy and friendship. And there are a number of men in the intellectual world who are willing to de-caste, de-race, and de-class themselves, who of course are born not by choice, but by accident, in their upper-caste, white, racist, and rich families. If they too find this essay useful for their self-transformation I will certainly feel heartened. As a rule however there are many Hindu intellectuals who invoke their armed gods—Brahma, Vishnu, Rama, Krishna, etc. to fight against me as I am, in their view, a 'Dushtashakti' (evil force). Against them I am certainly ready to fight back.

ON BEING BORN DALITBAHUJAN

I was not born a Hindu for the simple reason that my parents did not know that they were Hindus. This does not mean that I was born a

Muslim, a Christian, a Buddhist, a Sikh, or a Parsi. My illiterate parents, who lived in a remote South Indian Telangana village, did not know that they belonged to any religion at all. My parents had only one identity and that was their caste: they were Kurumas. Their festivals were local, their Gods and Goddesses were local, and sometimes these were even specific to one village. No centralized religious symbols existed for them. This does not mean they were tribals. My ancestors took to life on the plains about 500 years ago. They were integrated into the village economy, paid taxes to the village *panchayat* or to the state administration in whichever form the administration required. As long as they were shepherds, they paid the tax in the form of *pullara* (levy for sheep-breeding). In the years before I was born, they shifted the occupation from sheep-breeding to agriculture and paid land rent to the local landlord and to the *tehsil* office. Even in my childhood I remember my parents paying taxes both for sheep-breeding and for cultivating the land. But they never paid a religion tax, something which all feudal religions normally demand. Besides, they never went to a temple in which they could meet villagers belonging to all castes. Indeed, there was no temple where all the villagers could meet on a regular basis.

This does not mean that my family alone was excluded from this religious process because it was a family that could be ignored or neglected. Not so. Indeed, for two generations my ancestors had been the caste heads. My mother and her mother-in-law (that is, my grandmother) were members of a leading family of the Kuruma caste. Kurmas, Gollas, Goudas, Kapus, Shalas, Chakalies, Mangalis, and Madigas were caste groups that formed the majority in terms of numbers in the village economy. The entire village economy was governed by the daily operations of these castes.

The social structure in which I first became conscious of the world around me was Kuruma. My playmates, friends, and of course relatives, all belonged to the Kuruma caste. Occasionally the circle of friendship extended to Gouda and Kapu boys. We were friends because we were all part of the cattle-breeding youth. We took the cattle to the field and then played *chirragone* (our cricket), *gooliilu* (a game of marbles), *dongata* (a game of hide and seek), etc. However, surprisingly, whenever a Gouda friend visited my house he would eat with us, but sit slightly apart; when we went to Kapu homes their parents would give us food but make us sit a little distance away. While eating we were not supposed to touch each other, but could later play together and drink together from the rivers and streams. If we had carried our midday meal to the grazing field, we sometimes attempted to touch each other's food, but suddenly the rules that our parents had set out would surface: we would speak insultingly of each other's castes and revert to eating separately. Within moments, however, we were together again.

Agriculture being a collective activity of the village, the cows, bulls, and buffaloes were commonly owned as the property of many castes. This was perhaps a meeting ground for the village economy. Thus, when we went along with cattle, social life on the cattle ground became an inter-caste affair. But as we grew up, this life we had in common and the shared consciousness began splitting even in terms of production relations. My Kuruma friends and I withdrew from common cattle-tending activities and were trained in sheep-breeding, which is a specific occupation of Kurumas and Gollas alone. At the same time, my Gouda friends were drawn into toddy-tapping and Kapu friends into plough-driving.

THE TRAINING OF BOYS

Each one of us was supposed to imbibe the skills of his particular caste. I was introduced to the specific skills needed for the rearing of sheep. I was taught the different names of the sheep—*bolli gorre, pulla gorre, nalla gorre*, etc. I learnt about the diseases that afflicted sheep, how a delivery should be midwifed, how the young should be cared for, the best green grass for the sheep, etc. Goats required special treatment as they were to be fed with tree leaves (goats do not eat grass). We learnt what herbal medicines should be applied when sheep and goats are attacked by dis-eases. If the diseases were nerve-based ones, we learnt how to touch them with a heated iron rod at that particular spot. One of the most difficult and delicate tasks was shearing the wool from the body of the sheep. The scissors had to be handled with such care that they cut close but did not cut the skin of the sheep. All these was part of the expertise of a sheep rearer and we were carefully educated in them all.

BRINGING UP GIRLS

How were the girls educated or brought up? Whether they were my sisters or others, the pattern of training was the same. The elder girls were taught, even as they turned three, how to care for a younger brother or sister. Holding an infant requires skill and care, more so in the arms of a 3-year-old girl. This was the most important assistance the mother required when she left home for work early in the morning. Mothers would also teach their daughters how to powder chillies, husk the paddy, sweep the home and clean the eating bowls.

Besides this, a Kuruma woman teaches her daughter how to separate the wool from the thorns that stick to it and to prepare it for thread-making (*tadu wadakadam*). All these tasks are extremely skilled. By the age of 12 or 13 (by the time she has reached puberty) a Kuruma girl is supposed to know the basics of cooking. She begins with lighting the hearth and learning to tend to it. A Kuruma hearth consists of three stones with an extension on one side. On this extension stands a pot, known as a *vothu*, on which water is kept boiling. It requires a special skill not to upset or crack the *vothu* while cooking on the main hearth. Kuruma girls also learn how to manage the *kuradu* which is an important part of Kuruma cooking (as it is of all other Dalitbahujan castes). A Kuruma *kuradu* consists of *ganji*, water drained from cooked rice and then left to ferment slightly until it gives out a mild, sour aroma. While cooking rice or *jowar*, the *kuradu* is invariably used as the liquid (*yesaru*). *Kuradu* is considered good for health; in addition, it drives away evil spirits from the food. Every girl is initiated into these skills at an early age. First of all, handling pots that are vulnerable to breaking requires care and acquired skill. The only activity that was not taught to our girls which an urban girl might have to learn today was washing clothes. This is because washing was the washerman's/woman's task. A girl born in a Chakali (washerman) family learns all these activities in addition to learning how to wash various kinds of clothes.

The girls of these families are also taught, at an early age, how to seed the furrow by carefully dropping seed after seed. They are taught how to weed and even out extra growth in the crop; they learn how to plant with bent backs, moving backwards along the muddy land. Much explanation by the adults goes into the teaching of these activities to the young. Invariably there are experts in each activity who have earned a name for themselves in particular fields who the young are proud to emulate.

OF SEXUAL MORES

Sexual behaviour and manners are also taught as part of family and peer group life. A girl listens to older women talking to each other in groups about 'disciplined' women and 'indisciplined' women; their sexual lifestyles, their relations with husbands and others. A father does not hesitate to talk in front of his children about his approach to life or his relations with other women. More important than the father's is the mother's approach towards the children. A Dalitbahujan mother trains her children as a hen trains its chickens. She takes the children along with her to the fields, and sets them small tasks. While walking to the fields she often shares her problems with the children, particularly with the girls. It is not uncommon for her to talk to them about every aspect of her life. If any Dalitbahujan woman has a relationship with a man who is not her husband, the relationship does not remain a secret. The entire *waada* (locality) discusses it. Even the children of that family hear about it. In particular, when the father and mother quarrel, every aspect of life becomes public. Male children learn about women and about sex in the company of their friends, in the cattle-rearing grounds or sheep-feeding fields. All manner of sexual trials take place in the fields—the 'bads' and 'goods' of life learnt at quite an early stage. But this morality is not based on a divine order or divine edict. It is discussed in terms of the harmony of the families.

OF DALITBAHUJAN LANGUAGE

The languages of the Dalitbahujan are structured by their own grammars, designed for production-based communication. For example, a Brahmin might not understand expressions familiar to Kurumas, Goudas, or Madigas: *gorre unni kathiriyyi* (cut the wool of sheep), *or gorre pillanu kudupu* (allow the young sheep to suckle mother's milk) (Kuruma); *chettekki gela koyyi* (climb the tree and cut the *gela*) (Gouda); *toolu unu* (prepare the skin for shoe-making) (Madiga). Similarly, Brahminical statements like *sandhya vandanam cheyumu* (do the morning prayer of Sun) or *Sarvam daivadheenam* (everything runs according to God's will) might be incomprehensible to many Dalitbahujan. The basic difference in these two languages is that the Dalitbahujan language refers to productive work, whereas the Brahminical language refers to prayer and God. Though the Dalitbahujan have developed their language without the aid of writing, it is no less sophisticated than 'standard' Brahminical Telugu. Children's experience of language begins with fixing the names of things—birds, animals, trees, insects, everything that is around them. Every tree, every insect, every living and non-living being bears a name. These names are not taught through the written word but are repeated orally in communication that is use-based. The Kurumas have their own language, as do the Lambadas, the Erukalas, or the Koyas. Kurumas not only know about the sheep, goats, trees, plants, and so on, they know the names of every instrument used in wool-making and blanket-weaving. A Gouda knows the names of whole range of instruments, skills, and activities that are required for toddy-tapping. The specialization that one acquires in communicating these caste-occupational tasks is as much or more sophisticated than that possessed by a Brahmin who utters the several names of his Gods while reciting a *mantra*. What is ironic is that the recitation of several names of one God or many Gods is construed as wisdom, whereas knowing the language of production and the names of productive tools is not recognised as knowledge. The Brahmins have defined knowledge and defined it in their own image.

OF THE MADIGAS

My village used to have about 40 Madiga families who lived adjacent to the Gouda locality. Members of these two castes avoided physical contact with each other. I do not recall ever having had a childhood Madiga friend from my village. The Madiga boys younger than me were *jeetas* (very young children). Their familial and cultural practices were very similar to ours. What was different however was that from childhood they were taught to be always obedient, addressing the young and the old from the upper castes as *ayya banchan*. While they were *jeetas* (at the age of five) they were supposed to tend to the cattle and the buffaloes and guard the crops. Their childhood was much tougher than ours. They knew how to skin dead cattle, convert the skin into soft and smooth leather, and transform the leather into farm instruments and shoes. Their skill in playing the *dappu* (a special percussion instrument) was far beyond that of any one of us. Madiga boys and girls are taught, right from childhood, and as a matter of daily survival, to be humble in the presence of the landlord, Brahmin and Koomati. The same is true of the Chakali children and Mangali children. At home they live as equals, eating, drinking and smoking together. They are equals from childhood onwards. But the parents tell the children that 'you must shiver and shake before the upper caste master'. This is not because the Madiga parents, Chakali parents and Mangali parents have great respect or real love for the upper caste landlord, the Brahmin, or the Baniya, but because there is always the fear of losing one's job. They will say 'my son, be careful with that bastard, pretend to be very obedient otherwise that rascal will hit us on our stomachs'. The child pretends to be obedient as Gandhi pretended to be poor. But a pretence that starts at an early age becomes a lifelong behavioural trait. Fear of the upper caste *dora* is gradually internalized. Every Dalitbahujan family that teaches children about equality at home also teaches them about hierarchial life in society for the simple reason that otherwise terrible atrocities may follow. Apart from the fact that they are untouchables and live in appalling economic conditions, the Madigas are absolutely like the Kurumas, the Goudas and others. There is less religiosity among them than in any other caste. If the Kuruma, Goudas, Kapus, and Shalas have seven or eight goddesses and gods, the Madigas have one or two. They play the *dappu* for every occasion, but as a community they celebrate only the festival of Ellamma who is their *kuladevata* (caste goddess). For them even hell and heaven do not exist. A day spent starving is hell and a day's food a heavenly luxury.

Among all these castes what was unknown was reading books, going to temples, chanting prayers, or performing *sandhya-vandanam*. The Hindu religion and its Brahmin wisdom prohibited letters to all of us. Till modern education and Ambedkar's theory of reservation created a small educated section among these castes, learning the alphabet was a literally prohibited act. In addition, even the idol or *murti*-based *pujari*-centred temple was out of bounds for the Dalitbahujan. Today, some of them are allowed into temples but they can never relate to Brahminical gods.

OF SCHOOLING

As the first generation to see the slate and grasp the pencil, we jumped straight out of the 'jungle' into the schools. Even so, what was there in common between the Hindus and us? The Brahmin–Baniya children were the privileged ones. They were better dressed and better fed. We entered school with different cultures. Our eating habits are not the same. For all Dalitbahujan good food means meat and fish. We enjoy it, we relish it. For Brahmin–Baniya boys and girls even a discussion about meat and fish makes them feel like throwing up. For Madigas and Muslims beef is an item to be relished; for us it was prohibited but we never hated it as the Brahmin–Baniyas did. Our schoolteachers' attitude to each of us depended on his own caste background. If he was a Brahmin he hated us and told us to our faces that it was because the days were bad—because of *kaliyuga*—that he was being forced to teach Sudras like us. In his view we were good for nothing. Working in the field, in his view, was a dirty and unaesthetic occupation. Only mad people would work in dirty mud. Today we realize it was good that we were 'muddy'. We realize that mud is the birthplace of food and of working people's ideas. Who were the great ones according to them? The children who came from Brahmin, Baniya and of course from the upper-caste landed families. They did not do dirty farm work, their faces were cleanly washed, their clothes were cleaner, their hair carefully oiled and combed. They came to school wearing *chappals*, whereas those who feed cattle and those who make *chappals* from the skin of the cattle do not have *chappals* to wear. These were the reasons why we were ignorant, ugly, and unclean. It is not merely the teacher, even upper-caste schoolchildren think about Dalitbahujan children that way.

The textbooks taught us stories that we had never heard in our families. The story of Rama, poems from the Puranas, the names of two epics called *Ramayana* and *Mahabharata* occurred repeatedly. From the third class right up to the B.A. our Telugu textbooks were packed with these Hindu stories. For Brahmin–Baniya students these stories were stories from their childhood, very familiar not only in the story form but also in the form of the gods they worshipped. Whenever they went to temples with their parents they saw the images of these *devatas*. The boys bore the names of these gods; the girls the names of the goddesses. I distinctly remember how alien all these names appeared to me. Many of the names were not known in my village. The name of Kalidasa was as alien to us as that of Shakespeare. The only difference was that one appeared in Telugu textbooks while the other appeared in English ones. The language of textbooks was not the one that our communities spoke. Even the basic words were different. Textbook Telugu was Brahmin Telugu, whereas we were used to a production-based communicative Telugu.

To date I have not come across a Telugu textbook which is written in this production-based, communicative language. I have not encountered a lesson on Pochamma, Potaraju, Kattamisamma, Katamaraju, or Beerappa, the goddesses and gods whose names were familiar to us from childhood. This is not because these Gods and Goddesses do not have narratives associated with them. The simple reason is that no writer—and the majority of writers happen to be Brahmins—thought that these stories could be written down and form part of the lessons in school and college textbooks. No mainstream Telugu poet ever thought that going to people's culture meant talking about Dalitbahujan goddesses and gods. Even the poets and writers who were born Hindu, but later became communists, atheists, or rationalists, never adopted the culture of our daily lives. Actually, even the names of those revolutionary leaders sounded alien to us. For them Yellaiah, Pullaiah, Buchaiah, Buchamma, Lachamma were names of the 'Other'. Their culture was basically sanskritized; we were not part of that culture. They never realized that our language is also a language, that it was understood by every individual in our communities. And remember, these communities were not small in number; they were made up of lakhs and crores whereas the Hindu upper castes were few in number. If our parents had been conscious about the conspiracy, about this silent violence, they would have simply inhaled all the Hindus as *nasham* (as they normally inhale tobacco powder).

For a person—female or male—to become a complete human being, childhood formations are important. But our childhoods were mutilated by recurrent abuse and by a stunning silence. There was the conspiracy to suppress the formation of our consciousness. For hundreds of generations the violent stoppage of the entry of the alphabet into our homes nipped in the bud any possibility of self-consciousness. Even after schools were opened to us because of Independence or swaraj, a word which even today I fail to understand, the schoolteacher was against us, textbook language was against us. Our homes have one culture and the schools another.

What difference did it make to us whether we had an English textbook that talked about Milton's *Paradise Lost* or *Paradise Regained*, or Shakespeare's *Othello* or *Macbeth*, or Wordsworth's poetry about English nature, or a Telugu textbook that talks about Kalidasa's *Meghasandesham*, Bommera Potanna's *Bhagavatam*, or Nannaya and Tikkana's *Mahabharatam*, except the fact that one textbook is written using twenty-six characters and the other fifty-six? We do not share the contents of either; we do not find our lives reflected in their narratives. We cannot locate in them our family settings. Without constant recourse to a dictionary neither makes any sense to us.

Right from school 'their' children talked about 'their' initiation into the Hindu religion through the *upanayana*. From the day after the *upanayana* a white thread hangs around their body. When we first heard about that *upanayana* we too desired to have such a thread on our bodies. It is a different thing that many of us would have later thrown that thread out into muddy waters, as Basava did at the early age of twelve. But the fact is that at the age of seven or eight, to have an occasion when one is the focal point of the household and a priest comes to initiate us into religion would have given us confidence. Besides, when we learnt that in Brahmin,

Baniya, and other upper-caste families, initiation into writing takes place at the age of four and that it is also a festive occasion we greatly resented it. We have not yet acquired the consciousness to condemn the complete domination of Telugu-medium schools by the Hindu scriptures. Having had no alternative, we send our children to schools that teach only the *puranas*, or the Epics. This is a paradox and we live in many such paradoxes.

When we were told that the Hindu girls and boys were married even while they were children we recognized these practices as familiar since child marriage was also part of our lives. But when we read in the textbooks that the girls whose husbands died must remain widows and have their heads shaved; that they were to be clad only in white, we found it strange. In our families, girls whose in-laws did not look after them well got divorced very easily and soon second husbands were found for them. While marriages take place at home and are celebrated with one type of meal and drink, divorces also take place with meal and drink. Seeking divorce from an irresponsible husband is as much a sanctioned social act as getting married. In my childhood, when I read about Savitri struggling against the death of her husband simply because in the event she would become a widow, I was very happy that our women do not have to struggle like her.

Similarly, when we read that Hindu women were expected to die along with their dead husbands I was extremely happy that our women did not have to die like that. I was so glad that if suddenly my father died my mother did not have to follow suit. If she so desired she could get me a stepfather. What about history textbooks and Telugu textbooks that recounted innumerable stories about women who committed sati, without a single lesson about our women who still lived after their husband's death, who worked, brought up their children, and got them married. There was not a single lesson about women who found it difficult to get a divorce and had to struggle hard to obtain it. The textbook morality was different from our living morality.

HINDU IDEALS AND OUR IDEALS

In Brahmin *wada*s and families, narratives about heroes and heroines do not exist within a human context. This is because Brahmin life is alienated from the kind of socio–economic environment in which a real hero or a heroine can be constructed. Their social settings are the reading of *sloka*s or *mantra*s with proficiency. The greatest achievement is learning the whole of the *Ramayana* or *Mahabharata* or *Bhagvad Gita* by heart. Womanhood is discussed in terms of devotion to the husband and divine cooking. Indeed, Brahminical culture eulogizes negative heroes and negative heroines. For example, Krishna who encourages one to kill one's own relatives is a hero. Arjuna who killed his relatives is a hero. In these narratives, acquiring private property (the whole of the *Mahabharata* is constructed around land becoming the private property of minorities who are not involved in production) is idealized. But in Dalitbahujan *wadas* it is just the opposite. There are a number of real-life situations from which ideal heroes and heroines emerge. Their daily working interaction with nature provides the scope for their formation. One who kills relatives, for whatever reason, and one who commits crimes, for whatever reason, is a murderer or a crook. One who encourages killing is not a God but a devil worthy of condemnation. A Pochamma did not become our heroine because she killed somebody, a Kattamisamma did not become our heroine because she killed somebody; a Beerappa did not become our hero because he killed somebody. They became our heroines and heroes because they saved us from diseases or from hunger.

Hindu morality is just the opposite of our living morality. Take another example. An ideal woman in a Hindu text is one who does not eat and drink in the presence of elder women and men of all ages. A woman is not supposed to smoke and drink even if the man is a chain-smoker and the worst drunkard. But in our homes no one talks badly about a woman who smokes or has a drink. All our women drink toddy or liquor along with our men. Our women smoke *chuttas* at home and in the fields. They try to be at least notionally equal to men in all respects. Those who say that all of us are Hindus must tell us what Hindu morality is? Which values do they want to uphold as the right values? The upper-caste Hindu, unequal and inhuman cultural values or our cultural values? What is society's ideal today? What shall we teach the children of today? Shall we teach them what has been taught by the Hindus or what the Dalitbahujan masses of this country want to learn? Who makes an ideal teacher? Who becomes a good hero? One who produces a variety of crops, one who faces lions and tigers, or one who kills relatives and friends simply because what you think is dharma and what others think is *adharma*? Where do we begin and where do we end? We must begin by creating our history and we must end by changing this very social fabric.

The Brahmin–Baniyas think that their non-productive ritualistic life is wonderful and the Dalitbahujan non-ritualistic working life is mean. All this was proclaimed so consistently that it seemed true. Since our parents had been denied education, which alone could have enabled them to assess their own position realistically, whatever social status the Brahmin, parading as an *ayyagaaru* (priest), assigned to our parents they passed on to us. Right from childhood, in spite of our very considerable skills, we remained diffident. Once Brahminism had unnerved human beings who were so much mightier and powerful, the diffidence was passed on from generation to generation. All of us—the whole Dalitbahujan population— were made to see things upside down.

Brahmin–Baniya temples were not only far from us, but the Gods sitting, sleeping in those temples were basically set against us. Brahmin– Baniya houses were within our villages, but the very same houses built up a culture inimical to ours. The Brahmin–Baniyas walked in our village over the corpses of our culture. They were the gluttons while our parents were the poor starving people producing all that was necessary for the other people's comfort. Their children were the most unskilled gluttons, whereas our children were the real contributors to the national economy. Their notion of life was unworthy of life itself but they repeatedly told our parents that we were the most useless people. Having passed through all the stages of life, having acquired the education that enabled us to see a wider world, nothing but anger and anguish burn in our hearts when we reflect back on our childhood and its processes.

THE EVERYDAY ROUTINE

A Dalitbahujan couple rises every morning at *koodikuta* (cock crow). The man engages straightaway with his agrarian tasks, the woman with her household activities. Brahminical baths and prayers have no place in their life at that stage. The man has to feed his cattle and clean the cattle-shed. A Kuruma man hardly ever sleeps at home. Wherever the herd of sheep sleeps, that is his living place. Early in the morning he gets up, separates his sheep from the common herd. He then releases the younger ones from the *podi* (an enclosure where the young sheep are kept) and takes them to their mother to be suckled. The diseased cattle or sheep have then to be examined and medicines applied. A Gouda wakes up and straightaway puts on his toddy-climbing clothes and goes to the rows of toddy trees. He knows his toddy trees by name, as the shepherd knows his sheep or goats, and as the peasants know their cows, bulls and buffaloes. The Gouda climbs his first tree at sunrise. It is he who gets to see the beauty of nature at sunrise from the vantage of the tallest tree. Poised at the top, he skilfully chooses the point at which to make the first cut to his *gela* (a projection on the toddy tree from which the toddy is tapped). It is time now to take toddy that has accumulated in the *kallumuntha*; to check that the toddy drips from the *gela* without impediment.

The Malas or Madigas rise from their beds and begin either to clean and cure skins or prepare the leather for shoemaking. In the majority of cases, they then go to their master's fields to cut the crop or bundle it up or perform other sundry tasks. What these families must do every morning is not decided by them but by their masters. The women of these families get up and go to clean the master's cattle-sheds or to sweep the surroundings of the master's houses—but not, of course the inside of the house. They rush back home only to find empty cooking pots waiting to be washed, hungry children waiting for some food. They have no time to think about God, prayer, etc. The woman cooks some *ambali* (a sort of porridge), the food of the poor where even that one curry, as it is made in Kuruma house or Gouda house, does not exist. She must rush because she has to reach the working point in the fields much before dawn breaks. All Dalitbahujan men and women must do this. Their work never starts with a morning prayer or a cold water bath. The *sandhya vandanam* (morning prayer) of the Hindu finds no place in their day's timetable.

EATING TO LIVE; LIVING TO EAT

A Dalitbahujan woman gets up from her bed and picks up her water pot, fetches water for cooking, sweeps the house and *wakili* (the open place in front of the house), cleans the cattle-shed (if there is one), lights the hearth, pours out the *kuradu* water, and puts on the cooking pot. She then struggles hard to light the hearth that cooks the day's food. Unlike the Hindu woman she does not think about God before entering the kitchen, and does not think about maintaining the purity of *madi*. All this is a precondition for a Hindu woman making the *palaharam* (morning breakfast). For a Dalitbahujan woman cooking is a mundane activity, meant to feed the human body and keep it going, whereas for a Hindu, God is central even to the kitchen. A Dalitbahujan woman cooks some rice or *jowar* and one curry. If there is some buttermilk to add to it that day, it goes down well. A Hindu woman's cooking takes place primarily in the name of God. There is *palaharam, payasam,* a dozen curries, *daddoojanam, pulihoora, saambar, rasam* with *perugannam* (curd rice) to make up the eating process. All these are prepared with care and caution as food that is offered to God. But where does the concept of *prasadam* exist in our homes? The number of items of that godly food can be seen in any modern 'Brahmin' hotel that serves a *taalibhojanam* (plate meal). It is the God's duty to digest all these and also look after the health of the eaters. God must save them from overeating and from the diseases caused by their fatty diet. It is for this reason that all cooking and eating activity begins with prayer. The relationship between God and priest here becomes the friendly relationship between God and glutton. The case with Dalitbahujan castes couldn't be more different.

The moment the cooking activity of a Dalitbahujan woman is over, she feeds the children, swallows some food herself to satisfy her craving hunger, packs some food for her husband, and leaves for the field. The furrowing of land, its seeding and watering are all tasks collectively undertaken by both woman and man. It is not that the patriarchal 'strong' and 'weak' relations do not operate even in the field in these castes. They do, but they operate at a mundane level. Power relations between men and women are not 'sacred' and are, therefore, less manipulative amongst these communities. The divine stories do not structure them into an ideology that works on the human plane as male control over the female. To that extent this is a less complicated and less oppressive relationship than the relationship between man and woman amongst Hindus.

FEMALE AND MALE DOMAINS

In Kuruma, Golla, Gouda, Mala, Madiga and other castes the man does the work that is defined as 'male' work and the woman does the work that is defined as 'female' work. For example, in Kuruma families tending sheep, herding them, cutting the wool, milking the animals, are all male tasks. The women make the thread out of wool and attend to many other tasks that convert wool into blankets. By the time the crop comes into their hands, by the time the sheep deliver, by the time toddy is brought down, by the time the shoes are ready in these communities, both man and woman can claim to have contributed to its making—and for the making of the very professions. A peasant woman can at times move out of her traditional role of seeding and weeding to plough the land: a Kuruma woman can become a sheep-breeder in the absence of the man. However, a Brahmin woman can never become a priest. A Dalitbahujan woman within her caste–class existence is very much a political being, a social being, and an economic being. A Brahmin woman is not. The lower castes have a philosophy in performing their productive work which is distinctly different from the Hindus' philosophy. It is not a divine philosophy, but a mundane, human philosophy. It does not belong to the 'other world' and 'other life' but deals with this world. That whole philosophy is expressed in a single phrase that can be understood not only by these communities but also by Brahmins and Baniyas. The latter however do not want to take it seriously. Indeed do not want to even hear it. That simple phrase is *rekkaditegani bukkadadu* (unless the hand works the mouth cannot eat). This philosophical utterance is not speaking in terms of the hand that holds the bow and arrow as Rama did, or the hand that holds the *chakram* as Vishnu and Krishna did. It speaks about the hand that holds the plough to furrow the land and the hand that holds the seeds to seed those furrows and the hand that ensures that the plants grow out of those furrows and the hand that nurses them till they yield the crop.

Do these masses know that the Hindu text, the *Bhagavad Gita*, expounds a philosophy that is its very opposite? Do they know that that text also sets out its philosophy in a single poetic stanza? What is that philosophical stanza? 'You have the right to work but not to its fruits.' I myself would not have understood the meaning of this stanza if some foreigner had not translated that Hindu text into English. It is our people's misfortune that the priest who extracted *dakshina* from them on every occasion he visited them, never told them that this sentence establishes an ideology that advocates that our masses must work, but should not aspire to enjoy the fruits of that work. Where should those fruits go? The Hindu system established a network of institutions to siphon off the fruits of people's work into Hindu families who treat the work as mean and dirty.

CASTE AND POWER

The traditional Hindu understanding is that political power is to be held only by Kshatriyas, and that Brahmins are to assist them in ministerial positions. But this is an inadequate understanding. Power relations cannot be discussed merely in terms of institutions that relate to State. The Dalitbahujan life is intrinsically enmeshed in a certain framework of power relations. First and foremost, the caste system itself represents a certain framework of power relations. The Malas and Madigas, right from childhood, are brought up to obey and listen rather than to command and speak. The lower the caste of the person the higher will be the level of obedience, and the higher the caste the stronger the motivation to tell and command. Take for example the Kuruma, a middle-rung caste. Kurumas can command Malas, Madigas, Chakalies, Mangalies. Irrespective of their ages, people from the higher castes can address 'Dalitbahujan' castes demeaningly (a male person is addressed as *aré* and a female person is addressed as *yende, yevvative*, etc.) This itself establishes a certain power relation. The Kurumas have to behave differently in the presence of persons belonging to higher castes. Castes higher than the Kurumas, beginning with the Kapus, think that they have a right to humiliate and insult Dalitbahujan caste men and women. In all South Indian villages (this may be true of North India too), the Kshatriya caste that controlled the institution of state power has became dormant and a neo-Kshatriya force from the Sudra upper castes has begun to emerge. In Andhra Pradesh, for example, the Reddys, Velamas, and Kammas are increasingly beginning not only to believe that they form a part of the Hindu religion but also that they are castes imbued with the right to insult others. In spiritual terms they are not *dwijas*, or twice-born, but today in political terms they are attempting to play the role of the classical Kshatriyas by establishing their hegemony in all structures of power.

The neo-Kshatriyas believe that they are part of Hindu spirituality, and are becoming patrons of Hindutva. Hinduism believes in the theory of co-option and exclusion. The Brahmin–Baniyas are gradually co-opting the neo-Kshatriyas and excluding the castes below them. The surest way of structuring power relations and maintaining hegemony is by acquiring control of cultivable land and by systematically excluding the 'other' from controlling the land and land-related means of production. The neo-Kshatriyas have an added advantage in this as they are not yet entirely alienated from the agrarian production process and hence are culturally, and in terms of know-how, rooted in agrarian arts and agrarian science. There are some poor and semi-poor families who in caste terms belong to neo-Kshatriya groups such as the Reddys, yet their class position brings them into day-to-day contact with Dalitbahujan castes. These families function as connecting links between the Brahmin–Baniya nexus and the Dalitbahujan, maintaining the political hegemony of neo-Kshatriyas on a regular basis. Brahminism should have weakened substantially as a result of the spreading of modernity into the villages but for the emergence of the neo-Kshatriya cultural forms. The neo-Kshatriyas have become the saviours of Brahminism, reluctant to own up to the culture of Pochamma and Maisamma in which they are actually rooted; at the same time they are rebuffed by Brahminism which does not wish to extend to them the status of the *dwija* castes. Despite this, they continue to identify themselves aggressively with Brahminism. The Hindutva that this Brahminism has spawned is targeted at subverting those very social relations that imbue the Dalitbahujan Samaj and the existing socio-political system with its distinctive democratic character.

Indeed, the neo-Kshatriya castes are attempting to acquire for themselves a new cultural status. Their male children are brought up in an artificial heritage of martial culture. We find this in their names to which suffixes like Reddy, Rao, Patil, Patel, Singh, are increasingly added. In keeping with this, their women are being pushed into practising neo-*madi* cultural forms. A neo-Kshatriya wife addresses her husband in the plural, and in turn the husband addresses the wife not only in the singular but in demeaning forms (*yende, yeme*, etc). Distancing themselves from actual work in the fields and manipulating Dalitbahujan caste labour into doing all the hard work are some of the new arts being taught to their men and women. Like the Brahmin–Baniya, they seek to teach their female children to be docile and submissive sexual objects, trained to cook multi-itemed vegetarian and non-vegetarian meals. The notion of the sacred is beginning to enter into their cooking and eating habits. Particularly among women, a daily *pooja* is becoming part of their consciousness. Their ambition is not to Dalitize or democratize human relations, but to Brahminize them. This section of society understands the link between land and political power, and thus right from childhood neo-Kshatriya children are taught to acquire both, whatever the means. In this sense, Brahminical Kautilya-ism is a handy instrument. Their domination is evident in every aspect of day-to-day life, even in civil society, and politics and power an intrinsic and visible part of it. Yet because of their roots in agriculture, and their ambiguous, non-*dwija* spiritual status, their political moorings hover between democracy and dictatorship.

DALIT PATRIARCHAL DEMOCRACY

Among the Dalitbahujan castes, political relations within the family or community setting are basically democratic. In terms of the parent–children relationship politics operates in what might be termed 'patriarchal democracy'. The Dalitbahujan household is not essentially 'private'. Indeed the notion of private does not exist in Dalitbahujan consciousness. Among these castes, the home is essentially a social unit. This is an accepted norm. Wife-beating is a patriarchal practice that exists among all the Dalitbahujan castes. But the battered wife has a right to make the attack public by shouting, abusing the husband and, if possible, by beating the husband in return. Both the women and the men in the community have the right to interfere, arbitrate, and take the quarrel to the caste *panchayats*.

The caste *panchayat* pertaining to man–woman problems, inter- family disputes or intra-family disputes takes place in the open. Everyone present there has a right to be involved in arriving at a judgement. Dalitbahujan caste law does not stem from authority but out of the community. Its very openness act as a check against injustice. Since the notion of 'private' does not exist, every cause and consequence is debated. This does not mean that violence never occurs, but when there is brutality the positive dimensions of Dalitbahujan law prevails and the space for public outrage acts as a constant check.

One of the important mechanisms of this public outrage is found in the congress of women's deliberations popularly known as 'Ammalakkala Muchchatlu' (the deliberations of the mothers and sisters). These deliberations are open, political and juridical in nature, and adopt consensual methods for resolving problems. They take place in a variety of locations and at various times, in the mornings and evenings, within the village as well as in the fields, and have an inter-caste dimension. A careful observation of the Dalitbahujan caste *panchayat* juridical system and the Ammalakkala Muchchatlu indicates that the law of the Dalitbahujan castes does not distinguish between the public and private. Perhaps this is rooted in the very nature of Dalitbahujan caste existence which makes the notion of 'private' impossible, indeed unthinkable. The notion 'personal' also does not exist. Every 'personal' relationship among the Dalitbahujan castes is both social and political. Here, human bonds are structured in terms of 'we' not 'I'. Even if the concept 'I' exists, it does not have the same meaning among the Dalitbahujan castes as it has among the upper castes. For the Dalitbahujan, individualism is an expression of negative 'will'. There is nothing like 'mine'. Everything is 'ours'. Most Dalitbahujan are constantly struggling between the notion of 'private property' and 'communal property'. The higher up the caste hierarchy an individual rises, the greater the notion of private property becomes. For instance, the notion of private property is minimal among Madigas and Malas. Whatever the Dalitbahujan procure— whether a dead cow or bull—or when they slaughter a live sheep or goat, they divide it equally between themselves. In thousands of Dalitbahujan *wadas*, particularly scheduled caste *wadas*, equal distribution takes place in the form of *pogulu* or *kuppalu* or *pallu* (if it is mutton or beef, dividing it into as many equal shares as the number of families; or if it is grain, again equal shares). Those who work harder, say fetching the cattle or sheep, do not get more; the shares remain equal. In the post-colonial period the Government has been assisting these castes to some degree in order to enable them to acquire 'assets' (in a very limited way of course), but even these private 'assets' are within a very short span of time converted into public assets. The state agencies, and also the Indian upper castes, have been criticizing the culture of dispossession among the scheduled castes as 'spendthrift.' An incessant discourse among the upper castes, often expounded in abusive terms, is that these 'Dalitbahujan caste bastards' should not be given anything as they do not know how to retain or invest it. Such upper caste criticism is absolutely uncalled for. This culture is a remarkable legacy that India has, of a community that has lived for thousands of years with no notion of 'private property' and one that will quickly dispossess itself of it even if given to them in charity or the notion of welfare. The very concept of private property goes against its philosophy. It is not a weakness of a people but their strength, and it is here that the future of India lies.

DALITBAHUJAN GODDESSES AND GODS

What further separate the Hindu from us is the nature of his consciousness of the other world, the divine and the spiritual. For children from our castes, *Jeja* (the concept of God) is introduced in the form of the moon. As children grow up, they also get acquainted with Pochamma, Polimeramma, Kattamaisamma, Katamaraju, Potaraju, and other deities. Among the Dalitbahujan, there is no concept of a temple in a fixed place or form. Goddesses and gods take all forms and shapes, in a variety of places. Every Dalitbahujan caste child learns at an early age about these goddesses and gods. The children are part of the caste congregations during festivals such as Bonaalu, Chinna Panduga, Pedda Panduga, etc. Every Dalitbahujan caste child learns at an early age that smallpox comes because Pochamma is angry. The rains are late because Polimeramma is angry. The village tank gets filled or does not fill depending on the sympathies of Kattamaisamma. Crops are stolen by thieves as a result of Potaraju's anger. For Kurumas, prospering of sheep and the goats depends upon the attitude of Beerappa, a specific caste God. Thus there are common village Dalitbahujan gods and goddesses and caste-specific gods and goddesses. Of course, for us the spirit exists, as does the soul (*atma*), dead people return to relive in our own surroundings in the form of ghosts if they have not been fed well during the lifetimes. But there is no *swarga* (heaven) and there is no *naraka* (hell). All the dead live together somewhere in the skies.

This consciousness has not yet taken the form of an organized religion. The Dalitbahujan caste spirit is in essence a non-Hindu spirit because the Hindu patriarchal gods do not exist among us at all. We knew nothing of Brahma, Vishnu, or Eswara until we entered school. When we first heard about these figures they were as strange to us as Allah or Jehovah or Jesus were. Even the name of the Buddha, about whom we learnt later, as a mobilizer of Dalitbahujan castes against Brahminical ritualism, was unknown to us.

To appreciate the contrast between Dalitbahujan culture and Hindu Brahminical culture we should examine the goddess/god images that are popular among the village Dalitbahujan. It is significant that more goddesses than gods feature in Dalitbahujan narratives.

Pochamma is the most popular of Dalitbahujan goddesses in Andhra Pradesh (I am sure a Dalitbahujan goddess with similar characteristics exists all over India). Near every village, there is a small Pochamma temple. The notion of temple itself is very different in the case of this goddess. The temple is a place where the deity exists, but not in order that regular *poojas* be conducted for her. Pochamma is not made the object of a daily *pooja* by the priest. Once a year the masses (and this includes all castes except Brahmins and Banias) go to the temple with *bonalu* (pots in which sweet rice is cooked), wash the small stone that represents the deity, and clean the temple and its surroundings. The people can approach the goddess without the mediation of a priest. They talk to the goddess as they talk to one of themselves: 'Mother,' they say, 'we have seeded the fields, now you must ensure that the crop grows well; one of our children is sick it is your bounden duty to cure her. . . ' If one listens to these prayers, it becomes clear that they are a very human affair—nothing extraordinary about them. The people put small quantities of the *bonam* food on a leaf in front of the deity. Finally, the chicken or sheep they have brought there is sacrificed. The *dappulu* (percussion instrument) is beaten as the young dance and make merry.

What is their notion of Pochamma? She is the person who protects people from all kinds of diseases; who cures diseases. Unlike Sita, her gender role is not specified. Nobody knows about Pochamma's husband. Nobody considers her inferior or useless because she does not have a husband. The contrast between Saraswathi and Lakshmi on the one hand, and Pochamma on the other, is striking. Pochamma is independent. She does not pretend to serve any man. Her relationship to human beings is gender-neutral, caste-neutral and class-neutral. She is supposed to take care of every one in the village.

Before going to Pochamma everyone bathes, and puts on clean clothes. Those who can afford it, wear new clothes. While approaching Pochamma, one does not have to wear a *pattu vastram* (silk clothes), nor does one have to fast the whole day as one would be required to do when approaching the Hindu gods and goddesses. Pochamma does not specify what should be offered to her. That depends on the economic circumstances of the family. The rich take a sari and blouse piece with the *bonalu* and then take them back to their respective homes. Those who cannot afford such offerings can go to the temple empty handed. Pochamma's temple is not centralized like the Rama, Krishna, and Venkateshwara temples are. She is available in every village and people do not have to travel long distances to visit her. All these things have implications for peoples' social and economic lives, their time, and their psychological satisfaction. In other words, the spirituality that emerges around Pochamma does not divide people; it does not create conditions of conflict; it does not make one person a friend and another an enemy.

Pochamma is not a goddess who believes in communal conflicts among people. Religious distinctions have no meaning for her. If a pig passes by a Pochamma temple when the people are around it nobody objects; no animal, including pigs, is inauspicious in Dalitbahujan culture. There is not a single instance of communal riots being initiated from Pochamma temples. Such riots have been initiated from Rama temples, Krishna temples, Narasimha temples, just as riots have been initiated from mosques.

Is Pochamma literate or illiterate? Nobody knows, but the fact remains that she is not spoken of at all in relation to education. As the village masses—particularly women—are illiterate, they never relate to her or think of her in connection with education. The demands of the masses basically relate to production, procreation and sickness. In that sense she is, more than anything else, a materialist goddess.

A goddess whose popularity is second only to Pochamma, is Katta Maisamma. Katta Maisamma is a goddess of water, whose deity (a small stone) is kept on the bund of the village tank. She too does not require a big temple. The understanding of the people is that Katta Maisamma is responsible for ensuring that the tank is filled. She regulates the water resources. The Dalitbahujan believe that right from the seeding stage to the cutting stage, Katta Maisamma protects the crop. The paddy-fields below the tanks flourish because of her blessings. Today, that kind of belief is being slowly eroded. They now think that the quality of the crop depends on fertilizers and pesticides, and consequently even the average illiterate peasant uses fertilizers. In that sense, the Dalitbahujan mind is a scientific mind that can easily imbibe emerging technology and science. But in spite of this, Katta Maisamma continues to play an important role in their consciousness, and a whole range of rituals take place around her.

What is the social origin of Katta Maisamma? A primary investigation indicates that she is a Dalitbahujan woman who discovered the technology of tank construction. She must have wandered around and studied patterns of land and water very carefully. Perhaps she is the one who found out where to locate a tank, what kind of a bund to construct, and how much water to store. Naturally the discovery of such a system would have boosted agricultural production.

Yet another important goddess that the Dalitbahujan castes created and popularized among themselves is Polimeramma (the border Goddess). Polimeramma is supposed to guard the village from all external evils and to stop them at the boundary of the village. The duty that people assign to her is the protection of the entire village, irrespective of caste or class. Once in five or ten years, a buffalo is killed at the Polimeramma temple and the blood is mixed with a huge quantity of cooked rice, and the meat eaten by those who do—primarily Malas, Madigas, and Muslims. Muslims are in no way excluded from the ritual. The bloody mixture of rice is thrown on to all the roof-tops as *bali* (sacrifice). All the agrarian families, including Muslims who are part of the Dalitbahujan society of the village, demand such *bali*, but the Brahmins and Baniyas hold themselves aloof. Muslim men and women plant, weed and harvest alongside Dalitbahujan men and women, and share the food that the Dalitbahujans take to the fields and the agrarian skills they possess. The *peerala* festival (Moharram) is as much a Dalitbahujan festival as a Muslim one. The Dalitbahujans lead the *peeri* processions. They too hold the *peeri* on their body. On festive occasions the *biryani* that Muslims cook is sent to Dalitbahujan homes. In a situation of such close relationships between the Dalitbahujan and Muslims, all the agrarian festivals of Dalitbahujan are also Muslim festivals. The popular notion of *barkati* in Telangana villages is an adaptation of the Urdu word *barkat*.

After the *bali* is sprinkled on the houses, entry from the other villages into that village is closed for one week. The idea is that the diseases and evils from other villages should not enter. Similarly, for a week, the people belonging to that particular village cannot go to other villages, as such a journey would adversely affect the village's prosperity. During that period, there are debates about prosperity, about good and evil, all centred around production, procreation, and diseases.

There are several other village-specific, area-specific, caste-specific goddesses. Yellamma, Mankalamma, Maremma, Uppalamma, Sammakka, and Sarakka are some of them. None of these goddesses is said to represent delicate femininity. They are not shown sitting on lotus flowers, nor shown travelling on peacocks, or on *hamsas* or other birds. Not a single goddess is shown as a woman pressing the feet of her husband as Lakshmi and Saraswati do. Even Dalitbahujan men respect these goddesses. They are powerful and independent women. The Bengali Kali is depicted as a person killing a male. But the Dalitbahujan goddesses of South India do not represent that kind of violence. They are known as wise women who have discovered something for the well-being of the village; they are people who have saved the village from danger, or who constantly keep a watch over the village crops and wealth.

There are goddesses who were involved in wars to protect the entire area. Good examples are Sammakka and Sarakka, two tribal goddesses very popular in the Telangana districts. The story of these goddesses indicates that these militant tribal women opposed the Kakatiya kings' invasion of the Mulugu tribal belt during the twelfth and thirteenth centuries. Sammakka organized the tribal masses to defend themselves. The mighty Kakatiya army defeated these tribal armies; Sammakka, Sarakka, and Sammakka's brother Jampanna were killed near Jampannavagu (near Mulugu, Warangal district). From that point on, Sammakka and Sarakka became the martyr heroines of the tribes.

Though Sammakka and Sarakka emerged as goddesses from battlefield, unlike the Hindu gods, they are martyrs not victors and subduers. It is common for martyrs to be transformed into divine spirits. No Hindu god or goddess has martyred himself or herself in defence of the masses. All of them are ultimate winners, like the heroes in Hindi and other regional language films. In the Dalitbahujan tradition, in no story is violence privileged the way it is in Hindu narratives.

This is true also of the Dalitbahujan gods. Take for instance a common village god called Potaraju, who is very popular among the agrarian castes. Every peasant family keeps a stone painted white and daubed with turmeric in the field. This deity has no connection with a temple. It hardly occupies one square foot of land while the temples of the Hindu gods occupy several acres of useful agrarian and housing land. There are very few rituals that are associated with him. The people believe that Potaraju protects the fields from thieves and marauding animals. It is in the security of this belief that no peasant keeps a watch over the crop. This belief works among everyone, so nobody steals the crop since it will invoke the wrath of Potaraju. When a thief sees the image of Potaraju in the field he hesitates to touch anything there. What Potaraju expects from the people in return is very simple. After the crop is harvested, a chicken is sacrificed at the Potaraju image. The people believe that Potaraju is satisfied with this, and, of course, the chicken curry is relished by the people who do not place even a small quantity before the god.

No village goddess or god expects a *yagna* that involves priests. No *pulihoora*, *prasada*, *daddojanam*, ghee, or *perugannam* (the names of sundry varieties of rice foods) are offered to them. No oil, fat, or sweets are thrown into the fire to satisfy these goddesses or gods. Of late, through the influence of Brahminism, the peasants do break coconuts (which are indeed a symbol of a clean-shaven head with a scalp lock— *pilakajuttu*) to satisfy gods and goddesses. Sometimes the broken coconuts and cut limes are scattered at street corners to rid the village of evil spirits. Apart from this, no Dalitbahujan celebration involves any wastage of food or other produce.

As I have mentioned, there are number of caste-specific gods and goddesses such as Beerappa (a Yadava god), Katamaraju (a Gouda god). The stories of such caste-specific gods tell of the problems that these gods and goddesses encountered in building up that particular caste or profession. The narratives also detail how these gods and goddesses struggled to preserve the cultural tradition of those castes or professions. Take for example Beerappa who has a full-length narrative which is recounted to the people on every festive occasion by expert story-tellers. This story-telling is a ritual that has its own set of musical instruments—*dolu*, *talalu*. The story-tellers dress in the costume that Beerappa himself was said to have worn. The narrative is accompanied by a dance performed in an extremely pleasant rhythm and style. I have not met a single Brahmin or Baniya who knows the details of this famous story, but the story of Beerappa was part of our childhood. Many Kuruma and Golla (Yadava) boys treat Beerappa as their ideal, and many Kuruma and Golla girls regard his sister Akkamankali as the ideal woman.

What do all these Dalitbahujan goddess/god images, roles and narratives signify? The Dalitbahujan goddesses/gods are culturally rooted in production, protection, and procreation. They do not distinguish between one section of society and another, one caste and another. These stories do not entail the creation of an image of the enemies . Rituals are of a simple nature and do not involve waste of economic resources. Despite there being such a strong sense of the sacred, Dalitbahujan society never allowed the emergence of a priestly class/caste alienated from production or alienating the goddesses and gods from the people. There is little or no distance between the gods and goddesses and the people and, indeed, the people hardly depend on these goddesses/gods. To whatever extent they exist, and contact is needed, the route between the deity and people is direct. Barriers like language, *sloka*, or *mantra* are absent.

The Dalitbahujan goddesses/gods tradition is the exact opposite of the Hindu tradition in every respect. It is time that we confronted these differences and understood them. It is important that the scholars from the Dalitbahujan tradition enter into a substantial debate with Brahminical scholars. These Brahminical scholars and leaders who talk about Hindutva being the religion of all castes must realize that the Scheduled Castes, Other Backward Classes, and Scheduled Tribes of this country have nothing ·in common with the Hindus. Even today, no Brahmin adopts the names of our godesses/gods; to this day they do not understand that the Dalitbahujan have a much more humane and egalitarian tradition and culture than that of the Hindu. If Brahmins, Baniyas, Kshatriyas, and neo-Kshatriyas of this country want unity among diversity, they should join us and look to Dalitization not Hinduization.

BRAHMINICAL DEATH

Although it is not in our hands to decide where we should be born, it is certainly in our hands to decide how we should die. In the concept of death, and the experience of death, Dalitbahujan and Hindus differ markedly. In our country there is a Dalitbahujan death and there is Hindu— Brahmin, Baniya, Kshatriya, and neo-Kshatriya—death.

The difference between Hindu Brahminical death and Dalitbahujan death lies in the very concept of death itself. What is the Brahmin notion of life and death? A Brahmin believes that life must be lived for the sake of death which will bring him permanence and eternity. To live this way is to live a life that constantly thinks about death. This life in this universe must ensure a perennial life in the other world, i.e in heaven. The gods that he/she propitiates time and again are to provide two things. One, a happy life here on this earth, which in philosophical terms is a *kshanabhanguram* (a life that survives momentarily). At the same time, however, this short life on this earth must also be made to ensure a permanent life of privilege and pleasure. So, for a Hindu, death is a transition from this *kshanabhanguram* to eternity. But how does one spend this very short life here? In this life, one should eat in the name of that god who guarantees a permanent happy life. One should eat all the best things available on this earth to please the God who bestows the life of permanence. Though this body merely awaits day in and day out the transitory death that will carry it from the *kshanabhanguram* to eternity, it must eat rice, *dal*, milk, vegetables, ghee, fruit, and nuts in various forms. It must eat all this in the form of *daddoojanam, pulihoora, perugannam, pappu kuuralau,* and other curries in several flavours. Some curries should be sour; some should be sweet; ghee plays an important role in the cuisine. The vessel holding ghee has a special place in this impermanent life. All this must be followed by sweets—laddus, jilebis, fruit salad, etc. In the sweets too, ghee occupies the central place. In other words the *kshanabhanguram* body should be as fat as possible, with a rounded belly and unexercised muscles.

In the process of working for this most-needed death, two things are necessary: (i) leisure and, (ii) prayer. Leisure in this context is a divine leisure. It must keep the mind focused on acquiring the permanent life and partaking the pleasures thereof. However, this leisure is also used to develop skills that negate the 'others' (who, of course, are sinners because they produce the goods and commodities that prolong the *kshanabhan-guram* that a Brahmin would like to end as soon as possible). Why should he eat the products produced by the labour power of Sudra lower castes, which will prolong his life on this earth? In his notion he is not eating for his own sake but eating for God who alone can ensure him *moksha*, or release from worldly life. Why should he indulge in sex which only results in another life, like his own, which he himself wants to end? Even this he does for the sake of God's eternity which in turn becomes his own eternity. A son is essential if he is to enter heaven, and this son is a gift of God, who is also eager to take this *punyatma* (one who has done only good by not working at all) back to his kingdom. Why is the Brahmin a *punyatma*? Because he has eaten all that is produced by the Sudras and also treated all of them as untouchable rascals. Thus, for a Brahmin, that is for a Hindu, food and sex are two prerequisites for death. A Brahmin dies only to live long; a Hindu dies only to live long as a Hindu.

The life of leisure when supplied with food and sex, automatically ensures two things. One, it ensures that the *kshanabhanguram* is longer than the unsanctified life of Dalitbahujans because it gets the best of the foods. The emphasis on sex ensures the continuance of this life in his progeny. But this truth is systematically glossed over with the second instrument—prayer. Prayer provides legitimacy for all this drama. Prayer is a weapon in the hands of a Brahmin. It sets him apart from the rest of the masses. It is through this prayer that he establishes his hold over the rest of society. In a fit of madness, which might be a result of their lifelong alienation from work, life itself begins to appear to them to be meaningless. They call this madness the life of penance.

However, when this Brahmin, who does penance throughout his life and produces a son to ensure him a place in heaven, dies, according to the Brahminical notion, it is the day when God's call comes. This death appears very different from the death of a Dalitbahujan or lower Dalitbahujan. A Brahmin's death is adjusted to the movement of stars, *grahas* (planets), etc. Death is not supposed to be mourned. Immediately after the death of a person, the Brahmins around pour into the house. Some begin *poojas*, some begin *prardhanas*, some begin bhajans. The people around are not allowed to weep loudly; they can only sob. After the dead body is lifted, only men follow the funeral procession, women are not permitted to take part in the funeral procession.

From the day of the death of a Brahmin till the twelfth day, instead of mourning feasting takes place. When alive the Brahmin's body is sacred (this is why others may not touch them except when performing *padapooja*). After death that sacred soul begins its voyage to *swarga* and the body becomes untouchable (this notion got extended to Sudras and ati-Sudras too). The priests pray for their fellow priest's soul to be given a permanent seat in the other world. Even the death of a Brahmin is a tax on the already burdened Dalitbahujan. The living Brahmins will have more feasts which in turn will result in their extracting more from the Dalitbahujan masses. To begin with there is a daily *shraaddha*, gradually it becomes a monthly *shraaddha*, and thereafter every year at the death anniversary a *shraaddha* is performed. Even after the death the soul does not merge into the collectivity.

Is there any change in these notions of life and death among modern Brahmins? Not qualitatively. There are perhaps some quantitative changes, but the essence remains the same. Even today, an average urban Brahmin does not think differently from his ancestors. In post-colonial India, the Brahmins have very substantially urbanized themselves. The notion of *swarga* may not dominate their day-to-day life. There might be slight reversals in their notion of this life and the life after death.

Because of fast growing technology, an average Brahmin or Baniya publicly confesses that the life here should be lived with all the luxuries, but this does not mean that he or she reduces the emphasis on the permanent life in *swarga*. To achieve this, the discourse has been changed from dharma to merit. The state and the civil society are moulded to suit 'merit' in modern times just as it was moulded to suit dharma in ancient times.

The largest number of colour TVs are possessed by Brahmin and Baniya families. The largest number of private cars (perhaps about seventy per cent) belong to Brahmins and Baniyas. The largest number of people who travel by air in India are Brahmins and Baniyas. The highest number of people who travel in airconditioned trains and luxury buses are again Brahmin and Baniyas. Today they do all this in the name of service to the 'masses'. They did the same thing in ancient India calling it the service of God, done in the interest of *loka-kalyanam*. Nationalism reformulated Brahmanical philosophy, replacing the divine with the 'masses' as this was essential at a time when adult franchise was on the global agenda. The change from 'God' to 'masses' is a trick of the trade. Expanding the scope of the pleasures to be enjoyed in this world, pleasures increasingly on sale in a capitalist market, is an essential Brahminical desire, and hence the restructuring of Brahminism is paramount. During the post-1947 period, wielding political power became one of the pleasures of life.

This did not however diminish Hindu ambition for the permanency of life in the other world. As the Brahmins and the Baniyas exploit Dalit-bahujan from positions of political and bureaucratic power and industrial and capital markets, there is a growing sense of sin which, in their view, may precipitate early death. There is a danger that after death the sin may continue to haunt them in the other world. This was sought to be overcome by constructing posh temples and establishing puja rooms in their modern houses. Both in the temples and in the puja rooms of posh houses, Brahminical gods—Rama, Krishna, Shiva, Ganapathi, Lakshmi, Parvathi, etc.—are set up in modern shapes. All this is to facilitate exploitation and also to prolong life here and in the other world. Even in modern times death is mourned with feasting and feeding people from their own castes. After death, the third day celebrations, the eleventh day celebrations, monthly celebrations, anniversary celebrations, are all occasions for feasting. Those who have done little except cheat and eat during their lifetime are sought to be made historically important persons. Their biographies are written, their photographs are publicized, and their names appear in the media. Newspaper advertisements have become modern methods of upper caste celebrations of a person's death, and of the perpetuation of the dead man's memory. They have acquired crores to spend in this way. Even after a Hindu dies, living Hindus go on wasting social wealth on him. Obviously they think this social wealth is their (Hindu) wealth.

DALITBAHUJAN DEATH

For Dalitbahujans, life now and life after death have a different meaning from that of Hindus. For the Dalitbahujan, life is a one-time affair. This philosophy is expressed in the proverb, *puttindokasare saccindokasare* (we are born only once and die only once). A dying man/woman in a Dalitbahujan family is a loss in terms of productive work. Each person can potentially develop several productive skills of his or her own, and several instruments are employed that enhance production. A Kuruma man could have discovered new areas of sheep-breeding or developed better ways of cutting wool. A Kuruma woman could have added to the skills of spinning wool. In Dalitbahujan philosophy there is no concept of heaven or *swarga*. In their view, life here must be lived for life's sake. Further, life here is related to work. The more an individual works, the more sacred his or her life becomes. The proverbs, *panee prardhana* (work is worship), *panileeni papi* (one who does not work is a sinner) demonstrates that work alone makes life meaningful. In contrast to Brahminical notions of divine eating, Dalitbahujans consider eating as an intrinsic part of earthly life. Dalitbahujan women illustrate this philosophy, in which eating is considered to be a part of work, through the saying *anni panulu tiirinaayi, okka tinee pani tappa* (all my work is done; the only job left is to eat). The routine processes of cooking and eating have no relationship to God or to the sacred. Among the Dalitbahujan, there is quite considerable debate as to whether human beings eat in order to live or they live in order to eat. The life of the Dalitbahujan starts with work, and not with bed coffee or bed tea. It starts with sweeping, washing, taking the cattle to the field . The question of eating arises much later in the day. A Kuruma's day begins among the sheep or in the kitchen. A Gouda starts his day by reaching the toddy tree first, a Madiga takes his *aare* into his hands and sits at home making shoes They work first and eat later.

The act of eating itself is not elaborate. This philosophy of eating to live is exactly the opposite of Brahminical notions of living to eat. The gods and goddesses the Dalitbahujan worship—Pochamma, Maisamma, Potaraju, etc—do not need obeisance in daily puja; they do not demand divine feasting. All Brahminical festivals revolve round the number of items cooked on that occasion. The sequence of items—mostly food-stuffs—offered to gods is also the sequence of their eating. This is the reason why the Dalitbahujan proverb says *bammanollu bhojana priyulu* (Brahmins are lovers of food), whereas *sudrulu pani priyulu* (Sudras are lovers of work).

A festival for the Dalitbahujans is an inward-looking affair. They kill a lamb, a goat or a hen and give a small amount (*padi*) to the goddess or god once in a while, but prayer for prosperity in life or for heavenly death, does not figure in their relationship with divinity. (Fear is not totally absent, but fear is not given a philosophical justification.) One reason for this could be that the interaction of Dalitbahujans with the land, forests, animals, reptiles, water is aimed at getting something new out of these things. It is a scientific interaction. There is a constant intercourse with the new and the creative. This is the reason why in their day-to-day life the earth is referred to as mother earth, (*talli bhoodevi*), the forest is referred to as mother forest (*adavi talli*), the water is referred as mother Ganga (*Gangamma talli*). None of these forces demand prayer; they are forces with which Dalitbahujans constantly interact. Among the Hindus the land, water, and forest do not represent productive forces. For them these elements are not objects but subjects. Land is a spirit that gives *varam* (gift); it is a subject that produces objects. It is not an object that needs to be tilled and cultivated, but a spirit that has extraordinary, divine powers. The same is also true of water and forest. Even if Hindus signify them with mother images, such signification is different from the Dalitbahujan signification. Even the notion of mother signifies different things to Hindus and Dalitbahujan. For Hindus the notion of mother is symbolized in Lakshmi, Saraswathi, Parvathi, while for Dalitbahujans mother signifies Pochamma, Polimeramma, Katta Maisamma, and others who in turn symbolize natural forces. It is through the addition of labour (not leisure) that these forces yield socially useful products. A Hindu uses every one of these products, but thinks that they are products of prayer. A Dalit-bahujan knows that they are products of labour. Therefore, here labour is valued and leisure is condemned. Since this labour is always social, it produces a language, a grammar, and a literature—for example, a song is an integral part of labour. Therefore if any lower Dalitbahujan is not involved in work, such a person is known as *pani pata leenoodu* (a person without work or song). The parallel proverb of Brahminical Hindus is *caduvu sandhya leenoodu* (a person without education or prayer).

The son does play a role at the time of death in performing the ritual of *talagooru* (carrying a pot in front of a dead body and setting the body alight), but in Dalitbahujan society, the son is seen essentially as the caretaker of aging parents, not as one who ensures for his father a place in heaven. As the notion of *swarga* is not central to the Dalitbahujan, the question of whether there could be life after death is not important. Death is an end in itself. If a person plays a socially negative role, after death such a person becomes a ghost and keeps hanging around troubling people. According to the Dalitbahujan, a Brahmin ghost differs from Dalitbahujan ghost. A Brahmin ghost is a deadly ghost, always hungry, always after sucking the blood of others. A Dalitbahujan ghost on the other hand is one that hangs around the house and is easily satisfied by offers of simple food. Thus the difference between *punyam* (good) and *papam* (bad) is that *punyam* ends life forever, while *papam* turns a person into a ghost. Even though Dalitbahujans perform third day and eleventh day funeral ceremonies, the dead people lose their identities once the ceremonies are over. All the dead become part of the *peddalu* (elders).

Hindu and Dalitbahujan concepts of women's death also differ from Brahminical ideas. A Hindu woman does not find any important place in Hindu ritual hierarchy. A woman's death is mourned, but not eloquently. Among upper castes, if a man weeps loudly on the death of a woman he is said to be unmanly. But among the Dalitbahujan, weeping aloud is possible because all the people gather around the dead body, and generally the women outnumber the men. I remember when my mother died my father cried. The men around began to say 'You are a man, how can you cry like that?'. But the women intervened and said 'Let him cry; if he does not cry now when will he cry?'

After death, in the case of women too, the third day, the eleventh day, and the completion of a month after the day someone died, are observed as *mashikam*. After that, the dead person is only another of the dead elders. Among the Dalitbahujan, the bodies of married men and women are burnt to ashes. Children and unmarried women or men of whatever age are buried. This practice is an extension of Brahmin practice. But this is an unscientific way of dealing with dead bodies because it leaves no history in the form of fossils. If the whole world was to have done what the Brahmin rituals require, no fossil history of human bodies would have been available. Quite a lot of ancient and medieval history has been reconstructed on the basis of skeletons that could be studied centuries later. Burning human bodies destroys every evidence. I hope the Dalitbahujan will develop an alternative practice and cease to burn dead bodies. Today the practice of burning dead bodies is used by State agencies

like the police and the army to destroy evidence of torture and murder.
Brahminism must have evolved this practice in ancient India in order to
destroy all evidence of such torture and murder inflicted on Dalitbahujans
who revolted against Brahminical ritualism and inhumanity.

For a long time the Dalitbahujan did not believe in taking photographs
of themselves. Even today old people do not allow themselves to be
photographed. This is because the Brahmins did not allow them to
maintain any history. Though architecture, painting, and sculpture were
Dalitbahujan occupations, a painter or an artist never left a history or
a picture of his or her family, yet it was the Dalitbahujan who painted
and sculpted the family histories of the Brahmins and Kshatriyas. Many
a dead Brahmin's past record is kept in several forms by the Dalitbahujan.
Their own history and past record has however not been preserved by
them. Thus the Brahminical forces saw to it that their own writings were
preserved, their images were sculpted and their feelings painted. The
Kshatriyas also preserved their history in many ways. But the Dalitbahujan were not allowed to retain a sense of their past in any visible
form. This is another reason why with the death of a Dalitbahujan a
person dies forever. We must now change this situation. We must ensure
that dead Dalitbahujan live in the form of history, in art, in paintings,
in sculpture, and in literature.

We should change our relationship to Brahminism, but not by Hin-
duizing ourselves. We must change this relationship by Dalitizing the
Brahminical forces. Throughout Indian history the Dalitbahujan have
been the thesis and the Brahminical forces the antithesis. The relationship
between these forces in the form of thesis and antithesis has resulted in
producing a synthesis, but a mutilated synthesis. It is unnatural for a
section of human beings to acquire the role of antithesis and continue
to play that role forever. It is realistic and natural that all human beings
become thesis and confront nature as their antithesis. This is essential
if the relationship between Indians as human beings is to acquire a
positive homogeneity with plurality, and not a negative homogeneity
which would mean the very death of plurality.

7

'Rowdy-sheeters': An Essay on Subalternity and Politics*

VIVEK DHARESHWAR AND

R. SRIVATSAN

INTRODUCTION: DENIZEN AND CITIZEN

In the urban landscape of the Indian Modern, the 'rowdy' is a conspicuous, if inappropriate, figure. Cast out by the moral and political codes of modernity, he returns as the reified, estranged figure of modernity

* *Acknowledgments:* (Some names have been changed throughout the chapter to protect the identity of the collaborators.)

Our first acknowledgments go to Radhika and Venkatesh for their unflinching cooperation in engaging with us. We are indebted to their eloquent and clear formulations, which have taught us how not to look at the problem of subalternity. Our friend Shivaji obliged us to keep examining our own presuppositions; discussions with him, as those with Meherban, have been invaluable in shaping the argument of this chapter. We would like to acknowledge Lakshmi, Khaja, Satyamma, Krishnaveni, Shankaran, and Mohan Reddy for their time and cooperation despite demanding work schedules and commitments. Mr Basheeruddin has been an invaluable source of information regarding the actual process of employing and activating the police and criminal codes. We would like to thank Srinivas Reddy, Prithviraj Singh, and Krishna for sharing their views on the problem of criminality and rowdyism. Our progress would have been far more difficult and time-consuming, but for the helpful assistance in material and contacts provided by K. Lalita,

itself. This chapter seeks to investigate how the juridico–legal codes and
institutions inherited from the British define the referent for the category
'rowdy-sheeter'; how the police interpret and activate the 'rowdy' in our
specific historical conjuncture;[1] and finally, how the 'referent' (or the
potential referent) negotiates the institutional and cultural apparatus that
generate and demarcate his agency. In the final section we will briefly
discuss the politics of citizenship and its relationship to the political space
of the subaltern.

In the middle-class imagination, the 'rowdy' inhabits the dark zone of
the city, trafficking in illegal, immoral activities; a zone that is invariably
in need of law and order, and always threatening to spread to the safer,
cleaner habitat of the city. The term 'lumpenproletariat' (lumpen: shabby,
paltry; rabble or riff-raff), used as a category in Marxian social theory, also
situates them outside any social semiosis of class; a lumpen is precisely
one whose relationship to money is unmediated by any value; any bonds
of class solidarity or ties of community.[2] The 'lumpen', then, is subhuman,

---

Indira, Shivaji, Sunita, M.T. Khan, and K.G. Kannabiran. We are grateful to them.
For comments on the penultimate draft, we thank Partha Chatterjee, Shahid Amin,
and Dipesh Chakrabarty. The usual caveat, it should not go without saying, applies
more than usually.

[1] Also the media. However, from what one gathers, newspapers simply reproduce information doled out by the police. Of course, at a different level newspapers do contribute—indeed, fairly significantly—to the construction of
criminality, criminal space as object of both fascination and fear. The cinematic
interpellation of the 'rowdy' has produced one of the most durable figurations of
the popular imaginary. Raj Kapoor's 'Shree 420', to take the most celebrated example, situates the figure of the 'rowdy' squarely within the urban experience of
modernity, and uses that figure to question that experience and the commodifica-
tion that it entails.

[2] Marx's celebrated analysis of the lumpenproletariat is to be found, of course,
in his *The Eighteenth Brumaire of Louis Bonaparte*, in *Karl Marx: Surveys from Exile*,
ed. David Fernbach (Penguin, Harmondsworth, 1973). In that work Marx tried to
come to terms with a process that began with the promise of democracy and ended
with counter-revolution (infantry, cavalry, artillery, instead of liberty, equality ,
fraternity), thereby bringing to a close the age of democratic revolutions. What is
of interest to us is the way a gap seems to open up in Marx's analysis between
social classes and the formation of political identities. Indeed, Marx's very explanation of how Bonaparte succeeds in taking over the state by mobilizing the *lumpenproletariat* ('the scum, the leavings, the refuse of all classes') raises questions
about how to conceptualize the political and how political identities articulate
class-alliances and interests. For an elaboration of these questions and, in particular,
an acute analysis of Marx's representation of the lumpenproletariat *see* Peter

the 'other' (thus subaltern?) from whom the 'yuppie' (the unavoidable contemporary representative figure of the global middle-class) differentiates himself and his social space.

Our analysis of the figuration of the 'rowdy' or 'lumpen' in the contemporary Indian imaginary hinges on two interlocking sets of intuitions:

1. The figure of the 'rowdy' acquires semantic and ideological elasticity in the imaginary of the middle-class by becoming the focus of their anxiety about what they see as the 'criminalization' of politics ('*goondaraj*') and its threat to their precarious class-privilege. This very ideological social description then feeds into the everyday discourse of the ideologues of the middle-class, from Left to Left–liberal to liberal–Right, who invoke 'lumpenization of politics' as an explanation of all that they find disturbing in the social and political life of the nation.[3]

2. While narratives of nation, secularism, citizenship, public sphere are perceived as eminently suitable foci of our theoretical inquiries and deconstructive energies, the disciplinary and ideological structures that organize the space of our everyday and that differentiates 'us' from the subaltern classes, remain out of focus. If we take the term 'subalternity' as a shorthand for the critique of various 'norming' and exclusionary narratives, such as the nation, secularism, citizenship, etc. can one use that critique to interrogate the everyday practice of 'citizenship' (or 'democracy') that sustain and define our conception of the public sphere? In other words, can subalternity, as a critical category and as an approach, help destabilize existing political identities and conceptualize new ones?

This chapter is structured in two parts: in the first we look at the social institutions and practices that fix the referent of the category 'rowdy-sheeter'. This is a category we encounter most often in the crime page of a newspaper.[4] We read, for example, that the police have 'rounded up' hundreds of rowdy-sheeters in anticipation of 'communal tension' in the old city. The police of course 'know' them, 'recognize' them; after all, they have fixed the referent of the category in the first place. How do the police 'know' the rowdy-sheeter, what 'sociology' of class and gender, what 'anthropology' of caste and tribe, determine their notion of crime and criminality, and enable them to empirically fix the referent, making it a

Stallybrass, 'Marx and Heterogeneity: Thinking the Lumpenproletariat', *Representations* 31 (Summer 1990), pp. 65–94.

[3] 'Criminalization of politics' figured as a major theme of deliberation at the June 1994 session of the All India Congress Committee held in New Delhi.

[4] We are referring here to newspapers published in Hyderabad. As will be evident, all our 'field-work' was conducted in Hyderabad.

natural/social category of civil society? This 'official' knowledge about the 'rowdy-sheeter' and its reproduction by the newspapers determines the degree-zero of the category, its 'ground', as it were. Our interview with the police attempts to follow the discursive and institutional deployment of the category and how it is used as a means of social control.

In the second part, we present two of our conversations with the 'referents' or 'potential referents'—how we know the latter will be part of our ideological (self-) analysis—in which we try to understand their response to the material and ideological processes that position their agency in certain specific ways. While it is clear that the institutional and cultural power of the stereotype constrain their agency, we will have to find the language and perspective to understand the subject-position that enables them to negotiate (compromise, resist) the dominant stereotype and its practical consequences. What resources—cultural, political—do they draw from, what senses of agency does their milieu provide them? In what way can the discourse of their 'actions' be used to elaborate a political critique of the institutions of our civil society, the presuppositions and telos of our secular Left/liberal politics, and the horizons of our social imaginary that circumscribe and produce the phenomenon known as the 'rowdy'?

Thus we are seeking to outline the relationship between social representation and political identity. Ours is less a history of the present than an engagement with the political present, less a political theory of the lumpenproletariat than an analysis of the politics of representation.

DOCUMENT/APPARATUS/PROCESS

The rowdy-sheet is a record the police stations in the cities and towns of Andhra Pradesh (A.P.) keep of a rowdy. The term 'rowdy-sheet' seems to be specific to the police procedures of A.P., probably also Tamil Nadu and Karnataka, but the same function would doubtless be performed by a similar record of some other name in other places. The A.P. Police Standing Order No 742, dated 8 April 1971, defines the rowdy and prescribes that a rowdy-sheet may be opened for each rowdy under the order of a Superintendent of Police or a sub-divisional officer.[5] The closure of a rowdy-sheet must also be under the order of a gazetted officer in the police

---

[5] Cited in Padala Rama Reddi, *The Andhra Pradesh Police Code (in 2 vols)*, vol. 1 (Panchayat Publications, Hyderabad, 1991), pp. 556–7. *See* Appendix 1 for the format of the rowdy-sheet.

force, as also its retention beyond a period of two years. The characteristics of a rowdy are defined in this document as follows:

a.   a habit of committing, attempting to commit, aiding or abetting offences involving breach of peace.

b.   persons who have been bound over under sections 106, 107, 108(c), and 110(1) of the Code of Criminal Procedure 1973 (Act 2 of 1974), i.e. those who have been ordered to give security as a bond to keep the peace. These sections of the Cr.P.C. refer to any offence that includes assault (a gesture intending criminal force), use of criminal force (force with intent of committing an offence), mischief (actions causing loss or damage to person, property), and offences of criminal intimidation.

c.   Conviction more than twice in a period of two years under section 75 of the Madras City Police Act (Section 70 of the Hyderabad City Police Act), Section 3 clause 12 of the Towns Nuisances Act. (Committing public nuisance of any kind).

d.   Persons who habitually tease women or girls by passing indecent remarks or otherwise.

Perhaps the specific scale of offence targeted by the rowdy-sheet may be inferred from the description of the conviction particulars of the rowdy under the heading: 'Petty case number'.[6] A 'petty offence' is defined, according to the Code of Criminal Procedure 1973, as one that is punishable only by a fine not exceeding one thousand rupees (excluding some offences under the Motor Vehicles Act of 1939, or under any other law that provides for conviction of the accused in his absence on a plea of guilty).[7]

The last validating clause 'Persons who habitually tease women or girls by passing indecent remarks or otherwise' on the rowdy-sheet standing order, brings under police surveillance a category of offensive behaviour that seems related to an offence described in Section 509 of the Indian Penal Code of 1860 as 'Word, gesture or act intended to insult the modesty of a woman', punishable by fine and/or simple imprisonment for a period of up to one year. However, the police at a local level may interpret this clause in the standing order to construe as 'teasing' behaviour that may not necessarily be constituted as a punishable offence

[6] Ibid., vol. 2, pp. 517–18.

[7] Act No. II of 1974. Section 206, subsection 2. Cited in *Criminal Manual (Three Major Acts)* (Eastern Book Company, Lucknow, 1990). This definition of 'petty offence' is given in Sect. 206 entitled 'Special summons in relation to petty offences', and is qualified as being made for the purpose of this section.

under Section 509 of the Indian Penal Code (IPC).[8] The language of this clause seems to be slightly loose, in that it does not state specific pre-conditions such as being 'bound over' or 'convicted', as it directly does in the two other clauses. What this suggests is that the category 'rowdy' has a property that establishes for itself a specific relationship with (a certain construction of) femininity.

The historical location of the rowdy-sheet and its referent, according to the intention of the A.P. police laws, may be seen more clearly by setting it in a contrastive relationship with another document called the history-sheet, the different standing orders relating to which date from 20 February 1906 onwards. The A.P. Police Standing Order No 733 lays down that a history-sheet be opened for those who are habitually addicted to commit, or to aid or abet, crime.[9] The criminality envisaged in connection with the history-sheet marks out a domain that differs from, but has areas of overlap with, the rowdy-sheet. The defining characteristics of a person warranting the opening of a history-sheet are as follows:

Known depredators, i.e.

a)   Prisoners released from imprisonment for life, under chapters XII (Of offences relating to coin and government stamps), and XVII (Of offences against property) of the Indian Penal Code of 1860. Professional prisoners who have been convicted for dacoity, robbery, housebreaking, and theft.[10]

b)   A person who has twice been ordered to execute a bond for good behaviour on the apprehension by an Executive Magistrate that he is concealing his presence in the jurisdiction with the intention of committing a cognizable offence.[11]

c)   A person who has once been ordered to execute a bond on being apprehended by an Executive Magistrate as being, among other things, 'so desperate and dangerous as to render his being at large without security hazardous to the community'.[12]

[8] We are grateful to K.G. Kannabiran for pointing out that the Police Standing Orders are meant for the application at the local operational level by the police, and that the connection between them and the requirements of the IPC are likely to be indirect.

[9] Padala Rama Reddi, op. cit., vol. 1, p. 554.

[10] *Criminal Manual*. It is likely that the description 'professional prisoner' of the history-sheet standing order as reproduced in the *A.P. Police Code* is a misprint, a clerical error, or refers, inaccurately, to a recidivist offender.

[11] Sect. 109, Code of Criminal Procedure.

[12] The Code of Criminal Procedure, 1974, Sect. 110, clause (g). *Criminal Manual*, p. 48.

Persons who are 'such of those registered ex-notified tribe members under Order 736 for whom the Superintendent of Police or the Sub-divisional Officer thinks it advisable to do so on account of their active criminality'.[13]

Persons convicted under any section of the IPC and likely to commit crime again.

Persons, not convicted, but believed to be habitually addicted to crime. The areas of overlap between the history-sheet and rowdy-sheet seem to be clustered around offences involving breach of peace. The difference lies in the history-sheet's apparent special emphasis on offences against property, coin, and government stamps, while the rowdy-sheet's most distinctive characteristic seems to be its specific targeting of a gendered offender: a person who 'habitually teases women or girls' can only be a particular kind of male.[14] The rowdy-sheet format therefore has a sub-heading 'Son of:' in contrast to the more gender neutral 'Father's name/ Husband's name:' on the history-sheet. The tables recording the offences on the history-sheet do not have the qualifying tag 'petty', in contrast to the rowdy-sheet which does. The history-sheet requires a listing of con-victions, and of unsolved criminal cases in which the sheeter is definitely suspected; this is far more detailed than the information required to be gathered in the rowdy-form. The history-sheet consists of nine differen-tially detailed formatted 'pages' of information, each of which may consist of many leaves of paper, in contrast to the two-page format of the other.[15]

The deployment of class, community, and caste discrimination hetero-geneously within the institutionalized discourses on crime mark what appears undesirable immediately as, at least probably, criminal. The caste/tribe dimension in the police laws is rooted in the colonial defini-tions of some tribes as 'criminal' by nature—*vimukta jati* (ex-criminal tribes).[16] The rowdy-sheet too has a descriptive subheading 'Caste', which

---

[13] *The A.P. Police Code*, vol. I, p. 535.

[14] We do not have the space here to analyse the specifically post-colonial category of 'eve-teasing'. It is clear, however, that the 'rowdy' and 'eveteaser' are interchan-geable and both mark out a space in which 'citizens' and potential 'citizens' (col-lege-going, middle-class, upper-caste boys) will never appear.

[15] *See* Apps. I & II for the formats of the Rowdy Sheet and History Sheet.

[16] *Vimukta* literally means 'freed'. *See* S.O. No. 734(3) referred above. *Also* S.O. No. 806 specifies that a beat constable should gather specific information on the tribal origins of the criminal gang in a village. Cited in *Andhra Pradesh Police Code*, vol. 1, p. 577. Historians have now begun to investigate the colonial construction of 'criminality', 'criminal tribes and castes'. *See* Sanjay Nigam, 'Disciplining and

in current procedures is filled out rather disarmingly and alarmingly, as either 'Hindu' or 'Muslim'.[17] However, the tenacity of caste (in its current configuration), community and class as definitive factors in the production of the rowdy is attested to by the police and the media. They are clear about the fact that a rowdy is almost never an upper-caste Hindu. He is either a Scheduled Caste, Backward Class, or Muslim, all belonging to a socio-economic (non-) class which by definition resides in a *basti* or slum. The virulence of modern upper-caste sensibility is almost tangible in areas like Hyderabad, Vijayawada, and Delhi, where informal household discourse, media articles and police wisdom on criminality and its sociocultural origins all exhibit a neurotic predisposition to reproduce, either directly or in insinuation, the category of caste as constitutive of criminality.[18]

Mr Basheeruddin is a circle inspector with a heart disease for which he is contemplating treatment at Buffalo, New York. Elegantly clad in a safari suit he talked to us in his office about how the kinds of petty offences seen on the beat have changed over the past two decades. Pavement gambling, numbers games, even black-marketing of cinema tickets are, according to him no longer observable petty offences. In their place a different range of offences such as land grabbing (implicated frequently in communal 'riots') have arisen since the mid-1980s. Alongside official and unofficial discourses that have changed with the times, for example, to include the new term 'communal rowdy', more widely used since about 1985, the subjects described by the sheet, their suspect status, and the very way in which the form of the rowdy-sheet is used have also shifted in their function. There have been reports regarding communalization of the

---

Policing the "Criminals by Birth"', pt I & II, *The Indian Economic and Social History Review* 27: 2 (1990), pp. 131–64 and 27: 3 (1990), pp. 257–87; Sandria B. Freitag, 'Crime in the Social Order of Colonial North India', *Modern Asian Studies* 25: 2 (1991), pp. 227–61.

[17] This was seen in six rowdy-sheets which were shown to us during a visit to a police station.

[18] In Hyderabad, there is a whole settlement near the Santoshnagar Police Station inhabited by people who are informally described by the police as a criminal tribe. This was observed during the December 1990 riots, when one of the writers participated in a relief operation in this settlement.

In Vijayawada, the Erukula caste has been described, in connection with domestic theft, as habitually criminal by police officers.

The *Hindustan Times* (New Delhi, 3 April 1992 city edn), has an article entitled 'Police and People—East District: Warped Growth Leads to Crime', which cites the DCP East Zone, Mr Brar, on the subject of the 'criminals from the Bawaria tribes...'

police force, claiming, for example, that rowdy-sheets were being opened in the name of individuals just because their activity was simply 'is a Muslim'.[19]

There is, apart from the process of change briefly sketched above, evidence of another historical process of mutation and evolution, following its own time frame and compulsions, but interleaved with the former in a mutually productive way. News reportage on city crime seems to collapse the rowdy-sheeter and history-sheeter in their descriptions of arrests, shootouts, etc.: 'notorious rowdy-sheeter' and 'history-sheeter' are used interchangeably. This conflation was reflected in our conversation with crime reporters: to our question, 'who is a rowdy-sheeter', they responded with, 'he is the most hardened, desperate criminal whose record is kept in a police station'. References to attacks on the body, robbery, land grabbing, and terrorization by 'causing grievous hurt' (all of which would have come under the purview of the old history-sheet format) are made in connection with the rowdy-sheeter (who was, according to its format, initially conceived as a petty offender). News reporters deny any originality with regard to crime reporting and readily admit that they merely take down—even verbatim—whatever the Commissioner of Police or his representative say at the news conferences periodically held to disseminate news about the police's success in tackling crime in the city.[20] One police inspector's explanation is simply that the rowdy-sheet is the history-sheet, and that there is no difference between the two. He only differentiates between a 'potential' rowdy-sheeter and ordinary rowdy-sheeter—i.e. the adjective 'potential' describing one who has achieved the potential of the sheet and is filling the file with a police record of his exploits and punishments, and is therefore a testimony to police vigilance.[21] The rowdy-sheets themselves (in the police station we visited) show this collapse of function: one of the sheets we saw was used for a (lower caste?) Hindu rowdy who was clearly booked for offences against the body, i.e. stabbing, and another for a Muslim who was found instigating religious discontent and mischief during a communally sensitive period. The same sheet in more than one case has alternating entries of 'petty' and 'grave' offences. Other entries were of a 'petty' nature.

[19] Salahuddin Owaisi, the Member of Parliament representing the Majlis Itehadul Muslmeen party released a press note stating this about two or three months after the December 1990 riots in Hyderabad.

[20] Interviews with the crime reporters of three different newspapers in the city.

[21] One police inspector consented to be interviewed and also showed us his file of rowdy-sheets with full details for six men in his area.

These preliminary observations need to be verified by a broader sample of police opinion and crime logs before any theoretical arguments on their basis may be advanced. There is, however, another indicator of this tendency towards moving together of various domains of offences in what is termed the 'Andhra Pradesh Prevention of Dangerous Activities of Bootleggers, Dacoits, Drug Offenders, *Goondas*, Immoral Traffic Offenders and Land Grabbers Act, 1986'.[22] Evident in the title of the act itself, is a collapse of a wide variety of offences, variety of including the rowdy-sheet type and the history-sheet type under the umbrella 'prevention of dangerous activities', which in turn is defined in the act as 'acting in any manner prejudicial to the maintenance of public order'.[23] It is an act which permits the government to temporarily empower (with no limit on the number of empowerments or their 'spacing') the Commissioner of Police or District Magistrate to detain the specified 'undesirables' as a preventive measure. The document makes it clear that the reasons for its coming into being are the resources and influences of the offenders, the large scale of these activities, and the clandestine manner in which these dangerous activities are being carried out. In a first examination, however, it seems as if there is in the document, along with the agglomeration of these crimes, also (as apparent in news reporters' discourse and police practice) a de-differentiation of the treatment of the petty offender of the rowdy-sheet and the grave offender—i.e. there is (probably for very valid operational reasons) no clear mention of the scale of offence that will result in a preventive arrest. As the next section will attempt to show, much of the local political activity within a *basti* could directly be treated, in an 'eventuality', as within the purview of this act which is known in short as the 'Anti-*Goonda* Act'.

THE RETREAT AND RETURN OF THE ROWDY: TWO NARRATIVES

We present here the outcome of some of our attempts to interview men and women from some *basti*s in the city on the issue of rowdyism. The objective of these specific interviews was more to explore how 'normal' residents of the *basti* engaged with what we implicitly assumed was the disorder in their midst. We are using the word 'interview' for lack of

[22] Published in the *Andhra Pradesh Gazette*, Part IV–B, (Ext.), dated 28–02–1986. Rptd. in *The Andhra Pradesh Police Codes* . . . , vol. II, pp. 662–9.
[23] Ibid., p. 665.

anything better or more adequate. Perhaps it is best to begin by saying what it is not. We are certainly not attempting a 'thick description' of the *'basti'*, nor are we trying to present 'sensitive' ethnography of the lives of the people of the *basti* or of 'rowdies'. When we interviewed the police and journalists, we assumed a readily available role: scholars undertaking a sociological study of crime and criminality in Hyderabad. We asked them more or less predictable questions and received more or less predictable answers (even the routine of 'off the record' views, 'real' views as opposed to 'official' views, was understood and played fairly predictably). We did not expect anything different, given the 'public transcript' that allows for such transactions between citizens pursuing different professions. Even the 'hidden transcript' of our transaction (their 'real' opinions about us, the interview, and what we were attempting and vice versa) is equally predictable.[24] In any case, what we did with them could be easily classified as 'interview'.

No such 'public transcript' existed for our 'interview' with men and women, some of whom had no slottable identities and for whom 'scholars studying crime and criminality' was not a negotiable slot, even if they understood what that meant, as some of them obviously could and did. We, of course, did want to elicit narratives about the 'rowdy' figure from them; but we were really in no position to offer them a narrative—both plausible and politically scrupulous—about what we wanted from them and why. We had to patch together various kinds of explanations, the responses to which often obliged us to use or fall back on registers and subject-positions that we wanted to avoid (e.g. humanist social worker, compassionate employer, etc.). Some interviews 'failed' altogether; that is, they failed to elicit anything. Such failures, however, demonstrated very clearly that what we are up against is not (only) a problem of style or genre or of epistemological positioning, but of specifying a politics that engages with the question of subalternity in our everyday life. This does not obviously mean that the interviews that 'succeeded', that is, those which elicited some narratives, did so because we were able to 'position' ourselves properly.[25]

[24] The terms, 'public transcript' and 'hidden transcript', are taken from, James C. Scott, *Domination and the Arts of Resistance: Hidden Transcripts* (Yale University Press, New Haven, 1990).

[25] For someone who has been 'individualized' by the rowdy-sheet, to answer a question in the course of an interview is, formally, and in terms of its epistemology, to acquiesce to the kinds of disciplinary structure which he has spent his life rejecting: from well meaning questions, such as 'what is a nice boy like you doing in a place like this?' to such things as examination papers, parental interrogations,

At one end of the spectrum, we had Ramesh who understood 'where we came from' and who told us bluntly: 'Why do you want to write about rowdies? You are wasting your time'. In all our conversations, he not only refused any existing line of communication but also systematically subverted any attempt to construct a new, if provisional, transcript that would allow us access to the figure of rowdy on his terms. Indeed, it was obvious that he took some pleasure in baiting us.[26] At the other end, we had Narsamma, who worked as a maid for one of the authors. When we asked, 'what do you know about the rowdies in your *basti*', her first response was, *'Yemi antunaramma?'* ('What are you saying amma?') in puzzlement.[27] She initially did not seem to understand what it was we were asking her. Why should her (male) employer ask her about rowdies, when normally, the man of the house does not address her at all. We explained to her that our interest lay in those people who were constantly in trouble with the police (the problem here was that we had no way of drawing the 'subtle' distinctions between petty and cognizable offences in the Telangana dialect or in a paradigm that was accessible to her). Her first response was that as she no longer lived in the *basti* (a kind-hearted employer had given a one room tenement to live in with her husband and two children in return for her housework); she knew little about them: *'Naku yemi teluvadu'* ('I don't know anything'). Even when she did, she never raised her head outside the house, because she was mortally afraid. At that moment, however, she switched the conversation to the topic of black magic and *mantravadi*s. She became so engrossed in *mantralu*, and the killing of people through its medium that she continued to talk to us, compulsively and uncharacteristically, interrupting her sweeping and swabbing task many times and coming over into a different room in order

---

police beatings, and extortions of confessions, failed job interviews. There is no reason why he should see any difference between one interview and another.

[26] Interview questions addressed to 'rowdies' often elicit responses which derail the agenda. Sometimes, no answers are offered. At others the answer will be tangential, without directly approaching the topic. Often the answer is such that it sets up a counter question which puts you in a spot: 'What do *you* want to portray the rowdy as? Tell me that and I will tell you what you want to know'. He will signal his distaste for you by not even wishing you goodbye when you leave, having measured you up and found you wanting by a code of ethics he has learnt to live by. He will often say 'it is a very vast and complicated topic' and even refuse to elaborate the answer, switching the topic and asking the introducer a quite different question: e.g. 'Is this man a brahmin, or what?' or even 'Is he a reporter?'

[27] Narsamma often uses the feminine gender to address men in her conversation—it is not clear whether this is an idiosyncrasy or a dialectal variation.

to continue discussing a point she had started to make. Interestingly, in another interview too we found the topic of rowdyism straying into a discussion of *mantralu*.

When we asked another woman, Rashidabee, what she knew about the rowdies in her *basti*, she said that she never raised her eyes on the route between her place of work and home, because it was not her business. She flatly refused to say anything: *'Humko kai ku puchthe saab; ye baten sab mereko to kuch nahin maloom'* ('Why do you ask me all these saheb, I don't know any thing about these matters'), and ended the conversation abruptly, wishing us salaam. Another friend of ours, who had promised to ask a woman, working in the housing complex she lived in, to talk to us reported complete failure—the woman refused and brooked no negotiation in the matter. In yet another instance, asking a woman Mallamma to tell us about rowdies in her locality resulted in her clamping down completely: *'Ma basti la-aite yemi ledu; mundugala unde, kani ippudu anta sariga-ayi poyindi'* ('There is nothing of the sort in our *basti*; there was earlier, but everything has become all right now').[28]

Radhika is a Padmashali woman, belonging, in her words, to the highest of the *shali*s among this weaver community. She is married to a Harijan man. She says that she learnt the art of midwifery from her mother-in-law, and had attended to many deliveries even though such an activity was not her caste occupation. Indeed, on the appointed day she arrived late and sleepy-eyed, because she had attended to a difficult delivery that needed attention till dawn.

In response to our question about rowdies, she said now that the organized People's War Group (PWG) activity in her slum was at its lowest ebb rowdyism and gathering of *mamool* from the dwellers was high. However, she also said that even during 1987, when naxalism was at its peak, an increasing number of rowdies posing as radicals used to collect *mamool* from the slum dwellers. Speaking about the radical presence in the slum, she said that sympathy for the Left was very strong in the mid-1980s. The Warangal conference, organized by the PWG was, according to her estimates, attended by more than five thousand men and women from the slum: *'Memandaram, bus kiraya ma paisalato koni poyinam-ayya'* ('We all bought the bus fares with our money and went *ayya*'). At

---

[28] The question raised by all this is: what was the end result of these conversational dead ends—starting in good faith, but lapsing into awkward silences, evasive glances and sometimes downright hostility—with people who had no reason to distrust us? In complete contrast, we found people from our own milieu willing to discuss the topic endlessly.

that time, the support for the naxals was about '*rupayee ki aatana*' (fifty per cent). Since then, the enthusiasm has waned, primarily, according to her, because of increased police repression on naxalite supporters. At present the support, according to her estimation, would be less than 'four annas in the rupee' (twenty-five per cent). She is very proud that the radicals even now come to her house at midnight each May day, hoist the *lal jhanda*, and sing revolutionary songs. After that they go with whoever invites them and perform a similar revolutionary ritual at their houses. The number of houses that invite them have, according to her, come down to two or three from about thirty or so a few years ago; she and her husband remain the only really staunch supporters of the radicals.

Talking about the nature of rowdyism as she perceived it, she said that the trouble started most often because, for youngsters, solving disputes among neighbours was a way of seeking status and respectability. '*Yeppudu kotlata ayitundo, ee pillalu nadumatla vachhi, samadanam cheyaniki try chestaru—paisala koraku*' ('Whenever there is a fight, these youngsters intervene, and try to arbitrate between the parties for a sum of money'). Often the matter gets out of hand, and these youngsters would resort to physical violence in order to resolve the matter. The injured party would lodge a complaint at the police station, and the police would book a case against the youngster. Repeated offences would result in their being rowdy-sheeted. We asked her about the history of arbitration in the *basti* (because this aspect of rowdyism surfaced on at least two other occasions). She said that this was a respected practice started by the '*basti peddalu*' (community elders), and continued to this day. The most sought-after arbitrator was Municipal Rangaiyya, who was often appealed to when matters of dispute reached a head. Rangaiyya was the right-hand man of G.M. Maisaiyya, both of whom were among the original inhabitants of this Madiga *basti* in the mid-1970s. Since he was a lawyer, Maisaiyya was chosen as the leader to organize the *basti*'s resistance to eviction by the man who claimed to own the land and to lead the people in their *dharna*s and processions for water, electricity, and sewerage connections. By the early 1980s, the number of houses had risen from fifty or sixty to about six thousand. Each house was willingly contributing Rs 10 per month to Maisayya as a fee for legal and political representation. Today, however, his stature has fallen. People feel that he has become self-centred, and does not have the interests of the *basti* in mind. Others feel that they have no need for representation because their right to the land they live on has been recognized through the provision by government of power and water. (The recognition of their right by the government, ironically, seems to have worked against Maisayya, who led the struggle for this recognition, and has adversely affected his stature among the people in the *basti*.) Linked in an indirect way to this moment of legalization is the loss of legitimacy of the local arbitration process, and of the respectability conferred on the arbitrators by the *basti*. This is indicated by the institutionalized negation of the acts of arbitration attempted by other young educated men resulting in their becoming rowdy-sheeters and the general loss of confidence in the process of local arbitration itself, going by Radhika's account.) Radhika herself had once *gheraoed* an MLA who was visiting her *basti* and forced her to go round the *basti* to take note of the places needing water-connections.

Radhika admitted that her husband, her second, who has also married another woman, had his picture in the local police station for almost ten years—until about 1984 (this means that he was a rowdy-sheeter).[29] Her husband's explanation apparently was that he was standing beside a cart selling bananas, a fruit knife in his hand, when the police on a patrol of the area simply picked him up and hauled him off to the police station, and after a quick trial for a petty offence had a rowdy-sheet opened in his name. She said that the sub-inspector who was in charge of his surveillance, often protected him from policemen from other stations, when they caught him committing an offence in their territory. The reason for protection, according to her, was that she and her husband knew that the sub-inspector Yellaiah and his wife were *mantravadis*, who used to cure physical and mental illness with their black magic. '*Giraki deggara paisalu teesikoni, mantralato vallaku kavalisina mandini champesinru kooda*' ('They have taken money from customers to even kill people by *mantram*'). The sub-inspector protected him, according to her, because if her husband was caught, he would tell on the officer, thus jeopardizing his job. At this point, however, in response to some probing, she switched her story, or rather added another thorny branch to it. She said that one thing she knew about her husband all along was his habit of waylaying women at night and 'spoiling' them. Choking, she declared that she was not afraid to tell the world about this truth. He was rowdy-sheeted for this reason. Detailing the story, she said that she knew that the police officer too had a taste for

[29] Although the retention of the rowdy-sheet and history-sheet beyond two years requires the specific orders of a gazetted officer; knowledgeable sources say that these are either routinely granted or overlooked, so that the police may demonstrate their efficiency in keeping under surveillance and apprehending rowdies according to the needs of law and order. Rowdies are also objects of financial transaction: the patron has to bribe the police in order to release the rowdy each time.

young girls, because her husband had once taken her (before they were married) to him for a magical cure and the sub-inspector had tried to make a pass at her. According to this story, the reason why her husband was protected by the policeman was that he too was provided with women. Her husband collected the photograph from the rowdy-sheet, when it was closed, and it now hangs in the living room as a trophy.[30]

Venkatesh had come home at seven one morning in response to our request conveyed through a mutual acquaintance. As we groped for suitable opening narratives, which explained our interests and opened a mutually acceptable channel of communication, we arrived, by tacit understanding, at a framework of dialogue that positioned us as people interested in 'social welfare' and 'Dalit struggle'. He readily agreed to talk about rowdy-sheeters when we asked him to: *'Memu Mala vaallamu, Tuljapur—Nizamabad distritu ma ooru'* (We are Malas—we come from Tuljapur in Nizamabad district). Ramulu, his brother, was involved in starting up the Ambedkar Sangham there, around 1981–2. He was primarily concerned with resisting Reddy dominance. Ramulu lived a 'neat' life, challenging the landlords with his statements, acts, and style. *'Oka roju ayinanu donga ani pilichi, kotti, katti, kalichi champesinru'* ('They branded him a thief, beat him, tied him up and burnt him').

Two eminent civil liberties lawyers got involved and managed to ensure chief minister NTR's presence at a meeting at the press club. At that time many politicians with Dalit sympathies visited Tuljapur. An immediate grant of Rs 10,000 was secured for the next of kin, and two government jobs were promised. The collector came the next day and immediately gave the sister a job in the B.C. hostel there. Venkatesh who also qualified for a job, got employed as a cook in a hostel run by the state

---

[30] Radhika's account enables us to discern more clearly a few of the problems that may have caused many of our interviews to fail. Put schematically, we could renarrate Radhika's account to foreground her desire to participate in progressive politics. She sympathizes with the PWG; she agitates for social rights. But at the same time the embodiment of social undesirability in her through her husband—a *goonda*/pimp/rapist/tout/—is something which she does not want to suppress from her account of her life. Our renarration would have to face this mismatch between her desire to construct her life through progressive political action, on the one hand, and her ambivalent ties to her husband (he is a Left sympathizer too), on the other. (There is also her enigmatic references to black magic.) Some of our interviews 'failed', it seems to us now, because such difficult moments, rather than marking locations at which inadequate theories need piecemeal repair, demand to be met as nodes of resistance and elision that have the potential to inflect and change our existing public/political transcript.

government for handicapped students in Hyderabad. According to
Venkatesh, the sessions court had put the murderers away for life, but a
judicial enquiry later reversed the order and got them released in six
months. Venkatesh has been living in the Balamrai *basti* in Secunderabad.
Some twenty odd families used to live in a part of Balamrai called Am-
bedkarnagar by the residents, who have been there for about thirty years.
Some Gowds who owned part of this land, claimed all of it when it was
released by the cantonment. They collected rent from the houses built on
their land at the rate of Rs 10 per month over a long period. The Ambedkar
Sangham which was formed in 1982 stopped this. The two acres of land
left was claimed by the Sangham as theirs. In this area, there was a Madiga
family of five brothers; the rest were Malas. These people, Venkatesh says,
were professional rowdies, who 'earned' a living solely through *mamools*
and other 'illegal' sources.

Venkatesh says that the Sangham wanted to distribute the land they
had taken possession of, but the five brothers wanted to sell the land
for a profit. (A variation of the story is that the Sangham too wanted
to sell the land to earn some money for a community lavatory, which
was ultimately built. Government officials, who had never showed up
for decades, came by some two months later, razed it to the ground,
and replaced it with a 'bigger and better' lavatory. Venkatesh however
denies that the building of the lavatory had any thing to do with the
incident he was narrating.) Some land was distributed, some sold, and
things came to a head. The Sangham decided to have a showdown with
the family.[31] One of the rowdy brothers Acchaiah, who was having a
drink at the Kallu compound, began threatening to kill one of the
Sangham men. This news reached the Sangham from other visitors to
the bar. *'Memandaram, sangham pillalamu ready ayi poyinamu.'* ('We Sangham boys got ready'). A fight began, and Achaiah was stabbed with
a knife which went through his heart though there was no specific
intention to kill. He died on the spot. The police arrested all the men
(about twenty) present in the area during the fight, including Venkatesh
who was singled out as the principal organizer of the encounter. A boy
called Venu owned up to the murder (it is not known whether he actually
killed the man), so that the others might be let off. Venu, a house painter

---

[31] When asked whether Malas and Madigas fight each other, as is often believed,
Venkatesh said it was less frequent now than earlier because of the Ambedkar
Sangham. When they fight they do so because of Reddy patronage and incitement.
Reddy battles are fought on the field by Malas and Madigas—they are set against
each other.

by profession, was convicted and sentenced to imprisonment for life. He was due to be released in 1994.

Venkatesh says that his people live a rough life. With a salary of Rs 1500, they cannot afford to live in houses like ours, he said. They could barely afford to survive now. In the *basti*, people are not educated—children don't learn because they cannot go to school. Tuition is impossible because no one wants to come to a *basti* to teach. '*Ma pillalu aite polisulato kooda rough ga ne mataladutaru*', (our children talk roughly even with the police) because they know that they will be caught and thrashed anyway.

Illustrating this, he related an incident he had experienced on a bus. He was travelling on the Tank Bund towards Secunderabad. One man gave an 'RTC Staff' signal to stop the bus, got on, and sat behind the driver. The driver asked for his identity, and found that he was not on the staff of the RTC. There was an altercation, and the man got off at Raniganj. The driver however, continued to make a big fuss and all the passengers began shouting at him. '*Mana pillavadokadu*' (one of our boys) among the passengers, was a little more rude and used some rough language. The driver stopped at the James Street Police station and handed *this* boy over to the police—in place of the man who got off! When Venkatesh saw what was happening, he intervened and he too was taken in and locked up; both were thrashed. Venkatesh was booked under Section 70 of the Hyderabad City Police Act (committing public nuisance) and his watch was taken as a security in place of the fine which he could not pay there and then. So far, Venkatesh says, he has 'gone into' the police station three or four times, but his name is not on a rowdy-sheet, thanks to the intervention of some heavyweights.

According to Venkatesh, there are real rowdies who do nothing else for a living.[32] He cited examples of these types used by *sara* (cheap liquor supplied by the state government) contractors, who were usually *benami* (anonymous) representatives of major political figures. The rowdies were often used to scare away the competition. Other rowdies specialize in election manipulation, clearing land, etc. This last type usually receives a percentage of the money, or part of the cleared land as a fee.

---

[32] We had earlier scoured the newspapers for the story of Mohammed Sardar, a rowdy with a fierce reputation, whose killing by the police about three months before the communal riots of December 1990 led to speculations that they were sparked off by his death. Venkatesh's narrative of this 'real rowdyism', based on an intimate knowledge of Sardar's territory, has to negotiate this difficult knowledge that threatens to swallow the narrator. It seemed worth recording as a subaltern account of Sardar's life (*see* App. III).

Venkatesh too seems to believe in the existence of 'real rowdies'; he too wants to be able to distinguish between good beings caught in a web of criminality and real criminals. But who is this 'real rowdy'? Why does that figure seem to re-emerge or redouble just when we thought we could see it retreating?

THE CITIZEN AND HIS DOUBLE

If the political discourse of modernity created the ceremonies around the body of the citizen–subject, his rights and duties, his narratives of self-hood, it also effected a split, a doubling, between the legal–political–moral subject and the empirical subject of political technologies. The transmutation of the latter into the former, the world of subjection into the world of right, has been the 'unfinished' project of modernity. The figure of the 'rowdy' emerges, and constantly duplicates itself, in the very heart of the political discourse whose condition of possibility is, paradoxically, the split or doubling that it tries to overcome.

Thus, when we try to situate the 'citizen–subject' in relation to the world of disorder that constitutes the domain of his politics, we cannot fail to notice his seeming double presence. First, his presence outside, marking the *basti* with his interminable discourse as the site of *goonda*ism, irresponsibility, undesirability—and *excluding* it from his own domain of right, civility, and authority. These exclusionary discourses of the secular 'citizen–subject' emerge from many different institutional locations (the police codes, the media, upper-caste/middle-class Hindu households, family planning agencies, etc.), in connection with a variety of subjects of 'public' interest (criminality, communalism, population, law and order, health, development, etc.). Functioning in the very element of universality (rights, equality, etc.), this subject does not acknowledge its own particular political identity, seeking merely to extend its universality.[33] Paradoxically, the very attempt seems to posit or create zones negating universality.

---

[33] An almost perfect illustration is Amartya Sen's 'The Threats to Secular India', *Social Scientist* 238–9 (March/April 1993), pp. 5–23. Analysing the rise of Hindu extremism, he diagnoses illiteracy as a major factor (he is too careful a philosopher to say that it 'causes' communal fascism, even though that indeed is the upshot of his argument) in the rise of militant obscurantism: 'Obscurantism thrives on educational backwardness and gullibility' (p. 20). Sen's argument begs the question: why are 'illiterates' (assuming for the moment we know what that category refers to) *particularly vulnerable* (or 'gullible') to fascist propaganda or militant obscurantism?

The other presence of the 'citizen–subject' is visible in the narratives of Radhika and Venkatesh, *penetrating* them and splitting their discourse irretrievably into 'moral' and 'immoral', 'rational' and 'irrational', 'ignorance' and 'intelligence', 'correct' politics and 'incorrect' lives, etc. The proliferating contradictions of these terms, generated as much by our frame as by the content of their discourse, seems to seduce us subtly into a project of moral rehabilitation. It would be only too comforting to assume that the contradictory subjectivity that emerges in our transcript is something which they bring to us from their daily lives, fully formed, and which they deliver to us in its purity, in response to our questions. Should not this contradictory subjectivity presented to us be seen rather as a symptomatic product, crystallizing obediently within and according to the vectors of our interaction with them? Is it possible that the 'citizen–subject' was present *in* these interviews, invisible to us—because we were him—but very visible to both Radhika and Venkatesh in our bearing, compassion, and understanding? What other outcome could we expect from these interviews? As a double presence, both exclusionary and penetrating, the 'citizen–subject' positions himself above the rowdy and his milieu, not just through the content of civil discourse, but also through its very form. Thus, regardless of our intentions of 'not wanting to rehabilitate the rowdy', we, as sovereign authors of the good discourse of politics, tend to reproduce the split.

The most direct illustration of this emerges in the interview with Radhika. What is this 'interview', which in all its informality (we all sat on the floor and chatted over a cup of tea—no tape-recorder) seems to have perpetuated rather than destabilized the power relationships between us? What are these pathways of interaction that force us to revive and reinstate through our 'radical' practice, such implicit, oppressive, objectifying categories as 'interviewer', 'interviewee', 'illiterate', or, for that matter, even 'rowdy husband'? We have to consider the possibility that commonly used modes of political engagement and analysis, like interviews, fact finding missions, news conferences on atrocities, etc. are, in their present uncritically assimilated form, completely unsuited to a

---

Obviously, it will not do to say they lack secular education (literacy)! Let us note that 'illiterates' in Sen's account play the same role as 'lumpens' in Leftist accounts. For a mirror image of Sen's position but with considerably deeper insights in an understanding of modern politics—indeed of the modernity of politics *see* Ashis Nandy's 'Paradoxes of Secularism: The Buying and Selling of Religion', *Times of India*, 21 May 1994.

radical politics. Unsuited because they seem to reiterate existing political identities, thereby sanctioning their exclusionary practices. How, then, could this authority we inhabit be refused? How could a transcript be constructed that can exceed what that authority seems to reduplicate? We are not, obviously, calling for moral gestures; what we do need to take seriously is that our politics is not a matter merely of what we think, or the ideals we espouse (the ideals in the name of which we hold institutions accountable), but crucially involves what we are. We hope the previous section makes clear that these subalterns are indeed vulnerable, not to any particular politics but to social representations of all kinds, ranging from the disciplinary power of the 'rowdy-sheet', the developmental perspective of various institutions, to the homogenizing 'gaze' of the 'citizen'. The task, to which this chapter is an inadequate contribution, is to break and displace the power of representation embedded in various institutions and practices so that the question of the political identity of the subaltern can emerge precisely at the intersection of those institutions.

THE ROWDY AS CITIZEN? SUBALTERNITY AND POLITICAL SPACE

In our opinion the two narratives raise an important problem for the interpretation of politics and, more particularly, for a conjunctural analysis of political identities. When the term lumpenization of politics (or its variant, criminalization of politics and its obverse the politicization of criminality) begins to function as a signifier that simply overwrites the agency and activity of a particular space, in this case the *basti*, it cannot but disempower and demean that space and block off any attempt at evolving a perspective within which activities undertaken by those people can be seen as *political*.

To understand this state of affairs, it is worth analysing the function of invoking the 'lumpenization of politics'. The spectacular way in which this term has begun to organize and homogenize the perception of the citizen–subject (by definition the middle-class) attests, more than anything else, to a failure of democratic politics, as it has been conceived of and practised by the Left. For the Left (as for liberals) the problems stated in the discourses of the subaltern are not (yet) political problems; they will have to be rewritten or translated—they will have to come through to citizenship—before they become political.

Radhika and Venkatesh survive in a milieu that has been 'always already' criminalized. Any activity they undertake, indeed their very agency, almost inevitably gets written out of the public sphere by the disciplinary grid of legality. The discourse of citizenship has a narrow and precise meaning for them—captured accurately in the way the rowdy-sheet functions, symbolically and literally. It would be erroneous to isolate the pure literality of their problems and demands from the symbolic space that they inhabit, which is overdetermined, on the one hand, by the material violence of the legal apparatus, and, on the other, by the symbolic violence of the ideology of 'lumpenization, which is the definition with which the citizen–subject attempts to capture his double, the rowdy-sheeter.

It is the disengagement or disassociation of subaltern spaces by democratic politics that those wishing to occupy the subject position of the citizen–subject refuse to acknowledge. But this raises the important question—which has already surfaced in the last two sections—of how to conceive of democratic politics around the rights of citizenship if the very discourse of citizenship contains within itself a drive to differentiate, to double. This is an extremely elusive question to formulate because the very ideality of the discourse of citizenship makes it difficult to delineate its splitting or doubling as anything other than contingent by-product.[34] The logic and the consequences of putting into practice concepts and institutions of political modernity seem always to escape the self-understanding of those concepts or get posited as external to it. We cannot conceive of democratic politics simply as a fight for extending the rights of citizenship; what our interviews suggest is that we cannot any longer view the rights of citizenship as empty slots or counters that anyone can occupy.

What then are the prerequisites of citizenship? One such prerequisite

---

[34] The theoretical question here is whether the politics of citizenship as well as, more generally, the politics of rights, can ever overcome this doubling. For an understanding of the different dimensions of this difficult question, see Michel Foucault's discussion of the 'empirico-transcendental doublet' in *The Order of Things* (Tavistock, London, 1970), pp. 318–22, as well as his remarks on Kantorowitz in *Discipline and Punish: The Birth of the Prison* (Vintage, New York, 1979), p. 29; Michel Foucault, 'Governmentality', in Graham Burchell *et al.* (eds), *Foucault Effect: Studies in Governmentality* (University of Chicago Press, Chicago, 1991), pp. 87–104; Etienne Balibar, 'Citizen Subject', in Eduardo Cadava et al. (eds), *Who Comes After the Subject?* (Routledge, New York, 1991), pp. 33–57; Partha Chatterjee, 'Secularism and Toleration', *Economic and Political Weekly* 29: 28 (9 July 1994), pp. 1768–77; Vivek Dhareshwar, 'Caste and the Secular Self', *Journal of Arts and Ideas* 25–6 (Dec. 1993), pp. 115–26.

is obviously class. The point we are making, however, involves much
more than merely noting that a certain class position allows/prevents
people from occupying the slot or subject–position of citizenship. If one
of the major conditions of democratization is a certain disincorporation
of the subject's positivity—my particularity has no bearing on my participation in the public sphere—not everyone can participate equally in
the logic of disincorporation.

The empowering promised by the logic of disincorporation—I speak,
act as a citizen—has involved in India the deployment of discursive and
institutional strategies that have distributed the privilege of disincorporation in a highly uneven and unequal way; in such a way indeed that some
bodies—like the 'rowdy' or the 'lumpen'—will not disincorporate, so tied
are their shameful positivity to their bodies. Those strategies are, however,
an intrinsic part of the ritual of empowering the citizen. We thus have, on
the one hand, what we might call (in homage to Foucault's homage to
Kantorowitz) the *excessive* body of the rowdy, and on the other the disin-
corporated body of the citizen. Of course, the fact that some bodies can
reincorporate in the public sphere precisely as fantasmatic embodiments
or icons of power—for example, cine-stars and politicians (think of the
significance of the giant cut-outs)—far from disproving the logic of disincorporation proves to be one of its effects.[35] Therefore, the concept (if it
is one) 'lumpen' in the rhetorics of disincorporation as it has come to
operate in the discourse of citizenship in India names the 'excess' that will
not disincorporate; which indeed seems to proliferate because the logic
that creates a certain positivity as excess cannot be separated from the
discourse of citizenship.[36]

In sum, it seems to us that these concepts—citizenship, rights—themselves have a politics; there is, in other words, a *politics* of citizenship that
is not external to the forms of power that produces and reproduces the
'rowdy'. Thus when Radhika and Venkatesh try to occupy the subject–
position of the citizen they too end up reiterating the doubling. A recon-
ceptualiztion of democratic politics around the issue of citizenship then

[35] On disincorporation and democracy, *see* Claude Lefort, 'The Image of the
Body and Totalitarianism', in *Political Forms of Modern Society* (Polity Press, Cam-
bridge, 1986), pp. 292–306; *also see* the useful discussion in Michael Warner, 'The
Mass Public and the Mass Subject', in Craig Calhoun (ed.), *Habermas and the Public
Sphere* (MIT Press, Cambridge, Mass., 1992), pp. 376–401. For the reference to
Foucault and Kantorowitz, *see* the note above.
[36] On how the excess of identification works in the case of caste, *see* Vivek
Dhareshwar, 'Caste and the Secular Self'.

would have to be based on an analysis of the forms of power mobilized
by the concepts of political modernity and the effects they produce on
different institutional and discursive sites. If there is an aporia involved
in demanding that democratic politics interrogate our political modernity,
then it irreducibly defines our political present.

Appendix I

The A.P. Police Manual format for the Rowdy-Sheet:([1])

Form No. 88.   Order 742(1).

ROWDY-SHEET

Names and aliases: No.:   Date:

Son of: age/year of entry:

Caste: Occupation:

Native place, Police Station and District.
Type of offender, nature of rowdyism and
favourite localities for offences, etc.

Associates —

Name, Father's name and caste	Address	Instances of association	Sheet No., if any
etc.			

Reverse side of the form:

CONVICTION PARTICULARS

Serial No.	Petty case no.	Brief nature of offence and date, conviction details; Court and C.C. no.; police officers present.
etc.		

Remarks: (Here enter further details of rowdyism, details of petitions or complaints useful for a security case, and present conduct).

[1] Inspector-General of Police, Andhra Pradesh, Hyderabad, *The Andhra Pradesh Police Manual: Part II—Annexures and Forms* (Hyderabad Bulletin Press, Secunderabad (undated)), pp. 1045–6. Also reproduced in Padala Rama Reddi, *The Andhra Pradesh Police Codes: (2 vols), vol. II* (Panchayat Publications, Hyderabad, 1991 (rpt.)), pp. 517–18.

Appendix II

The A.P. Police Manual format for the History-Sheet:([2])

Form 87(c)
[Orders 733, 894 & 1002(11)]

History-Sheet

SHEET 1

1. Name and aliases
2. Father's name/Husband's name
3. Caste
4. Trade or Profession
5. (a) Native place (district and police station)
   (b) Identifying witnesses (two or three), their fathers and addresses
6. (a) Place of residence with dates and periods
   (b) Places visited with dates and periods
7. Class of offender. (Append notes showing MO details, means of transport used, kinds of property stolen, etc., in all case which any such features are distinctive.)

SHEET 2

8. Description (delete what is not applicable). If nothing extreme under the head, delete all sub-heads. (Underline any very distinctive point.)

   Approximate year of birth.
   Also refer to list of physical peculiarities and Criminal Characteristics

---

[2] From the *Andhra Pradesh Police Manual: vol. II*, reproduced in **Padala Rama Reddi, *The Andhra Pradesh Police Codes: (2 vols), vol. II*, pp. 514–17.**

given under Order 893(3) of the Andhra Pradesh Police Manual Part-I while filling this sheet.

Height	(which may be classified as tall 5'8", 6' and above, medium 5'4", short 5'4" and very short below 5).
Build	Thin, Medium, Fat.
Hair	Colour-Black, Brown, Greying, Grey, Curly (no note about straight hair) Baldness-Frontal, rear.
Fore-head	Broad, Narrow, Wrinkles (Horizontal, Vertical).
Eye brows	Arched, Straight, Joined, Thin, Thick, Bushy.
Eyes	Black, Brown, Blue, Small, Large, Sunken, Building, Special peculiarities (Squint, Blood-shot, One-eyed, Blind, Artificial).
Nose	Snub, Pointed.
Nostrils	Wide, Narrow, Straight, curved (Parrot like), Sunken at the root, Special peculiarities.
Ears	Large, Medium, Small, Lobe, Large, Small, Hanging, Pierced, Special Peculiarities (Hairy).
Lips	Thick, Thin, Hare lips, Protruding Upper lip.
Teeth	Small, Large, Protruding, Overlapping, Special Peculiarities, Missing, Gold Pointed, Silver Pointed.
Chin	Double, Dimpled, Square, Pointed.
Face	Square, Oval, Round, Prominent, Cheek-bones, Prominent Jaw, Flabby Cheek, Sunken-cheek, Pock-pitted.

Moustaches/Beard.

Complexion—Fair, White, Brown, Black.

Legs—bow-legged, knock-kneed.

Feet—Flat foot, Toe missing, Extra toe, Special peculiarities.

Speech—Stammer, Nasal, Feminine, Fast.

Deformities—Hunchback, Stopping, Lameness, Pot bellied, six fingers and other Peculiarities:

Habit

SHEET 3

9.   Relatives (those he is likely to visit to be underlined or starred).

Name and Relationship if any	Residence Police Station	Occupation	Reference to History-Sheet

10. Associates (those he is likely to visit to be underlined or starred).

Name, Father's name and caste	Residence Police Station	Occupation	Nature of association & reference to History-Sheet if any

SHEET 4

11. Exact information regarding known methods of disposal of stolen property (cite cases) and names and residence of receivers.

SHEET 5

12. Particulars of past arrests, when and where, and by whom harboured.

13. Localities in which he has committed crime. (Specify any favourite locality and cite offences committed in particular localities.)

14. History of how he became criminal, etc.

SHEET 6

15. Particulars of cases in which definitely suspected, with clear reasons for suspicion, and miscellaneous information useful for a security case.

Section, Modus Operandi and G.I.F. No.	District, Station and Crime Number	Kind of property	Summary

SHEET 7

16. Particulars of convictions and cases in which acquitted, or discharged (including compounded cases).

Section M.O. and & G.I.F. number	Station and Crime No.	Kind and value of property		Court, C.C. number, date and sentence	F.P. Bureau serial no. and date; identifying witnesses; jail number; date of release and return
		Lost	Recovered		

SHEET 8

17. Current doings

SHEET 9

18. Photograph sheet

Profile left.   Profile right.

Full face.   Full length.

Head and shoulders.

Close up photographs of physical deformities with descriptions.

Appendix III

The Story of Mohammed Sardar (as narrated by Venkatesh):

Sardar started out as an auto driver, who lived in 'Pinchum' Lines in Bowenpally. He became friends with Raju, a rowdy-sheeter. Progressing through the stage of being a drinking buddy, he slowly began getting involved in some petty cases. They were both caught for some offences. Raju absconded from the trial, and the police began putting pressure on Sardar. One day Sardar, who was having a drink at a bar in Bowenpally, encountered Raju and his gang of ten friends there. He asked Raju to come and talk to the police as they were harassing him for Raju's absence. Tempers flared and the ten men beat up Sardar, who managed to escape and ran home to fetch a knife. Meanwhile eight of the friends decided to go home, while Raju and another person decided to go after Sardar. They met in a graveyard halfway between the bar and Sardar's house. Then Raju's friend saw the knife and ran away. Raju tried running away, stumbled and fell into a grave. Sardar finished him off and gave himself up to the police. Raju had a friend called Chakali Krishna who was a 'technical mind', or a master strategist, mediating between rowdies and politicians like Channa Reddy, etc. Chakali Krishna ensured that Sardar got life imprisonment. He was earlier an employee of Mushtaq who owned two hundred acres of land in Ailapuram. Chakali managed to acquire the title deed for the land by duping Mushtaq's, and got the land registered in the name of Chanchalguda Ravi, Master Pehlwan, and Rajesh. The case is still on in the Sanghareddy courts. Mushtaq wanted to finish Chakali. He befriended Sardar in prison and waited till six months leave had accumulated at the rate of about fifteen to twenty days a year. He then got him released on parole with a bond of two lakh rupees. Mushtaq's college-going son, who had a gang of college-going rowdies, gave him bombs, guns, etc. As soon as Sardar was released, Chakali tried to have him put back, but Mushtaq managed to get him out again. Sardar first went to Master Pehlwan's *adda* in Begum bazaar and threw a bomb and ran away. (The Begum bazaar bombing incident figures prominently in the fact finding reports of the communal riots of 1990.) He created a lot of trouble everywhere, but the police did not catch him out of fear. One day, he went to Balanagar to collect *mamool* (protection money) on some land. A police *jamadar* tried to catch him, without heeding Sardar's warning. Sardar shot the policemen dead. After this, there was a police hunt on for him, but they did not succeed in catching him. Chakali had a heart surgery planned in Madras. Sardar passed word to him that he would be waiting for him in Madras. Chakali cancelled his trip. Then a few days later, Sardar went to the Paradise area and was speaking to the owner of Zam Zam bakery. Chakali happened to arrive at Paradise with his body-guards. Sardar threw a bomb at the group of ten men, and another one in the drain to kill those who were hiding there. As one innocent man, who was dressed like one of the bodyguards, ran towards the Central Telegraph Office, Sardar caught up with him and shot him dead. Venkatesh claims to be a witness to this incident, standing as he was near a cart selling bananas. Then Sardar went to Chanchalguda Ravi and collected two lakh rupees for Mushtaq's land. Chakali prepared to go to Madras, but died of fright in his own house. Three days later Sardar was shot dead by the police. His body, when taken to Bowenpally, was not recognized as his by his wife and son. They refused to accept that Sardar was dead. (Sardar's death was a cause of a great deal of tension in the Bowenpally area.) However Venkatesh says that there was absolutely no link between Sardar's death and the riots, which he felt were part of a political game to topple Channa Reddy.

8

Problems for a Contemporary Theory of Gender[*]

SUSIE THARU AND

TEJASWINI NIRANJANA

I

Suddenly 'women' are everywhere. Development experts cite 'gender bias as the cause of poverty in the Third World'; population planners declare their commitment to the empowerment of Indian women; economists speak of the feminization of the Indian labour force. In 1991–2, for instance, the People's War Group of the CPI(M–L) found themselves drawn increasingly into women's campaigns against sexual and domestic violence, dowry, and the sale of arrack or country liquor. Upper-caste women thronged the streets in the anti-Mandal protests; women are among the best-known leaders of the Ramjanmabhoomi movement; the BJP have identified women and Dalits as the principal targets of their next election campaign. Film after film features the new woman, who also

[*] This chapter was first presented as a paper at the Anveshi/Subaltern Studies conference on Subalternity and Culture held in Hyderabad in January 1993. An earlier version has appeared in *Social Scientist*. We thank K. Lalita, Veena Shatrugna, Mary John, V. Geeta, Parita Mukta, and Lata Mani for discussing the paper with us, Mr Dasgupta and the staff of the *Eenadu* library for letting us use their collection of press clippings, and Anveshi Research Centre for Women's Studies for creating a context where such issues are engaged. Our thanks to Dipesh Chakrabarty and Shahid Amin for useful editorial comments.

figures prominently in Doordarshan programmes. In overwhelming numbers, women joined the literacy campaigns in Pondicherry and parts of Andhra Pradesh. The anti-arrack movement initiated by rural women destabilized the economy of Andhra Pradesh.

How might we 'read' the new visibility of women across the political spectrum? What does it represent for gender theory and feminist practice today? For all those who invoke gender here, 'women' seems to stand in for the subject (agent, addressee, field of inquiry) of feminism itself. There is a sense, therefore, in which the new visibility is an index of the success of the women's movement. But clearly this success is also problematic. A wide range of issues rendered critical by feminism are now being invested in and annexed by projects that contain and deflect that initiative. Possibilities of alliance with other subaltern forces (Dalits, for example) that are opening up in civil society are often blocked, and feminists find themselves drawn into disturbing configurations within the dominant culture. We attempt in this chapter to understand the implications of this phenomenon. We feel our task is all the more urgent since the crisis in feminism is clearly related to the crisis of democracy and secularism in our times.

In the 1970s and 1980s, an important task for feminist theory was to establish 'gender' as a category that had been rendered invisible in universalisms of various kinds. In Hyderabad, for example, the campaign against 'eve-teasing' taken up by women students in the early 1970s brought into the open the hostile and sexually threatening conditions all women had to deal with everyday, not only in the university, but also on the streets and in every kind of work-place. Through public interest litigation, as in the cases of injectable contraceptives (Net-Oen) and police rape, and appeals against a variety of judgements—on custodial rape, family violence, restitution of conjugal rights—we demonstrated the asymmetries and inequalities in gender relations that underwrote the notion of rights and the legal process. We demanded changes that would make the law more sensitive to the cultural and economic contexts of women's lives. Women's groups investigating 'dowry deaths' demonstrated how the designation of the family as private domain restricted women's access to protection against domestic violence. They exposed the collusion of the law, police, medical system, and the family in classifying these deaths as suicides. Feminist scholars worked to salvage gender and women's issues from being subsumed by class analysis, sought to extend the Marxist understanding of labour to include domestic production, and pointed out the marginality and vulnerability of women in the workforce; disciplinary formations such as history or literature were critically discussed, and alternative narratives produced that foregrounded women. We demonstrated gross inequalities in women's access to health care systems or to 'development', and examined patriarchal ideologies as they worked across a wide range of institutions. These initiatives extended our understanding of the micro-politics of civil society, showing how pervasively mechanisms of subjugation operated, and how processes of othering functioned in relation to women.

In the late 1980s and the early 1990s—the Mandal/Mandir/Fund–Bank years—however, we face a whole new set of political questions.[1] Entering into new alliances we have begun to elaborate new forms of politics. These have demanded engagement with issues of caste and religious affiliation/community and with new problems emerging from the 'liberalization' of the economy, creating contexts in which the contradictions implicit in earlier initiatives have become increasingly apparent. For example, feminists calling for a uniform civil code in the context of the Shah Bano case soon realized the difficulty of distinguishing their position from that of an aggressively anti-Muslim lobby, and began to downplay the demand as 'Shah Bano' became the rallying cry for Hindutva. Similarly, in Chunduru, sexual harassment was cited as justification for the punishment meted out to Dalits by upper-caste men. More recently, leftist women's organizations in Hyderabad were placed in a dilemma about joining in a protest against the arrest and torture of a Muslim student accused of 'eve-teasing'. Debates around the introduction of hormonal implants and injectables into the national family planning programmes reveal analogous contradictions that underlie notions such as women's freedom, self-determination, or their right to choose. We feel that the kind of contradictions that confront gender analysis are structurally similar to those that face class analysis, caste initiatives and, more broadly, democracy and secularism today. In this chapter, our concern is to investigate the relationship of these contradictions to the gender, caste, class, and community composition of the 'subject' in the dominant order. Historically, this citizen–subject has been underwritten, and naturalized, by the 'humanism' that presents it as politically neutral.

[1] We use 'Mandal' to refer to the anti-Mandal (anti-reservation) agitation, 'Mandir' to refer to the Ramjanmabhoomi movement to build a Ram temple in Ayodhya–Faizabad, and 'Fund–Bank' to refer to the era of structural adjustment policies promoted in India by the International Monetary Fund and the World Bank.

II

Gender analysis, like class analysis, had revealed how the humanist subject and the social worlds predicated onto it functioned in such a way as to legitimize bourgeois and patriarchal interests. What has never been really apparent, however, is the way in which both Marxist and feminist politics continue to deploy other dimensions of the hidden structuring (such as caste or community) of the humanist subject, as well as the premises of secularism–democracy invoked by it. We have been unable, therefore, to critically confront inequalities of caste or community implicit in that subject or its worlds. We have also found it difficult to radicalize the concepts of secularism and democracy to meet the political requirements of our times. We shall be arguing in this chapter that these tasks call for an investigation and critique of the humanist premises that not only underwrite the politics of dominance but also configure the 'subject of feminism'.

The notion of the 'human' as it appears in political theory, and more importantly in humanist common sense is inextricable from what has been termed the metaphysics of substance. Framed by this metaphysics, the human appears as a substantive base that precedes and somehow remains *prior* to and outside of structurings of gender, class, caste, or community. In liberal political theory, it is this human core that provides the basis for legal personhood. Humanist Marxism offers a critique of the class invest-ments of liberal individualism, but preserves the normative idea of a human essence, principally in the concept of alienation and in teleological notions of history but also in the notion of ideology as false consciousness. Humanist feminism, too, is predicated on notions of female alienation from a putative human wholeness. Even across significant political and theoretical divides, the notion of a human essence that remains resolutely outside historical or social coding continues to operate as 'common sense'. It is not difficult to see that these theories, and their politico–legal deriva-tives, actually produce what they claim to recognize. For example, by basing the *rights of the individual* on the fiction of a substantive human core,[2] the law creates that core, or more precisely, a core-effect; the idea of *alienation* gains force only as it measures itself against a human fullness; *teleological narratives of history* find resolution only in a fully and recog-nizably human world.

---

[2] For a relevant discussion of the metaphysics of substance and the question of rights, *see* Mary Poovey, 'The Abortion Question and the Death of Man', *in* Joan Scott and Judith Butler (eds), *Feminists Theorize the Political* (Routledge, London, 1991).

Thus produced, this human subject, on whom the whole question of 'rights' is predicated, was imaged as the citizen–subject and the political subject. This imaging, (a) articulated gender, caste and community (and initially even class) only in the realm of the social; (b) marked these as *incidental* attributes of a *human* self; and, (c) rendered invisible the historical and social/cultural structuring of the subject of politics. The shaping of the normative human–Indian subject involved, on the one hand, a dialectical relationship of inequality and opposition with the classical subject of Western liberalism and, on the other, its structuring as upper-caste, middle-class, Hindu, and male. The structuring was effected by processes of othering/differentiation such as, for example, the definition of upper-caste/class female respectability in counterpoint to lower-caste licentiousness, or Hindu tolerance towards Muslim fanaticism, and by a gradual and sustained transformation of the institutions that govern everyday life.[3] Elaborated and consolidated through a series of conflicts, this structuring became invisible as this citizen–self was designated as modern, secular, and democratic.[4]

Our strategy in this chapter will be to examine certain 'events', such as Mandal or the rise of the Hindu Right, in which contemporary feminist analysis is coming up against certain impasses. These impasses indicate, on the one hand, a fracturing of the humanist consensus that has been the basis of left- as well as right-wing politics and, on the other, an opening up of possibilities for new political alignments and initiatives. These events, it seems to us, characterize the moment of the contemporary and might be investigated as metonyms of gender in which cultural meanings are being contested and refigured.

[3] The historical emergence of the citizen–subject in India has been explored in the impressive work of scholars like Kumkum Sangari, Uma Chakravarti, Lata Mani, Partha Chatterjee, Gyanendra Pandey, and others. *See* Kumkum Sangari, 'Relating Histories: Definitions of Literacy, Literature, Gender in Nineteenth-Century Calcutta and England', *in* Svati Joshi (ed.), *Rethinking English: Essays in Literature, Language, History* (Trianka, Delhi, 1991); Sangari and Sudesh Vaid, 'Introduction' to Sangari and Vaid (eds), *Recasting Women: Essays in Colonial History* (Kali for Women, Delhi, 1989); Uma Chakravarti, 'Whatever Happened to the Vedic Dasi? Orientalism, Nationalism and a Script for the Past'; Lata Mani, 'Contentious Traditions: The Debate on Sati in Colonial India'; Partha Chatterjee, 'The Nationalist Resolution of the Women's Question', all in *Recasting Women*; Gyanendra Pandey, *The Construction of Communalism in Colonial North India* (Oxford University Press, Delhi, 1990).

[4] For a fine account of how Satyajit Ray effects the consolidation of this human, citizen–subject in the freshly-minted realism of the Apu trilogy, *see* Geeta Kapur, 'Cultural Creativity in the First Decade: The Example of Satyajit Ray', *Journal of Arts and Ideas* 23–4 (Jan. 1993), pp. 17–50.

Obviously, each of these metonyms has a separate and particular history. But since our focus here is on the contemporary moment, we are concerned less with the emergence of these 'events', more with the impress of history on the present. In a strict sense, then, our approach is genealogical. We wish to explore historical conflicts as they structure everyday life and affect political initiatives in our time. The aim is to initiate a polemic that will render visible the points of collision and the lines of force that have hitherto remained subterranean, and construct instruments that will enable struggles on this reconfigured ground.

III

Our first metonym is Mandal–Chunduru, where we investigate the articulation of the gender question in the hegemonic culture of the 1990s. In both Mandal and Chunduru, 'women' were foregrounded, although in different ways. 'Women' came to be invoked here as, in a sense, feminist subjects: assertive, non-submissive, protesting against injustice done to them *as women* (Chunduru) or *as citizens* (the anti-Mandal agitation). An examination of the hidden structuring of this feminist subject would, we believe, reveal its similarities with the subject of humanism, marked—in a way that requires the occlusion of the marking—by class, caste, and community.

Mandal

The background is one familiar to most of us. The then Prime Minister V.P. Singh's announcement on 7 August 1990, of the implementation of the Mandal Commission recommendations for reservations of 27 per cent for Backward Castes, apart from 22.5 per cent for SC/STs in government service and public sector jobs, sparked off student riots, primarily in North India, but also in Hyderabad and a few other places. The methods of protest ranged from street-cleaning and boot-polishing to self-immolation; the discourses deployed most significantly were those of Unrewarded Merit and the Salvation of the Nation.[5] The actual course of events is too well-known to require recounting here. What we would like to focus on is the imaging of women in the anti-Mandal agitation, preceded by a

[5] These activities were designed to signify that meritorious men and women, who would otherwise occupy white-collar positions, would be forced as a result of the reservations policy to earn a menial's livelihood.

brief discussion of the way in which the agitation itself was represented in the media.

Indian Express editor Arun Shourie, rousing the upper-caste youth to action in his editorials, spoke of 'the intense idealism and fury' of the students (*Indian Express*, 29 Sept. 1990). A well-known intellectual denounced the reservations for OBCs as a 'transgression of moral norms' and as a political practice that would 'destroy the structure of democratic politics' (Veena Das, *Statesman*, 3 Sept. 1990). She spoke of the 'hidden despair' of the 'youth', and the government's refusal to recognize that 'people' 'may be moved by utopias, not interests'. The media's invocation of *students, youth,* and *people* was marked by a strange consensus on usage—these terms were obviously unmarked, yet referred only to those who were upper-caste or middle-class. An editorial in the *Independent* bemoaned the fact that the middle-class now had no place in India (4 Oct. 1990), suggesting that somehow they were the only legitimate political subjects/actors in a democracy. Only the subject of humanism could claim the utopias of the Enlightenment.

The Nation was a central figure in the anti-Mandal discourse. Claiming the heritage of Jawaharlal Nehru (a 1950s speech of Nehru's that was widely circulated, asserting that reservations would produce a 'second-rate' nation), the anti-Mandalites saw themselves as the authentic bearers of secularism and egalitarianism. Equality, they argued, would be achieved by a transcendence or a repudiation of caste, community, and gender identifications. For feminists who had struggled for years to inscribe gender into the liberal model, the Mandal issue posed a difficult question. Young middle-class women began to declare that they were against the reservations for women that had been announced in Andhra Pradesh for instance, as well as against the idea of reserving seats for women in public transport. Reservations (like subsidies) were *concessions*, and would make women 'soft', they said, reducing their ability to be independent and strong. In the anti-Mandal protests, women often appear not as sexed beings but as free and equal citizens, as partners of the rioting men, jointly protesting the erosion of 'their' rights. The nearly unanimous media celebration of the upper-caste students framed them within a non-sectarian nationalism and humanism; these young men and women were truly egalitarian and therefore anti-Mandal, whereas pro-Mandal groups were accused of supporting a resurgent casteism.

We asserted earlier that 'the Indian' comes into being in a dialectical relationship of inequality with the Western subject of humanism. In the first two decades or so after Independence, the post-colonial 'Indian' lays claim to a more egalitarian liberalism than that produced in the age of empire and in the heart of empire. Nehruvian socialism takes shape after the Soviet example of state planning, although allowing for a 'mixed' economy that retains large numbers of middle-class professionals in the public sector. In the global configuration that has emerged after the collapse of the second world, in the context of economic 'liberalization' in India and the gradual erosion of the public sector, the neo-nationalist Indian subject proclaims its Indianness even as it internationalizes itself. Now claiming equality with the Western subject of humanism on the latter's own terms, the 'Indian' aggressively demands the rejection of everything that would come in the way of its achieving an equal place in the new world order.

Whereas in the Nehru years the retarders of progress were seen as casteism, fundamentalism, or feudalism, and the role of the state was to help overcome these, in the Fund–Bank years these 'evils' are imaged as being located in welfarism and in the state-controlled public sector itself. The 'failure' and 'inefficiency' of the public sector is seen primarily as the outcome of the reservations policy; if becoming 'efficient', therefore, is the only way of integrating India into the world economy, then the obvious means of achieving this is to abolish reservations and establish a meritocracy. The sociologist André Beteille argued recently that no one wants to defend a caste hierarchy today;[6] but what he did not add was that the new secular hierarchy—a meritocracy premised on efficiency—refigures, transforms, and redeploys caste. In an article written during the anti-Mandal agitation, BJP leader K.R. Malkani mentioned 'a vice president of the IBM' who 'joked that they have so many Indians, and they are so good, that they in the IBM have decided not to employ any more, since they could just take over the IBM! Read the Brahmin for the educated Indian, and you have some idea of our wealth and brain power' (*The Daily*, 11 Oct. 1990). After the self is marked upper class/upper caste, the process of marking, as we have already suggested, becomes invisible. The recomposition of the middle class, the secular class that stands in for the nation, is thus predicated on the redeployment and othering of caste.[7] Professing secularism enables a displacement of caste (and also community) from the middle class sphere, so that it gets marked as what lies *outside*, is *other*

[6] In a public lecture on caste in modern India, delivered at the University of Hyderabad, January 1992.

[7] The media always uses the term 'caste groups' or 'caste organizations' to refer to *lower-caste* groups. As K. Satyanarayana has pointed out, 'caste' usually refers only to lower caste.

than, the middle class. In the consolidation of the middle class and in the othering of caste, 'women' play a crucial role.

Not only were women visually foregrounded by the media during the agitation, they also took part in large numbers in the struggle to do away with reservations for backward castes and Dalits. A report in the *Free Press Journal* says: 'The girls of Jadavpur University were the most militant and wanted to blockade roads and defy the law' (15 Oct. 1990). In many cities, hitherto 'apolitical' women students participated enthusiastically in demonstrations and blockades, mourning the 'death of merit' and arguing the need to save the nation. Wives of IAS officers demonstrated in the capital on behalf of their children, who they claimed were being denied their rightful share in the nation. The fact of women 'taking to the streets' became in the hegemonic culture iconic of an idealism that recalled the days of the freedom struggle. The marking of 'women' as middle class and upper caste has a long genealogy that, historically and conceptually, goes back into nationalism as well as social reform.[8] Marked thus, 'women' are seen as morally pure and uncorrupted—hence the significance of their protest, which becomes a 'disinterested' one since they have no place in the organized political process.[9] However, as a powerful strand of nationalism asserts, it is women who are entrusted with the task of saving the nation. In actuality, the nation is frequently imaged as 'woman' (Bharatmata, Mother India).

The re-emergence of women in the public sphere as claimants to the nation and to citizenship results in a masculinization of the lower castes. To rephrase the title of a well-known feminist book, in Mandal—Chunduru, all the women are upper caste (and, by implication, middle-class Hindu) and all the lower castes are men. As we argued earlier, in the anti-Mandal agitation, 'women' feature as citizens and not necessarily as gendered beings. But the representation in the media of their well-nourished faces and fashionable bodies visually defined the lower castes as Other. The photographs of the anti-Mandal women suggested that caste (read lower caste) is defined against 'women', and against the assertive and articulate humanist–feminist subject. As Sangari and Vaid have argued, 'the description and management of gender and female sexuality

[8] *See* the articles in *Recasting Women* by Partha Chatterjee and Uma Chakravarti, as well as the introduction to Susie Tharu and Lalita K. (eds), *Women Writing in India: 600 BC to the Present*, vol. II (Feminist Press, New York, 1993).

[9] That 'this student movement' 'articulates political processes that lie outside the domain of organized politics' was Veena Das's characterization of the anti-Mandal agitation in 'A Crisis of Faith' (*Statesman*, 3 Sept. 1990).

is involved in the maintenance and reproduction of social inequality'.[10] Sexuality was a *hidden* issue in Mandal, as an interview with an anti-Mandal woman student suggested. The student had held in a demonstration a placard reading: 'We want employed husbands.' When asked why, she said that reservations would deprive their men of employment. In that case, why should they not marry 'backward' boys? '"But how can that be . . . ", her voice trailed off' (Jyoti Malhotra, *The Independent*, 26 Aug. 1990). The anti-Mandal women had learned to *claim* deprivation and injustice, now not as women but as *citizens*, for to ground the claim in gender would pit them against middle-class men. The claiming of citizenship rather than sisterhood now not only set them against Dalit men but also against lower-caste/class women.

Chunduru

Interestingly, it is the claim to sisterhood that accomplishes the same effect in Chunduru. To sketch the context: in the culmination of a series of hostile encounters spread across at least two to three years, on 6 August 1991, in the village of Chunduru in coastal Andhra Pradesh, thirteen Dalits were murdered by upper-caste Reddys. The catalyzing 'event' appeared to be the incursion into the cinema hall space reserved by tradition for members of the upper castes by a young Dalit graduate, who was later beaten up, forced to drink liquor, and marched to the Chunduru police station, where he was 'accused of harassing upper-caste women in an inebriated condition'.[11]

After the carnage of 6 August, the mourning Dalits organized a funeral procession, during which some haystacks and thatched roofs were set on fire. Most of the Reddy males had left Chunduru to avoid arrest. The upper-caste women who stayed behind complained loudly of harassment by the Dalits, suggesting that their present accusations stemmed from a long history of grievances against Dalit men. The women claimed that they had been tied to trees and kerosene poured over them, and only the arrival of the police saved them from death.

Shortly after, the Reddys of the region formed a 'Sarvajanabhyudaya Porata Samithi' along with the Kammas, Brahmins, Kapus, Rajus, and Vaishyas, and organized processions, *dharnas*, and roadblocks to protest their 'oppression' at the hands of Dalits.[12] The upper-caste women, they

[10] *Recasting Women*, p. 5.
[11] We base this narrative of the events on Samata Sanghatana's report, published in *Economic and Political Weekly* XXVI: 36 (1991), pp. 2079–84.
[12] For this information, we are indebted to K. Balagopal's report, 'Post-Chunduru

contended, had been systematically harassed by Dalit men. Accusations of eve-teasing and assault multiplied, post-Chunduru. On 13 August in Kollipara village near Tenali, a Dalit boy was beaten up by upper-caste boys for teasing 'a schoolgirl'; a report dated, 11 August 1991, said that earlier in the month, a Dalit student was stabbed on the pretext that he had teased 'three girls'. The original cinema hall story was recorded as one about 'a Harijan youth putting his feet up on the seat in front in the cinema hall occupied by a caste Hindu girl' (*Statesman*, 9 Aug. 1991). In Chunduru itself, the story went, just before 6 August, when Dalit labourers were no longer employed for transplantation and women from the landlords' family had undertaken the task, Dalit men were supposed to have accosted the women one day, quarrelled with them, stripped them naked, and forced them to remove the transplanted seedlings and re-plant them. Enraged upper-caste women attacked the convoys of Chief Minister Janardhana Reddy and former Chief Minister N.T. Rama Rao, blaming the State for not providing them protection from the Dalits.

Years of sexual abuse of Dalit women by upper-caste men appear under the sanction of 'custom' while the alleged 'eve-teasing' of upper-caste women by Dalit men invokes the horrors and prohibitions/punishments of major transgression, the penalty of death. Chunduru drew the attention of urban women's groups, but especially for those feminists who had refused to be part of the anti-Mandal agitation and were attempting to build fragile alliances with Dalit organizations, the hegemonic articulation of the gender issue as one of 'molestation' (of upper-caste women) was deeply problematic. But to counterpose this against the molestation of Dalit women was equally problematic.

Feminists can grapple with this problem only by addressing the key role played by caste in the making of the middle-class woman. In the nineteenth-century *bhadralok* campaigns against Vaishnav artistes, as much as in the anti-nautch initiatives in Madras Presidency, the virtue and purity of the middle-class woman emerged in contrast to the licentiousness of the lower-caste/class woman. It is a logic that continues to operate, as for instance in the cases of Rameeza Bee and the Birati rapes: the women crying rape were 'prostitutes' and therefore had no right to complain of sexual harassment.[13] A woman's right over her body and

and Other Chundurus', in *Economic and Political Weekly* XXVI: 42 (1991), pp. 2399–405.

[13] *See Report of the Commission of Inquiry into the Rameeza Bee and the Ahmed Hussain Case* (Government of Andhra Pradesh, 1978), and Tanika Sarkar, 'Reflections on

control over her sexuality is conflated with her *virtue*. So powerful does this characterization become that only the middle-class woman has a right to purity. In other words, only *she* is entitled to the name of woman in this society. Again we see, as in Mandal, the masculinization of the lower-castes—the Dalits only male, the women only upper-caste. The category of 'woman', and therefore in a very important sense the field of feminism as well as the female subject, emerge in this context by obscuring the Dalit woman and marking the lower caste as the predatory male who becomes the legitimate target of 'feminist' rage.

IV

The introduction into national 'family welfare' or population control programmes of long-acting hormonal implants and injectables, and possibly also of RU 486, the abortifacient pill, is the metonym through which we would like to explore contradictions implicit in feminist demands for freedom, choice, and self-determination.

Women's groups and health activities in India have opposed these contraceptives on several grounds. They have commented on the dangerous side-effects (disturbed menstruation, hypertension, risk of embolism, nervousness, vomiting, dizziness, etc.) and contra-indications (these drugs may not be used by women with any history of liver or heart problems, diabetes, clotting defects, cancer, migraine, recent abortion, irregular cycles, or smoking). They have pointed out that the administration of such contraceptive technologies depend on well-equipped health-care systems. Existing public health facilities in India are nowhere near adequate for screening potential users, inserting and removing implants, and providing continued monitoring of user health. They warn of the risks involved in using drugs not developed or standardized for women in India. They argue that hormonal contraceptives should not be introduced before conducting epidemiological and biochemical studies that take into account differences in weight, diet, and so on, between Indian women who will use these contraceptives and the 'average' Western woman.[14] All told, it becomes evident that considered as contraceptives

---

Birati Rape Cases: Gender Ideology in Bengal', *Economic and Political Weekly* XXVI: 5 (1991), pp. 215–18.

[14] The high costs of the contraceptives (one set of Norplant implants will cost the Indian government around Rs 750) and the profits that will accrue is also an important issue, but was not raised by activists.

for Indian women who are not part of the urban middle class, the profiles of Norplant, Net-Oen and RU 486 are abysmal.

International organizations such as Planned Parenthood and the Population Council who fund research on these contraceptives and promote their use, as well as the multinational corporations that manufacture them, invoke the founding demands of the women's movement itself as they market these drugs. Women's lives, rights of self-determination and choice, privacy, autonomy, and empowerment is now on the agenda of multinational capital. What is more, powerful feminist lobbies such as the Feminist Majority in the USA endorse these claims. Consider a widely publicized statement by Werner Foros, president of the Washington-based Population Institute, released in Bombay as part of an initiative to counter efforts by Indian women's groups to oppose Norplant. While Foros does cite resource shortage in third world countries as an important factor in population planning, he seems far more distressed that a majority of women in such countries had no control over their fertility, that the important right of 'choice' was not available to them. In the same statement, he quotes a survey in which 300 million women worldwide had said that they hadn't wanted their last child; 'women today do two-thirds of the work, earn only one-tenth of the money and own less than one per cent of the property. So the empowerment of women is perhaps the most important intervention we can pursue.' His goal was a population programme in which the 'poorest of poor couples has the means to make a choice'.[15]

Similarly, the scientist Etienne-Emile Baulieu—consultant and spokesperson for the multinational Roussel-Uclaf who have developed the abortifacient pill, RU 486—speaks of it as the 'moral property of women'. It is a duty, he claims, to make the right to this property available in the third world: 'Denying this pill is basically signing the death warrant

[15] 'Men's attitudes are big hurdles', interview with Sonora Jha Nambiar, *The Sunday Times (of India)*, 1 Nov. 1992, p. 11. In what appeared to be a well organized campaign, Fornos, Sai, and other functionaries of these and similar organizations seemed to have been brought to India principally to endorse the government's Norplant programme, stalled by a writ filed by some feminist organizations. They were provided high profile coverage in the press (Rahul Singh, Bachi Karkaria, Darryl D'Monte, Rashme Seghal interviewed them and discussed Norplant). The articles invoked the horrors of an expanding India, welcomed scientific advances such as Norplant and decried women's protest against it as 'vociferous and clearly misguided', misinformed, 'unfortunate and politicized', and as holding up progress when the country was on the brink of disaster.

for the 200,000 women who die [worldwide] annually from abortion.'[16] Fred Sai, president of Planned Parenthood, feels that the most serious problem facing India's otherwise praiseworthy efforts at population control is the lack of 'contraceptive options' that are offered to the Indian woman and the consequent limits to the choices she can make as an individual with an individualized profile of requirements.[17]

The feminist credentials of those who research into and promote these contraceptives are further consolidated when their initiatives are presented as enabling and empowering women in conservative or religion-bound contexts. Thus the campaign for the abortifacient pill stressed the fact that women would initiate and control the abortion process themselves, and that they could do so without telling anyone else in the family. In brief, the promise was of technologically bypassing social or legal prohibition: 'What could be more private than taking a pill, how could a state control swallowing?'[18] In the USA the Feminist Majority spoke of anti-abortionists as the common enemy of women and science, since 'both women's health and freedom of research are being sacrificed by allowing anti-abortion extremists to block the production and distribution of RU 486'.[19] Proponents of Norplant and Net-Oen in India argue that long-acting implants or injectables that do not interrupt intercourse and do not require women to do anything on a regular basis are particularly suitable for an illiterate and backward population. They also point out that these drugs expand the options open to women, and allow Indian women to take decisions about contraception that do not require the cooperation of their husbands or the sanction of their families. Choice and privacy are both invoked in the battle which is set up as one between the good, progressive, pro-woman scientists and promoters of these contraceptives, and their conservative, anti-woman opponents. Thus the 'limited options' offered by our population programme are attributed 'to the conservative Indian medical mindset, which has reservations about hormonal contraceptives' (*Times of India*, 1 Nov. 1992), while the stalling of Net-Oen and

[16] Fern Chapman, 'The Politics of the Abortion Pill', *Washington Post*, 3 Oct. 1989, p. 13. Cited in Renate Klein, Janice G. Raymond and Lynette J. Dumble, *RU 486 Misconceptions, Myths and Morals* (Spinnifex, Melbourne, 1991).

[17] Quoted by Sara Adhikari in 'Countdown to Disaster', *The Sunday Times (of India)*, 1 Nov. 1992, p. 11.

[18] Ellen Goodman, 'Moral Property', *The Boston Globe*, 17 July 1989, p. 11. Cited in Klein, et al., p. 25.

[19] Klein, et al., pp. 5–6. The recent decision to make RU 486 available in the USA was seen as a feminist victory.

Norplant, first by feminist litigation and later by the drug controller who has called for fresh trials, is decried respectively as 'unfortunate and politicized (*The Independent*, 22 Oct. 1992), the handiwork of a few 'vociferous and clearly misguided' groups (*The Week*, 16 Nov. 1992), and as inefficiency and 'procrastination that hinders real progress' (*Times of India*, 1 Nov. 1992).

The figure of the woman that is being liberated and endowed with rights in these discourses requires scrutiny. The use of these contraceptives is premised on the notion that wise planning and scientifically developed products can fulfil women's demands for liberty and self-determination (and catapult them into modernity) without changes in existing family relations or in society at large; in other words, the promise is of a technological fix that can bypass sexual politics and indeed the network of relations in which women are gendered and subjugated. For example, most of the women who die attempting abortion die not because existing methods are unsafe but because abortion is *illegal*, and has to be done furtively in ill-equipped places and possibly by untrained personnel. This fact finds no place in these statements; neither does the fact that problems arise even in countries like India where abortion is legal, because a 'standardized' medical education does not train doctors to perform abortions. The abortifacient pill is not going to change that situation; indeed, as a technology it is designed to evade such issues and ends up, (a) placing the entire burden for what continues to be a difficult and often illegal procedure on the individual woman; (b) putting women's health in considerable danger; and (c) ruthlessly expanding what might be thought of as 'reasonable' risk and 'tolerable' pain or discomfort to make up for the irrationality of the system.

Norplant was developed as a drug that could be used on unruly and recalcitrant populations not only in the third world but also in the first. It targets the woman, is long-acting, does not need a literate or numerate user, does not require the user's cooperation after it has been implanted, and can be monitored by the authorities with just a glance at the woman's arm. Despite the huge investments in propaganda about woman's choice, Norplant's potential as an instrument of control was clearly recognized. In the USA, less than a month after it was passed by the Food and Drug Administration, a judge ordered that a convicted woman should not be let out on probation unless she agreed to have the implant. A newspaper editorial suggested that because of growing poverty among the blacks, welfare mothers should be offered incentives to use Norplant (*Philadelphia Inquirer*, 12 Dec. 1990). Norplant is now promoted in much-advertised population control programmes in some of the most coercive regimes in the third world—Chile, Indonesia, the Philippines, China—and the somewhat less obliging Indian government is described as 'lacking political commitment' or indulging in 'procrastination . . . that hinders real progress when the country is 'hurtling towards disaster'.

Women's freedom, agency, and choice is invoked only within the closed-off, private domains of the family and of reproduction, which are in turn imaged as extremely—and unchangeably—conservative and chauvinist. These assumptions underlie the production and marketing of the contraceptives, but they are socially endorsed, elaborated, and reproduced in the family welfare programme as a whole through advertising campaigns, institutional arrangements and attitudes. In addition, the wide range of sexual and familial relations that exist in the country and the variety of subject–positions that are therefore available to a woman are, in the process, homogenized and naturalized in a conservative mode. For example, these contraceptives assume that women have no control over the conditions in which they get pregnant; that contraception cannot be negotiated or discussed by the couple; that the woman has no right to refuse sex. No attempt is made to reinforce or envisage more egalitarian relationships or place responsibility on the man. In the world of the family welfare programme, a man who is not a male chauvinist is a contradiction in terms. No questions are asked about the nature and quality of existing health care systems and the complex factors that mediate different women's access to them. The politics of the private is not addressed, and no questions are asked about the contradictions between various women's requirements and the national and internationalist agendas of population control. Women's freedom begins to look alarmingly like the freedom to consume these expensive and dangerous products in a climate of disinformation that makes a mockery of 'consent'. These discourses continue to address the question of women's rights and invoke women as free agents in vocabulary drawn from feminism, but only within the once again depoliticized and privatized domains of the family and of reproduction.

The problem is that a whole range of issues that constitute the subjugation of women, and indeed their differential subjugation in relation to class, caste, and community, are naturalized in the 'woman' whose freedom and right to privacy is invoked and who becomes the bearer of the 'right' to choose. The very same move also makes it possible to bring this individual's rights into alignment with the interests of population control and multinational profit. For instance, hormonal injectables/

implants might be considered as expanding contraceptive options for women in situations where they have ready access to an efficient and well-equipped medical set-up. To put it in different terms, for a woman whose caste, class, and community positioning matches that of the citizen–subject, hormonals might be regarded as genuine 'choices'. Yet, ironically, these contraceptives were never developed for this woman. They were intended for 'less desirable' demographic groups: the teeming millions of the third world, non-white immigrants in the first world, criminals. Corresponding, in our national context, are the rural 'masses' and the urban poor, a majority of whom are Dalits and Muslims, and of course Muslims in general. Feminists using arguments about women's health have been able to drive a wedge into one fault-line in this structure. Yet untouched however are issues of caste, class, and community that require us to expand the problematic beyond that of the 'rights of the liberal body'. Women—as individuals or in groups—have to bear the increasingly heavy burden of these contradictions as they invent resources with which to negotiate their ever more demanding citizenship and to survive.

V

Hindutva Women

Women on the Right have also opened up a space that might in many ways be regarded as feminist. As Tanika Sarkar points out in a study of the Rashtrasevika Samiti (the women's wing of the RSS), women are 'active political subjects' not only in the Samiti, but also more generally in the domain of communal politics.[20] The women leaders of the BJP are not daughters, wives, or mothers of deceased male leaders. They are there in their own right and seem to have carved out distinctive political roles and identities for themselves. Equally significant is the articulate and often passionate involvement of women who otherwise seem to have little interest in public life in issues such as reservations, the appeasement of Muslims, or corruption in the bureaucracy. Riots now have a new profile, with women, sometimes even middle-class women, actively participating as in Bhagalpur in 1989, Ahmedabad in 1990, or Surat in 1992. News photographs showed a sizeable number of women among those arriving

---

[20] Tanika Sarkar, 'The Woman as Communal Subject: Rashtrasevika Samiti and Ram Janmabhoomi Movement', *Economic and Political Weekly* XXVI: 35 (31 Aug. 1991), p. 2062. Henceforth cited in the text as TS.

for the 1992 Ayodhya *kar seva*. Several papers carried reports of Sadhvi Rithambara and Uma Bharati cheering on the crowd that tore down the Babri Masjid.

More striking—and in some ways more disturbing—than the appearance of this militant individual on the public battlefields of Hindutva is her modernity and indeed her feminism. The new Hindu woman nearly always belongs to the most conservative groups in Indian society—upperclass/caste, middle-ranking government service or trading sectors—but she cannot be regarded as traditional in any simple sense of the term, any more than Hindutva can be read as fundamentalist.[21] There is very little talk of going back to tradition. The focus is on injustice, for which the Babri Masjid serves as symbol. At issue in the war of Hindutva, which is defined after Savarkar as love for the motherland, is not Hinduism, but the Indian nation.

Predictably, self-respect is an important theme. However, hitched into women's aspirations for self-respect is the idea of Hindu self-respect. One account of the origin of the Samiti is that Lakshmibai Kelkar founded it after she saw *goondas* (interestingly not Muslims) raping a woman in the presence of her husband. Since Hindu men (who are in this story both lustful and weak) could not protect their wives, Hindu women had to train to do so themselves (TS 2061). As in authoritarian politics the world over, the emphasis is on discipline and on purging or cleansing the social body of corruption, using force if necessary. While the immediate object appears to be Indian society, the Muslim enemy is very close to the surface here. In the RSS/VHP/BJP imaginary, the *matrabhumi* is presented as a repeatedly raped female body and the myth of the enemy within and of Muslim lust play key structural roles. Thus, for Muslims '*aurat matrabhumi nahin hai, bhog bhumi hai*' (Woman is not the motherland, but the earth to be enjoyed).[22] The violence women experience and their need to fight against and gain respect within their own society is all but obscured as the well-made enemy steps in, suggesting that self-respect is best gained in the protection of the motherland. The fact that in the projected Hindu

---

[21] Each one of the office-bearers of the Rashtrasevika Samiti, Tanika Sarkar points out, denounced sati. What about voluntary sati? 'A young activist said with genuine revulsion: *Woh ho nahin sakta. Aurat jalengi kyoon?*' (That can never happen. Why would a woman burn herself?) Shakha members do not use their caste names and everybody eats together. The Samiti is not against inter-caste or even inter-community marriage—provided the families agree (ibid.).

[22] Pradip Datta, Biswamoy Pati, *et al.*, 'Understanding Communal Violence: Nizamuddin Riots', *Economic and Political Weekly* XXV: 45 (10 Nov. 1990), p. 2494.

rashtra Muslims would not be allowed four wives was regarded by *kar-sevika*s at Ayodhya as index of the respect women would receive in that utopia (TS 2062).

Like the anti-Mandal agitation, Hindutva would seem to have enabled an articulate, fighting individualism for women and for men. Its power is productive in the Foucauldian sense, inciting its subjects to speak out and act, to become independent, agentive, citizen–individuals. One notices increasingly the confident exponents of Hindutva (students, otherwise unremarkable middle-class men and women) who intervene at seminars and public meetings. These subjects are marked as authentically Indian and as having found an ethos within which their natural—and national—expressive selves can emerge and be sustained.

It is important to understand that though this new Hindu self is represented as discriminated against and embattled, it has the confidence of occupying a 'neutral' ground that provides the basis for a new moral authority. Hindutva, for example, is represented as a potential national ethos within which all other religions and communities might be justly housed. The claim is commonly backed by two arguments. One, a re-deployment of nationalist versions of Indian history in which Hinduism is represented as having a long tradition of tolerance; the other an invocation of Western nation-states and their endorsement of dominant religious traditions in the secularism they practice. The history of violence through which those national bourgeoises established authority is never discussed. The new Hindu subject speaks the voice of a reason that opposes false dogmas (such as Western theories, pseudo-secularism), challenges the bias of existing institutions (the courts, the constitution) on the ground that they are not sensitive to the desires of the majority and appeals to truths that are self-evident to genuine Indians. Thus Girilal Jain writes about the 'bloated rhetoric of secularism, constitutionalism and the law' (*Times of India*, 12 Dec. 1992), while Swapan Dasgupta comments after the demolition of the Masjid:

In effect the *kar sevak*s presented Hindu society with a *fait accompli*. They could either disown the illegal act on account of both politics and aesthetics. Or they could come to terms with their own assertiveness, equate it with the storming of the Bastille and the collapse of the *ancient regime*, and prepare to face the consequences. [*Sunday*, 20–6 Dec. 1992, p. 9.]

In moves that are surprisingly quickly effected and apparently hold conviction for increasingly large numbers of Indians, the virulent anti-Muslim history of Hindutva, a political agenda focused on pulling down a mosque and building a temple, and a record of communal violence, is gilded over and legitimized as Hindutva reoccupies the discourses in which bourgeois nationalism established authority in its European birthplace—and, more important from the point of view of our argument in this chapter, the forms of subjectivity that emerged in tandem with it. Thus L.K. Advani (invariably represented in the press as mature, soft-spoken, and charming) insists that his is actually the only 'secular' party. The demolition of the Babri Masjid is only a 'temporary setback'. A.B. Vajpayee (honourable, reasonable, cultured) exonerates the real BJP by locating communalism only in its 'young and overenthusiastic party workers' (*Indian Express*, 26 Dec. 1992).[23] The angle on neutrality that appears in the context of the gender question is more telling. Members of the Rashtrasevika Samiti distinguished their position from that of other women's organizations by saying, 'when we arbitrate we do not always take the woman's side. We are neutral. . . . *Hum ghar torne-wale nahin hain.*' (We are not home-breakers) (TS 2062). Similar evidence of 'neutrality' in relation to caste or class is not difficult to locate.

The politics of this neutrality-effect demands closer scrutiny. The BJP/VHP/RSS combine are pressing in on a whole set of existing figures, logics, and institutions as they lay claim to the nation and to neutrality. As their allusions to European history and to first world nationalism also indicate, a figure that is repeatedly referenced is the bourgeois citizen–subject and the world that was 'legitimately'—and ruthlessly—recast in his interests and in his singular image. Closer home is the neutrality of the Nehruvian state and of planned development in which the 'social' problems of caste, class, and gender, and colonialism are addressed and analysed by scientific planners and handed over to the bureaucracy for redress. The problem, briefly summarized, is that though this state acknowledges social disbalances and accepts responsibility for righting them, it functions on the basis of an executive centrality in which the state is authorized to speak and act for the people. It is becoming increasingly clear that the task of shaping this executive centrality and a social imaginary that authorized it, dominated cultural politics in the immediate post-Independence period. Identities that had taken shape in major pre-Independence class, caste, and gender struggles, and which might have provided the basis for another social imaginary

---

[23] The Left Front government in West Bengal distinguished itself at the time of the Bantala and Birati rapes by very similar evasions. *See* Tanika Ṣarkar, 'Reflections on the Birati Rape Cases: Gender Ideology in Bengal', *Economic and Political Weekly* XXVI: 5 (2 Feb. 1991).

of the nation, were fractured and disorganized as they were rewritten
into narratives of humanity and citizenship. The task, however, is an
ongoing one, for hegemony is continuously under threat. Films, novels,
histories, television programmes, the press in general, the curricula, and
a range of their institutions of civil society address potentially rupturing
questions of caste, gender or community and rework them into narratives
that legitimate the middle-class, upper-caste Hindu, patriarchal and
internationalist markings of the hegemonic subject.

As a result of this alliance with the subject of humanism, the common
sense of the new Right has a much greater hold than the formal/electoral
support received by the BJP might suggest. Thus, whether one looks at
the mainstream press or at the apparently non-political programmes put
out by Doordarshan (the morning chat shows, the evening serials, the
children's programmes, the afternoon women's programmes), or ways of
thinking, feeling, reasoning, and arriving at conclusions that govern the
daily lives of the growing consumer population, Hindutva seems well set
to becoming hegemonic. Powerful new discursive articulations are thus
effected between this individualism and organic–conservative themes of
religion, tradition, nation, family, personal integrity, order, and discipline.
The discussion on minorityism, injury/appeasement, pseudo-secularism,
and nationalism have brought these subjects into focus in a virulently
anti-Muslim frame and as it feeds directly into a genealogy of modern
Indian womanhood that marks it not only as Hindu, but as upper caste/
class, the Muslim woman is caught in a curious zero-zero game. Either
way she loses. She cannot really be woman any more that she can be
Indian. As woman and as Indian, she cannot really be Muslim. As for the
women on the Right, they are indeed empowered by these new movements, but in a way that sets up the feminist project as one that endorses
caste/class hierarchies and the othering of Islam.

VI

We have been arguing that the hegemonic articulation of the gender issue
sets up the feminist subject in an antagonistic relationship with, for example, class–caste (Mandal–Chunduru), or religious identity (women on
the Right), and in such a way as to aid the reabsorption of this subject
into consumer capitalism. We now turn to our last metonym, the anti-
arrack movement in Andhra Pradesh. The various ways in which the
movement has been interpreted and 'women' have been represented seem

to work in such a way as to erase and delegitimize earlier feminist initiatives. The process is not a simple one, and we do not claim that we have
been able to map all—or even most—of its complicated strategies and
effects. Media depictions of the anti-arrack movement annex its initiative
into a variety of contemporary discourses about the nation, its women,
and the purification of the former by the virtue of the latter. Feminist
theory and practice are caught in a curious set of contradictions. The
portrayal of the anti-arrack women as the only authentic feminists, paradoxically also involves, (a) a denial that their struggle is concerned specifically with *women's issues*, and (b) a reinscription of it as an anti-feudal
struggle, or as a struggle to cleanse the body politic and save the nation.
What seems to enable both the denial and the reinscription is the invoking
of the anti-arrack woman as the subject of humanism. Interestingly, in
terms of the positions offered to the female/feminist subject, there is little
to distinguish the articulators of the women's issue in a conservative, high
nationalist mode from those who invoke it as part of the class (or specifically anti-feudal) struggle. As these diverse writers seek to separate the
anti-arrack movement from historical feminism, they obscure crucial dimensions of the radical egalitarian potential of actually existing feminism.
At the same time, they make invisible dimensions of the anti-arrack
movement that find resonance with other feminist initiatives.

What are the facets of the anti-arrack struggle that become visible as
we contest these dominant representations of it? What implications do
they have for contemporary feminist practice and gender theory? We
begin with a brief narrative of the movement.

A series of struggles centred around government-backed sales of arrack (*sara* in Telugu) have been taking place over the past decade or so in
various regions of Andhra Pradesh. In each region, different local configurations have sustained arrack as an issue; while in the Telengana
region and in a few other districts the CPI(M–L) groups have initiated or
supported the agitation, in some of the coastal Andhra districts the movement seems to have emerged in conjunction with other events, such as
the adult literacy programme. Women all over rural Andhra Pradesh
attacked excise department jeeps and police, burned arrack packets, pun-
ished arrack sellers, and fined the men who continued to drink. After
September 1992 the movement appears to have gathered rapid momentum, spreading from village to village in a manner that no organized
political party has been able to predict or control. Since the article which
was the basis for this chapter was originally written in December 1992,
there have been further developments: the Andhra Pradesh government

announced a ban on arrack in Nellore District from 15 April 1993, and throughout the state from 1 October 1993. The ruling Congress–I claimed the ban as a pro-people initiative on its part. Enormous coloured hoardings depicted the evils of arrack, portrayed smiling rural families freed from the menace, and Chief Minister Vijayabhaskara Reddy gazed benevolently on the scene from gigantic cut-outs towering above the hoardings, which were put up at major intersections in the capital city of Hyderabad.[24] The audio-visual publicity machinery of the government ventured into remote areas of Andhra Pradesh to spread propaganda about the need to stop drinking arrack. In the Assembly elections of November 1994, the Congress suffered a major defeat, and the Telugu Desam Party (which had earlier introduced the government-sponsored distribution of arrack) returned to power. The new Chief Minister, N.T. Rama Rao, declared within minutes of taking office that prohibition of all liquor would immediately come into force in the state. He was only acceding, he said, to the demand of the sisters who had voted for him.

Each political organization, however, seemed to appropriate the *sara* women, laying claim to their struggle, and configuring them as the true subjects of feminism. The range is an astonishing one: from the Gandhians to the Lohiaites to the Telugu Desam to the BJP/RSS; from the Marxist–Leninist parties to the traditional Left (CPM and CPI) to the Dalit Mahasabha; not to mention women's organizations across the spectrum: from the Arya Mahila Samiti to the socialist Mahila Dakshata Samiti, from the A.P. Mahila Sangham to the two Progressive Organizations for Women backed by different M–L parties. The woman in the anti-arrack struggle appeared as a Romantic subject, and predicated onto her were an assortment of complex narratives of which she was sole heroine.[25]

The BJP MP, Uma Bharati, praising the anti-arrack women, wanted 'women' 'also [to] campaign against dowry, craze for foreign goods and corruption'; she felt they should 'help create national awakening (*swadeshi jagran*)' (*The Hindu*, 20 Oct. 1992). The BJP in Nellore District where the movement was very strong are said to have named the women as Shakti, Kali, and Durga, just as the all-India vice-president of the BJP, Jana Krishnamurthy, declared that '*matru shakti* [mother's strength, power] had

[24] Government Order (G.O.) No. 402 dated 24 April 1993. Announcing the ban, Vijayabhaskara Reddy said that total prohibition was the 'policy of the Congress Party right from the start' and the ban had nothing to do with the crusade launched by the Telugu Desam.

[25] They use the word 'Romantic' as shorthand for the free, agentive, expressive, spontaneous rebel subject typical of the nineteenth-century literary–cultural movement of Romanticism.

caused others to fall in line' (*The Hindu*, 12 Oct. 1992). Taking a slightly different but related stand, Dalitbahujan theorist K. Ilaiah spoke of the movement as asserting 'the mother's right to set the family right'.[26] Va-vilala Gopalakrishnaiah, an elderly freedom fighter, argued that the anti-arrack movement was 'similar to the freedom movement' and that 'care should be taken to see that it will not be politicized' (*The Hindu*, 16 Oct. 1992).[27] 'Mothers with babies in their arms walk miles to come for de-monstrations, wrote Vimala of the POW (*Nalupu*, 1–31 Oct. 1992). The imagery was that of woman 'who has come out into the street [*veedhiloki vacchindi*]' (film actress Sharada, in *Eenadu*, 5 Oct. 1992); and, as in the anti-Mandal agitation, or in the nationalist movement, this woman be-came the icon of purity and idealism.

In trying to explain why women were out on the streets, writers seem to obscure many factors that might have enabled the rebellion to find articulation, such as the withdrawal of the rice subsidy, the carefully planned increase in arrack sales, the literacy classes and the stories about arrack in the literacy primers. What is offered instead is the picture of the village woman's eternal tears and suffering, and how *sara* 'sucks the blood of the poor' (*Nalupu*, 1–31 Oct. 1992). When driven to extreme despair, suggest the dominant narratives, the woman's human essence asserts itself and allows her to claim the status of citizen–subject.[28] Interestingly, the assertion of her 'civility' is premised on her being wife and mother, on her concern for her children and husband. What the woman desires, as Sharada would have it, is 'happiness in the family' (*Eenadu*, 5 Oct. 1992) and that the auspicious marks of her marriage (*paspu-kumkumam*) not be taken from her. This refiguring of the authentic subject of feminism seems to be an implicit critique, for example, of urban feminists as they are customarily imagined in the dominant cultural representations of our time. This authentic feminist subject is characterized by a retired judge as a rural woman with 'a specific nature of her own'; 'she lives as a slave to custom as long as she can, and when she cannot tolerate that life any more and begins to break barriers, neither men nor the urban women can imagine the manner in which she will struggle. She has nerve' (Justice

[26] K. Ilaiah, 'Andhra Pradesh's Anti-Liquor Movement', *Economic and Political Weekly* XXVII: 43 (1992), p. 2408.
[27] There are interesting parallels with the anti-Mandal agitation, which many intellectuals acclaimed as a manifestation of nationalism, at the same time warning against any attempt to 'politicize' it.
[28] 'The tears of thousands of families are pushing them into the struggle', says the actress Sharada (*Eenadu*, 5 Oct. 1992).

Arula Sambasiva Rao, in *Eenadu*, 6 Oct. 1992). The woman's militancy is coded as that spirit which makes her a good wife and mother; the true sati demonstrates her *paativratya* or devotion not by being passive but by acting aggressively to save her husband from an untimely death.

By emphasizing the 'familial' impulse behind women's militancy, dominant explanatory narratives deny the status of the *political* to their actions and seek to contain their scope. A celebratory report in *Indian Express* (13 Oct. 1992) described the anti-arrack issue as 'a burning social question'; N.T. Rama Rao of the Telugu Desam Party invoked the memory of Gandhi's desire to impose prohibition and his (Gandhi's) opinion that 'only womenfolk could bring about this social change' (*Indian Express*, 15 Oct. 1992). Ramoji Rao, editor and publisher of *Eenadu* Telugu daily that gave extensive coverage to the *sara* struggle, said: 'Every individual who keeps trust in the values of social life should wholeheartedly welcome the Great Movement [*Mahodyamam*]. . . . Everybody with flesh and blood, who has a sense of shame, and humanism, is cheering the struggle' (*Eenadu* editorial, 25 Oct. 1992). Analysts on the Left seemed to veer between interpreting the movement as one for social reform (personal conversation with CPM members) and seeing it as 'part of the anti-feudal struggle' (*Nalupu*, 1–15 Nov. 1992). That the movement was perceived by some as 'leaderless' helped to push towards a characterization of it as 'non-political'. As Ramoji Rao put it in an editorial, the movement had 'transcended caste, religion, class and party' although after it had gathered momentum various 'political parties and women's organizations are now hurrying after it' (*Eenadu* editorial, 13 Sept. 1992).

The obverse of the refusal to image the women as political actors is the bestowal on them of a social role, that of rescuing not only their families but also 'saving the nation'. The hegemonic narratives *authorize* the women, give them 'moral authority' to *cleanse* a body politic 'stinking of *sara*' (*Eenadu* editorial, 13 Sept. 1992). Once again, the consensus in terms of analysis and solution is stunning. Across the political spectrum, writers set up an elaborate demonology in which the valiant women battle the forces of evil, represented by the politicians, the arrack contractors, government officials, industrialists, and the whole 'corrupt' apparatus of state and civil society.[29] The meaning of *sara* (K. Balagopal calls it the 'obscene fluid') here becomes that which is unnameable and disgusting beyond belief, stands for the 'uncivilized politics'[30] abhorred

---

[29] *See*, for instance, civil liberties activist K. Balagopal's 'Slaying of a Spirituous Demon', *Economic and Political Weekly* XXVII: 46 (1992), pp. 2457–61.

[30] The phrase is from the AP Civil Liberties Committee press statement, issued

by the enlightened secular humanist. Repeatedly, *sara* is evoked not only as being 'responsible for all the violence and atrocities on women' (Suman Krishna Kant, Mahila Dakshata Samiti chair, in *Eenadu*, 3 Oct. 1992) but also as signifying the source of all evil and corruption; and it is rural women who are 'blowing the conch-shell of battle to destroy the atrocious *sara* demon' (*Eenadu* editorial, 25 Oct. 1992). As K. Balagopal puts it, 'The supreme courage and tenacity of thousands of rural women has pitted itself against the abysmal humbug of the state's rulers . . . [and the women] have taken up sickle and broomstick to drive the obscenity out of all our lives' (*Economic and Political Weekly*, 14 Nov. 1992, p. 2457). The anti-arrack movement will 'cleanse us of corruption' (A CPM supporter, in personal conversation); a polity that has fallen away from the idealistic days of nationalism will have its moral impurity washed away by the *sara* women.

What other readings might be possible both of the problem and the struggle? We would want to contest the dominant representations, for example, by suggesting that the *sara* movement is a significant elaboration of the politics of everyday life, and that in such a reading questions of gender, class, caste, and community come into a radically different configuration, where the emphasis shifts from moral purity to economic exploitation or the aspiration for physical well-being.

The observations that follow, necessarily impressionistic, are based on our visit to twelve villages in three *mandals* of Nellore District in November 1992.[31] While the women's success in reducing or even preventing arrack sales directly affected the State and can be seen without much effort as a 'political' action, the movement also seemed to have resulted in a reconfiguring of power—and gender relations—within villages. Women did not usually confront individual men in their homes but attacked the local *sara* shop and the excise jeeps that supply liquor. The women also seemed to articulate many domains of their life in political terms or as political issues (even areas that class analysis would see as 'economic'). As Kondamma of Thotlacheruvupalli put it: 'Why does the government send us *sara*? Let them give us water instead, and we could have two crops a year. Now we have nothing.' Commenting on the State's indifference to their lives, she pointed out that while they had 'home delivery'

by K.G. Kannabiran and K. Balagopal (*Eenadu*, 18 Sept. 1992).

[31] We were part of a team sent to Nellore by Anveshi Research Centre for Women's Studies, Hyderabad. Our account of the movement draws heavily on the Anveshi report of the visit.

of arrack they had to go nearly twenty miles to the nearest town to treat a simple case of diarrhoea. In this village (Udaygiri Mandal, Nellore District), the women had pulled down the arrack shop and collected donations to build a stone platform over it which they used for public meetings. 'Why should we care', said Kondamma, 'if the government is losing money on *sara* because of us. When they had profits, did we see any of it? If the government has losses, let them cut *your* salaries.' Marvelling at the state's obtuseness, she remarked: 'You should feed a buffalo before you milk it, otherwise it'll kick. And we've kicked.' 'This year we won't vote for anyone', she continued. 'They're all the same. And if our men want to vote, there'll be war between us.'

Other women, in the village of Kacheridevarayapalli (Anantsagar Mandal, Nellore District), drew up a figurative balance sheet that assigned a different set of meanings to *sara*. The *cost* of the government's Rs 850 crores of excise revenue was death (caused by the men's drunkenness—the deaths were those of themselves as well as of the women, the latter often suicides), hunger, ill-health, lack of education for the children, constant debt, their belongings—all the pots and pans and all their clothes—pawned for buying *sara*, their mental anguish. When they got rid of *sara*, said the women, they began to eat twice a day, the village streets were clean ('no drunks vomiting all over the place'), everyone's health improved ('the men are getting fat and contented'), they had peace of mind ('*ippudu manasushanti undi*'), freedom from abuse, and solvency. The village landlords expressed the fear that labourers who had stopped drinking *sara* and were now able to save a little would not come to them for loans. Agricultural wages would now have to be paid in real money rather than partly in packets of *sara* obtained at a discount. Women's growing control over wages was beginning to undermine long-standing structures of dependency. What is seldom noted in the celebratory accounts of the origin-stories of the anti-arrack movement is the Congress government's withdrawal of the rice subsidy for low-income families. The movement could be seen then as a critique, in a sense, not only of the State but also of the priorities of the globalizing economy and the effects on everyday life of structural adjustment and the contemporary reorganization of markets.

Many of the women in the movement spoke of the significance education, or literacy, has for them. One of the stories we heard about the beginnings of the movement was about an inaugural function in Ayyavaripalli village for the government-initiated Akshara Deepam programme designed to eradicate illiteracy. The function, attended by a State Cabinet

Minister and the District Collector, was disrupted by some drunken men. The women of the village, as in all other villages the only ones who attended the night classes, demanded the closure of the local *sara* shop so that their classes could be held in peace. Willing to promise anything to ensure the success of the literacy programme, the officials complied. This and other narratives about women's achievements were written into the post-literacy primers; stories such as the one about Dubagunta village ('*Adavallu Ekamaithe*'—If Women Unite) where three drunken labourers lost their way and drowned in a tank. A hundred women first stopped the local arrack cart from entering the village; then they turned back 'a jeep full of *sara* packets'; after this, the lesson goes, the police arrived to enforce the right of the contractor to sell arrack. The women stood their ground, saying they would go to the Collector if necessary. 'This year', the lesson concludes, 'no one came forward to bid for arrack in our village'.[32] Women also spoke of other lessons, charts, and topics for discussion in their literacy primers, such as 'Seethamma Katha', 'Unity', and 'Who's Responsible for this Death?', which inspired them to join the struggle against arrack. 'We want our children to go to school', said Kondamma of Thotlacheruvupalli. This claiming *from below* of the right to education makes evident one of the most important agendas of the anti-Mandal agitation, the denial of education to the lower castes.[33] The upper-caste anxiety about educated Dalits, as in Chunduru, is to prevent them from occupying the space of the modern as it has been marked out in the post-colonial nation. The *sara* women's claiming of education seemed to recognize this logic and challenge the exclusions of modernity itself. The Dalit and Muslim women engaged in the struggle seemed to be articulating a claim on the rights of the citizen, from a critical perspective not necessarily predicated on their 'human essence'.

In spite of the fact that the women in the movement were predominantly from the Scheduled Caste, Backward Caste, and Muslim communities, their jointly undertaken efforts to stop the excise officials received the tacit support of the upper-caste women of their village. Although it is an understanding obtained from the women's perspective that allowed them to claim *sara* as 'their' issue, the movement seldom pitted them against individual men, or against women from other castes/communities.

---

[32] *Chaduvu Velugu* and *Akshara Deepam* literacy primers. We are grateful to T.S.S. Lakshmi and K. Sajaya for providing translations of the lessons.

[33] A popular anti-Mandal refrain was that educational opportunities for lower caste people would wean them away from their traditional occupations, turn them into clerks, and thereby destroy the handicrafts and textiles that symbolized Indian culture.

A unique feature of the anti-arrack movement was the refusal of the women to take up initiatives beyond their village. As Mastan-bi of Kacheridevarayapalli put it, 'Are the women of the other villages dead? Why should *we* go there to fight against *sara*?' In relating their initiatives to the specificity of their location (their slogan is *Maa ooriki sara vaddu*— 'We don't want sara in our village'), in demarcating a domain over which they can exercise control, the anti-arrack women seem to be envisaged, and engaged, in a politics of the possible.[34]

VII

It seems to us that the early 1990s represent a turning point for Indian feminism. Each of the metonyms we have chosen for analysis focus on hegemonic mobilizations of a 'feminist' subject specific to our times. Each displays the contradictions that emerge within feminist politics and the challenges that confront gender analysis in the context of the refiguring of dominance in a rapidly globalizing Indian economy. Clearly the metonyms evidence an undertow in existing Indian feminism of structures of domination. Yet the anti-Mandal agitation, the politics of contraceptive choice, the feminism of the Hindu Right, or the representations of the anti-arrack movement provide us also with configurations that crystallize and precipitate the possibilities of new and more radical alliances. This chapter has been primarily concerned with the exploration of factors that disable alliances between feminism and other democratic political initiatives, but we regard this as a crucial first step in the shaping of a feminism capable of a counter-hegemonic politics adequate to our times.

It is possible that in this essay this concern has not allowed us to focus richly enough on the democratic potential of actually existing feminism. Yet it is clearly this potential that both demands and empowers the kind of critical engagement evident in our argument. It is also precisely this democratic potential that has enabled us as feminists to support Dalit movements or take part in anti-communal initiatives today. By confronting the specific genealogy of the woman–subject and its impress on contemporary politics, we have tried also to open up for investigation the subject of democracy–secularism in India.

---

[34] We take this phrase from Kumkum Sangari's well-known article, 'The Politics of the Possible', reprinted in Tejaswini Niranjana, P. Sudhir, and Vivek Dhareshwar (eds), *Interrogating Modernity: Culture and Colonialism in India* (Seagull Books, Calcutta, 1993).

9

Discussion Outside History: Irish New Histories and the 'Subalternity Effect'

DAVID LLOYD

This essay has a threefold agenda. I hope first to provide an account of recent shifts in Irish historiography that align some of its practitioners, implicitly if not programmatically, with the kinds of questioning that have been associated with *Subaltern Studies*. Secondly, I wish to explore the implications of such historical work for Irish cultural studies, concentrating on the ways in which the study of subaltern groups in Ireland as elsewhere has entailed equally a critique of the 'modernizing' or enlightenment assumptions that structure a state formation largely inherited from British imperial institutions. Thirdly, I want to engage with criticisms of such a critique of enlightenment, in particular with those from a feminist perspective, in order to nuance the kinds of exploration that may be undertaken under the rubrics of subalternity or 'post-colonialism'.

That some of these issues will seem familiar to readers of *Subaltern Studies* and of associated work helps to underscore two linked remarks of a theoretical nature that from the outset I wish to make. The first relates to the designation of Ireland as 'post-colonial'. This cannot, under present political conditions, be an innocent categorization, since it implies that

that portion of the island under British rule is, properly speaking, still colonized. This assertion will be hotly, if not always rigorously, contested by some, and particularly by those who seek to defend the normative status of British 'civil society' in Ireland. Clearly, for them the expression 'post-colonial' used of any part of the island seems to legitimate the view that the current conflict is a final stage in the history of Ireland's de-colonization and must accordingly be contested. In so far as it relates to contemporary issues, this chapter will take as its premise that Ireland has been and remains a site of colonialism and anti-colonial struggle but will suggest that that struggle needs to be articulated around a far broader interpretation of the concept of the 'post-colonial' than one defined prin-cipally by national independence or unification. I will return to this point in greater detail below.

But the designation 'post-colonial' will also be contested for different reasons, especially by those who would argue that Ireland's location on the western edge of Europe properly links its history to European national struggles, to Young Italy, or to Polish and Hungarian nationalism, for example, rather than to those of the so-called Third World. By the same token, Ireland's increasing participation in the European trading block seems a strong argument against any analysis of its current condition as 'post-colonial'. There are indeed strong arguments on any side of this debate; too many to explore fully here, and it is part of Ireland's anom-alous state to have the social and cultural forms of both a small European country and a decolonizing nation.[1] The social contradictions consequent on this anomaly have inspired a number of recent projects in various cultural and intellectual spheres that seek to explore Irish history in the comparative frames offered by Third World experiences. Such projects can evidently be read as antagonistic to recent trends towards increasing

[1] For a critical approach to the term 'colonial' as used of Ireland, see Bartlett, 1988. See also Tom Dunne's summary (1992) of arguments that Ireland's condition is that of an outlying territory gradually absorbed into an expanding European monarchy rather than a colony, and of counter-arguments that to view Irish history thus is to risk omitting the traumatic effects of British rule. For strong contrary arguments, based primarily on cultural grounds, see MacSiomoin (1994) and Kiberd (1994); Crotty (1986) provides a thorough economic analysis of relations between Ireland and other countries that have undergone what he terms 'capitalist colonial under-development'. India is his principal comparative instance. Lustick (1993)'s com-parison of Ireland with Algeria in the process of state formation, while taking issue with the 'internal colonialism' model developed by Hechter (1975), implicitly relates Irish history to that of one of the most striking instances of post-war decolonization; one that gave rise to Frantz Fanon's foundational texts on colonialism.

integration into Europe, and accordingly to both the economic logic of integration sponsored by the Irish state and the political logic of regionalism as a solution to partition; a solution espoused by the British and Irish states as also some Northern Irish nationalists.[2] Historiography informed by the lessons of dependency theory, by critiques of neo-colonialism and, indeed, by subaltern histories is less sanguine about the implications of super-state formations and the fate of regions within them. It would, accordingly, be disingenuous to pretend that the debate about Ireland's colonial history could be resolved through empirical means: what is at stake in the terminology is at once political, that is, regarding the ends of the state, and always already methodological.

This brings me to the second point: the apparent familiarity to subaltern historians of Irish discussions derives not from any given analogies between Irish and Indian history or historiography (though at some level of analysis such analogies may certainly be maintained) but from what we might call a 'subalternity effect'.[3] That is, the social space of the 'subaltern' designates not some sociological datum of an objective and generalizable kind, but is an effect emerging in and between historiographical discourses. Those of us who have been interested in learning from *Subaltern Studies* in some form have been so interested precisely because that lesson transforms the kind of questions we pose to Irish history and culture, and enables a rearticulation of political possibilities. Both the terms 'post-colonial' and 'subaltern' designate in different but related ways the desire to elaborate social spaces that are recalcitrant to any straightforward absorption—ever more inevitable though this often seems—of Ireland into European modernity. A project of historical representation or denotation addressed to differently constituted objects of research combines with a performative engagement which could be seen, borrowing Raymond William's triadic structure, to desire the derivation of emergent from residual practices.[4] This is not, however, to seek to legitimate contemporaneous acts or practices by appealing to past forms,

---

[2] John Hume, leader of the moderate Northern Irish nationalist party, Social Democratic and Labour Party (SDLP), has for some time been arguing the regionalist position. *See* for example, his long article entitled 'Time for all sectors to reflect deeply on the legacy of Irish nationalism', *Irish Times*, 13 April 1994. For an overview of 'regional' solutions, *see* Kearney and Wilson (1994).

[3] On parallels between Ireland and India, *see* Cook (1993) and Crotty (1986). I use the term 'subalternity effect' by analogy with the late Joel Fineman's use of the term 'subjectivity effect' in relation to the emergence of the western subject, as he argues, in literature and especially in Shakespeare. *See* Fineman (1992).

[4] On these terms and their historical relations, *see* Williams (1977: 121–7).

opposing thereby an alternative but no less spurious mode of historical continuity to that of dominant narratives. Indeed, the interesting question to pose, to take one forceful example, would be not whether the Provisional Irish Republican Army (PIRA) is in fact continuous with the nineteenth-century Fenian movement, but how non-élite struggles, including these, operate through discontinuities. The object is, accordingly, to reapprehend social processes in terms of the uncloseable struggle between the 'self-evidence' and continuity of dominant representations and those other cultural forms whose apparent 'irrationality' and sporadic temporality is as much the effect as the cause of their marginalization. The study, for example, of popular movements for their forms of practice as well as for their simple occurrence not only recalls instances of resistance that have often been erased from canonical narratives, but also questions the temporality that underpins dominant historiography. I shall argue later that this question of forms of temporality is crucial to the political dimension of historiography in a post-nationalist moment.[5]

I

Ranajit Guha, in his well-known preface to *Subaltern Studies*, projects subaltern historiography as the elaboration of precisely such spaces, constituted ambiguously by previous modes of historiography and/or by the statist orientation of colonial and nationalist politics as marginal. In this sense, the preface partially follows its ostensible mentor, Antonio Gramsci, in understanding the intimate relation between élite historiography and

---

[5] A crucial precursor for such historiography in Ireland may well be James Connolly. Though, like Gramsci, he was an activist intellectual rather than a professional historian, his historical works, especially *Labour in Irish History* and *The Re-Conquest of Ireland*, are pioneering attempts to trace the episodic insurgencies of working-class elements within and beneath the more familiar history of nationalist movements. Also like Gramsci, he sees working-class history as one that ultimately overcomes the 'episodic and fragmentary' nature of Irish history:

Without this key to the meaning of events, this clue to unravel the actions of 'great men', Irish history is but a welter of unrelated facts, a hopeless chaos of sporadic outbreaks, treacheries, intrigues, massacres, murders, and purposeless warfare. With this key all things become understandable and traceable to their primary origin . . . (Connolly, 1922: 215).

As with Gramsci, however, the implications of his critique of orthodox historiography may be more suggestive in the present moment than his desire to recreate a unitary history.

the state formation. In another sense, as I have argued elsewhere, the subaltern project thus described deviates significantly from Gramsci's Hegelian Marxist one in refusing to reinscribe the end of subalternity in the capture of the state (Guha, 1988: 35; Gramsci, 1971: 52–5; Lloyd, 1993: 126–8). No less than Indian historiography, the course of Irish history writing has been bound to state formations. Irish cultural nationalism could be said to have articulated itself from the 1840s around the contestation of a Whig historiography for which Ireland's successive civil struggles culminated in its benevolent absorption into the British constitution. But nationalist historians, lacking perhaps Gramsci's elegant interpretation of their dilemma, were unable to produce Irish history without remarking constantly on its peculiarly *discontinuous* narrative, on its untotalizable tale of spasmodic uprisings and defeats, or its 'fragmentary and episodic' cultural forms. As Gramsci might have predicted, only the admittedly partial capture of an independent state ushers in the heyday of nationalist histories whose teleological version of the Irish national struggle became the staple of the national curriculum. To quote from one such text, Edmund Curtis's standard *A History of Ireland*, first published in 1936:

To make a country's history intelligible, the historian naturally seeks for some point of unity, and this has been long deferred in Ireland's history. . . . For the establishment of a central government representing the nation and able to rule justly over all its elements, Ireland has had to wait till the present generation. (Curtis, 1961: vi)

Henceforth, however, Irish historiography has not followed the pattern ascribed by Guha to Indian historiography. For the contestation of nationalist histories, until relatively recently, came not from anything akin to *Subaltern Studies* but rather from a large and impressive body of historical work that has become known as 'revisionist history'.[6] The focus of this work has been less on the epic of national struggle and more on the emergence under British administration of modern state institutions in Ireland: the national education system, national police force, the legal apparatus, and so forth. Though it has perhaps been

---

[6] For a fuller survey of this tradition and its recent critics, *see* Dunne (1992). For a defence of revisionism, *see* Michael Laffan's essay 'Insular Attitudes: The Revisionists and their Critics', in Ni Dhonnchadha and Dorgan, 1991, 106–21; for critical positions, especially in relation to Roy Foster's recent work, *see* Seamus Deane, 'Wherever Green is Read', *in* ibid., 91–105, Brian P. Murphy, 'Past Events and Present Politics: Roy Foster's *Modern Ireland*', *in* O Ceallaigh (1994: 72–93) and Donal McCartney, 'History Revisions: Good and Bad', *in* ibid., pp. 134–56.

superseded by R.F. Foster's *Modern Ireland, 1600–1972* (1989), F.S.L.
Lyons's *Ireland Since the Famine* (1971) is still a summary instance of the
tendencies of this group of historians, synthesizing into a larger narrative
much of the work on nineteenth- and twentieth-century institution building that had been produced in individual monographs. The methodological and political underpinnings of this historiography are inextricable
from the consolidation in Ireland of institutions of higher education and
the revisionist emphasis on the emergence of modern state institutions
as the proper object of history is itself an instance of the material
parameters of discursive formations. Indeed, the supercession of an
avowedly political nationalist historiography by a professionalized and
empirically sceptical methodology occurred for the most part through
the retraining of Irish historians in British institutions. (Dunne, 1992;
Stewart, 1993)

In the wake of a still dominant 'revisionist' history, Irish historiography has yet to produce anything as self-conscious and theoretically
reflective as *Subaltern Studies*. Nevertheless, it is clear that the last fifteen
years or so has seen the emergence of a large corpus of non-élite histories:
histories of agrarian movements, local histories, social histories of the
complex intersections of class and colonization in rural Ireland, women's
history, in the form both of biographical work and, more recently, of
studies of women's movements and social history. The historiographical
influences and analogues of these studies have been various, but include
in particular the 'history from below' of Thompson and Hobsbawm or
the social and gender history of journals like *History Workshop*, on the one
hand, and French everyday and local histories, on the other. It would thus
be wrong to seek to homegenize either the impulses behind or the products of the new Irish histories.[7]

The cumulative effect of this historical work has, however, been to
shift significantly the narrative axes of Irish history. The concentration of
nationalist and revisionist historiography on state seizure and state building is displaced by histories (the plural is deliberate) whose narrative telos
has ceased to be the state. Clearly, for example, the 'ends' of the Irish
labour movement have not been, nor were ever assumed to be, coincident
with the foundation of the Irish state. The same holds true for the various
movements for women's emancipation that have emerged since the mid-
nineteenth century: it is probably no accident that the major feminist

[7] For a useful survey of such new histories and the current historical debates, *see*
the section 'New Histories: Visions and Revisions' of *The Irish Review*, No. 12
(Spring/Summer 1992).

contributions to Irish history of the past decade have been biographies of the principal women figures of the first quarter of this century whose active involvement in the national, labour, and women's movements issued in their corresponding opposition to the conservative Catholic state that actually came into being. It is indeed precisely the inadequacy of the organizing narrative of state formation to represent such struggles, and the failure of the state itself to respond even to that dimension of feminist and labour demands whose expression takes shape within the forms of legal discourses on rights and citizenship, that has required the opening of further studies in the longer duration of labour and women's history. What such studies may yet clarify is the extent to which the failures of the state lie in the peculiar conjunction of modernity and non-modernity that forms the cultural substrata of the post-1922 Irish states. To the implications of such contradictory formations for the understanding of a gender history of Ireland we will return later.

II

But it is at this point that the significance, at once political and epistemological, if that distinction still has any meaning, of invoking Ireland's *post-colonial* status makes itself felt and that the performative nature of historical discourse, including that of subalternity, manifests itself. For the *anti-colonial* nature of the Irish nationalist struggle is not expressed through any 'objective' decision as to the political status of Ireland within the United Kingdom or the British Empire. It is located rather in the peculiarity, within the Western European frame, or the typicality within the context of global anti-colonial struggles, of Irish nationalism's appeal to its pre-modernity as the site of significant cultural differences on which to found a distinct but no less *modern* state formation, equivalent to if not identical with that of Britain. Or, to put it differently, Irish nationalism appealed to the very characteristics that were, to imperial eyes, the marks of the people's underdevelopment and inherent dependence to provide the very grounds of its claim to independence. The state is, accordingly, founded upon a fetishization of invented traditions that are constitutively rather than contingently (as might be argued for the 'traditions' of metropolitan states) in contradiction to the state's need to form abstract political subjects as citizens. Many of the social contradictions that have attended Ireland's entry into the European Community circulate around this ideological necessity by which the state was constituted around a conservative

268   DAVID LLOYD

cultural identity whose traditionalism conflicts with concepts of abstract
individual rights that are fundamental to the idea of the modern state.

The conclusion to be drawn from these observations is not, however,
that Ireland accordingly must be seen to have undergone a so far incomplete modernization, as if modernity had some discernible if Platonic ideal
as its telos.[8] On the contrary, we can recognize that the form in which
Ireland entered its modernity was constitutively contradictory, on both
sides of the border. One of the most striking symptoms of Ireland's
colonial history is the virtually chiasmic relation between the two post-
treaty states: where the Republic constituted itself around conservative
traditionalism in order to forge a modern democratic state, Northern
Ireland sought to legitimate its separation by appeal to the values of civil
society, yet, since these values were explicitly derived from Protestantism,
succeeded in constituting a violently sectarian state.[9] Not untypical of the
dynamic of colonial history generally, this instance of contradictory modernity helps us to trouble the distinction usually made, and constantly
invoked in Irish debates, between the matrix of modernity, state institutions, rationality and historiography itself, on the one hand, and that of
traditionalism, tribalism or localism, irrationality and mythology, on the
other. For if the state relies in the post-colonial moment on the canoniza-
tion of a certain selection of practices then termed tradition, and forges
that canon through nationalist histories, it relies equally on a violence
proportional in intensity and kind to the resistance it meets in order to
repress or erase the traces of other practices and narratives. In Northern
Ireland that violence has been manifest in the massive deployment of the
repressive state apparatuses; in the Republic, due to the eventual incorporation after a brief civil war of the political opposition to the Free State
under De Valera and, no less significantly, to massive and continuing
emigration, the violence has been largely a function of the ideological state
apparatuses.

Cliona Murphy has remarked that 'The controversy regarding revisionism in Irish history is ironic considering the narrowness of the
history that has been at the centre of the dispute—nationalist history'
(Murphy, 1992: 21). While the focus of both nationalist history and revisionism has been on nation–state formation, with a shift of focus from
heroes to bureaus, the multiple foci of the new histories have been on the

[8] For a critique of the notion of 'incomplete modernity' in the Indian context, see
Chakrabarty (1994).
[9] For some of the contradictions attendant on the close relation between sectarianism and the secular claims of the Northern Irish state, see Todd (1988).

sites and narratives that state formation constitutively occludes. The shift of focus entails equally the production of various subjects and various temporalities while simultaneously bringing into play the ideological location of the historian. As Murphy herself points out, the very project of women's history, even before the question of a specifically feminist perspective, questions not only the contents of previous histories and their principally male protagonists, but also the institutional construction of objectivity: what is objective is not merely a function of empirical method but is bound to the modes of narrative verisimilitude which, as with the literary canon, divide significant from insignificant, major from minor subjects. Crucial to the self-evidences of historiography, as she elsewhere points out, is the normativity of historical 'periods' (Luddy and Murphy, 1990: 3). To take up an earlier point, women's history in Ireland as elsewhere has had to move gradually from studies devoted to figures active in the arena of the state—nationalists and suffragists—to studies increasingly devoted to the 'daily life' of women in Ireland, as if the former studies legitimated the latter (Luddy and Murphy, 1990: 2; Cullen, 1994). A not dissimilar set of observations about the institutional construction of histories that matter can be made in relation to the recent upsurge of local histories, many, if not most, of which have been undertaken by non-professional historians, or by academics from other disciplines. In this case too, the subjects of history, in the sense of its writers as of its agents, have changed together with implicit assumptions both regarding what counts as history and what historical processes 'seem like'.[10]

The shifts in perspective that the new histories imply are numerous, and akin to many with which readers of *Subaltern Studies* will be familiar. Among these might be included a rethinking of popular culture not in terms of tradition or its 'betrayal', but in terms of its capacity to conjoin processes of adaptation and resistance, the refunctioning of printed ballads or of melodramas—commodity forms principally emanating from Britain—for purposes of agitation being but two instances; the study of social formations that proved insusceptible to absorption into the state formation or the nationalist movements that shaped it, such as the agrarian movements of the eighteenth and nineteenth centuries and the short-lived soviets of the 1920s; the examination of the ways in which the daily lives, especially of working class women, cut across the neat division of gendered social spheres on which the Republic's constitution itself is

---

[10] Kevin Whelan pointed out to me that this disdain for local histories is closely related to the traditional historiographer's suspicion of non-written sources such as ballads and tales that are, nonetheless, crucial to subaltern historiography.

founded.[11] It is for this reason that any hard and fast distinction between the 'new histories' and cultural studies is difficult to maintain.

In each of the above instances, what is troubling is not merely a set of assumptions as to the 'proper' content or object of history, but its narrative ends. Popular culture can no longer be seen in relation to a putative adherence to or deviation from a resurgence of national consciousness embodied in traditions, nor can its insurgencies be seen merely, in Hobsbawm's terms, 'proto-nationalist', awaiting their full significance in absorption into the nationalist struggle for the state (Hobsbawm, 1990). Whether we are speaking of agrarian struggles, women's history, or of non-élite cultural forms, what this implies is the recalcitrance of each of these historical sites to the formation of abstract political subjectivity in which, for all its ideological traditionalism, official Irish nationalism conjoins with the project of modernity. At the same time, however, it is also the case that in the final analysis it is equally impossible to narrate the histories of non-élite social and cultural formations in abstraction from the narrative of state formation. For the latter narrative certainly relates, from the perspective of state and modernity, the story of successive attempts to incorporate recalcitrant formations, implying that the history of non-élite formations is always at least partially the history of their constitution and emergence as resistant, if not always openly, to state formation. I emphasize this in order to insist on the *contemporaneity* of non-élite formations to those that are taken by élite historiography to represent modern forms that supersede outmoded or primitive 'traditions' (Lloyd, 1993: 149). In contradiction to such narratives, we may assert that the practices of non-élite groups represent, no less than those canonized in state-oriented histories, responses of adjustment and resistance to the 'modern' social transformations whose institutions they may often have provoked, and as such constitute spaces outside and adjacent to rather than 'prior' to the state formation itself.

It is in this sense that we can begin to comprehend a phenomenon that we might term 'oscillation' that Luke Gibbons captures so well in reference to popular understandings of traditional ballads like 'The Lass of Aughrim'. Discussing this and similar ballads, Gibbons points to the difficulty of knowing when such a figure is to be seen as an individual and historical person, and when as a refunctioning of traditional allegories (Gibbons, 1992: 366–7). The oscillation between allegorical and historical

---

[11] For some instances of these conjunctions between cultural studies and new history, *see* Herr (1991), Lloyd (1993), Rockett (1989), O'Connor (1988), Cahill (1990), Luddy and Murphy (1990).

interpretations of the latter takes place precisely in the shift of social location that the interpreting subject occupies at any given moment. The fading of the allegorical mode of understanding is, as it were, a function of the accession of the subject to the symbolic modes proper to the representative histories of the nation–state formation. But it is important to stress that it is a fading that takes place in time with the emergence of a dominant social narrative and from the latter's perspective: the space occupied by the non-élite social formation is occluded rather than erased or superseded by the dominant and persists even in that occlusion. Rey Ileto's work on the Philippines is analogously instructive here in ways that might be useful to the furthering of new Irish histories. As he argues in 'Outlines of a Non-Linear Emplotment of Philippine History', in the shadow of the dominant national and imperial narratives of modernity, and, specifically, outside the colonial formations of the metropolis and the pueblo, existed another social space and formation, depicted from the centre as 'banditry'. The bandit, accordingly, becomes 'the emblem of disorder, of the fundamental discontinuity of any pueblo-based history', and must be reincorporated by 'linear history' as 'an inchoate form of peasant unrest' that will give rise to a nationalist oriented peasant movement later in the century (Ileto, 1988: 145–6). It is important, however, not to dissolve the formal discontinuity emblematized by the bandit (or in the Irish context, agrarian movements or women's culture, for example) in emphasizing their 'always already thereness'. Constituted in simultaneity with and difference from modern civil society, and representing in a certain sense the 'constitutive other' of modernity, these spaces that are the object of 'new histories' are not therefore to be conceived as alternative continuities, parallel to dominant narratives and only awaiting, in Gramsci's sense, to attain hegemony in order to be completed. On the contrary, and at the risk of deliberate hypostasization, we might argue that the apparent discontinuity of popular or non-élite history furnishes indications of alternative social formations, difficult as these may be to document and decipher for the disciplined historian, as well as the formal grounds for their persistent inassimilability to the state. Of course, the sporadic appearance of popular resistance is always in part a function of the historians' own perspectives, but I would argue, if tentatively, for the more substantive claim that popular memory constitutes a repertoire of narratives, mythemes, rumours, retained and reconstellated, that flash up, like Benjamin's dialectical images, in moments of danger (Benjamin, 1973). Like Benjamin's image, the constellations of popular memory are spatial more than temporal formations, whose very 'failure' to totalize and whose formal hybridity allow for the accommodation of multiple locations among which the non-élite subject oscillates. Among those locations are those sites in which that subject is indeed interpellated, if incompletely, as citizen–subject. The insubordination of such formations is in precise differentiation to the narrative forms of official histories.[12] For the latter, faced with the impossibility of totalizing societies whose mode of rationalization is simultaneously and paradoxically disintegrative and homogenizing, endow totality with a narrative structure that, though never itself finally closed, continually subordinates social groups which cannot be included systemically to the status of the pre-rational and primitive. The recurrent insurgence of those groups correspondingly appears as sporadic and irrational violence and as an index of the failure of Irish society, in this instance, to have fully emerged into modernity. It is the implicit and explicit project, on the other hand, of post-colonial, subaltern, or simply 'new' histories to open the spaces within which unsubordinated narratives can resonate. That resonance is the effect of the excess of possible histories, subject positions, affects, affiliations or memories over the singular history through which the state seeks to incorporate and regulate its political subjects.

III

The position on modernity and the state formation that I have been drawing out of the Irish new histories has been contested from a number of positions, of which the feminist version is the most coherent. Such critiques generally have a dual focus: on the one hand, on the conservatism of both the Irish states, on the other, the presumed conservatism of Irish communities. Although the former focus targets appropriately the deployment of tradition and sectarianism, respectively, by hegemonic state nationalisms, the latter focus firstly presumes the accuracy of representations of Irish communities as conservative and secondly misreads what I would term the *performative* intervention of the critique of modernity.[13]

---

[12] *See* Ranajit Guha, 'The Prose of Counter-Insurgency', in Guha (1988), for a magisterial analysis of the formal elements of dominant historiography. I would want to suggest here, in the spirit of Ileto's work on the *pasyon* (Ileto, 1979), that the formal analysis of popular or subaltern cultural forms suggests equally the outline of other semiotics of organization and movement.

[13] It should also be remarked that the often unintended tendency of the criticism

Among the effects of the new histories has been to challenge both the assumption of the inherent conservatism of the Irish populace and that of the traditionalism of Irish republicanism in general; assumptions that structure, to different ends, both nationalist and revisionist historiographies. As one of two salient instances, the long-standing understanding of the 1798 uprising as resulting from an incongruous alliance between enlightened and mostly middle-class Protestant republicans, on the one hand, and a traditionally minded Gaelic and Catholic peasantry, on the other, has recently begun to crumble as more research has been done not only on the social composition of the 'peasant' rebels but also on intellectual contacts, through priests and schoolteachers, between Ireland and the continent outside élite circles.[14] The implications of this research may well be carried forward to new understandings of subaltern radicalism through the nineteenth century and into the post-Independence period.

A second instance of the questioning of such assumptions involves continuing research on the effects of emigration on the social and political composition of rural Ireland during the post-Famine consolidation of larger landholdings that enabled the emergence of what Emmet Larkin referred to as the 'nation-building class', the small farmers. The relation between this class and the social and cultural conservatism of the Irish nationalism that founded the Irish Free State in 1922 is not far to seek, but cannot be extended to Irish society as a whole.[15] As the historian Joseph Lee has recently been arguing, the apparent relative economic and political success of Ireland with regard to other decolonizing societies must

---

of both states is to legitimate unionist arguments for preferring the association with a 'more modern' British civil society to unification with the conservative Irish Republic.

[14] For some recent work on 1798 and the United Irishmen, see, for example, Smyth (1992) and Dickson et al. (1993).

[15] Continuing resistance by conservative if rural-based parties to the Irish Labour Party's moves to extend voting rights to recent emigrants is a pragmatic acknowledgement both of the radicalizing effects of emigration on many and of the way in which the emigration of the working classes has historically consolidated conservativism in 'independent' Ireland. On patterns of emigration and their relation to Irish politics, see Mac Laughlin (1991, 1993a, and 1993b). Irish music, which has in any case historically emerged from and been transformed by the experience of emigration from the mid-nineteenth century, continues to be an excellent register of the radicalizing potential of migration. For two notable instances, see the London based group, Marxman, *33 Revolutions per minute* (Phonogram, London, 1993) and the New York based Black 47, *Fire of Freedom* (SBK, New York, 1993).

necessarily be understood in relation to decades of emigration that have
maintained Irish population levels at around five million rather than the
fourteen million that might have been reasonably projected at the moment
of Independence. Given that circumstance, the degree of Ireland's continuing structural dependence and underdevelopment becomes all the
more remarkable, even as the social stability of the Republic becomes more
explicable for reasons indicated above. Again, despite the predominant
image of the Irish male emigrant, recent research indicates that the impact
of emigration may have been greater on Irish women than on Irish men,
although partially disguised by the vocational nature of much female
emigration: missionary, educational and nursing work dominating alongside domestic service.

The patriarchal conservatism of the post-Independence state accordingly needs to be understood in terms of a longer history involving the
pre-Independence class formations that brought bourgeois nationalism
into dominance, the contradictions of post-1920s populism through
which De Valera gained and maintained power despite the often socially
disastrous effects of his isolationist economic policies, and the persisting
importance of emigration as the means to maintaining social and economic stability by diffusing conflict. In the light of such histories, it
might become apparent that, however paradoxically, a socially conservative or 'traditionalist' state was the instrument by which post-Independence Ireland negotiated its entry into global capitalism and modernity. In a certain sense, this very paradox permitted Ireland's rapid
transition through the 1960s and 1970s from an isolated economy to a
classic instance of 'dependence': the depletion of organized labour and
the 'traditionally' highly gendered division of labour furnished ideal
conditions for multinational corporate investment akin to those of other
Third World sites, but advantageously located within the European
Community. The impact of the cycle of state-subsidized foreign investment in largely assembly-oriented industry, short-term surplus-value
extraction and subsequent plant-closure has been especially severe on a
predominantly female workforce in a fashion strikingly correspondent
to the situation of women elsewhere within the larger structures of
post-Fordist global capitalism.[16] And, as in those other locations in the
third world, the Irish post-colonial state's sponsorship of traditionalist
social relations, especially in the domain of gender relations, has

[16] For a survey of the history of women's labour in modern Ireland, *see* Beale
(1987: 139–63).

contributed substantially to the possibility of hyperexploitation of labour in general and women's labour in particular in the present.

Currently the increasing integration of Ireland within the political and legal as well as economic framework of the European Community is accentuating the contradictions between the state's traditional ideology and its modernizing forms. The European Court at Strasbourg offers a court of appeal for civil liberties beyond the Irish (and, it must be noted, British) courts. In this respect, Europe certainly offers the possibility of extending the realization of those civil rights promised by the modern political state into domains of the family and sexuality where they have largely been denied both by the Irish constitution, as in the case of abortion and divorce, and by related legislation. Accordingly, the completion of a project of modernity and the full extension of rights of citizenship are linked in the struggle against patriarchal conservatism. As Clara Connolly put it in her review of recent Irish critiques of the universalism of western modernity:

We know that all over the contemporary world, these notions [of abstract humanity] are being replaced by the most frightening forms of communalism, and 'difference'-based ethnic exclusivism. In that scenario, women are merely the property of the group, the symbol of the nation's future, to be protected or defiled according to their belonging. The concept of equality enshrined in 'citizenship' offers more to women than that. (Connolly, 1993: 109)

However, the long history of modernity and of nationalism in Ireland has not involved any simple opposition between abstract universalism and reactionary particularism. On the contrary, as much of the new history is already demonstrating, each enfolds the other while producing contemporaneous and resistant alternatives. That is, in certain respects, the universalizing project of imperial modernity, so well detailed in much revisionist history, is at one with the needs of nationalism to produce the modern citizen–subject as the subject of the nation–state. Hence the assiduous preservation of the apparatuses, ideological and repressive, of the British state after 1922. At the same time, that state nationalism has redeployed ideas of tradition and racial stereotypes that were equally crucial to the maintenance of an imperial discourse on modernity and identity, redefining them only to mark its difference within the same forms. The consequence has been an effort, common to imperialism and the national state, to marginalize inassimilable and recalcitrant social groups, cultural forms, and political projects.

Nowhere has this been more apparent than in the complex history of gender in Ireland. Briefly, since the full history of gender relations in modern Ireland has scarcely been broached, Irish nationalism and British imperialism largely concur in the late nineteenth-century in associating self-government and 'manliness', at the level of the individual person as at that of the nation. In reaction to 'celticist' stereotypes of the 'feminine Celt' produced by Matthew Arnold and others, Irish nationalism reacts by seeking to produce a rigorous re-engendering of social spaces in Ireland, culminating in the constitution of 1937 with its explicit division of masculine and feminine spheres. The process is clearly analogous to processes that Ashis Nandy has described within the Indian context in *The Intimate Enemy*. That project, however, would appear to have worked against the grain of Irish sociality and to have failed to grasp the social and economic consequences of imperialism. The stereotype of Irish 'femininity' is not merely an invention, but is a refraction into terms that legitimate empire of what must have been marked differences in the codings of gender, its economic and social significance, and the articulation of affect or what Williams has termed 'structures of feeling' (Williams, 1977: 128–35). At the same time, given the terms of Victorian and modern constructions of gender, the structural position of Irish males, as dispossessed and disenfranchised, corresponds in part to the position generally designated feminine, while few women can have simply occupied domestic spaces. The contradiction between the assumptions and project of the modern state, as indeed of capitalist gender relations, and the historical and material conditions of Irish men and women has been profoundly productive of anomic masculinity in Ireland. What has yet to be adequately documented and analysed is the emergence of differently articulated male and female homosocial spheres in colonial and post-colonial Ireland, though these doubtless exist and have probably profoundly affected political and social life in Ireland. It is an open question whether these spheres will appear to historical research merely as effects of colonial damage or as resources for alternative visions of cultural and social life.

The consideration that in fact social forms regarded as damaged, whether from a perspective that sees them as remnants or residues of past forms or from one that sees them as inadequately developed, may nonetheless represent resources for alternative projects, is fundamental to the possibilities I am seeking to draw from Irish subaltern historiography. The implication of the new Irish histories is that the resistances inscribed in non-élite histories represent not a mere adherence to often outmoded cultural traditions, but sites of a complex intersection of individual and communal locations that resist reduction to the form of civil subjectivity which dominant narratives prioritize. The *performativity* that I seek to draw from this currently fluid, and by no means integrated body of researches, involves the attempt to produce and theorize dialectically out of such materials the possibility that social and cultural forms that are necessarily relegated to residual status by dominant historiography might generate forms for emergent practices even where their apparent content may be in some views simply conservative.[17] Where the emancipatory claims of both nationalism and Marxism have been predicated effectively on the need to erase and surpass contemporary social and cultural forms and to seek the resources for social transformation in a dialectical relation to the deep past, it may be possible to locate in the marginalized forms of lived social relations the contours of radical imaginaries. The insistence of the new histories on the *contemporaneity* of marginal and dominant social forms, and on their differential construction, is in this respect a profoundly instructive corrective to the self-evidences of developmental historiographies which over and again relegate difference to anteriority.

---

[17] The attempt to derive the forms of radical ideologies from actual social relations has been a long-standing tradition of Irish national Marxism and feminism. James Connolly, again, is a principal figure here. For some preliminary explorations of these traditions, *see* Gibbons (1991 and 1992); Lloyd, 'Nationalisms Against the State'; Coulter (1993).

Select Bibliography

Althusser, Louis, 'Ideology and Ideological State Apparatuses (Notes towards an investigation', in *Lenin and Philosophy and other Essays*, Ben Brewster (trans.)) (New York: Monthly Review Press, 1971).

Bartlett, Thomas, 'An End to Moral Economy: The Irish Militia Disturbances of 1793', *Past and Present*, No. 99 (May 1983), pp. 76–136.

——, '"What Ish My Nation?": Themes in Irish History 1550–1850', in *Irish Studies: A General Introduction* (ed.) Thomas Bartlett, et al. (Dublin: Gill and Macmillan, 1988), pp. 44–59.

Beale, Jenny, *Women in Ireland: Voices of Change* (Bloomington: Indiana University Press, 1987).

Beames, Michael R., *Peasants and Power: The Whiteboy Movements and their Control in Pre-Famine Ireland* (New York: 1983).

Benjamin, Walter, 'Theses on the Philosophy of History', *in Illuminations* (ed.) Hannah Arendt, trans. Harry Zohn (London: Fontana, 1973), pp. 256–66.

Boland, Eavan, *Outside History: Selected Poems, 1980–90* (New York: Norton, 1990).

Cahill, Liam, *Forgotten Revolution: Limerick Soviet, 1919, A Threat to British Power in Ireland* (Dublin: O'Brien Press, 1990).

Chakrabarty, Dipesh, 'Hindu Extremism and Post-modernism: An Indian Debate on the Politics of Knowledge' (TSS 1994; forthcoming in David Lloyd and Lisa Lowe (eds), *Other Circuits*).

Connolly, Clara, 'Culture or Citizenship? Notes from the "Gender and Colonialism" Conference, Galway, Ireland, May 1992', *Feminist Review* 44 (Summer 1993), pp. 104–11.

Connolly, James, *Labour in Irish History and The Reconquest of Ireland* (Dublin: Maunsel and Roberts, 1922).

Cook, S.B., *Imperial Affinities: Nineteenth Century Analogies and Exchanges Between India and Ireland* (New Delhi: Sage, 1993).

Coulter, Carol, *The Hidden Tradition: Feminism, Women and the State in Ireland* (Cork: Cork University Press, 1993).

Crotty, Raymond, *Ireland in Crisis: A Study in Capitalist Colonial Underdevelopment* (Dingle: Brandon Books, 1986).

Cullen, Mary, 'History Women and History Men: The Politics of Women's History', in O Ceallaigh, 1994, pp. 113–33.

Curtis, Edmund, *A History of Ireland* (London: Methuen, 1961).

Dickson, D. et al. (eds), *The United Irishmen: Republicanism, Radicalism and Rebellion* (Dublin: Lilliput, 1993).

Donnelly, James S. Jr., 'The Whiteboy Movement, 1761–5', *Irish Historical Studies*, 21, no. 81 (March 1978), pp. 20–54.

Dunne, Tom, 'New Histories: Beyond "Revisionism"', in *The Irish Review*, no. 12 (Spring/Summer 1992), pp. 1–12.

Fineman, Joel, *The Subjectivity Effect in Western Literature* (Cambridge, Mass.: M.I.T. Press, 1992).

Foster, R.F., *Modern Ireland, 1600–1972* (New York: Penguin, 1989).

Gibbons, Luke, 'Race against Time', *Oxford Literary Review*, no. 13 (Spring 1991).

——, 'Identity without a Centre: Allegory, History and Irish Nationalism', *Cultural Studies*, 6.3 (Oct. 1992), pp. 358–75.

Gramsci, Antonio, 'Notes on Italian History' in *Selections from the Prison Notebooks*, ed. and trans. Quintin Hoare and Geoffrey Nowell Smith (New York: International Publishers, 1971), pp. 52–120.

Guha, Ranajit and Gayatri Chakravorty Spivak, *Selected Subaltern Studies* (Oxford: Oxford University Press, 1988).

Hechter, Michael, *Internal Colonialism: The Celtic Fringe in British National Development, 1536–1966* (Berkeley: University of California Press, 1975).

Herr, Cheryl (ed.), *For the Land They Loved: Irish Political Melodramas, 1890–1925* (New York: Syracuse University Press, 1991).

Hobsbawm, E.J., *Nations and Nationalism Since 1780: Programme, Myth, Reality* (Cambridge: Cambridge University Press, 1990).

Ileto, Reynaldo Clemena, *Pasyon and Revolution: Popular Movements in the Philippines, 1840–1910* (Manila: Ateneo de Manila, 1979).

——, 'Outlines a Non-Linear Emplotment of Philippine History', in Lim Teck Ghee (ed.), *Reflections on Development in Southeast Asia* (ASEAN Economic Research Unit: Institute of Southeast Asian Studies, 1988), pp. 130–59.

Kearney, Richard and Robin Wilson, 'Northern Ireland's Future as A European Region', *Irish Review* 15 (Spring 1994), pp. 51–69.

Kiberd, Declan, 'Post-colonial Ireland: "Being Different"', in O Ceallaigh, 1994, pp. 94–112.

Lloyd, David, *Anomalous States: Irish Writing and the Post-Colonial Moment* (Dublin: Lilliput Press, 1993).

Luddy, Maria and Cliona Murphy (eds), *Women Surviving: Studies in Irish Women's History in the 19th and 20th Centuries* (Dublin: Poolbeg, 1990).

Lustick, Ian, *Unsettled States, Disputed Lands: Britain and Ireland, France and Algeria, Israel and the West Bank-Gaza* (Ithaca: Cornell University Press, 1993).

Lyons, F.S.L., *Ireland Since the Famine* (London: Weidenfeld & Nicolson, 1971).

Mac Laughlin, Jim, 'Social Characteristics and Destination of Recent

Emigrants from Selected Regions in the West of Ireland', *Geoforum*, 22.3 (1991), pp. 319–31.

Mac Laughlin, Jim, 'Ireland: An "Emigrant Nursery" in the World Economy', *International Migration Quarterly Review*, 31.1 (1993), pp. 149–70 (1993a).

——, 'Place, Politics and Culture in Nation-Building Ulster: Constructing Nationalist Hegemony in Post-Famine Donegal', *Canadian Review of Studies in Nationalism*, 20.1–2 (1993), pp. 97–111 (1993b).

MacCurtain, Margaret and Donncha O'Corrain (eds), *Women in Irish Society: The Historical Dimension* (Westport, Conn.: Greenwood Press, 1979).

MacSiomoin, Tomas, 'The Colonized Mind: Irish Language and Society', *in* O Ceallaigh, 1994, pp. 42–71.

Markievicz, Constance, *Prison Letters*, with a Biographical Sketch by Esther Roper and Preface by President De Valera (London: Longmans Green & Co., 1934).

Murphy, Cliona, 'Women's History, Feminist History, or Gender History?', in *The Irish Review*, no. 12 (Spring/Summer 1992), pp. 21–6.

Ni Dhonnchadha, Mairin and Theo Dorgan (eds), *Revising the Rising* (Derry: Field Day, 1991).

Norman, Diana, *Terrible Beauty: A Life of Constance Markievicz* (Dublin: Poolbeg, 1991).

O Ceallaigh, Daltun (ed.), *Reconsiderations of Irish History and Culture* (Dublin: Leirmheas, 1994).

O'Connor, Emmet, *Syndicalism in Ireland, 1917–1923* (Cork: Cork University Press, 1988).

O'Neill, James W., 'A Look at Captain Rock: Agrarian Rebellion in Ireland 1815–45', *Eire-Ireland*, 17.1 (Autumn 1982), pp. 17–34.

Smyth, Jim, *The Men of No Property: Irish Radicals and Popular Politics in the Late Eighteenth Century* (London: Macmillan, 1992).

Stewart, A.T.Q., 'A Scholar and A Gentleman', interview with Hiram Morgan, *History Ireland*, 1.2 (Summer 1993), pp. 55–8.

Todd, Jennifer, 'The Limits of Britishness', *Irish Review*, no. 5 (Autumn 1988), pp. 11–16.

Ward, Margaret, *Maud Gonne: Ireland's Joan of Arc* (London: Pandora, 1990).

Whelan, Kevin, 'Come All Ye Blinkered Nationalists: A Post-Revisionist Agenda for Irish History', *Irish Reporter 2* (2nd Quarter, 1991), pp. 24–6.

——, 'The Power of Place', in *The Irish Review*, no. 12 (Spring/Summer 1992), pp. 13–20.

Williams, Raymond, *Marxism and Literature* (Oxford: Oxford University Press, 1977).

Glossary

Adi-Dravida	A term adopted by the British to refer to both tribal and low-caste Hindu groups; (lit.).
adivasis	A word often used by forest communities to describe themselves, literally 'original inhabitants'.
AJGAR	Refers to the coalition of Ahir, Jat and Gujar castes that comprised the Hindu mob in Mewat.
anna	1/16 of a rupee.
arrack	Country liquor, sold through government-approved outlets which are auctioned periodically.
auliya	A saint.
ayya banchan	An expression in Telugu, meaning 'my lord we live at your feet'.
barkati	Telugu for the Urdu word *barkat*, meaning prosperity.
basti	A slum.
begar	Forced labour.
bhadralok	Respectable person of middle-class origin.
bhagat	A priest.
bhauband	Brotherhood of chiefs.
bhet	gift.
bīghā	5/8 of an acre.
chapati	Unleavened bread.
charkha	A spinning wheel.
chutta	A smoking pipe made of leaf.
chutti/choti	The tuft of hair worn by Hindus.
daftar	records.
dakshina	Payments made to priests for services rendered.
dal	Lentils.
dang	Hills.

dappu/lu	A percussion instrument played by Malas and Madigas (q.v.).
desh	The plains.
Devdasis	A particular caste of women dedicated to the service of Hindu temples from early childhood; often erroneously called prostitutes.
dhani	A hamlet.
dhāṛ	A mob.
dharna	Agitation, a sort of a 'sit in'.
doha (pl. *dohe*)	A couplet.
gadi	Seat of power.
gangā jal	Sacred water of the Ganga river.
gherao	Surrounding a person in authority so as to enforce one's demands—a form of agitation.
giras	A due collected from villages around the Dangs.
goonda	A man who disrupts law and order, i.e. a rowdy.
got	An exogamous subdivision of a caste group.
haks	Dues/rights.
jāgir	Grant of land or village.
jāgirdār	A holder of a village or a land grant.
jajmān	A patron.
jeeta	A farm servant/household servant.
hullar	A colloquial term for the violence accompanying the Partition of India.
kallu compound	A toddy or palm liquor drinking shop.
kaliyuga	The name of the last and worst of the four *yugas* or ages, at the end of which the world is to be destroyed.
karbhari	Assistants to chiefs or village headmen.
karkun	A clerk.
kar seva	Performance of service or labour in a religious cause.
khair	*Acacia Catechu.*
khadi/khaddar	Homespun cotton cloth.
khakhra	*Butea Frondosa.*
killedar	A fort commandant.
kos	A measure of distance, approximately 2 kilometres.

kumkum	Red powder used to mark the hair parting and/or forehead of an auspicious, married woman.
kuradu	Starch taken out of cooked rice, used for further cooking.
lakh	100,000.
lal jhanda	Red flag.
lambardārs	Headmen.
lāthī	bamboo stave.
madi	Wet clothes donned by upper caste Hindus while cooking and eating, signifying a state of purity.
Madiga	Caste name for a cobbler in Telugu.
mahua	*Bassia Latifolia.*
Mala	Omnibus caste name of people who perform different menial tasks in the Andhra region.
mamool	Protection money.
mantralu	Sorcery.
mantras	See *slokas* (q.v.).
mantravadi	A sorcerer.
mela	A fair, usually associated with pilgrimage.
mlechha	A derogatory term for a Muslim, implying ritual pollution.
Mirasis	A caste of Muslim musicians and bards.
morchā	A military front.
nagaras	Drums.
pagdi	A turban.
pāls	The thirteen territorial clans of the Meos.
panchayat	An assembly of caste or village elders.
Padamshali	Caste name for weavers in Telugu.
patti	A subdivision of the village.
pooja	Worship; adoration (of a deity etc.).
prardhana	Prayers (in Telugu).
prasadam	Food ritually offered to Hindu deities.
rānī	Queen.
safāyā	Euphemism for the ethnic cleansing operation undertaken by the Alwar state.
saintālīs	'47 or 1947 AD.
sadado	*Terminalia Arjuna.*

saheb	A term used for a powerful man from outside the Dangs.
sandhya vandanam	Morning prayers.
sara	Country liquor (q.v. *arrack*).
satyagraha	The form of non-violent political protest used by Gandhi; (lit.) 'truth force'.
satyagrahi	One who offers satyagraha.
seekhel bhanel lok	Educated persons.
shali	The level or sub caste used by *Padamshalis* (q.v.), to describe hierarchies within the caste group.
shela	Shawl.
shraadha	A Hindu ceremony in honour and for the benefit of deceased relatives, observed at fixed periods.
slokas	Vedic hymns. See also *mantras* (q.v.).
shuddh	Pure.
shuddhi	The campaign launched by the Arya Samaj for conversion/reconversion to Hinduism.
sikka	Seal.
sipai	Sepoy.
sirkar	Government/state.
sirpav	A set of clothes given on ceremonial occasions.
sisu	Blackwood tree: *Dalbergia Sisu*.
toṛedars	Muzzle loaders.
upnayana	Hindu ceremony of investiture with the sacred thread.
vahivat	custom.
wada	A locality.
yagna	A sacrifice, and rituals accompanying it.